# The Middle East Military Balance 1999–2000

# BCSIA Studies in International Security

Michael E. Brown, Sean M. Lynn-Jones, and Steven E. Miller, series editors

Karen Motley, executive editor

Belfer Center for Science and International Affairs (BCSIA)

John F. Kennedy School of Government, Harvard University

Allison, Graham T., Owen R. Coté, Jr., Richard A. Falkenrath, and Steven E. Miller, *Avoiding Nuclear Anarchy: Containing the Threat of Loose Russian Nuclear Weapons and Fissile Material* (1996)

Allison, Graham T., and Kalypso Nicolaïdis, eds., *The Greek Paradox: Promise vs. Performance* (1996)

Arbatov, Alexei, Abram Chayes, Antonia Handler Chayes, and Lara Olson, eds., *Managing Conflict in the Former Soviet Union: Russian and American Perspectives* (1997)

Bennett, Andrew, *Condemned to Repetition? The Rise, Fall, and Reprise of Soviet-Russian Military Interventionism, 1973–1996* (1999)

Blackwill, Robert D., and Michael Stürmer, eds., *Allies Divided: Transatlantic Policies for the Greater Middle East* (1997)

Brom, Shlomo, and Yiftah Shapir, eds., *The Middle East Military Balance 1999–2000* (2000)

Brown, Michael E., ed., *The International Dimensions of Social Conflict* (1996)

Brown, Michael E., and umit Ganguly, eds., *Government Policies and Ethnic Relations in Asia and the Pacific* (1997)

Elman, Miriam Fendius, ed., *Paths to Peace: Is Democracy the Answer?* (1997)

Falkenrath, Richard A., *Shaping Europe's Military Order: The Origins and Consequences of the CFE Treaty* (1994)

Feldman, Shai, *Nuclear Weapons and Arms Control in the Middle East* (1996)

Forsberg, Randall, ed., *The Arms Production Dilemma: Contraction and Restraint in the World Combat Aircraft Industry* (1994)

Hagerty, Devin T., *The Consequences of Nuclear Proliferation: Lessons from South Asia* (1998)

Heymann, Philip B., *Terrorism and America: A Commonsense Strategy for a Democratic Society* (1998)

Kokoshin, Andrei A., *Soviet Strategic Thought, 1917–91* (1998)

Lederberg, Joshua S., ed., *Biological Weapons: Limiting the Threat* (1999)

Shields, John M., and William C. Potter, eds., *Dismantling the Cold War: U.S. and NIS Perspectives on the Nunn-Lugar Cooperative Threat Reduction Program* (1997)

# The Middle East Military Balance
# 1999–2000

## Shlomo Brom and Yiftah Shapir
### Editors

BCSIA Studies in International Security

**Jaffee Center for Strategic Studies**
Tel Aviv University

The MIT Press
Cambridge, Massachusetts
London, England

Library of Congress Cataloging-in-Publication Data

The Middle East military balance, 1999–2000 / Shlomo Brom
and Yiftah Shapir, editors.
p.   cm.—(BCSIA studies in international security)
Includes bibliographical references and index.
ISBN 0-262-02478-0 (hc. : alk. paper)
1. Middle East—Armed forces. 2. Middle East—Strategic aspects.
I. Brom, Shlomo. II. Shapir, Yiftah. III. Series.
UA832.M5223   1999
355'.033056'09049—dc21                                                          99-049269
                                                                                CIP

*Jaffee Center for Strategic Studies*
The purposes of the Jaffee Center are: first, to conduct
basic research that meets the highest academic standards on
matters relating to Israel's national security as well as to Middle
East regional and international security affairs; and second, to
contribute to the public debate and governmental deliberation of issues
that are—or should be—at the top of Israel's national security agenda.
The Jaffee Center seeks to address the community of
scholars in the field of security studies in Israel and abroad, as well as
Israel's policy-making and opinion-making elite and its public at large.
The Center relates to the concept of strategy in its broadest
sense, namely, the complex of processes involved in the identifica-
tion, mobilization, and application of resources in peace and war, in
order to solidify and strengthen national and international security.

This book was typeset in Israel by Kedem Ltd., Tel Aviv, and was
printed and bound in the United States of America.

*Cover photo:* Development Options for Cooperation: The Middle East/East
Mediterranean Region 1996. Government of Israel, Jerusalem: August 1995.

# Contents

## Part III: **Charts and Tables**

## Part IV: **Glossary of Weapons Systems**

## Abbreviations                                                     475

# Preface

During 1999, the Middle East has once again witnessed some interesting developments. In three of the region's states, important changes in government have taken place: in Jordan and Morocco, the deaths of King Hussein and King Hassan were followed by the crowning of King Abdullah and King Muhammad, respectively. In Israel, Ehud Barak defeated Benjamin Netanyahu's bid for re-election as Prime Minister. As this volume goes to print, the latter change has created new hopes that the Middle East peace process will be restarted.

The previous year manifested another US attempt to renew Israeli-Palestinian negotiations. This effort led to the signing of the Wye River Memorandum. But internal developments in Israel led to a suspension of the memorandum's implementation and the Netanyahu government fell soon thereafter.

In late 1998, the efforts to prevent Iraq from rebuilding its weapons of mass destruction capabilities reached a new peak. Iraq's continued efforts to curtail the international inspections and the monitoring of its activities in this realm led the US to launch Operation Desert Fox. But the immediate result of this operation was an end to Iraq's supervision by the United Nations Special Commission (UNSCOM), leaving considerable uncertainty regarding the future of the efforts to contain Iraq.

Other conflicts - some active, others latent - also left their mark during the past year. These include: the guerrilla campaign conducted by the Hizbollah against Israel in South Lebanon; Turkey's efforts to battle the Kurdish movement in the eastern part of the country; the usually dormant conflict between Syria and Turkey; the conflict between Greece and Turkey over Cyprus; and, the civil wars in Afghanistan, Algeria, and southern Sudan.

Thus the Middle East continues to be a hotbed of conflict and war. This merely re-emphasizes the importance of gaining familiarity with, and understanding of the various facets of the military balance in the region: standing armed forces, paramilitary organizations, weapons of mass destruction and ballistic missiles.

This volume provides our best estimate of the military forces currently possessed by the states of the Middle East. Part I of the book, edited by Brig. Gen. (res.) Shlomo Brom, presents a qualitative assessment of these forces in the land, sea, and air. It also addresses the evolution of defense budgets in the region and a new facet of Middle East terrorism: the "Afghanistan Alumni." Parts II, III and IV of the volume, prepared by Yiftah Shapir, provide the most detailed data available in the open literature regarding the composition of these military forces.

The Jaffee Center launched its study of military forces in the Middle East in the early 1980s. The first volume analyzing these forces was published in 1983, and beginning in 1985 such a volume was produced on an annual basis. Until 1995, these volumes were printed and distributed by the Jerusalem Post, while the 1996 and 1997 volumes were published by Columbia University Press.

*The Middle East Military Balance 1999–2000* is the first published by MIT Press in the framework of the BCSIA Studies in International Security. The publication comprises another facet of the growing relationship between Tel Aviv University's Jaffee Center for Strategic Studies and the Belfer Center for Science and International Affairs at Harvard University's John F. Kennedy School of Government. We are grateful to Prof. Graham Allison, Director of the Belfer Center, and to Dr. Steven Miller, Director of the International Security Program at the Center, for having initiated an exciting relationship that has resulted in the production of this volume.

With the inauguration of this new series, we have introduced a number of innovations into the annual *Middle East Military Balance*. First, the *Balance* will be updated until the beginning of the publication year. Thus, this year's volume provides our estimate of the military forces possessed by the region's states in early 1999. Since changes in the region's military balance rarely develop overnight, we expect the *Balance* to remain accurate during most of the following year. Hence, we named it *The Middle East Military Balance 1999–2000*.

Second, in addition to detailing the inventories of the military forces possessed by the region's states, the volume provides a qualitative analysis of these forces. This will not be repeated every year. Rather, such analysis will be provided when sufficient qualitative changes merit a "new look." From time to time, different approaches to such analysis will be introduced. On other occasions, the strategic context within which the region's military balance should be assessed will be provided.

It should be emphasized that the qualitative analysis of the military forces in the Middle East provided here employs different methodologies. There is, in fact, no single agreed upon method for evaluating military forces. Thus, Col. (res.) Dr. Shmuel Gordon uses an innovative approach to assessing the region's air forces while Col. (res.) Moshe Matri and Navy Capt. (res.) Eli Oren, use more traditional methods for analyzing the quality of the region's land forces and navies, respectively.

Finally, we would like to express our gratitude to those who made the preparation of this volume possible. Moshe Grundman, assistant to the JCSS Head of Center, coordinated every aspect of completing this volume and bringing it to press; Carol Cook, Steven Rodan and Emily Landau made invaluable contributions in editing the text; Tamar Malz and Avi Mualem did a masterful job of entering the editing changes into the text. Martin Kat translated the Hebrew version of the articles. Yoel Kozak and Tamir Magal performed the difficult task of compiling, updating and setting the data on the region's military forces. Helpful assistance and comments were provided by JCSS research assistants and documentation managers: Orna Zeltzer, Avi Mualem and Ori Slonim. We are also deeply indebted to Karen Motley, Executive Editor at the Belfer Center, for the time and energy she invested in supervising the entire production process and for the extreme care and patience she demonstrated during the difficult months that resulted in the publication of this volume.

**Brig. Gen. (res.) Shlomo Brom**
**Editor**
**Senior Research Associate**

**Prof. Shai Feldman**
**Head of Center**
**Jaffee Center for Strategic Studies**

# The Middle East Military Balance

# 1 9 9 9 – 2 0 0 0

# Introduction

## Shlomo Brom

Countries usually define their military requirements on the basis of their strategic goals and the threats with which they must contend. The nature and rate of the Middle East arms buildup results from the interaction between the military requirements of the region's states and their ability to meet those needs.

There is a correlation between important political and strategic developments in the Middle East, and changes in the nature and rate of military buildup in the region. Thus, for example, progress in the Israeli-Arab peace process has led to a slower pace of arms acquisition in most of the states involved: Israel, Jordan, and Syria. On the other hand, the 1991 Gulf War led to an acceleration of the arms buildup among the Gulf states, except for Iraq, which has been made subject to international sanctions. In general, postwar periods have been marked by an accelerated arms race between the belligerents. This is motivated by the need to replace losses, to implement the lessons of the war, and to be better prepared for the next round. The defeated side has a strong incentive to enhance its capabilities, while the winning side strives to maintain its advantage.

Political and strategic developments have also led to changes of emphasis in armament programs. Israel, for example, has been affected by two important developments in the past decade. The first is the advancement of the peace process, which has reduced the sharpness of the conflict with Israel's immediate neighbors. The second is the heightened political hostility of the second and third tier states – those with which Israel does not share a border – and their enhanced ability to reach Israel with strategic weaponry (surface-to-surface missiles and long-range aircraft).

These developments have led to a major change in the characteristics of Israel's arms procurement. In recent years, Israel has invested considerable resources in obtaining the capability to confront distant threats and punish the states that pose those threats, at the expense of other military requirements. To that end, Israel is procuring long-range attack aircraft, acquiring intelligence-gathering satellite capabilities, and developing an early-warning and defense infrastructure against long-range surface-to-surface missiles. At the same time, Israel is examining possible changes in its defense policies and military doctrine, aimed at meeting the new threats.

Algeria furnishes a different example. There, the main strategic threat to the regime is internal, reflected in a civil war that has been raging for several years. Obviously, under such circumstances, investment in the capacity to deal with internal subversion takes precedence over a buildup of military forces geared to meet external threats. Not surprisingly, the Algerian armed forces have not been expanded in recent years.

Lately, significant changes have taken place in the ability of Middle East states to allocate the resources required for an arms buildup. The decline in oil prices, along with structural problems in the economies of the region's states, and the increase in civilian needs due to the rate of population growth, have reduced most states' ability to allocate resources to the military. The only states that still manage to arm at a pace commensurate with their perceived requirements are either recipients of external aid, or oil-producing states with populations small enough to enable them to rearm, despite the fall in oil prices. Yet the sources of external aid have also contracted. The dissolution of the Soviet Union has left only one superpower in the Middle Eastern arena – the United States – which is willing to help finance the buildup of forces of its client states, mainly Israel and Egypt, and to a lesser extent, Jordan.

When contemplating the Middle East in the broad sense of the term, there is little meaning to the idea of a military balance involving all the region's states. Morocco, for example, is not concerned about threats from Israel or Iraq, when it decides upon the size and composition of its armed forces; and vice-versa. For a better understanding of the way in which military power develops in the Middle East, the area may be divided into three sub-regions, each with its actual or potential rivalries and its local arms race: the Persian Gulf, North Africa, and the region of the Israel-Arab dispute. This, of course, is not a perfect breakdown: there are states that play a significant role in more than one sub-region. A good example is Iraq, which is a central actor in the Gulf area but also has a role in the Israeli-Arab conflict. Moreover, some Middle Eastern states cannot be easily assigned to any of the three sub-regions. An example is Yemen, whose force structure is affected by the potential threat of Saudi Arabia, which we define primarily as a Gulf state. However, countries on the Horn of Africa, such as Eritrea and Ethiopia, also constitute potential threats to Yemen.

The division we propose is relevant mainly when considering potential high-intensity or low-intensity military conflicts. It is less relevant when considering strategic capabilities – surface-to-surface missiles or weapons of mass destruction. The long range of the strategic platforms makes conflict possible between states that are not in the same sub-region, for example Israel and Iran. Despite these qualifications, a division of the Middle East into these three sub-regions provides an appropriate framework for an analysis of the Middle Eastern military balance.

The qualitative assessment of Middle East armed forces presented in this volume examines these forces according to the three generally accepted spheres of warfare: land, air and sea combat. Such a division is convenient because it fits the manner in which the armed forces are divided in most military establishments. But this division is not without problems, because a real battlefield involves combined combat; each of the armed services can operate in virtually all spheres of combat. There is also a synergistic effect between the services, the most salient of which is combined army-air force operations on the land battlefield. But this difficulty can be overcome, if, when examining the balance between the land forces of two sides, the air capability that affects ground combat is taken into account. On the other hand, a land-sea-air division has the advantage of permitting a professional evaluation of each sphere of warfare.

In assessing the strength of military forces, additional methodological difficulties are encountered. These derive primarily from the complex of factors that impact the effectiveness of military power, and from the difficulties of measurement, especially of qualitative factors. Sometimes it is even difficult to compare two weapon systems of the same type. A combat aircraft and a battle tank are both complex systems, each of which comprises a fairly large number of sub-systems. Their characteristics can be gauged, but it is not easy to arrive at the aggregate of these characteristics. An aircraft has a maximum speed, some capacity for maneuver, a payload capacity, a radar with detection and fire-control capabilities, ordnance, guidance systems of given capabilities, and various warning systems. A tank has armor of a given quality, a gun of a certain diameter, shells of various capabilities, a fire-control system, and a mechanical system that determines the characteristics of propulsion and maneuverability. It is difficult to decide, on the basis of a point-by-point comparison of characteristics, which aircraft or tank is superior to its counterpart, and by how much. When factors such as the quality of crews and commanders are added, along with the quality of organization and training, and such force multipliers as $C^4I$, the difficulties of measurement become insuperable.

In more purely technological spheres, methods of quantitative measurement are more applicable. The contributors to the *Middle East Military Balance 1999–2000* have chosen different methods for examining the balance in the various spheres. Only in that of air warfare has Col. (res.) Dr. Shmuel Gordon endeavored to develop a quantitative method for gauging air power, which is described in his article; his analysis of the air forces of the region is based on that method. The other authors, Col. (res.) Moshe Matri in the sphere of land combat, and Navy Capt. (res.) Eli Oren in the sphere of naval power, have preferred an analysis based on the authors' qualitative judgment. In the future, it may be possible to develop, on the basis of Dr. Gordon's work, a similar quantitative method for examining naval forces, which are also highly technological.

The past year saw a continuation of the political and strategic trends that affected the development of military forces in the Middle East since the beginning of the decade. To varying degrees and in different ways, this is true for all three sub-regions of the Middle East. Naturally the Israeli-Arab sub-region is influenced considerably by the progress and setbacks of the Israeli-Arab peace process, while the Gulf area is still immersed in the consequences of the Gulf War and its lessons, and the North African states are pre-occupied with their internal security problems.

The United States continues to function as the only superpower in the Middle East, focusing its activities on the Persian Gulf and the Israeli-Arab peace process. One of its tools is the extension of US military assistance to Middle Eastern states. Russia, especially under Primakov, first as foreign minister and later as prime minister, attempted to "return to the Middle East." It has been able to obstruct US policy related to Iraq by exploiting its status as a permanent member of the UN Security Council. It also transfers technology of surface-to-surface missiles and weapons of mass destruction to Iran. To date, at least, the European Union has not translated its solid economic position in the Middle East into strategic and political influence.

The states involved in the Israeli-Arab conflict have continued to adhere to the peace process during Netanyahu's term as prime minister of Israel despite the deadlock in negotiations between Israel and both Syria and the Palestinians. Clearly, the decision of Arab states to continue to pursue this approach was influenced by their recognition that Israel's military superiority rules out a military option for resolving the conflict. At the same time, as long as these states continue to adhere to the peace process, they have preferred not to increase military spending at the expense of other national or regime priorities.

Economic conditions in these states have continued to impose severe constraints on the level of their military spending. Israel and Egypt, which enjoy considerable assistance from the US, have managed to finance substantial buildup programs, and Jordan too has obtained increased US aid in the wake of its peace treaty with Israel. Yet this falls far short of meeting Jordan's military requirements after years of budgetary drought. A similar drought continues in Syria, where procurement of new weapon systems has been undertaken only sparingly; an expected breakthrough, involving large-scale arms transactions, mainly with

Russia, has not yet materialized. Under these circumstances, Syria continues to give priority to those components of its military that enhance its strategic deterrence, and thus persists in allocating resources to the development and manufacture of surface-to-surface missiles and chemical weapons.

Problems of "current security" continue to concern some states involved in the Israeli-Arab conflict. Israel is bogged down in a guerrilla war in southern Lebanon, waged by the Hizballah with the help of other Lebanese organizations. On the other hand, cooperation between the security services of Israel and the Palestinian Authority (PA) has reduced terrorism originating in the PA - controlled areas to an exceedingly low level. Jordan continues to face a security problem along its border with Iraq, involving mainly smuggling and infiltration, which have been increasing under the pressure of the sanctions applied against Iraq. Syria was preoccupied by the possibility of a conflict with Turkey, stemming from the infiltration into Turkey from Syria of members of the Kurdish Workers Party (PKK), and the fact that Syria had given asylum to PKK leader Ocalan. Syria's eventual expulsion of Ocalan and a Syrian undertaking to stop supporting the PKK have lowered tension with Turkey.

The Persian Gulf continues to be troubled by the ongoing conflict between Iraq and the United States, supported by the other Arab Gulf states. Iraqi efforts to free itself from UNSCOM's supervision and the international sanctions led, in late 1998, to the most severe clash between Iraq and the United States since the Gulf War. The results of Operation Desert Fox were mixed. On the one hand, targets in Iraq, particularly those related to the development and manufacture of surface-to-surface missiles, sustained substantial damage. In addition, the United States adopted a policy of immediate attack when evidence of Iraqi avoidance of its obligations to refrain from producing weapons of mass destruction (WMD) are detected. On the other hand, UNSCOM supervision has been discontinued, and there is concern that Iraq is about to exploit this to renew its programs for the production of WMD and surface-to-surface missiles. International sanctions, however, prevent Iraq from acquiring modern weapons. The depreciation of existing weapon systems and the impossibility of conducting training exercises in various military spheres on a regular basis have probably also led to a continuing erosion of Iraq's military capabilities.

Iran continues to experience severe economic difficulties, and is incapable of implementing its arms buildup program. Its conventional military forces suffer from a low budget, while the Iranian government has decided to allocate resources to weapons of mass destruction and surface-to-surface missile programs. A milestone in Iran's long-range missile program was its first test launch, in the second half of 1998, of the Shihab-3 missile.

The internal power struggle between the revisionist camp of President

Khatami and the conservative camp of the religious leader Khamenai has raised hopes for change, and for a thaw in relations with the West. Yet to date, there is no evidence of change in Iran's military policies or in its programs related to the development of surface-to-surface missiles and weapons of mass destruction. Neither is it certain that a victory for the Khatami camp would lead to desired changes in these areas.

The Arab Gulf states, apart from Iraq, have continued to implement their broad force buildup programs, which were largely affected by their lessons of the Gulf War. This has been the case despite the financial liquidity problems they experienced, caused periodically by falling oil prices. These liquidity problems resulted in some delays in weapons acquisition but did not affect the overall programs. Despite the fact that in certain spheres, particularly in the air and at sea, the Arab Gulf states enjoy both qualitative and quantitative superiority over the two regional "giants," Iraq and Iran, the Gulf states have limited confidence in their ability to face these two powers. Hence, they continue to rely on the United States, which maintains a permanent naval presence in the Gulf and a forward deployment of forces and equipment in several Gulf states. Despite the cash-flow problems they sometimes face, the financial strength of these states enables them to procure the best weaponry offered by the United States and Western Europe. There is still a considerable gap, however, between the quantity and quality of the weapons in their possession, and their ability to employ them effectively.

By contrast, the armed forces of North Africa are in a state of arrested development. Most of the states in this sub-region have been suffering from economic difficulties and internal problems. Algeria is bogged down in a civil war and Morocco in a guerrilla war in the Sahara against the Polisario. Libya has been damaged, mainly by a drop in oil prices, but also by sanctions imposed in the aftermath of the Lockerbie affair. As a result, the Libyan armed forces have earned the nickname "the world's largest scrap-yard."

The 1991 Gulf War has had a deep impact on the subsequent development of the armed forces of the region. One clear direction is the increased emphasis on surface-to-surface missiles and weapons of mass destruction. Yet the clear, brutal demonstration of Western technological superiority over an awesome regional power like Iraq was also significant. Such technological capability is an indication of what has come to be called the Revolution in Military Affairs (RMA). The demonstration raised anxiety among the main military establishments in the Middle East that what transpired in the Gulf War was not a one-time event, but rather an indication that the gap in military capability between the advanced Western armed forces and the other nations of the world will widen. Such a gap has far-reaching strategic and military significance.

Hence it is important to ascertain whether there are states in the Middle East that are capable of narrowing this gap by having their armed forces integrate elements of the RMA. The most important of these elements are the military information revolution, modern sensor technology, precision-guided ordnance, C⁴I systems, and the adoption of appropriate military organization and doctrine. According to most military observers, Israel enjoys a considerable advantage in these spheres. It has an adequate technological base and well trained manpower, as well as the resources required for absorbing and integrating these new technologies.

Doubts exist, however, as to whether other Middle Eastern states are capable of making the required changes in the foreseeable future. For that reason, the trend in most Middle Eastern armed forces has been to develop other types of capabilities, which could provide asymmetrical responses to the RMA. Yet as noted earlier, many Middle Eastern states have been experiencing difficulties in financing any type of conventional arms buildup. Moreover, they understand the limitations on the employment of regular military forces in a world where there is only one superpower, and where the international system imposes stronger constraints against military aggression. Consequently, there has been a search for alternative methods for advancing political and strategic interests. This search has led, in some cases, to a preference for low-intensity conflict (LIC), on the one hand, and an effort to obtain weapons of mass destruction, on the other. The assumption is that such weapons will compensate for an unfavorable balance in conventional weaponry and deter outside intervention. In turn, these developments have led to changing priorities in the structure of other armed forces of the region. The latter are giving higher priority to contending with irregular forces, and to providing a response to surface-to-surface missiles and weapons of mass destruction. These trends cut across all the sub-regions of the Middle East.

Multilateral discussions on arms control and regional security (ACRS), initiated in the aftermath of the 1991 Madrid peace conference, were discontinued in 1995 and have not been renewed. Thus, disarmament and arms control agreements cannot be expected to influence the Middle East military balance, barring changes in the policies of the main actors in the region. Neither, for the time being, have the nuclear tests of India and Pakistan had a significant impact on the Middle East. Thus far, there have been no indications of technology transfers from those states to the Middle East; nor are there indications that these tests have led to any change in the perception of Middle Eastern states concerning weapons of mass destruction. While expectations of pressure on Middle East states to reach arms control agreements have not been realized, Iran stands out as an exception. Despite its deep involvement in WMD and surface to surface missile development, it is very active in various global non-proliferation regimes, demonstrating a surprising willingness to undertake various disarmament commitments. The most important development in this realm has been Iran's decision to sign, ratify and begin implementation of the Chemical Weapons Convention.

The creation of coalitions or alliances can influence the balance of forces in the Middle East. The growing cooperation between Turkey and Israel in recent years is a salient case in point. While the strength of these ties, and their impact on the Middle East balance of power has been exaggerated, these ties clearly enhance the deterrent posture of both parties, engendering anxiety among their Arab neighbors. The connection with Israel has strengthened Turkey militarily, because it provided it with military technologies not available from other sources.

It is within the context of the various strategic developments identified here, that the military forces of the Middle East are detailed and evaluated in this volume. As the *Middle East Military Balance 1999–2000* goes into print, further developments–particularly in the Arab-Israeli subregion – loom on the horizon. The impact of these developments on the future of the region's military forces will be ascertained in the following volumes of this annual assessment.

# PART I

# QUALITATIVE DIMENSIONS

# The Balance of Land Forces

## Moshe Matri

The structuring of military forces is a process that takes years, starting from the definition of threats and operational requirements, through negotiations for the supply of weapons, and finally, their delivery and deployment. A parallel process is the military recruitment and training of manpower, the formation of combat units and the imposition of structural reform in a drive to integrate new weapons systems and maximize their effectiveness on the battlefield.

The Gulf States, for example, have begun these processes as a result of the lessons they have drawn from Operation Desert Storm in 1991. After the war, they decided to significantly expand their military forces and began receiving new weapons in the mid-1990s – systems that were not expected to reach operational maturity before the end of the decade. The process has been slow, however, because of manpower constraints as well as the failure of these states to fully exploit the technological potential of advanced Western weaponry.

The United States has emerged as the world's leading power and accounts for more than 50% of arms sales in the region. It determines the rules of the arms race and links military aid to the support a client state demonstrates for US regional interests, including the Israeli-Arab peace process. The result has been a steady supply of weapons to the Gulf states, massive aid to Israel and Egypt and a renewal of military aid to Jordan, after it signed a peace treaty with Israel in 1994.

Concerned by the threats to the Gulf and the Arabian Peninsula, the United States formulated the doctrine of dual containment, the term given to the policy that prevents either Iran or Iraq from dominating the region. Within the framework of this policy – which prevailed until recently – Washington embarked on the massive supply of modern weapons systems to the land and air forces of Bahrain, Kuwait, Saudi Arabia and the United Arab Emirates. A key concern that has limited this effort is that advanced US technology might fall into the hands of hostile regimes. Another limitation is the difficulty of these Middle East states to absorb new weaponry.

Still, the main element in the doctrine of dual containment centers on America's ability to project power in the Gulf region. Within the framework of CENTCOM, the United States has deployed brigade-sized formations in Kuwait and Qatar, and prepositioned additional equipment for ground forces on board vessels deployed in the Persian Gulf.

The drive toward arms procurement by Gulf states has also attracted other Western suppliers. Swiss and Canadian weapon contractors have joined their British and French counterparts in the competition for arms deals in the Gulf and Arabian Peninsula.

By contrast, Russia's role in arms transfers to the region has diminished considerably. After the end of the Cold War, Moscow changed the terms under which it was willing to sell arms. Russia now demands cash and the settlement of past debts, and the result has been a halt of weapon sales to Middle Eastern states that had been Soviet clients in the 1980s. Indeed, the greater a state's previous military dependence on the Soviet Union, the greater the damage to that state's military procurement in the 1990s. For Syria, as well as Iraq and Libya, Western arms sanctions during the 1990s have also denied them alternative sources of armaments.

At the same time, Russia's insistence that economic considerations dominate its arms sales policy has created opportunities for other former republics of the Soviet Union. Consequently, Ukraine, Moldavia, and Georgia have launched efforts to market Soviet weapons systems in the Middle East.

Before proceeding to analyze the buildup of ground forces in the region, a word on methodology may be appropriate. It is difficult to monitor the development of militaries in the Middle East by comparing them over time. Often, changes in published military balances from one year to the next reflect changes in assessment rather than new data. Consequently, the analysis of trends in this chapter is based on an overall perspective of arms transactions and the processes of force structure, rather than on a comparative examination of multi-year data related to the orders of battle.

In any discussion of ground forces, it is best to divide the Middle East into three sub-regions. Most of the states in the region are limited in their ability to send ground forces far from their borders; hence, the need to examine the balance of power separately for each subregion.

**The Israel-Arab subregion** – This subregion comprises states that directly border Israel and have been at war with it: Egypt, Jordan, Lebanon, Syria, and Israel itself. The subregion continues to harbor the potential of a ground war that could draw in additional states in the absence of a breakthrough in Israeli-Syrian negotiations. Egypt and Jordan have signed peace treaties with Israel, but both still regard Israel as a potential rival. Israel views its Arab neighbors in the same fashion.

The Persian Gulf and Arabian Peninsula – This subregion includes states with vast oil reserves that were involved in regional wars over the last two decades; the subregion continues to contain the seeds of future conflict. The military and political power of states in this subregion affect the balance of power in the Israeli-Arab dispute, particularly in the areas of surface-to-surface missiles and weapons of mass destruction (WMD). But the ability of some of these states, particularly Iraq and Saudi Arabia, to send expeditionary forces to states fighting Israel, is currently limited.

North Africa and Sudan – The level of investment in the military by states in this subregion has been declining in the 1990s, mainly because of economic difficulties and internal disputes. The potential for military conflict in this subregion is lower than in the other two areas. The militaries of North African/ Sudan area affect the balance of power in the Israeli-Arab conflict less than the militaries of the Gulf states. Indeed, states from the North African region would send no more than a token amount of ground forces in any future Israeli-Arab war.

Dividing the Middle East into three subregions also provides a clearer picture of threat assessments and the resulting military buildup. Saudi Arabia, for example, perceives threats from Iraq, Iran and the Arab states that border the kingdom. Israel is perceived as a lesser threat.

Iraq is unique in the Persian Gulf subregion. It has historic ambitions of regional hegemony, even at the price of war. Baghdad has also participated in Israeli-Arab wars, sending forces to Jordan and Syria and launching missile attacks on Israel during the 1991 Gulf War. Thus, Iraq can be described as both a state in the Gulf subregion as well as an influential factor in the Israeli-Arab conflict.

This example underlines the importance of geography in specific scenarios of military confrontation. Contrary to the contention that in an age of surface-to-surface missiles borders and territory have little meaning, geography significantly affects the capacity of Arab states to play a role in Israeli-Arab war scenarios. First, geography dictates the ability to exploit military power in ground combat. For example, combat between Israel and Syria in the narrow area of the Golan Heights is entirely different from that in the vast spaces of the Sinai Peninsula. Military forces would be used differently, the room for maneuver varies widely, and the ability to launch a deep-strike offensive differs.

Second, geography can determine the ability of expeditionary forces to join an Israeli-Arab war. For example, a war along the Israeli-Jordanian border could increase the prospects that forces from the Persian Gulf and Arabian Peninsula, particularly Iraq, would participate. Fighting along the Israeli-Egyptian front could result in the deployment of forces from Libya and other countries in North Africa. By contrast, Arab countries would find it difficult to join an Israeli-Syrian war because of the small area of the Golan front.

Moreover, the cost of sending forces by sea or air to Syria from either the Gulf region or North Africa, would be high. An attempt to station these forces in Syria before the outbreak of war could alert Israel. But sending these forces to Syria after the beginning of hostilities would not allow them to participate in the fighting during the crucial early days of the war. These prospects are important when considering the effect of an Iranian expeditionary force to Syria or Lebanon during a war in which either or both of these countries would be engaged with Israel.

The current geopolitical realities in the Middle East make the creation of a broad Arab coalition against Israel unlikely. The peace treaties Israel has signed with Egypt and Jordan prevent the movement of forces from states like Iraq, Iran or Libya to Israel's borders. There are also strict limits on the amount of troops and weapons Egypt can deploy in the Sinai peninsula. For its part, Jordan has pledged not to allow foreign forces into its territory. These constraints will apply as long as the peace treaties are observed.

The 1991 Gulf War proved that the geopolitical relationships in the region limit the use of force. Israel demonstrated restraint in using Jordanian and Saudi air space to attack Iraq despite Baghdad's nearly daily missile attacks on the Jewish state. This restraint was induced primarily by Israel's interest in maintaining the Allied coalition against Iraq.

Two areas whose significance has increased in recent years due to the low intensity conflicts (LICs) conducted in proximity to Israel's heartland are South Lebanon and the West Bank and Gaza. In the first, Israel is fighting Hizballah – a competent Shi'ite guerrilla organization. In the second, the Palestinian Authority (PA) maintains large forces for internal security. These forces constitute a potential threat to Israel in scenarios of war with the Arab states.

Geography dictates that, in the event of war, Israel would maintain control over southern Lebanon and the Palestinian territories – areas close to Israeli population centers. This mission may tie down Israeli forces and hamper the mobility of troops that head toward the main battlefronts.

As long as the Middle East peace process is kept alive, a major ground threat to Israel is unlikely. If the circumstances change, however, the Middle East can expect a realignment of both Arab-Israeli as well as inter-Arab relations. Longtime Arab rivals are likely to participate in a military coalition against Israel.

# Procurement and Force Structures

## *The Arab-Israeli Subregion*

This subregion is divided into two groups. The first is comprised of states forced to reduce or even cancel their military buildup. For Syria and Jordan, the reason is economic; for Lebanon, the reason is instability. The second group contains states that receive a constant level of US military aid. Such assistance permits Egypt and Israel to increase their armed forces through multi-year programs and helps them manufacture and export weapons.

Egyptian and Israeli procurement includes six elements: procurement of new systems, some of them export versions specifically configured for the Middle East; indigenous production of weapons systems; weapons received from US surplus military stocks; the upgrade of US weapons systems; in the case of Egypt, the assembly of weapons; and, the lease of US weapons.

The following is a survey of developments in procurement and force structure in each of the states in the subregion.

### Syria

Syria has failed to conclude any major arms deals since 1993. This appears to have been caused primarily by disagreements with Moscow over Syria's $12 billion debt to Russia. Syria's poor economy and Western sanctions have also prevented Damascus from turning to other suppliers – either in the former Soviet Union or elsewhere.

As a result, Syria has not procured major military platforms or changed its order of battle. Instead, Syria has focused on upgrading portions of its tank corps. Ukraine has modernized 200 of Syria's T-55MV tanks and Iran also provided some assistance to the modernization of Syria's tanks.

In addition, Syria purchased some anti-tank capabilities; in 1998 it began to take delivery of the Kornet (AT-14) anti-tank missile from Russia. The contract involved 1,000 laser-guided missiles with a range of 5.5 kilometers. The procurement is expected to improve Syria's efforts to confront Israeli armor. Much of Syria's anti-tank arsenal is based on older generation Russian and French anti-tank missiles.

Meanwhile, the Assad regime attempted to maintain the combat readiness and training of its troops in both Syria and Lebanon. Syrian forces in Lebanon comprise part of Syria's defensive posture against an Israeli attack. By contrast, the role of those forces in Lebanon's internal security has declined significantly.

At the same time, Syria continues to expend considerable efforts in developing and expanding its arsenal of Scud-based surface-to-surface missiles. The effort has been carried out in cooperation with North Korea and perhaps Iran.

## Jordan

Jordan's main effort has been devoted to maintaining the readiness and professional standards of its small military, while ensuring its loyalty to the Hashemite regime. Since 1996, Jordan has been engaged in a gradual restoration of its military ties to the United States. Washington has sent relatively small quantitites of arms to Amman, primarily a squadron of F-16 A/B aircraft. The aid package also included 50 M-60 A3 tanks, 40 of which were delivered in 1998, 18 self-propelled artillery pieces, and a small number of Black Hawk UH-60A helicopters.

Jordan has increased its tank fleet by 100 since 1996 but has not instituted changes in its ground forces. The United States can be expected to continue to strengthen Jordan's military in the post-Hussein era, given Amman's support of the Middle East peace process.

## Egypt

Egypt continues the buildup of all branches of its armed forces. The process, based mostly on US-made weapons, is largely financed by the annual $1.3 billion in US military aid. During the 1990s, Egypt has taken delivery of more than 500 M1-A1 tanks assembled in Egypt in the framework of modernizing its armored corps. One armored division has already been equipped with these tanks and a second division is in the process of being converted. Currently, negotiations are proceeding for an additional 200 M1-A1s, 340 M-60 A1 tanks from US Army surplus stocks, and the upgrade of M-60 A1 tanks to M-60 A3s.

The army's armored and mechanized formations are completing their conversion to Western systems by replacing other components of their force structure as well. In 1998, the Egyptian army was to have received 24 SP-122 (122 mm) self propelled artillery pieces assembled in Egypt. Cairo has also ordered AN/TPQ–37 artillery radars and 540 TOW-2B anti-tank missile launchers. For its land-based air defense system, Egypt has ordered 50 mobile Avenger batteries, which include Stinger anti-aircraft missiles and anti-aircraft machine guns installed on Hammer vehicles. Procurement of Chinook CH-47D helicopters from the United States is also being planned.

Egypt is also producing Scud-B surface-to-surface missiles, apparently with the aim of upgrading them to Scud-C missiles, with a range of 540 kilometers. The effort has been launched with North Korean assistance. Unconfirmed reports assert that Egypt's Scud-B force has increased by 24 launchers.

Egypt has also pursued a methodical training program, an important part of which has been joint maneuvers with the United States as well as with European and Arab states. The United States views Egypt as a main pillar of its Middle East policy, an assessment that was bolstered during the 1991 Gulf War.

Washington has pressed for interoperability between US and Egyptian forces through joint training and combat doctrine.

Egypt's armed forces also serve as the backbone of the regime. In the mid-1990s, military units were deployed on a number of occasions in the campaign against Islamic militants when the government decided that its internal security forces needed reinforcements.

### Israel

The Israel Defense Forces (IDF) continues to implement its multi-year buildup program, *Mirkam*. The program was first formulated in 1991 and was updated several times during the decade. The program's operational priority is to enhance ground warfare capabilities, particularly against Syria. The IDF's procurement policy and combat doctrine development are aimed at maintaining an edge in the battlefield; facilitate day and night as well as all-weather combat; and improve intelligence for ground warfare. These aspects of the program have been implemented by modernizing the tank fleet and improving capabilities of artillery, anti-tank weapons, and helicopters. The military has also expanded the use of precision-guided munitions (PGM) by its air and ground forces. The IDF has been implementing the program while reducing the manpower of the standing military, retiring aging equipment, and reducing the training time of reserve forces. At the same time, a comprehensive reorganization of the logistics structure has been carried out.

The IDF also continues to consolidate the Ground Forces Command, established in the 1980s. Indeed it now considers making the command into a fully independent service. The process was bolstered when Lt.-Gen. Shaul Mofaz became the IDF Chief of Staff in the summer of 1998. Mofaz also plans changes in the command structure of infantry divisions and brigades.

The *Mirkam* program aims to introduce Israeli developed weapons systems, complementing the weapons obtained from the United States. This includes the Merkava Mk-III tank and its auxiliary systems. The Merkava tank has been in service for some 20 years, and comprises 30% of the IDF's active tank force. The latest model – the Merkava Mk-IV – is under development. Israel also continues to manufacture fire-control and target-ranging systems for tanks as well as kits for improving the protection of armor on tanks and APCs. In addition, the IDF has improved the capabilities of combat engineering units to remove obstacles and clear minefields. The military has also developed the use of tanks as heavy armored personnel carriers, particularly in LIC missions in Lebanon.

The IDF's artillery corps are also modernizing by obtaining 48 MLRS launchers and upgrading their command and control systems. The *Mirkam* program also stresses the upgrading of anti-tank capabilities, both airborne, with combat helicopters, and land-based, with modern anti-tank missiles. In this framework, the IDF has announced that it is equiping infantry battalions with the 2-5 km range Gil anti-tank missiles, manufactured by Rafael–Israel's Armament Development Authority, which also produces the Spike and NTD-Dandy anti-tank missiles for export. Israel has also ordered TOW-2A anti-tank missiles.

The ground-based air-defense capabilities of the army formations were strengthened in 1998, with the deployment of the *Mahbet* air defense system, which incorporates both Stinger anti-aircraft missiles and the M-163 Vulcan SPAA anti-aircraft gun. The Israeli-designed *Mahbet* system is based on the integration of systems obtained from US military surplus stocks. The IDF air defense capabilities will be further reinforced with Chaparral anti-aircraft short range missiles, also from surplus US stocks.

The Israeli Air Force helicopter fleet took delivery in 1998 of 15 Black Hawk UH-60L helicopters. They joined 10 Black Hawk UH-60A already in the service. In addition, it continues to upgrade its CH-53 helicopters, to be renamed *Yassour 2000*. In 1998, Israel also obtained US permission to purchase AH-64 Apache Longbow helicopters.

## *The Persian Gulf and Arabian Peninsula*

The lessons of the Gulf War and the rising military power of Iran are the critical factors influencing the accelerated arms buildup of the Arab states. These states have signed huge arms deals with US and other Western companies, including Britain, Canada and France. The transactions involve tanks, APCs, artillery, and anti-tank missiles.

### Saudi Arabia

Saudi Arabia has managed to implement a vigorous buildup program in all branches of its armed forces, through a constant supply of US and other Western-made weapons. But that buildup has been hampered by budgetary and manpower constraints. Consequently, the Saudis failed to implement their plans to base their land forces organization on divisional level formations. Hence, the brigade continues to comprise its basic formation.

The Saudi Army has been slow in deploying the hundreds of tanks it has purchased in the 1990s. The army is preparing to deploy 315 US-manufactured Abrams M1-A2 tanks and 400 Bradley M2/M3 APCs, but must first complete the training of a sufficient number of crews. The Saudis had planned to order additional Abrams tanks to replace their aging M-60-A3s. Meanwhile, the army has retired its older AMX-30 tanks.

The Saudis have invested considerable resources in their National Guard. After the formation of its third mechanized brigade in the mid-1990s, the National Guard took delivery of wheeled (8X8) armored personnel carriers, the Canadian version of the Swiss Piranha APCs, manufactured by GM Canada. The contract comprised 1,100 vehicles, more than half of which have been delivered, partly to replace the wheeled V-150 Commando APC. In addition, the National Guard has procured 27 towed M-198 155 mm artillery pieces and 120 TOW anti-tank missile launchers from the United States. Some 50-200 Saudi-manufactured Peninsula Shield armored vehicles are likely to join the order of battle.

The Saudis have continued to invest in their combat helicopter fleet, organized in Army air wings. Germany appears to have begun delivery of 12 Cougar helicopters. The Saudis are also negotiating for the acquisition of 12-24 Apache helicopters from the United States. They already received 12 such helicopters in 1993.

**Kuwait**

Having recovered from the Iraqi invasion of 1990, Kuwait is in the process of rebuilding its military. It has wide access to Western arms but the emirate is hampered by manpower constraints that have slowed the pace of procurement and deployment in all branches of the military.

Nevertheless, Kuwait continues to mechanize its army. In this framework, 220 Abrams M-1 A2 tanks were purchased from the United States. In addition, it is integrating the British-made tracked Desert Warrior APCs, 250 of which have been delivered since 1994. These vehicles join 150 APCs procured from Russia and Egypt.

In 1998, the Kuwaiti National Guard continued to take delivery of US-made wheeled (6X6) Pandur APCs – the US version of an Austrian APC. By early 1999, half of an order of 200 of these vehicles have been delivered.

The Kuwaiti artillery corps is receiving more pieces in the framework of its plans to establish three more battalions. China plans to deliver 27 PLZ-45 155 mm artillery pieces, and the United States was to have sent 48 Paladin M-109A6 self-propelled guns until the Kuwaiti parliament froze the transaction in late 1998. The deal with the United States had also included AN/TPQ-36 artillery radar and some 30-100 120 mm self-propelled mortars. From Russia, Kuwait has taken delivery of long-range (70 km) Smerch MLRS. By early 1999, it also ordered anti-tank missile launchers – TOW-2B from the United States and HOT from France.

Kuwait is also building a fleet of helicopters. The first component of the fleet will be 16 Apache Longbow combat helicopters from the United States, adding to the 16 French-made Gazelle combat helicopters it already possesses. The second component is an order for Dolphin SA-365 naval attack helicopters from France. The third component will be combat transport helicopters: negotiations have begun for 20 Black Hawks (UH-60A/L) from the United States and 20 Cougars (SA-532) from France.

### Other GCC States

The *UAE* is continuing its military procurement from a variety of sources. Negotiations with Washington have been tough because of Abu Dhabi's insistence that the United States transfer sensitive technologies. At the same time, the UAE has been trying to diversify its procurements, negotiating with Britain, Holland and Russia to equip its land forces. These talks have improved the UAE's bargaining position in negotiations with the United States.

Since 1995, the army has taken delivery of an order of 390 French Leclerc main battle tanks. So far, about 250 have been delivered and 150 have been deployed. The army has ordered 460 modern APCs, of which 200 are US-made Bradleys (M-2/M-3), 140 are Turkish AAPC FMC-Nurols (deliveries were expected to commence in 1999), and 120 Russian BMP-3s (the status of this order is uncertain). In the realm of self-propelled artillery, in 1998 they renewed the acquisition of 85 M-109A3 self-propelled guns, upgraded in the Netherlands. Orders were also placed for multiple rocket launchers (MLRS) from the United States.

The UAE continues to develop its helicopter fleet, ordering 10 Apache combat helicopters. They will join the 20 Apaches that it received in 1993. In addition, the UAE has ordered Panther AS-562 naval attack helicopters. During the 1990s, the emirate also took delivery of medium and light transport helicopters.

An examination of the other oil-producing Gulf states yields a similar procurement pattern. *Bahrain* is continuing to integrate its M-60A3 tanks. The sheikdom took delivery of 70 of these tanks in 1998, thus doubling its corps since 1996. Earlier in the decade, it integrated the Dutch-manufactured YPR-765 APCs, and self-propelled M-110 (203 mm) artillery pieces and MLRS from the United States. Bahrain has also ordered TOW-2A anti-tank missile launchers from the United States while continuing the formation of a squadron of 14 Cobra AH-1E combat helicopters. In 1996, it had also taken delivery of several Black Hawk transport helicopters.

*Qatar* has also taken delivery of 10 AMX-30 tanks and has begun to take delivery of the first of the 40 Piranha P-2 wheeled APCs ordered from Switzerland. It has also ordered French VAB and Egyptian Fahd APCs. The emirate may also be upgrading 20 French self-propelled 155 mm MK F-3 artillery pieces. Negotiations are currently being conducted with Britain for the purchase of 50 modern Challenger tanks, and with France for the purchase of 50-100 Leclerc tanks.

There were no significant developments during 1998 in the *Omani* ground forces. They have apparently begun the integration of 80 British-manufactured (and Swiss-developed) wheeled (8X8) Piranha APCs. These APCs were purchased in a 1995 transaction that includes the option of an additional 40-50 APCs of the same model. Oman might also purchase 18 British-manufactured Challenger tanks, in addition to the 18 already procured in 1995. But the deal could be suspended because of Oman's economic woes.

### Iran

Iran aspires to become a major power in the Persian Gulf region, with the ability to project power far beyond its borders. However, the Iranian military buildup has been limited by political and economic constraints. In 1998-99, no significant new Iranian arms transactions were reported. Nor have there been any significant developments in the order of battle of its land forces, either in its operational formations or main weapons systems. At the same time, Iran has continued the modernization of its tank fleet, the main element of which is an order for several hundred T-72S tanks. It has also been progressing with its program to manufacture 150 Zulfikar tanks, based on the chassis of the M-47/48 tank and equipped with a Russian gun. Production has been slow – about 20 tanks a year – and by early 1999 only about 40 have been manufactured. In addition, the Iranian ground forces have procured several dozen locally-manufactured Boragh APCs.

Iran's main supplier is Russia, which provides systems for Tehran's air force, air defense forces, and army. Other states in the CIS, particularly Georgia, also supply weapons to Iran.

Iran continues to invest in surface-to-surface missile development, both strategic and tactical. It has purchased Scud B/C model missiles and has increased the number of launchers. In July 1998, it test-launched the Shihab-3 missile, with a range of 1300 km.

### Iraq

Iraq is attempting to preserve its military capabilities while having to contend with both external military threats and domestic threats to its regime. However, saddled by international sanctions that preclude the acquisition of modern equipment, Iraq has not recorded any new procurements. Hence, its over-all military capabilities are eroding. It continues to maintain its ground forces by cannibalizing weapons systems. At the same time, it has preserved the infrastructure and technology for the manufacture of ballistic missiles. But US and British air attacks in late 1998 and early 1999 have further damaged Iraq's air defense system as well as its infrastructure for the repair and manufacture of weapons.

### Yemen

The 1994 civil war exacted a heavy toll from Yemen's armed forces, which had just been through a major transformation in 1990 as a result of the unification of North Yemen and the Democratic Republic of Yemen. The war resulted in an erosion of the order of battle and manpower, and the country's helicopter fleet and the ground forces weaponry were damaged. In its efforts to rebuild its forces, Yemen may renew its arms procurement ties with Russia, as was indicated by the 1998 negotiations for the purchase of advanced Su-27 aircraft.

## *North Africa and Sudan*

In 1998-1999, only a few significant developments were reported in the armed forces of North Africa and Sudan. The absence of arms buildups in these countries was caused by economic constraints on the one hand, and the collapse of the Soviet Union, on the other. In the cases of Algeria and Sudan, the civil wars in which the two countries were engaged presented added difficulties to the modernization of their military forces.

*Algeria* is in the process of renewing procurements from Russia. Several contracts have been signed, including for the supply of attack helicopters. The West, particularly France, continues to maintain close security relations with Algiers in an attempt to help the regime fight Muslim fundamentalists.

The Algerian civil war has led to an increase in the components of military power that are relevant to the conduct of the war. Algeria has increased the number of artillery pieces, APCs, and helicopters. It has placed orders for 200 Egyptian-manufactured Fahd APCs after taking delivery of 200 such vehicles in the early 1990s. According to unconfirmed reports, Algeria has also ordered from Turkey 700 Akrep wheeled reconnaissance vehicles. It has also ordered 47 MI-8/17 attack helicopters from Russia and pilotless drones from South Africa.

*Libya* has reportedly failed to complete a major arms transaction over the past decade. All branches of the Libyan armed forces show signs of erosion, particularly affecting such weapons systems as tanks, artillery, and combat helicopters.

Similarly, *Tunisia* has not reported significant arms deliveries for its land forces in recent years. Its recent orders have been limited to some M-109 self-propelled artillery pieces, as well as tank carriers, from the United States.

*Sudan* announced a program to increase conscription and the order of battle of its land forces. It is an ambitious program which highlights the government's problems in contending with the People's Liberation Army (SPLA) in the south of the country. While Sudan has not recorded any significant military procurements in recent years, in 1998 it acquired 6 MI-24 (Hind) combat helicopters from Belarus and ordered additional helicopters from Russia. These purchases will help offset the erosion of its helicopter fleet. Sudan also procures from Iran spare parts for its Russian- and Chinese-made weapons.

## Turkey

The Turkish military is one of the leading combat forces in the Middle East. Turkey is a member of NATO, and is a signatory to the Conventional Forces in Europe Treaty (CFE), which sets limits on weapons systems deployment in the European theater. Until the dissolution of the Soviet Union, Turkey had formed an important part of NATO's southern flank. Currently, it sees itself at the center of a triangle of instability, comprising the Balkans in the west, the Caucasus in the east, and the Middle East in the southwest. Turkey's defense policy is based on the assessment that it can lower external threats and increase influence by promoting military ties with states in the Balkans, the Caucasus and the Middle East.

The Turkish Armed Forces (TAF) have undertaken an ambitious and comprehensive modernization program, the implementation of which will be spread over the next decade. The military continues to rely primarily on conscripts; career officers and NCOs comprise only about 10 percent of the armed forces. Women have been commissioned in TAF land forces since the early 1990s.

Turkey's military procurement program places a high priority on domestic production of weapons systems, in an effort to advance its industrial and technological infrastructure.

Turkey developed its military ties with Israel in the mid-1990s. Strategic cooperation between the two countries is based on the common threats they perceive in Syria, Iran, Iraq, and Islamic fundamentalism, as well as on the close relations both countries have with the United States. The two countries also have similar modernization requirements for their armed forces. At the same time, Turkey also continues to maintain defense ties with Saudi Arabia and Jordan.

Turkey plans to manufacture 1,000 main battle tanks, to be undertaken jointly with overseas companies selected in competitive bidding. The TAF also intends to upgrade M-60 tanks, some 1,000 of which are currently in active service.

Since 1997, the TAF has been absorbing into its order of battle AAPC/ACV tracked APCs, manufactured in Turkey by FMC-Nurol in a joint project with the United States. So far, some 1,200 of the APCs, in various configurations, have been delivered, out of a total of 1,700 planned by the year 2000. The project has led to a substantial increase in the Turkish APC fleet, which had previously been based on 2,800 M113 A1/A2s.

Turkey's artillery arsenal includes both towed medium artillery and 155 mm self-propelled guns, 500 of which (models M52T and M44T) are being upgraded with the assistance of German companies. Turkey is also interested in procuring Eryx anti-tank rocket launchers. But a joint project with France for the manufacture of the launchers in Turkey was frozen in 1998 for political reasons.

The TAF continues to absorb US-manufactured ATACMS tactical surface-to-surface missiles into its order of battle. Some 40 missiles have been delivered since 1997, out of 72 ordered. The missiles are fired from MLRS launchers. Turkey possesses 12 such launchers; the ATACMS has a range of 150 km and is very accurate.

The TAF helicopter fleet includes a relatively small number (45) of combat helicopters, all of the Cobra family. Only a few of these are Super Cobras (AH-1W/1P) integrated into the TAF land forces. The acquisition of 145 modern combat helicopters is being planned; bids were examined in 1998 by Turkish Military Industries Agency (SSM), but a contractor has yet to be chosen. The first 50 helicopters are scheduled for delivery in 2002.

Turkey is also strengthening its fleet of transport helicopters. In 1998, the air arm of the army took delivery of 30 Cougar AS-532 helicopters, joining 20 that are already in its service since the mid-1990s. The helicopters are being produced in a joint project of French and Turkish aircraft industries. Most of the helicopters will be for the Turkish Air Force and used for reconnaissance and rescue missions.

Turkey is also considering procurement of additional heavy-lift helicopters for transporting ground troops and equipment. It also possesses 50 Black Hawk helicopters, 35 of which are in the service of the gendarmerie, which until 1998 was responsible for operations against the Kurdish insurgency, led by the Kurdish Workers Party (PKK). The Turkish Army published a tender in 1998 for 23 UAV pilotless drones, two-thirds of which are designated for long range (more than 300 km) and the remainder for medium range (200-300 km).

Turkey perceives threats from Greece in its dispute over the Aegean Sea, as well as from Syria. Its most serious internal threat is posed by the PKK, which has engaged in an insurgent activities for the last 15 years in the southeast of the country. Syria and Iraq have provided the PKK assistance and refuge; in 1998 this led to the transfer of responsibility for the war against the PKK from the gendarmerie to the army.

## Over-all Trends

An analysis of the quantitative buildup of land forces in the Middle East reveals several developments and trends:

**Mechanization.** Arab armies are continuing to mechanize their ground forces – an effort that began after the 1973 Arab-Israeli war – by turning infantry divisions into mechanized and armored divisions. Particularly noticeable in recent years has been a growth in the Arab arsenal of self-propelled artillery and anti-tank capabilities. The combined effect of these trends has been to offset some of the operational advantages the IDF had traditionally enjoyed in offensive ground combat.

**Combat Helicopters.** Helicopters have become increasingly important in land warfare in the Middle East. Their presence in the region began in the late 1970s. Helicopters were used in the 1980-88 Iraq-Iran war and the 1982 war in Lebanon, but Operation Desert Storm in 1991 marked a watershed in their use in ground combat. Subsequent to the introduction of anti-tank helicopters – manufactured in the Soviet Union, France, and Germany – the states of the Arab-Israeli subregion and the Persian Gulf have procured advanced US combat helicopters in the 1990s. The Apache Longbow, a long-range helicopter that can operate under all weather conditions, is expected to make its appearance in the years ahead.

Almost all states in the Middle East are now investing heavily in combat helicopters. The number of such helicopters in the service of the IDF has grown by 250 percent since 1984, and has doubled in the Arab orders of battle during the same periods. Several more large procurement transactions of combat helicopters are expected in Saudi Arabia and Kuwait. Israel's intensive employment of these helicopters in Lebanon has contributed to refining the doctrine governing their use in battle, as well as enhancing their integration with ground forces, and command, control and intelligence systems.

**C⁴I: Command, Control, Communications, Computers, and Intelligence.** Amid the information revolution, C⁴I systems have become increasingly important in the military. The 1991 Gulf War illustrated that in order to destroy masses of ground targets, possessing the means for destroying such targets is not sufficient. Rather, the capability for identifying and locating these targets accurately and in real time, and for assessing the damage they sustained, is critically important. This requires appropriate sensors and the capability to process and analyze the data obtained in real time. The capacity for synthesis and analysis of information is critical in an attack on ground targets, highlighting the importance of C⁴I systems in ground battle. While the Middle East is no exception, these systems have been more widely employed by air and naval forces in the region than by ground command. The integration of C⁴I systems into the land arena still constitutes a significant challenge to the armed forces of the Middle East. Egypt, Saudi Arabia, Israel, and Turkey make the widest use of such systems.

*Egypt* has used C⁴I systems to integrate information sources with the command and control systems of its air defense command, and Saudi Arabia has also equipped itself with C⁴I systems for air defense. The Gulf War and the subsequent buildup of military forces exposed the vital need for such systems.

Consequently, the Saudis have completed the Peace Shield project, which makes use of airborne early warning and control systems integrated with Patriot anti-aircraft missile batteries. The Saudi system is expected to be linked to the Kuwaiti air defense system within the framework of the Gulf Cooperation Council. At the same time, the Saudis are expected to remain dependent on the United States for operating and maintaining the Peace Shield system.

*Israel* has major advantages in the development and absorption of military C⁴I systems. It has long recognized the need to develop C⁴I systems to defend its air space, maximize the use of air power, exploit intelligence and ensure accurate firepower. These systems comprise the backbone of Israel's effort to preserve and expand the qualitative advantage it enjoys over Arab armed forces.

The multi-year *Mirkam* program has placed a high priority on the attainment of real-time battlefield intelligence capabilities. Advanced ELINT and COMINT systems, and increased reliance on visual intelligence (VISINT), from airborne and other platforms, have increased the need for accelerated filtering, processing, and transmission of information in combat. Israeli companies are also engaged in the export of C⁴I systems to a number of countries worldwide. At the same time, the Ofek reconnaissance satellite, currently in orbit, provides Israel with independent strategic intelligence.

The modernization program of *Turkey*'s armed forces places high priority on integrated communications systems (TAFICS) and command and control systems. In addition, Turkey is considering the acquisition of communications and intelligence systems that rely on satellite communications for its air force. In the land arena, Turkey plans to emphasize C⁴I-based fire control systems that rely on local area networks (LANs). In the sub-system for artillery, Turkey will continue to rely on command and control systems ($C^2$).

In Israel and Turkey, there is a clear awareness of the need to construct C⁴I systems for land forces, in a variety of configurations, from the level of the artillery battery and tank and infantry battalion, up to the division level. Foreign sources report that the IDF is equipping itself with a combat vehicle integration system (CVIS), apparently at the tactical level, for ground warfare. Other armies in the region have not been as involved in this sphere. Therefore, Israel currently enjoys considerable advantages in contending with battlefield information over other states in the region. It possesses the technology as well as the personnel to exploit this technology to the maximum.

**Organization and Manpower.** It is difficult to assess the changes in the manpower and organization of armed forces in the Middle East. It would be difficult to gauge, for example, changes in the level of motivation or in the capability to operate modern weapons systems. Information concerning manpower mix in the region's armed forces is insufficient in comparison to data pertaining to arms transactions with Western states.

Nevertheless, certain important conclusions can be inferred from data pertaining to developments in the manpower structures of the armed forces of the Middle East in recent years. With a much higher birth rate than in the developed Western countries, most Arab states have sufficient manpower reservoirs. The significant buildup in the armed forces of the Gulf region and the Arabian Peninsula – associated with procurement and integration of new equipment – have indeed resulted in increased manpower levels in the standing forces. In Saudi Arabia, Kuwait, Bahrain, and Qatar, a rise in manpower levels was detected in 1995. In the UAE and Oman, the increase began in 1997. Nevertheless, limitations in manpower and training have hampered the absorption of new systems in Saudi Arabia. Not surprisingly, Saudi military leaders have defined the element of manpower – including a plan to draft university graduates into the military – as the principal component of the 1996-2000 five-year plan.

In the Arab-Israeli subregion, the data on organization and manpower is mixed. Syria and Egypt, which have adopted general draft systems, have nevertheless experienced a decline in their standing force during the years 1993-98. The decline in Egypt reflects a comprehensive streamlining of manpower implemented simultaneously with the force buildup program. In Israel, there was a gradual increase in the number of draftees resulting from an increase in the manpower pool. At the same time, an effort has been made to reduce the number of career officers and NCOs in order to reduce costs. In the Jordanian military, based solely on professional personnel, manpower levels have remained constant.

It appears that the economic burden involved in maintaining large standing forces has been the determining factor in restraining manpower levels. The Arab armed forces failed to establish reserve units. The Syrians, who attempted in the 1980s to form two reserve armored divisions, are gradually turning these skeleton units into regular armored divisions. Jordan and Saudi Arabia have retreated from plans to launch a general draft, which could have created the basis for reserves. In Saudi Arabia and Kuwait, manpower limitations have apparently blocked the ability to absorb weapons systems for the army and air force. By contrast, through a well-developed reserve force, Israel is preserving its ability to counter the numerical advantage of its Arab rivals, whose populations are growing much more rapidly than that of Israel.

# *Comparative Strengths*

An examination of the balance of military power in the Middle East at the end of the 1990s should include a comparative analysis of the armed forces of states that have the potential for clashing with one another. The following remarks do not address the likelihood of war between these states; instead, it analyzes the strengths and weaknesses of these states in possible conflicts among them.

The political rivalries in the region provide numerous possibilities for conflicts between Israel and Arab states, among Arab states, and between non-Arab Muslim and Arab states. The end of the Cold War has not prevented Arab or Muslim states from engaging in such conflicts. Nevertheless, in the post-Soviet era, the United States has much greater freedom to intervene militarily in the region, possibly to limit the magnitude of these conflicts. The different conflict configurations will be addressed here by dividing them along the three subregions discussed earlier in this chapter: the Arab-Israeli subregion, the Persian Gulf and Arabian Peninsula, and North Africa.

## *The Arab-Israel Subregion*

Four main scenarios will be addressed within the framework of the Arab-Israeli subregion: (a) a war between Israel and Syria; (b) an "eastern front" conflict with Israel; (c) a comprehensive Arab war against Israel; and (d) a war between Syria and Jordan.

### Syria versus Israel

Under current geostrategic circumstances in the Middle East, this is the most likely war scenario in the Arab-Israeli subregion. Should Syria launch the war, it would try to recruit other Arab states such as Iraq, Iran, and Libya to supply it with weapons and spare parts, both during and after the fighting.

Syria and Israel have roughly the same number of mechanized and armored divisions. Syria has a quantitative advantage in the number of tanks and artillery pieces, but Israel's fleet of main battle tanks is of higher quality. Israel enjoys an advantage in mobility given its arsenals of APCs and self-propelled artillery. Syria maintains an advantage in tactical surface-to-surface missiles with conventional warheads, a factor likely to affect Israel in the early stages of combat.

Israel enjoys an advantage in the air, including in the number and quality of multi-role combat aircraft, combat helicopters and transport capabilities. Its cumulative advantages in the air, in advanced munitions, and in C⁴I systems, would offset Syria's quantitative advantages in the early stages of the ground battle and would provide Israel with a clear-cut advantage.

Land fighting between Syria and Israel would be waged in a relatively small area – the Golan Heights – and probably in Lebanon as well. Syria's aim would be to repeat the surprise attack of 1973. The main problems which the IDF would have to contend with in this scenario are: the need to mobilize reserves and move them to the front under fire; combat in a battlefield saturated with targets such as tanks, artillery batteries, command positions and logistic sites; and the need to move to the offensive within a matter of days. Although the modernization of the IDF is expected to improve these capabilities, Syria's defense capabilities should not be underestimated. Damascus is bound to commit troops to the Golan as well as around Damascus in an effort to block an all-out Israeli offensive.

### "Eastern front" versus Israel

In this scenario, which is based on past Israeli-Arab wars, ground forces from Jordan, Iraq, and Saudi Arabia would support the Syrian campaign. These states would also use combat jets, helicopters and surface-to-surface missiles during the war. Iran would contribute weapons and spare parts.

Jordan plays a major role in this scenario. The key question is whether the Hashemite Kingdom would allow the other Arab armies or air forces to use its territory or air space. Should Jordan allow the use of its territory, Israel would face a wide and powerful "eastern front." If Jordon refrained from becoming a launching pad for an Arab invasion, then this scenario would differ little from a Syrian-Israel war limited to the Golan Heights.

The addition of Iraqi, Jordanian, and Saudi forces would place Israel at a quantitative disadvantage. The Arab states would have numerical superiority in troops, armored and mechanized forces, and combat brigades, as well as in main weapons systems such as tanks, APCs, artillery pieces, and tactical surface-to-surface missiles. The Arab force would also wield superiority in combat helicopters. Yet, Israel would be able to counter these disadvantages with its air superiority and with the qualitative advantage of its ground forces.

Israel would continue to enjoy a qualitative and quantitative advantage in combat aircraft, even if the aforementioned Arab states supported the Syrian effort. But it would be difficult for the Israeli air force to support the ground campaign on the eastern front. This is because the Arab expeditionary forces would saturate the battlefront with surface-to-air missile launchers, both mobile and stationary.

It should be emphasized, however, that the establishment of an "eastern front" would require dramatic changes in the political landscape of the Middle East. Such changes are unlikely to occur soon.

### A broad Arab coalition versus Israel

In this scenario, Egypt and Jordan would violate their peace treaties with Israel to join an attack on Israel by Syria, Iraq, Saudi Arabia, Libya, and Kuwait. Algeria and Morocco would contribute to the war effort as well. Non-Arab Iran would send surface-to-surface missile units and helicopters to the Syrian front.

From Israel's standpoint, this is the worst-case scenario. Israeli troops would be heavily outnumbered in a two-front war and the Arab states would have between a two- to three-fold advantage in the number of divisions. They would also have greater quantities of main weapons systems such as tanks and artillery pieces. The Arab coalition would also enjoy a clear advantage in APCs, combat helicopters, and anti-tank missiles.

Egypt's participation in such an Arab coalition would be the most significant factor. The Egyptian military would alter the balance of land power and confront Israel with a formidable air force. The Egyptian Air Force is equipped with advanced US aircraft and support systems and operates according to Western combat doctrine. Israel would have great difficulty defeating an Arab coalition that operates on several fronts. Indeed, even if the task were limited to defending the country, Israel would be hard pressed to do this along a number of fronts simultaneously.

As in the two preceding scenarios, Israel would need to contend with two additional but minor fronts. In Lebanon, the IDF would be confronted by the Iranian-backed Hizballah as well as by other militias. The Hizballah is equipped with a varied arsenal, from light weapons and night-vision equipment, to anti-tank rockets, anti-helicopter missiles, and artillery. In the West Bank and Gaza Strip areas that are controlled by the Palestinian Authority (PA), the IDF would face regular forces as well as guerrillas aligned with the PA. These forces could hamper the movement of IDF troops to the front lines. Still, although the weight of these forces would be greater than during previous wars, the Lebanese or Palestinians are unlikely to have more than minimal influence on the course and the outcome of a comprehensive war.

### Syria versus Jordan

In a conflict between Syria and Jordan, the balance of power – on land, in the air, and in surface-to-surface missiles – would clearly be in Syria's favor. But Syria would not be able to exploit its superiority without moving troops away from the Israeli front – clearly a risky proposition. Syria would succeed in attaining certain objectives in northern Jordan, but Jordan could make Syria pay a high price for such success, especially if the help of other countries is summoned. Indeed, as the confrontation between the two countries in 1970 has shown, Israeli troop movement may be enough to prevent Syria from concentrating sufficient forces to defeat Jordan.

## *The Persian Gulf and Arabian Peninsula*

Iraq or Iran may initiate conflicts in the Gulf subregion. Iran is building its forces while Iraq's military strength is declining. Both countries are aware that any conflict in the Gulf would involve a US response. The inclusion of US military forces alters the balance of military power in the region and serves as a powerful deterrent to Iraqi and Iranian aggression.

### Iraq versus Iran

Despite the losses sustained by the Iraqi army in the 1991 Gulf War, and its subsequent military stagnation, Baghdad still wields a land force superior to that of Iran. The Iraqi army has 10 armored and mechanized divisions compared to four for Iran. The basic combat formation of Iraq's Republican Guard is the division, while that of Iran's Revolutionary Guards is the brigade. Iraq's fleet of 800 T-72 tanks comprise some 40 percent of its armored corps. Iran has only about 200 such tanks. The Iraqi order of battle includes 900 BMP APCs, compared to Iran's 400.

The Iraqi army would be more proficient in a campaign that involves mechanized and armored divisions and corps formations. Both armies, however, possess only a small arsenal of self-propelled artillery – about 150-200 pieces each.

An Iran-Iraq war would be waged mainly on land, along the two countries' 1,000 kilometer common border. The war would most likely be static, although both countries would try to launch major offensives in the southern and central sectors of the front. Iran enjoys an advantage in infantry that could be exploited mainly for defensive operations. In the immediate aftermath of the Gulf War, Iran worked to reduce Iraq's advantage in armor, but in recent years this effort has encountered increasing economic constraints.

The air forces of both countries are weak and are not likely to influence the outcome of the ground battle. Iraq lost a significant portion of its advanced combat aircraft during the 1991 Gulf War. Some of these aircraft were destroyed during the war; other aircraft were flown to Iran in an effort to save them from Allied air strikes. Iran has managed to integrate only a small portion of these jets, mainly Su-24s, into its order of battle.

The Mig 21, which is being retired by many former Soviet clients, comprises the backbone of the Iraqi Air Force. Hence, its capacity to participate in the land battle is very limited. Iraq enjoys some advantages over Iran in the sphere of air defense that derive from a dense array of surface-to-air missiles, supplemented by interceptor aircraft. Nevertheless, the erosion of Baghdad's C$^4$I systems creates weak points that the Iranian Air Force could exploit in offensive operations against Iraq.

As long as Iraq is limited in its ability to manufacture surface-to-surface missiles, Iran will have a relative advantage in tactical surface-to-surface missiles with conventional warheads: the Iranian order of battle contains 30-40 Scud launchers. These missiles could easily bypass Iraq's air defense system. In contrast, Iraq probably possesses no more than a handful of Scud launchers.

### Iraq versus the GCC

Hostilities could erupt between Iraq and the members of the Gulf Cooperation Council (GCC) – along Iraq's border with Kuwait or Saudi Arabia. Iraq could attempt to invade these states with ground forces and special forces and then assume a defensive posture. With forces already in the Gulf region, the likely US response to such an attack would be quick, and Iraq would be more vulnerable to such a response than in the past.

Despite the buildup of forces implemented by Saudi Arabia and other members of the GCC throughout the 1990s, Iraq still enjoys a quantitative advantage in ground forces. The Saudi Air Force would play a larger role than before, in defensive missions and ground support. Saudi Arabia's array of advanced Patriot surface-to-air missiles and C$^4$I systems dedicated to air defense would reduce the damage caused by the Iraqi Air Force, severely weakened since Operation Desert Storm.

A broad Arab coalition, including Bahrain, the UAE, and Egypt, could be expected to mobilize in a common front against Iraq. But Egypt's support might not be meaningful since its troops would be unlikely to arrive in time to make a difference.

## North Africa

The states of North Africa have a long history of intra-regional conflict. But the likelihood of military confrontation between these states appears to have diminished. Should such confrontations nevertheless erupt, they would be influenced by three main variables:

- The rising power of Egypt, and the weakening of Libya;
- The weakening of the Algerian armed forces due to the civil war;
- The loss of Soviet support for the Libyan and Algerian armed forces.

### Egypt versus Libya

An Egyptian-Libyan war would be waged far from the strategic centers of either country. The Egyptian armed forces enjoy an immeasurable quantitative and qualitative advantage on land and in the air over the Libyan armed forces. The basic formation in the Egyptian Army is the division – either armored or mechanized – while in Libya, the basic formation is the battalion, or, at most, a shaky brigade-like structure.

In the Western Desert, combat would probably spread over a vast expanse, with small units exchanging fire. In such desert combat, Egypt's helicopter fleet would allow the military to transport troops quickly and conduct special operations involving forces larger than battalions deep inside Libyan territory. Nevertheless, Egypt would find it difficult to operate its forces at the distances necessary to bring about Libya's strategic defeat.

## Algeria versus Morocco

The overall quantitative balance of forces between Morocco and Algeria clearly favors the latter. Although the Moroccan armed forces probably enjoy a considerable qualitative edge over Algeria's forces due to their Western training and doctrine, this advantage does not seem large enough to overcome the quantitative gap favoring Algeria. In an Algerian-Moroccan war, most of the fighting would take place in the desert, involving sporadic battles in isolated sectors. As a result, some of Algeria's military superiority would not be exploited. As in the previous scenario, fighting could be protracted, without a clear outcome.

## *Other Potential Conflicts*

It is worth noting how the balance of power in the Middle East might affect a number of other scenarios in the region at-large:

### Turkey versus Syria

In the second half of the 1990s, the Turkish armed forces made several impressive demonstrations of strength along the Syrian border, exacting a political price from Damascus that reflected Turkey's superiority over Syria in all spheres – on land, in the air, and at sea. Syria, which has focused on its border with Israel, had left its border with Turkey denuded of land forces. The Turkish armed forces are equipped with modern weapons systems and enjoy superiority in battlefield mobility.

The armed forces of both countries operate accurate tactical surface-to-surface missiles with conventional warheads, which can be employed against infrastructure and command installations. Turkey is equipped with ATACMS missiles while Syria possesses SS-21 missiles. In a conflict, Turkey would seek to exploit its air superiority; Turkey's F-16 aircraft would play a central role in interdiction missions as well as in support of ground forces.

### Turkey versus Iraq

Turkey and Iraq have never engaged in a direct military confrontation, yet both countries perceive such a confrontation as possible. The Turkish army is clearly superior to that of Iraq in all spheres. Turkey possess Western armor, modern APCs, and self-propelled artillery. The main front in such a confrontation would probably be the border region of northern Iraq and southeastern Turkey. The terrain is mountainous and armored movement would be slow. This would prevent Turkey from making full use of its superior army and air force.

### Iraq versus Syria

A confrontation between Iraq and Syria would be limited to the land and air arenas. Both countries would have a problem in concentrating forces. For Syria, this would mean having to withdraw forces currently positioned opposite Israel on the Golan Heights and in Lebanon. For Iraq, such a move would mean a redeployment of troops that now face Iran. In addition, both Iraq and Syria could not sustain a long war because their armed forces are deteriorating and suffer a shortage of spare parts.

Iraq has larger ground forces, but Syria has an advantage in mechanized and armored formations. The Syrian air force also enjoys a clear advantage over Iraq's air force that was severely damaged in the Gulf War. Syria also has an edge over Iraq in tactical surface-to-surface missiles.

### Iraq versus Jordan

The Iraqi army has a significant quantitative advantage over Jordan's ground forces. But the Jordanian air force has a certain qualitative edge stemming from its F-16 aircraft and its superior pilots. Still, Iraq has the overall advantage in air power; its quantitative advantage is too large for Jordan's qualitative edge to overcome.

## Conclusion: Current Threats to Israel

In conclusion, a few remarks may be appropriate regarding the implications of the preceding analysis on Israel's strategic net assessment. Clearly, Syria remains the primary military threat still confronting Israel. The Iraqi threat has been reduced considerably. Egypt and Jordan appear unlikely to join a military coalition against Israel. Still, Israel is confronted with emerging threats from surface-to-surface missiles and weapons of mass destruction.

The core of Syrian power is its ground forces. However, there has been a considerable decline in Syria's ability to attack Israel. Its Soviet strategic umbrella is gone and the likelihood that it could recruit other Arab states to support its war effort is also low.

The Iraqi threat has also declined for the short- and medium-term. US containment policy is preventing an Iraqi arms buildup. At the same time, the range of external and internal threats to Saddam Hussein's regime requires Iraq to maintain a military prepared for combat.

In an Israeli-Arab war, Iraq could be counted on to send ground forces to the Syrian front. Such a force would be supported by combat helicopters, air defense and air force units. Despite their longtime enmity, Iraq will become Syria's ally in any war with Israel. And unlike the Gulf states, the Iraqis would relish the prospect of joining such a war, tempered only by the considerable military and financial limitations imposed by international sanctions.

The surface-to-surface missile threat facing Israel is growing. The Arabs enjoy an advantage over Israel in conventional surface-to-surface missiles and launchers. These weapons are likely to damage Israel's military power and create an even greater disruption in Israeli cities, particularly during the early stages of fighting.

Israel is on the threshold of an initial capability to intercept surface-to-surface missiles, in the framework of the *Homa* project and its centerpiece—the Arrow ATBM. However, the project is not likely to check the efforts of Arab and Muslim states to procure tactical surface-to-surface missiles, or missiles with ranges of 500 km and above.

Israel retains its air superiority over Syria, a significant factor in winning the ground war. But the threat to Israel has expanded to include other Arab states armed by US-manufactured weapons systems. These systems have been deployed by the air forces of Egypt and the states of the Gulf subregion.

# The Balance of Air Forces

## Shmuel Gordon

Modern wars have demonstrated the primary role of air power: in high intensity conflict (HIC) such as the Gulf War, and low intensity conflicts (LIC) like the conflict in Southern Lebanon, air power has become a key to achieving not only military objectives but political goals. The emphasis in modern conflict on the limited use of power sometimes obscures the need to make a comprehensive measurement of the balance of aerial power.

Traditional assessments of military and air power have been based on the quantification of major platforms and combat units. Implicit in such an analysis is the assumption that the number of platforms (e.g., aircraft, helicopters and missile launchers) and units (e.g., wings, squadrons) are the principal criteria for measuring the strength of an air force. However, this assumption is only partially valid. In the past 20 years, air forces have experienced a revolution, applying advanced technologies to a wide range of munitions, weapons systems, avionics, sensors, and command, control, communication, computer and intelligence ($C^4I$) systems. These technological advancements and their implications are as crucial to air power as is the number of aircraft and squadrons.

Modern technology influences every aspect of warfare, improving the quality of weapons systems, enhancing manpower quality and affecting doctrine, tactics and organization. These elements combine to form synergetic effects, and enable air forces to reach high standards of planning and execution. Advanced technologies and their synergetic effects can offset disadvantages in pure quantitative balances, and allow a smaller force to perform a larger number of missions.

Hence, the analysis that follows attempts to emphasize the importance of evaluating an air force's capacity to integrate a broad array of systems. It comprises a comparative assessment of qualitative capabilities: state-of-the-art technology, advanced armaments, C⁴I systems and manpower. Although it is commonly assumed that quality cannot be measured accurately, the underlying premise of this analysis is that most elements of quality can be quantified by evaluating systems performance, and by examining the ability of advanced systems and integrated forces to execute defined missions.

Variations in the organizational frameworks of different air forces make it difficult to compare them. In Egypt, for example, unlike Israel, the airborne platforms and the ground-to-air defense systems do not operate under the same arm. To overcome this problem, the following analysis encompasses all the elements involved in air warfare, regardless of their organizational subordination.

A comparative analysis requires a model that measures the relative power of the adversaries. The first section describes the methodology used to develop the model. The second section uses the model to compare the strength of the Israeli Air Force with a coalition of Arab air forces. This section illustrates in some detail the various insights that can be derived by using the model. The final chapter employs the model to assess the relative strength of other air forces, or coalition of air forces, in the Middle East.

At the outset, it should be emphasized that the model used here is still at the research and development phase. In addition, important data required in order to make the analysis complete are not yet available. Hence, the results derived and presented here should be regarded as tentative.

## *Methodology*

The model ascertains the major roles of an air force, and attempts to measure the operational capabilities required to fulfill these roles successfully. Two categories of roles are used for this purpose: (a) Defensive air superiority in the air; and (b) Offensive air superiority on the battlefield, i.e., the capacity to destroy surface targets.

The first role of any air force is defensive air superiority – defense of the homeland and its armed forces. This role can be performed by using different platforms or combinations of platforms: (a) interceptors, or "search and destroy" platforms, which are assisted by intelligence gathering, command, control, and electronic warfare; (b) surface-to-air missile (SAM) systems, assisted by sensors and command systems; and, (c) a combination of interceptors and SAM systems.

Offensive air superiority on the battlefield (OASB), the second role of the air force, is aimed at achieving control of the ground battlefield and obtaining freedom of action and maneuver for ground forces. Its missions include: defeat, destruction and neutralization of enemy ground forces, elimination of weapons of mass destruction and surface-to-surface missiles (SSM), and the destruction of strategic targets, C⁴I systems, and other essential ground targets. The model excludes missions in which the air force is under direct control of the ground commander, such as close air support (CAS) and special operations. An example of the set of missions included in the OASB is the independent air campaign executed by the coalition forces in the Gulf War.

The basic assumptions of the methodology used in the development of the model are that: (a) the experience and professionalism of high quality analysts are indispensable to evaluating air power; (b) the accumulated experience of high quality analysts can be weighted by using expert systems and Delphi-like methodologies; and (c) the use of a model that enables integration of quantified professional assessments with the available data on air forces will significantly improve the comparative evaluation of air forces.

During the long process of developing this model, the parameters of aerial power were defined, data and information on most of these parameters were gathered, and the relative importance ("weight") of each parameter was assessed and calculated.

At the outset, a group of military experts was chosen to take part in the classification and selection of the parameters of aerial power. A detailed list of parameters was prepared and the experts were asked to grade each of them according to their importance to aerial power. The results were calculated, the low-grade parameters were re-evaluated, and, as a result, some of the parameters were removed from the list.

The remaining parameters were divided into several groups, such as: systems, manpower, and infrastructure. Each group was divided into several sub-groups. For example: the group "systems" was divided into two sub-groups: fighting systems and support systems. Finally, the sub-groups were further categorized. For example: fighting systems include aircraft, helicopters, and munitions, etc. Chart 1 illustrates a partial "tree of parameters":

## Chart 1: Parameters of Offensive Superiority

| | | Support Systems | Helicopters |
|---|---|---|---|
| | Systems | | |
| | | Weapons Systems | Aircraft |
| | | Warriors | Air-to-Air Munitions |
| | Manpower | | |
| | | Support Manpower | |
| **Offensive Superiority** | | | Air-Ground Munitions |
| | | Physical | |
| | Infrastructure | | |
| | | Logistics & Supply | |
| | | Synergy | |
| | System of Systems | Rate of Operations | |
| | | Perseverance | |

Once developed, the model was distributed to several experts in air warfare, intelligence, air power assessment, and weapons systems. These experts were asked to assess the relative importance (weight) of each parameter. The sum of the weights of the parameters in each sub-group is always 1. Consequently, the high rating of one parameter is assigned at the expense of the other parameters in the same sub-group. For example, if a grade of 0.6 is assigned to "weapons systems," the parameter "support systems" cannot get a grade other than 0.4. Chart 2 illustrates a partial sample of the answers.

In order to calculate the weight of each parameter, the weight of the parameter was multiplied by the weight of its sub-group. Then, the result was multiplied by the weight of the group. The final result is the relative weight of the parameter in the total power of an air force. For example: the final weight of "aircraft" is 0.096. This is derived by multiplying the weight of "aircraft" (0.4) (representing the relative importance of "aircraft" in comparison to other "weapons systems") by the weight of "weapons systems" (0.6) (representing the importance of "weapons systems" in comparison to "support systems"). The result of this multiplication (0.24) is then multiplied by the weight of "systems" (0.4) (representing the importance of "systems" in comparison to other factors that comprise "offensive superiority").

## Chart 2: The " Weight " of Parameters

| Offensive Superiority | | | | | | |
|---|---|---|---|---|---|---|
| Systems | 0.4 | Support Systems | 0.4 | Helicopters | 0.2 |
| | | Weapons systems | 0.6 | Aircraft | 0.4 |
| | | | | Air-to-Air Munitions | 0.1 |
| Manpower | 0.3 | | | Air-Ground Munitions | 0.3 |
| Infrastructure | 0.1 | | | | |
| System of Systems | 0.2 | | | | |

The results imply that the parameter "aircraft" represents 9.6% of the total power of an air force. Yet, this percentage is considered very high on the hierarchy of parameters of aerial power. Since the determination of the combined weight is an essential element of the model, the results were reexamined exhaustively until they represented as accurately as possible the evaluation of the experts. The end product of this phase was a list representing the importance of each parameter of aerial power.

At this stage, the required quantitative data – platforms, manpower, and airfields – had been gathered, verified and added to the model. Some data, e.g., on synergy, could not be quantified. In these cases, the same experts were asked to grade the capability of each air force. The results of this method were also carefully reviewed, until they represented the evaluation of the experts. The product of this phase was a set of tables that consist of the quantitative data, and the results of the expert assessments of the other parameters of all air forces in the Middle East. The model mainly makes use of the JCSS database presented in part II of this volume. Regarding advanced weapons, essential data were also obtained from the SIPRI Arms Transfer Project.

For the purpose of evaluating the data, an expert system used by government and military organizations was chosen. The system is designed to be utilized by analysts and researchers in many fields. It enables individuals and groups to perform structured analyses of defined parameters, evaluating alternatives, and analyzing and recording the conclusions. The system features the ability to combine personal knowledge and accumulated experience within a formal procurement process: the user can integrate raw data with personal or group judgment to enhance the decision-making process.

After some technical tests, the expert system and the model were used and improved in the framework of several projects, including two decision-making games, carried out at the IDF's National Defense College. After further development, the methodology was defined as "operational." It played a pivotal role in a decision making process in Israel's Ministry of Defense regarding the possible development of a weapon system, as well as in the context of another choice made which invoiced many parameters of aerial power.

The model was then tested by constructing two "virtual" air forces and evaluating their relative power. Finally, the model's reliability, validity, and accuracy were verified by using sensitivity tests, and the availability of the required data was ascertained. The tests examined four types of variables used in the model: (a) the impact of changes in the weight of each parameter (the results of the expert assessments); (b) the effects of changes in a single expert's view; (c) the influence of changes in the quantitative data (number of aircraft, missiles, etc.); and (d) the impact of changes in the expert assessments of the non-qualitative parameters (synergy, perseverance, etc.)

During the process of constructing the model, the system was run hundreds of times. At each intermediate stage, the results were studied and necessary corrections and improvements were made. The process was applied separately to the two principal roles of air forces: defensive air superiority and offensive air superiority. The most serious shortcoming that emerged was the absence of sufficient quantitative data, mainly regarding precision munitions. This forced a further gathering of data. After achieving satisfactory results, insights, consequences, and conclusions were drawn.

The model used here, like any methodology of military power assessment, has some drawbacks. First, it does not use scenarios, which are employed frequently by military establishments in evaluating their military capabilities. Second, the model provides an evaluation of aerial power alone, and does not relate to other factors that influence the results of air campaigns, such as weather and geo-strategic and political factors. Third, it requires detailed and accurate data which are not always available. Finally, the model is sensitive to the accumulated experience and talents of the experts selected to take part in the exercise.

On the other hand, by allowing the incorporation of qualitative factors, the method has a clear advantage over traditional military balance analyses that rely solely on a quantitative comparison of weapon platforms and units. Intuitively, it is often clear that one air force is superior to another despite its smaller size. The model allows us a scientific method for verifying or disproving such assessments, and for making propositions about the relative strength of air forces.

# The Arab-Israeli Aerial Balance

The insights that can be derived from the methodology used here can be best demonstrated through a comparison of the strength of the Israeli Air Force (IAF) with the strength of a coalition of the Syrian, Egyptian, and Jordanian air forces plus an expeditionary force comprising of 20% of the Iraqi Air Force. This coalition could potentially represent a formidable opponent to the IAF.

Indeed, in order to fully appreciate the utility of the model, its outcomes should be compared to the results of applying traditional balance of power analysis – focusing on quantities of weapons – to the participating air forces. The illustration is limited to a comparison of weapons systems. Chart 3 compares numbers of airborne platforms – aircraft and helicopters – possessed by the Israeli Air Force and the coalition of Arab air forces.

## Chart 3: IAF-Coalition: Quantities of Main Platforms

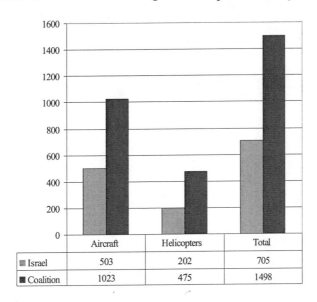

|  | Aircraft | Helicopters | Total |
|---|---|---|---|
| Israel | 503 | 202 | 705 |
| Coalition | 1023 | 475 | 1498 |

Chart 3 indicates that the coalition has an advantage of 1:2 in numbers of aircraft and 1:2.4 in helicopters. But this does not represent the real relative strength of the rivals. Most military observers would argue the opposite proposition, i.e., that the IAF is superior. Chart 4 demonstrates a more detailed evaluation that compares the quantities of different classes of aircraft, thus introducing a qualitative dimension to the analysis.

## Chart 4: IAF–Coalition: Aircraft by Classes

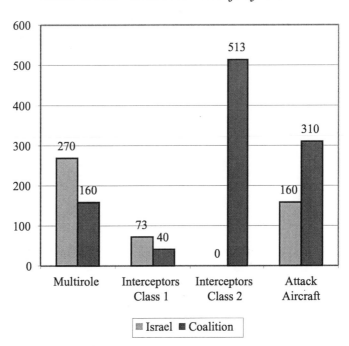

Yet, Chart 4 delivers a complex message. The IAF enjoys an advantage in high-quality aircraft, but the coalition has a decisive advantage in medium-quality aircraft. The chart does not lead to a clear conclusion as to the balance of the two air powers. If other weapons systems – helicopters, missiles, and UAVs – were added, the resulting portrait would be even more complicated and confusing.

By contrast, the model that has been developed allows for a clear comparison of the relative strength of the air forces, and presentation of this comparison in either a general or detailed form, depending on the purpose of the analysis. Chart 5 provides the evaluation yielded by the model regarding the fighting systems deployed by the Israeli Air Force and those deployed by the Arab coalition. It demonstrates clearly the superiority of the Israeli Air Force in weapons systems. It offers an integrated evaluation of the quantities and the qualities of weapons systems, and represents them in a simple chart.

## Chart 5: IAF–Coalition: All Fighting Systems

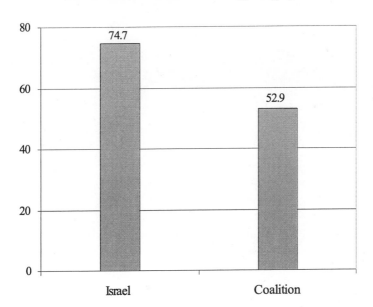

Chart 6 illustrates the relative over-all power of the IAF and the air forces of the broad Arab coalition when "defensive air superiority" and "offensive superiority on the battlefield" are differentiated. It demonstrates clearly the superiority of the IAF in weapons systems. It offers an integrated evaluation of the quantities and the qualities of weapons systems, and represents them in a simple chart.

## *Chart 6: IAF–Coalition: Aerial Power*

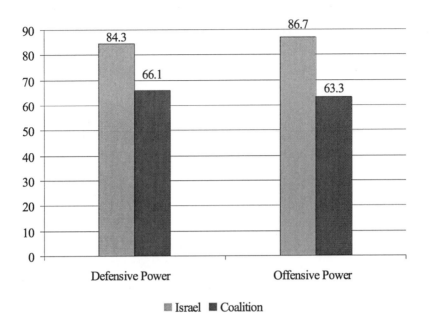

The chart demonstrates the substantial advantage of the IAF in both defensive and offensive roles. This is impressive because quantitatively, the IAF suffers a 1:2 disadvantage in total number of aircraft, attack helicopters, and airborne support systems, such as intelligence gathering and countermeasure systems. The ratio is even higher for SAM systems and precision guided munitions (PGM). The IAF is at a 1:1.7 disadvantage in air crews, and 1:5 in the number of air bases. But despite these gaps in quantity, the IAF enjoys superiority in the two main roles presented in the chart. This superiority is derived from its sophisticated C⁴I systems, "system of systems," its professional, highly motivated personnel, and superior weapons systems. This is illustrated in Chart 7 that focuses on the most important parameters.

The following sections elaborate how the two sides fare with respect to the four most significant families of parameters: 1) systems (weapons systems and others); 2) manpower; 3) infrastructure; and 4) "system of systems" which represents synergy, integration, perseverance, and rate of operations.

## *Chart 7: IAF–Coalition: Offensive Superiority*

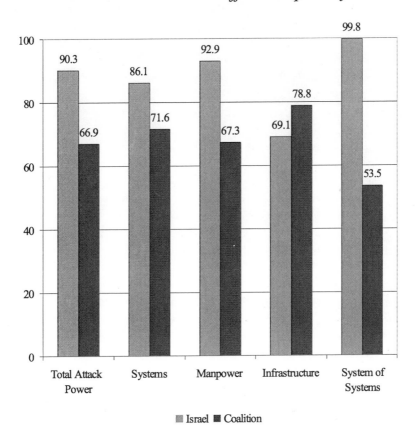

Israel ■ Coalition

### Systems

The rivals differ in the capabilities of their systems. The quality of the IAF systems overwhelms the quantitative advantage of the coalition. This qualitative advantage is most salient in multirole aircraft, first line interceptors, air-to-air missiles and air-to-ground guided munitions. The IAF procures advanced systems and weapons developed and produced by Israeli defense industries as well as from the US. In certain areas, Israeli military industries are among the most advanced in the world. This is reflected in the production of the Arrow Anti-Tactical Ballistic Missile (ATBM) system, the Silver Arrow long-range UAV, and PGMs for attack helicopters and aircraft.

The Egyptian air arm, the pivot of an Arab war coalition, is completing a long process of transformation to Western systems and technologies. It has procured various modern systems, such as aircraft, attack helicopters, air-to-air and air-to-ground guided munitions, C⁴I systems, early warning systems, and electronic warfare systems.

The modernization of an air force is often limited by economic constraints. This is clearly reflected in the Syrian Air Force which lags behind in modernization and procurement of modern aerial systems. The Iraqi Air Force is in even worse shape, with the UN sanctions applied against Iraq hindering any effort at reconstruction.

## Manpower

Manpower is another realm in which the IAF has a significant advantage. This is due to the fact that in this realm the qualitative dimension is of paramount importance. However, some quantitative dimensions of manpower are also significant: (a) the number of aircrews is crucial to sustain and endure high intensity conflict (HIC); (b) the ratio of air crews to aircraft and helicopters is also important, because aircraft fatigue is slower than the fatigue experienced by air crews. Thus, a higher ratio translates into a capability to fly more missions. The coalition's 1:1.7 advantage in this realm is therefore significant.

By contrast, the total number of personnel in the various air forces is of little significance. An air force is an organization that relies on the professionalism and motivation of its manpower – technicians, logistics workers, C⁴I operators, and fighting men. Air forces capitalize on cutting edge technologies, which demand a few high-quality operators rather than many low quality personnel. There is a synergistic effect in integrating modern technologies and quality manpower. This effect enhances the impact of the IAF's advantage in manpower on the over-all balance of air power. From this perspective, the IAF's advantage is probably even greater than the model indicates because experts tend to underestimate the quality of their own air force.

Quality is not an abstract term. Most parameters of quality are measured by quantitative parameters, and the end results of quality are measured quantitatively. Better pilots fire their munitions more accurately and kill more targets. They react more quickly to new threats and they have better odds of surviving – allowing them to participate in additional missions. Better technicians accomplish their duties quickly, and their work is more reliable.

## Infrastructure

Most estimates of air power ignore infrastructure as a significant family of parameters affecting air force strength. This probably stems from insufficient data, leading analysts to overlook the importance of infrastructure for offensive and defensive capabilities. Infrastructure of air bases, C⁴I centers, communication, fuel, and logistics is essential for air warfare. In addition to accelerating the rate of operations, the importance of infrastructure increases as: (a) the war progresses; (b) the intensity of fighting grows; (c) an air force struggles to survive under concentrated attack. In this realm the IAF, despite its modern infrastructure, is vulnerable. The coalition air forces have more assets and fighting men, and they are better dispersed.

## "System of Systems"

This family of parameters encompasses almost purely qualitative factors, including synergy, force multipliers, rate of operations and force preservation. These parameters depend heavily on the quality of manpower – particularly commanders, fighting men, operations planners and developers of C⁴I systems. The term "system" has two meanings: technological and organizational. "System of systems" is a complex consisting of platforms (aircraft, helicopters, UAVs, satellites, SAM systems), weapons systems, and C⁴I systems and centers, which integrate with operational organizations, doctrines, concepts of operations, processes of planning, command in real-time, and debriefing. The challenge is to transform a variety of technological and organizational systems into a workable, effective, efficient "system of systems."

Only a few air forces around the world have demonstrated a successful, modern "system of systems." None of the Arab air forces are among this group. By contrast, it is in this realm that the IAF enjoys the most formidable advantage. With this advantage, the IAF can exploit its relatively limited resources remarkably well and achieve two contradictory goals: a high rate of offensive operations and force preservation.

Among Arab states, the Egyptian Air Force has made noticeable progress in this realm, due to its close relationship with the US Air Force and the procurement of US-made systems. The Syrian Air Force has only a modest capability in "system of systems," but despite its continuing failure to compete with the IAF, it has acquired valuable experience in its encounters with Israel's air force. Jordan's Royal Air Force is assumed to have acquired a better "system of systems" capability than other Arab air forces, but it is too small to affect the over-all balance of power. The Iraqi Air Force contributes very little to total coalition strength in this category.

Finally, it should be emphasized that the diversified doctrines and tactics of different air forces, and the dissimilarities of equipment, probably degrade the power and capabilities of the coalition's combined strength in the "system of systems" realm. Consequently, the coalition faces a problem of coordination between forces, between aircraft and SAMs, between different $C^4I$ systems, and problems of electromagnetic interference among the different systems.

## Chart 8: IAF–Coalition: Offensive Air Superiority Sample of Parameters

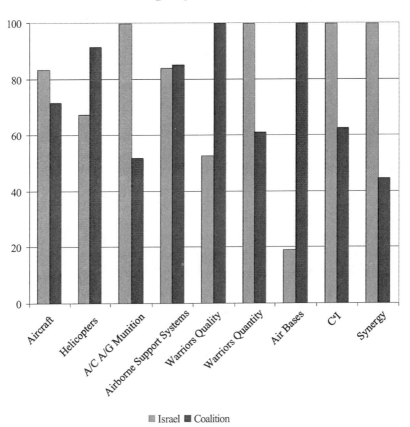

■ Israel ■ Coalition

## Over-all strength

The model utilized here improves our understanding of the components of the IAF's superiority – defensive and offensive – over a coalition of potential opponents. It also enables a refined evaluation of the strengths and weaknesses of the air forces involved.

It should be clear that despite its defensive air superiority, the IAF cannot prevent sporadic penetration by aircraft, helicopters and gliders into Israeli airspace. In addition, its ATBM defense is based on systems (the Arrow and *Homa* systems) that are only beginning to approach initial operational capability (IOC). On the other hand, the IAF has developed, deployed and currently utilizes a formidable defensive "system of systems" that challenges any attempt to threaten the state of Israel and its armed forces from the air.

The IAF's offensive superiority on the battlefield can be utilized to cause much destruction to ground forces, SSMs, national command systems, and other important elements of the coalition "war machine." Consequently, during the last few years, the IAF has become even more dominant in the IDF's operational offensive doctrine. As a result, more resources have been devoted to enhancing its offensive power.

The last two modern air wars in the Middle East (the Lebanon War and the Gulf War) are used as models for the IAF's doctrine, training, R&D and procurement. However, compared to its defensive superiority, which is overwhelming, the IAF's offensive superiority is not sufficient for performing all the missions that would be required of it. This is due to its relatively small size and its limited capability to operate at long ranges.

The coalition air forces apparently lag behind in the requirements of modern aerial offensive warfare. In order to play a substantial role, an air force should construct an effective "system of systems" capable of reacting in near real time as the situation changes. Yet, the coalition air forces are likely to suffer limited integration. In addition, their shortage of modern air-to-ground munitions, and the IAF's superior defensive power, combine to place serious limitations on the over-all performance of the coalition air forces' offensive operations.

Finally, the result of the comparison between the IAF and the air power of the broad coalition stipulated here implies that the IAF would enjoy an even greater advantage over a narrower Arab war coalition. As Chart 9 illustrates, this advantage would be even more dramatic should the conflict be limited to one between Israel and Syria–the IAF is twice as strong as the Syrian air force.

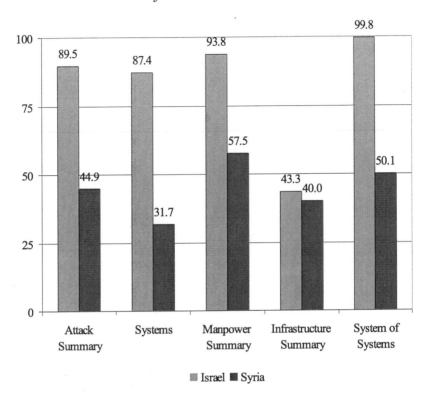

*Chart 9: IAF–Syrian Air Force: Main Parameters*

# Other Aerial Balances

This chapter briefly illustrates the main outcomes of the model when applied to other aerial balances in the Middle East. For this purpose, potential conflicts between different coalitions and nations were considered and the balance of the air powers participating in each conflict was evaluated. Before presenting these balances, the relative capabilities of the different air forces of the region are illustrated. Chart 10 relates to defensive superiority on the battlefield, and Chart 11 to offensive superiority.

## *Chart 10: Defensive Air Superiority*

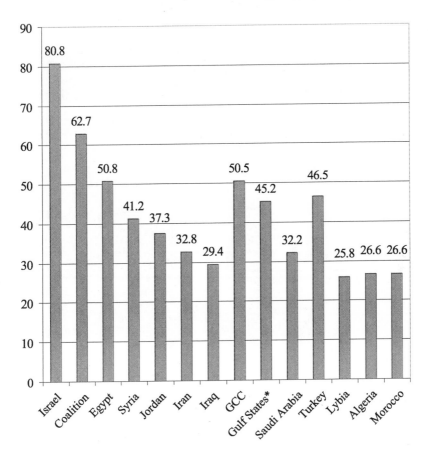

* Gulf States refers to the combined forces of the GCC states except Saudi Arabia.

## *Chart 11: Offensive Air Superiority*

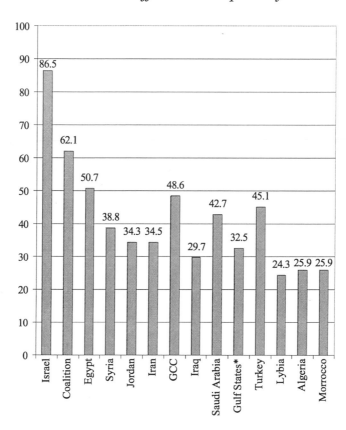

## *Primary Insights*

A brief observation of the two charts reveals the following insights:

- Most air forces have acquired a balanced capability. That is, their strength in defensive air superiority and offensive superiority on the battlefield is more or less symmetric.
- Rivals like Iran and Iraq, and Algeria and Morocco, enjoy an equilibrium in air power.
- The combined strength of the air forces of Saudi Arabia and the Gulf States is superior to that of the Iraqi Air Force.
- The IAF is superior to the other air forces of the region.

---

* See note on p. 65

A plausible explanation for the first two points may be found in the emphasis of the model on qualitative factors such as manpower, "system of systems," and technology. This emphasis reduces the weight of the differences in quantity on the final analysis of the relative capabilities of air forces in the Middle East.

## *Iraq versus GCC*

This section refers to the balance of air forces between Iraq on the one hand, and Saudi Arabia and the smaller members of the Gulf Cooperation Council (GCC) on the other.

Iraq retains sizable ground forces, but its air force suffered a crushing defeat in the Gulf War. Since then, the sanctions applied against Iraq made any rebuilding of its air force impossible. The Gulf states and Saudi Arabia, acknowledging the remaining Iraqi threat, attributed high priority to the modernization of their air forces and to coordination among them.

### *Chart 12: Iraq-GCC: Aerial Power*

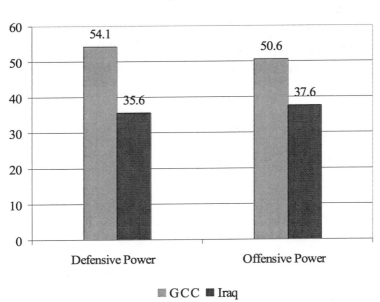

Chart 12 illustrates the relative power of the GCC air forces and the Iraqi Air Force. It demonstrates the substantial advantage of the GCC air forces in both defensive and offensive roles, providing a deterrent against Iraq. The GCC air forces are superior in both quantity and quality of weapons systems, advanced munitions, airborne support systems, and the quantity of active air crews. Chart 13 illustrates the balance of power in the main families parameters.

## *Chart 13: Iraq–GCC: Comparison of Main Parameters (Offensive Superiority)*

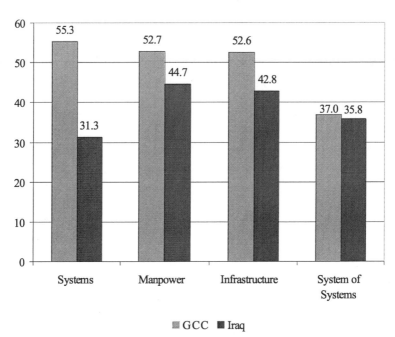

### Systems
The GCC air forces enjoy a decisive advantage in weapons systems over the Iraqi Air Force. The latter's advantage in number of aircraft does not have much effect, due to the substantial qualitative advantage of the GCC states. These states possess sufficient resources and enjoy access to Western military markets. They continue to modernize their air forces in order to deter Iraq from attacking, and to defend themselves if deterrence fails.

### Manpower
The approximate balance in number of aircrews is 1:1.8 in favor of the GCC. The quality of both sides' aircrews is much more difficult to estimate. However, the relationships of GCC air forces with Western air forces probably provide the

former with better training and doctrine. The platforms-aircrews ratio is similar, meaning that the rate of missions per aircraft and helicopter that the Iraqi and GCC air forces can perform is about the same, assuming that asymmetric logistical constraints do not change this balance. The advantage of the GCC in manpower is based on a preponderance of personnel, not on a qualitative edge.

### Infrastructure

The quality of GCC infrastructure is higher than that of Iraq. This advantage may enhance force preservation in case of a surprise attack by the Iraqi Air Force, and will help maintain the rate of operations in defensive and offensive warfare.

### "System of Systems"

Both sides suffer serious weaknesses in this realm. The Iraqi Air Force does not possess modern $C^4I$ systems or personnel qualified to operate such systems. The Gulf War has degraded Iraq's "system of systems" capabilities substantially, and UN sanctions prevent it from improving, even minimally, its capabilities in the parameters of synergy, rate of operations and force preservation.

### Conclusion

Saudi Arabia and the smaller Gulf states have significantly improved their ability to defend themselves against an Iraqi aerial attack. Iraq lost most of its offensive air superiority in the Gulf War and its aftermath, and its air force does not permit it to dominate the battlefield. The Gulf states have acquired sufficient air power to deter Iraq or to confront an Iraqi invasion without the involvement of outside powers.

## Turkey versus Syria

As a NATO member, Turkey is in a unique position in the Middle East. It controls part of Cyprus, and its relations with its neighbors–Greece to the west and Syria, Iraq, and Iran to the south and to the east – contain the roots of potential military conflict. Its growing relations with Israel may further increase tensions with its Arab neighbors.

A number of Turkey's air bases are used by the United States Air Force (USAF) for operations against Iraq, and some of its air space and air bases are used by the IAF for training. Turkey's potential military conflict with Syria is indicative of other conflicts in which Turkey may be involved without direct US military assistance.

## *Chart 14: Turkey-Syria: Aerial Power*

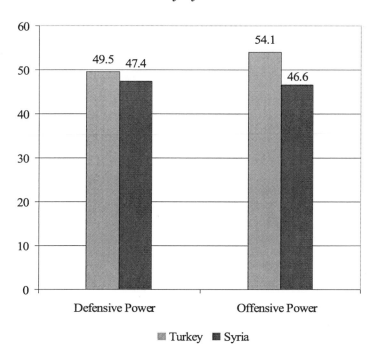

After the 1982 Lebanon War and the later disintegration of the Soviet Union, Syria did very little to modernize its air force. It has built and deployed its air force mainly to meet the IAF challenge.

Chart 14 illustrates the balance of power between the Turkish Air Force and the Syrian Air Force. The chart reflects the superiority of the Turkish Air Force – an interesting result, considering that quantitatively, it is inferior to Syria's air force in the number of aircraft, attack helicopters and aircrews. This is explained by the significant qualitative edge of Turkey's Air Force. Chart 15 illustrates the balance of power between the two air forces in the main families of parameters.

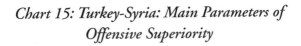

## Chart 15: Turkey-Syria: Main Parameters of Offensive Superiority

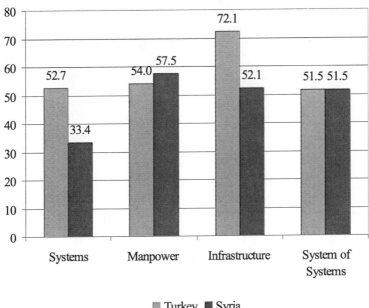

### Weapons systems

The Turkish Air Force has a considerable advantage in weapons systems due to the higher quality of its aircraft and its air-to-surface munitions. For example, its fleet of 175 multirole fighter aircraft has no Syrian equivalent. Turkey also possesses airborne support systems that are superior to the Syrian Air Force by a factor of almost three.

It should be noted that the defensive air doctrines of the two air forces are substantially different. The Turkish doctrine is based on the integration of fighter aircraft and deployed SAM systems, and emphasizes the use of interceptor aircraft. In the Syrian doctrine, the use of SAM systems is given high priority, while fighters are considered secondary and are used only to guard the flanks. Chart 16 provides the balance of power of the aircraft and SAM systems within the defensive air superiority role.

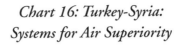

*Chart 16: Turkey-Syria:*
*Systems for Air Superiority*

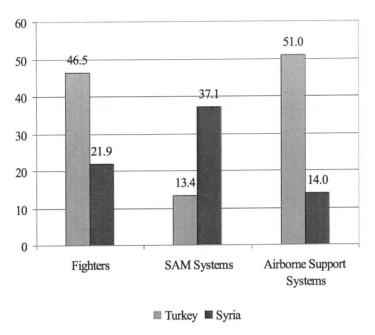

Turkey ■ Syria

Quantitative assessments, based on comparing the number of platforms, reveal that the aircraft ratio is 1:1.2 in favor of the Syrian Air Force. By contrast, the model used here, which integrates quantitative and qualitative evaluations, shows that the Turkish Air Force enjoys a dramatic over-all advantage over the Syrian Air Force. This is explained by the higher quality of fighter aircraft possessed by the Turkish Air Force and by its superiority in airborne support systems. The balance in the case of SAM systems is different: while the quantitative comparison favors Syria by only 1:1.2, the model presents a much greater Syrian advantage.

The Turkish Air Force is historically dependent on USAF assistance, systems and training. Recently, a new source for advanced systems – the Israeli defense industries – assisted in the modernization of the Turkish Air Force, in projects such as the upgrading of the F-4 fighters fleet. This upgrading includes some unique Israeli systems which were developed based on the IAF's combat experience gained in operations conducted against Syria.

## Manpower

The Syrian Air Force suffers a long-standing weakness in manpower quality. Exposure to Western technologies and training is considered essential for improvement in this sphere, but this has not materialized thus far. The Turkish Air Force has adopted NATO standards, and trains accordingly. This must have had considerable impact on the quality and professionalism of its personnel, but this qualitative edge is not sufficient to balance the Syrian advantage in size.

## Infrastructure

In infrastructure, the two air forces enjoy equal strength. The Turkish Air Force has an advantage in logistics, due to improvements it implemented prior to Desert Storm and in its aftermath, in order to meet the requirements of the USAF deployed in Turkey. But this advantage is balanced by Syria's superior early warning systems and its better logistics infrastructure in SAM systems.

## "System of Systems"

The two air forces probably fare similarly in this family of parameters. However, a shortage of relevant data inhibits a conclusive comparison in this realm.

## Conclusion

Syria has built its air force primarily to confront Israel. Recognition of the inherent inferiority of its air force has led to an emphasis on defensive aerial power and on SAM systems for air defense. Consequently, the organization, doctrine and weapons systems of the Syrian Air Force may not be suitable for a confrontation with its northern neighbor. By contrast, the Turkish Air Force, with assistance from the United States and Israel, appears to have increased its capacity to face the Syrian Air Force.

## *Libya versus Egypt*

Chart 17 illustrates the relative strengths of the Libyan Air Force and the Egyptian Air Force. The chart demonstrates the unequivocal dominance of the Egyptian Air Force in the defensive as well as the offensive role.

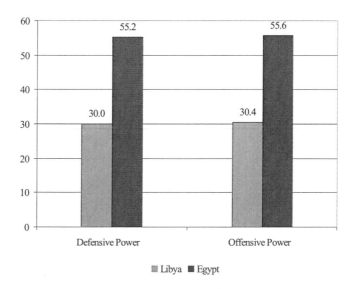

*Chart 17: Libya-Egypt: Aerial Power*

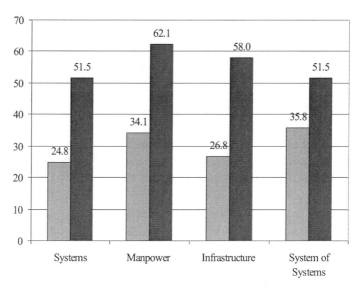

*Chart 18: Libya-Egypt: Main Parameters of
Offensive Air Superiority*

Chart 18 illustrates the ratio of power in the main families of parameters. It shows that based on a qualitative advantage in weapons systems, manpower and synergy, the superiority of the Egyptian Air Force is overwhelming in each family of parameters.

## Iran versus Iraq

Iran and Iraq are long-standing rivals, and the war in which they were engaged in 1980-1988 permits a close assessment of their qualitative parameters of power.

### Chart 19: Iran-Iraq: Aerial Power

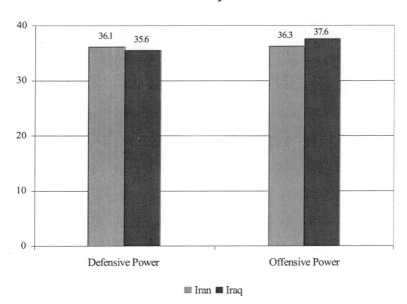

Chart 19 illustrates the relative strength of the two countries' air forces. It displays a slight superiority of the Iranian Air Force in defensive roles and a slight superiority of the Iraqis in the offensive roles. A closer observation reveals a much more intricate balance of power. Chart 20 illustrates the balance of air power between Iraq and Iran in the main families of parameters.

The results revealed in this chart are mixed. The Iranian Air Force has an advantage in weapons systems, manpower and "system of systems," mainly due to its qualitative edge in these realms. By contrast, the Iraqi Air Force is superior in infrastructure due mainly to its 1:1.8 advantage in air bases. The

## Chart 20: Iran-Iraq: Main Parameters of Offensive Air Superiority

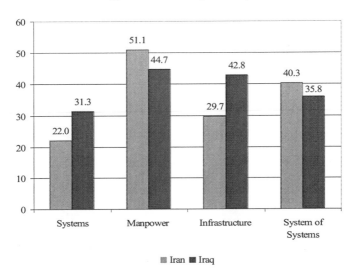

Iranian Air Force enjoys a better technological infrastructure due to its advantages in R&D and production of Iran's defense industries. Moreover, the military results of the Gulf War, the passive role of the Iraqi Air Force, and its inability to oppose the USAF in more recent operations, have probably had a negative impact on the morale and quality of the Iraqi Air Force's personnel.

### Algeria versus Morocco

On the western edge of the region, the two more powerful armed forces are those of Algeria and Morocco. The air forces of the two countries will probably play an important role in any military conflict between them. Chart 21 illustrates the relative power of the Moroccan Air Force and the Algerian Air Force.

## *Chart 21: Algeria-Morocco: Aerial Power*

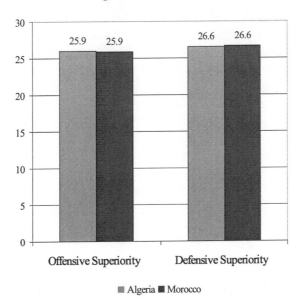

The chart shows that over-all, the two air forces are of equal strength. Similar results appear in Chart 22, which displays the main parameters of aerial power.

## *Chart 22: Algeria-Morocco: Main Parameters*

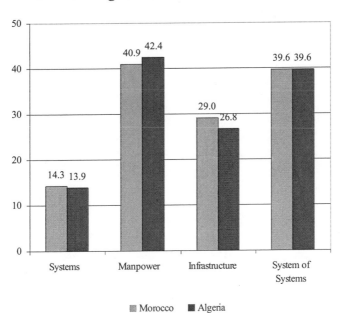

# *Concluding Remarks*

A number of concluding remarks are appropriate. The first concerns the importance of economic factors in affecting aerial power. The size and quality of most of the air forces in the Middle East did not change significantly in the past few years. This is due primarily to the severe economic constraints experienced by most of the region's states. It should be noted, however, that due to the absence of sufficient data, the model utilized here does not take into account the allocation of financial resources as a measure of air power strength.

The second remark concerns the role of surface-to-surface missiles (SSM). Ballistic missiles comprise an important factor in the Middle East military balance. These systems often compensate for the lack of offensive and deterrent power of air forces. SSMs are considered by some of the region's states (e.g., Iran, Iraq and Syria) as an "equalizer" against the offensive superiority of the IAF and the USAF. At the same time, defensive and offensive systems are being developed to counter the SSM threat. In the coming decade, technological and operational competition – between SSMs and weapons systems designed to reduce their threat – will become a crucial element in the regional balance of power.

The third remark highlights the similarity between the relative defense power and the offensive power of the region's air forces. Air forces have various roles and missions. However, the assessment of the balance of air forces is limited to only two pivotal roles: defensive air superiority and offensive superiority on the battlefield. These roles are associated with different requirements: weapons systems, intelligence gathering systems, platforms, doctrines, tactics, and training. But these roles differ even more in the type of targets on which they focus: defensive air superiority aims at the enemy's penetrating aircraft, while offensive superiority on the battlefield aims at the enemy's ground forces, C⁴I systems, SSMs and strategic assets. Consequently, an analysis of at least these two roles was required in order to estimate the balance among the region's air forces. This estimate demonstrates that air forces in the Middle East have developed a more or less balanced composition of forces, allowing them equal levels of offensive and defensive capabilities.

The final remark concerns the Israel Air Force. The IAF remains the dominant air force in the Middle East. This dominance results largely from its dramatic superiority in the "system of systems" parameter. In turn, this superiority stems from the IAF's high quality personnel, doctrine, and indigenous development and production of C⁴I systems. But, since the IAF comprises a central element of the IDF, and has a dominant role in Israel's defense doctrine, its real test is not whether it can defeat the other air forces in the region, but whether it can realize the expectation that it will have a decisive impact on the land battle and will be capable of destroying or suppressing strategic threats. In the latter realms, the IAF continues to suffer significant deficiencies. For example, its ability to destroy or suppress SSMs remains limited.

The analysis presented here is based on an innovative approach to the evaluation of air power. As is the case with other methodologies, the approach is not free of deficiencies. Hopefully it will continue to be modified in order to diminish its remaining drawbacks.

# The Balance of Naval Forces

## Eli Oren

Two events shaped the naval environment in the Mediterranean and the Middle East over the past decade: the first is the decline of Soviet power around the world. Indeed, the collapse of the Soviet Union left the United States and its allies in control of the naval arena. The second is the central role played by multinational naval forces in the two major conflicts during the past decade: the Gulf War and the war in the former Yugoslavia.

The Soviet Union's naval presence in the region had been based on friendly maritime facilities and fleets built with generous Soviet aid. The fleets relied on East Bloc weaponry and assistance in logistics, training, and operation. The disintegration of the Soviet Union and the enormous difficulties Russia encountered in maintaining the worldwide military deployment it had inherited led to the collapse of this support infrastructure. Russia changed its policies and sold weapons strictly on a cash basis. The result was that Moscow's weapons became unaffordable to most former Soviet clients in the Third World.

The collapse of the Soviet naval network also led to a reexamination of Western military budgets. Western powers, particularly the United States, began to reorganize their militaries, cut their budgets and reduce their forces. These budget cuts particularly hurt the naval component of the force structures. Many of these services simply could not afford to maintain their fleets and were forced to retire ships and offer them for sale, mainly to states in Asia, Africa, and South America.

The United States Navy was no exception. The reform in the US military resulted in many ships being sold at bargain prices to allies. The victims of this policy were the naval industries of Europe, which in recent years registered a significant decline in orders for new ships.

In the 1990s, navies have also demonstrated an unprecedented degree of cooperation. Multinational military operations have become the norm. Many Western fleets have been involved in the establishment of multinational naval forces and have been trained to operate under unified command. The WEU naval force that operated in the Persian Gulf, and the joint WEU and NATO naval force that operated in the Adriatic, were established on an ad hoc basis. Other fleets operated as permanent naval forces – such as NATO's standing naval force in the Mediterranean, and the EuroMarFor – the multinational naval force established in 1993, comprised of units from France, Spain, Italy, and Portugal.

On the eve of the third millennium, and after 50 years as an arena of great-power rivalry, the Mediterranean is once again a Western Mare Nostrum. Indeed, Russia's withdrawal from the Mediterranean appears irreversible, at least for the foreseeable future.

The decline of the navies of Algeria, Libya and Syria was caused primarily by the end of Soviet assistance. Another factor has been international sanctions imposed on these nations, denying them access to Western arms markets. On the other hand, the navies of the Mediterranean states that enjoy US and Western European support have continued to develop. Cooperation between these navies and those of the United States and European states has become closer; bilateral and multilateral maneuvers have become the norm in the eastern Mediterranean.

The situation differs in the Persian Gulf, where Iran is developing an effective naval force. The Gulf's distance from the home ports of the US and European fleets – constraining their ability to maintain a continuous naval presence there – has also led to a less stable environment.

## *The Eastern Mediterranean*

The balance of naval power in the eastern Mediterranean mainly involves the navies of Israel and Egypt. Both are allied with the United States, are recipients of US aid, and enjoy a strong working relationship with the United States Navy and the Sixth Fleet. Although Israel and Egypt signed a peace treaty 20 years ago, they remain rivals in the sea, and their navies view one another as a threat.

### *The Israeli Navy*

The role of the Israeli Navy has been succinctly stated by one of its commanders-in-chief: "Open seas and safe coasts." This reflects the two main threats that the Israeli navy confronts. It also serves as the basis for the navy's force development plans.

- **The threat to Israel's shipping lanes.** This threat was manifested in the Israeli-Arab wars of 1956, 1967, and 1973 when Egyptian forces blockaded the Israeli port of Eilat. Since then, blockade scenarios have determined the navy's policy on offensive warfare as well as its requirements for an independent capability for securing important shipping lanes, including those far from Israel's shores.

- **The threat of sea-borne terrorism** against population centers and infrastructure along the coast. The vulnerability of Israel's so-called soft underbelly to infiltration from the sea resulted in numerous terrorist attempts to penetrate the country's array of detection systems and naval patrols. After Israel had experienced several painful sea-borne terrorist raids in the 1970s, the navy enhanced its detection and interception capabilities. Coastal defense was based on an integrated system of land stations, and air and sea patrols. These patrols were carried out mainly by small patrol vessels of the Dabur- and derivative classes.

Israel's current naval development plan began after the 1973 Yom Kippur War. Unlike the ground, air, and intelligence arms, the navy performed well in that conflict, and its combat doctrine proved effective. The Israeli navy routed its counterparts in Egypt and Syria. But ironically, the navy's success almost led to its downfall. The IDF's top command and Israel's senior defense officials attached a lower priority to the navy. Decisions on procurement programs were repeatedly delayed or modified. After several unsuccessful trials with Flagstaff-class hydrofoils, built by the United States and Israel, and improvements of the Sa'ar-class vessels, the navy's procurement programs settled on the following components:

- **Surface Combat Vessels:** The most important component are the three advanced-model Sa'ar 5 corvettes, built in the United States according to an advanced design that emphasizes stealth. The vessels are equipped with advanced electronic systems, mainly of Israeli manufacture, and with the Barak missile defense system.

  Along with the Sa'ar 5s, the navy is equipped with smaller Nirit-class missile boats, of Israeli manufacture. These platforms, based on the hull of the Sa'ar 4.5, are equipped with some of the electronic systems developed for the Sa'ar 5, including a state-of-the-art mast, and the Barak system. The navy also continues to possess a number of older model missile boats, some of which have been refitted for anti-submarine warfare.

- **Submarines:** This component comprises three Gal-class submarines, built in the United Kingdom according to German design (IKL 500) more than 20 years ago. Since then, they have been upgraded, including the installation of the Sub Harpoon underwater-to-surface missiles. Three larger and more advanced Dolphin-class submarines built in Germany are gradually replacing this force. The original program consisted of construction of hull sections in German shipyards and assembly in shipyards in the United States. The plan, however, was shelved in the late 1980s. In 1991, it was revived after the German government announced its willingness to finance the construction in Germany of two submarines for the Israeli navy. In 1994, an agreement was reached for the construction of a third submarine, to be jointly financed by Germany and Israel.

The three Dolphin-class submarines, expected to enter active service by the year 2000, are among the most advanced conventional submarines in the world, with operational capabilities considerably superior to those of their Gal-class predecessors.

- **Helicopters:** The sea arm of the Israeli Air Force includes three Israeli-manufactured Westwind fixed-wing naval patrol planes and AS-565SA "Atalef" (Bat) naval helicopters. These operate from the decks of some classes of naval vessels. The development program for a helicopter drone – the HellStar – fell victim to budget cuts.

- **Coastal defense:** This is based on relatively small and simple Israeli-built vessels – the Dabur- and Dvora-class vessels. These vessels have been upgraded over the years, especially in their propulsion and detection capabilities.

Investment by the navy in the areas of anti-submarine warfare and mine countermeasure warfare has been more modest, reflecting the service's emphasis on offensive missions.

Much of the navy's equipment and ordnance are of Israeli development and manufacture. However, the growing dependence of the IDF's budget on US assistance has led to an increase in procurement from the United States. The strengthening of strategic ties between Israel and the United States is reflected in the close relations between the Israeli navy and the US Sixth Fleet, which includes the conduct of joint maneuvers.

The navy also has a role in developing Israel's relations with other states in the region. It conducts joint maneuvers with the Turkish navy, and has participated in three-way search-and-rescue (SAR) exercises – Mermaid 98 – with the Turkish and US fleets.

Israel and Jordan also conduct a brisk relationship – which includes SAR exercises – and cooperation in the Gulf of Eilat. By contrast, despite a peace agreement between Israel and Egypt, ties between the two countries' navies are virtually non-existent.

To summarize, the Israeli navy is undergoing a dramatic upgrading, especially of its surface vessels and submarines. Although the buildup will be slower than originally anticipated, it will allow the Israeli navy to maintain the qualitative advantage it enjoys in the eastern Mediterranean.

## The Egyptian Navy

The Egyptian navy is responsible for securing a 2,000-kilometer coastline along two seas. The navy has been given priority in recent years to ensure its central role in Egypt's military and strategic ties. This includes the service's participation in naval maneuvers with other countries both within and outside the region. For example, when Cairo sought to respond to Israeli-Turkish-American maneuvers, it arranged a similar exercise – Alexandria 98 – with the Greek navy.

The development of the Egyptian naval forces over the last 20 years stems from Cairo's relationship with the United States, which began when Cairo signed a peace treaty with Israel in 1979. In 1991, Egypt became a leading US ally when it joined the Western-led coalition against Iraq in Operation Desert Storm. In turn, the United States, which views Egypt as a strategic partner, recognizes the importance of a strong, friendly naval force, capable of helping to secure the international trade and oil-export routes from the Persian Gulf to the Mediterranean. Consequently, in recent years Washington has made considerable efforts to help the Egyptian navy in procurement, maintenance, instruction, and training. With its assistance programs, the United States has become virtually the sole supplier of the Egyptian navy.

When Cairo signed the peace treaty with Israel in 1979, Egypt's navy was just beginning to replace its Soviet-made vessels, regarded as inferior to those of the Israeli navy or to those of the Western-oriented Saudi navy. Subsequently, Egypt took advantage of its new access to Western arms markets. It bought from Britain six Ramadan-class missile boats, five smaller 6 October-class vessels, and two Descubierta-class missile frigates that were originally ordered by the Spanish navy. Egypt also upgraded its older vessels by installing new equipment, including Western radar and electronic warfare systems.

This breakthrough, however, did not stop the erosion of Egypt's second-line surface vessels or of the underwater fleet. China helped Egypt to address this problem by providing its navy with 24 inexpensive low-technology vessels in the first half of the 1980s, including four new submarines similar to those of the Romeo-class built in the Soviet Union in the late 1950s.

The Egyptian navy's next leap came in the late 1980s when it turned to the United States. When Egypt upgraded the four Chinese-built Romeo-class submarines, the United States agreed to furnish it with weapons systems and technologies never provided to an Arab navy. Thus, state-of-the-art US and

European weapons and detection systems were installed in the submarines. The systems gave these submarines the capability of launching underwater-to-surface Sub Harpoon missiles similar to those of the Israeli Gal-class submarines. Indeed, the Egyptian effort was planned after the Israeli navy announced that it would upgrade its submarine fleet. Thus, the modernization project, completed in 1996, assures the Egyptian navy a submarine fleet of reasonable capabilities for the next decade.

In recent years, the Egyptian navy has begun to explore the possibility of a further modernization of its submarine fleet. Within this framework, the procurement of two modern submarines is being considered. Egypt could acquire these vessels from the United States or from other potential suppliers. Yet purchasing the submarines from the US involves a major obstacle: US security assistance to Egypt is already over-committed due to prior long-term Egyptian orders from US arms manufactures. Outside the US, there are three possible means for obtaining the desired subs:

1. Purchasing two Dutch Zwaardvis-class submarines, decommissioned from the Dutch navy;
2. Building Moray-class submarines in the Netherlands;
3. Constructing German submarines similar to the Dolphin-class being built in Germany for the Israeli navy.

The Egyptian navy also seeks to enhance the anti-submarine warfare capabilities of the surface fleet. This fleet is threatened by traditional rivals – the Israeli and Libyan submarines – as well as by Iran's Russian-made Kilo-class submarines that operate in the southern approaches of the Red Sea.

The decommissioning of US naval vessels, subsequent to the Pentagon's Bottom Up Review, gave the Egyptian navy an opportunity to fulfill its military requirements within the framework of US aid programs. The resulting availability of naval platforms has led the Egyptian navy to alter the priorities of its buildup program. In 1994, under a lease agreement that eventually changed to purchase, the Egyptian navy obtained two Knox-class frigates built in the early 1970s. Between 1996-99, four modern Oliver Hazard Perry-class (OHP) frigates joined these vessels. The Egyptian navy also obtained 10 Super SeaSprite helicopters for reconnaissance and ASW missions. Additional modern weapons systems were also obtained, among them surface-to-surface and surface-to-air missiles, anti-submarine torpedoes with advanced capabilities, and Harpoon air-to-surface missiles for F-16 aircraft employed to operate against surface vessels. The Egyptian navy has also shown an interest in modern missile boats, as possible replacements for aging vessels.

The new systems enhance the Egyptian navy's capabilities in the following areas:

- **Operation of autonomous surface task forces on the high seas.** This is based mainly on OHP-class frigates and to a lesser extent on Knox- and Descubierta-class frigates. Armed with Harpoon missiles, these modern vessels possess state-of-the-art over-the-horizon surface combat capabilities, submarine detection and ASW capabilities (with both ship-borne systems and helicopters), as well as integrated defense against threats from the air (surface-to-air missiles).
- **Operation of airborne systems as integral components of a task force.** Such systems include helicopters for ASW tasks, detection, and over-the-horizon targeting; special fixed-wing aircraft for reconnaissance and over-the-horizon targeting; and F-16 combat aircraft with air-to-surface missiles.
- **Submarines.** Upgrading of Romeo-class submarines, enhancing their ability to detect surface vessels and providing them with underwater-to-surface missiles. This has increased the capabilities of Egypt's underwater fleet against surface vessels. By contrast, this upgrading has done little to reduce the signature of the submarines, thus leaving them exposed to enemy ASW systems.

The Achilles' heel of the Egyptian navy remains the quality of its personnel. The challenge faced by the service's instruction and training systems is greater than ever. This is further exacerbated by the fact that the Egyptian navy maintains a very large number of different systems of various origins, and at widely different technological levels.

The variety of systems employed by Egypt's navy also presents it with a difficult logistical burden. It employs three main types of Western missiles against surface ships: the Harpoon (in surface-to-surface, underwater-to-surface, and air-to-surface versions), the Italian Otomat, and the French Otomat (in surface-to-surface and air-to-surface versions). This is in addition to several types of Chinese and Soviet surface-to-surface missiles and a variety of surface-to-air missiles (SM-1 and ASPIDE). The variety is just as great in the sphere of underwater weaponry, propulsion, and electronic systems.

Consequently, despite massive US support, including the establishment of a training and maintenance infrastructure, the Egyptian navy still falls far short of realizing the full potential of its weapons systems.

## The Turkish Navy

The challenge facing the Turkish navy is daunting. Turkey's maritime border spans more than 8,000 kilometers, in the Aegean, Black, and Mediterranean seas. Its navy has played a leading role in its dispute with Greece in the Aegean, in the conflict in Cyprus, and in the tension with Syria. The Turkish navy is also involved in a range of international activities. It participates in NATO – the commander of the Turkish navy served also as the naval commander of the Northeast Mediterranean Area, within NATO's Southern Command. In addition, Turkey seeks to advance naval cooperation in the Black Sea and the eastern Mediterranean.

Most Turkish naval vessels and ordnance are of US and German origin. Nevertheless, some of its vessels and equipment are manufactured by Turkey's well-developed naval and defense industries, under license and in accordance with designs by foreign companies.

The navy maintains an order of battle balanced between surface combat vessels, submarines, and amphibious, mine warfare, and air arm units. The delivery in 1998 of three Oliver Hazard Perry-class (OHP) frigates – decommissioned by the US navy – was part of a multi-year force renewal and buildup program. This program will include additional frigates and other improvements in the fleet's operational capabilities.

The underwater component of the Turkish navy comprises obsolete US-manufactured diesel submarines and more modern German vessels, most of which have been built in Turkey under license. The scope of Turkey's underwater fleet – 15 submarines – is considerably greater than that of any other country in the eastern Mediterranean basin.

In summary, the Turkish navy is proficient in dealing with short-range threats. Once its force modernization program is completed in the early years of the 21st century, it will be better equipped to deal with distant threats, such as the securing of sea-lanes, and participation in long-range multinational operations.

## The Syrian Navy

Like this country's other armed services, the Syrian navy is based on Russian equipment and weapons systems, technicians and advisors. Tartous harbor, the southernmost of the Syrian navy's three bases, was one of the most important Soviet bases outside the Soviet Union, and served for many years as the home port of the Soviet Mediterranean fleet [Sovmedron]. The collapse of the Soviet Union, and the continuing disagreement with Russia over Syria's $12 billion debt, have hampered the efforts to resume procurement.

Syria's perception of its naval threats are based on the lessons of the 1973 Yom Kippur War and the 1982 Lebanon War. In 1973, Syria was unable to repel

Israeli warships that blockaded its coast. It also failed to prevent Israeli naval attacks on strategic facilities in Syria and Lebanon and the landing of Israeli troops along the Lebanese coast in 1982.

Damascus has low expectations from its navy, which ranks lowest in priority among Syria's armed services. This is because Syrian ports are far from Israel, and Damascus has land routes that serve as alternatives to sea traffic. Consequently, the only task expected of the navy is to defend the Syrian coast in coordination with land forces, naval helicopters, and attack aircraft.

The navy's modest responsibility has required minimal investment in front-line vessels and more substantial funding for detection capabilities and coastal weaponry. The latter systems include mainly mobile coast-to-sea missile launchers, such as the SSC-3 Styx for short-to-medium range, and the SSC-1B Sepal for medium-to-long range missiles. The navy has also sought to maintain its ASW capabilities by employing helicopters and surface vessels.

In the framework of its modest investments in its naval arm, Syria has nevertheless made some improvements in its fleet since 1973. Its Osa I and Osa II missile boats are newer and slightly upgraded versions of those deployed during the Yom Kippur War. The missiles on board these ships are updated versions of the SSN-2, developed in the late 1950s. The inferiority of these weapons prevents the Syrian navy from confronting its Israeli and Turkish neighbors.

Several years ago, Syria purchased three obsolete Soviet Romeo-class submarines, but failed to establish an underwater arm. Maintenance was so poor that the underwater fleet was badly damaged before the submarines could be deployed. Syria is said to be seeking modern Russian Kilo-class submarines, but Damascus probably lacks the funds required for such a transaction.

As a result, the Syrian navy does not pose a real challenge to any adversary. Its capacity to defend Syria's territorial waters and coast are somewhat better, but only if supported by its air force. Syria's ASW capabilities are also limited and will deteriorate further unless Damascus solves its maintenance problems and obtains modern submarines.

## The Lebanese Navy

The efforts to reestablish a central government in Beirut and to rebuild Lebanon's armed forces included a reexamination of the navy. The military has designated its naval arm as an important tool in law enforcement and the control of Lebanon's coast, which has been dominated for years by private militias.

Lebanese naval forces now include several patrol vessels obtained from Great Britain, and 24 small boats obtained in early 1994 from the United States. It also possesses two French-built landing craft, which survived the civil war.

### *The Jordanian Navy*

Jordan's naval force is responsible for securing the short Jordanian coastal strip between the borders with Saudi Arabia and Israel. The Jordanians deploy three Hawk fast patrol vessels of British manufacture, and several smaller patrol vessels for coastal defense.

In securing the Gulf of Aqaba, Jordan's small naval force cooperates with the navies of Israel, Egypt and Saudi Arabia. It also conducts joint exercises with the United States and other Western navies.

## *North Africa*

Until the early 1990s, the navies of North Africa played a role in the Mediterranean naval balance. At that time, Soviet support ended, and the region became embroiled in domestic conflicts. The best examples of the latter are the insurgency in Algeria and the war in the southern Sahara. These conflicts have drained national resources and led to the decline of North African naval power.

At the same time, the naval presence of the West in the region has been greatly strengthened. Libya perceives this presence as a threat, particularly after the establishment of the multinational European forces – EuroMarFor and EuroFor – in 1993.

### *The Libyan Navy*

In the early 1980s, at its peak, the Libyan navy had the largest fleet of missile boats in the southern Mediterranean. It included both Western and Soviet models of missile boats as well as submarines, amphibious forces, and other units. But the navy was dependent on foreign assistance for maintenance and operations.

At that time, Libya was able to pose a threat to navigation in Mediterranean. This led to the 1986 clash with the US Sixth Fleet. The clash stemmed from Libya's claim to the Gulf of Sidra, and its attempt to limit the freedom of navigation of the Sixth Fleet. At the end of the battle, two Libyan naval vessels were sunk and several were damaged.

This was the beginning of the decline of Libya's navy. In 1992, Moscow suspended its weapons supply to Tripoli in wake of sanctions imposed by the United Nations in connection with the explosion of the Pan Am jet over Lockerbie in 1988. Western-made vessels became the first victim of the sanctions, followed by Libya's submarines. Finally, Libya's Soviet-supplied surface vessels were disabled. They were able to survive the longest because it is easier to maintain surface vessels; Tripoli employed technicians from the former Soviet Union for this purpose.

By the late 1990s, none of the Foxtrot submarines procured from the Soviet Union in the late 1970s and early 1980s remain serviceable. Thus, Libya's underwater capabilities, which in the 1980s had caused much concern to Western navies as well as to those of neighboring states, ceased to exist.

Similarly, only a small fraction of the dozens of missile-carrying vessels in the Libyan navy remain capable of sustained patrols along Libya's long coast. Nevertheless, the naval infrastructure remaining at Libya's disposal would enable it to conduct terror operations, such as the clandestine mine-laying of the Red Sea in 1984, or attacks on civilian vessels.

## The Tunisian Navy

Tunisia's small navy focuses on guarding its territorial waters. It fulfills this mission with an antiquated force comprising of three French-built Combattante III missile boats, 20 patrol vessels from China, Britain, and France, and some 20 coast guard boats. Ten of the coast guard boats belonged to the former East Germany and were donated by the Federal Republic of Germany.

Tunisia's naval order of battle also includes a number of auxiliary vessels donated by the United States.

## The Algerian Navy

In the early 1980s, the Algerian navy launched an effort to close the gap with neighboring navies and to enable it to become a regional naval power. The buildup involved the procurement of frigates and missile boats from the Soviet Union, and the establishment of an amphibious force based on two British-built LSTs and a Soviet-built LSM. Algeria acquired patrol vessels from Britain and produced boats indigenously, based on foreign designs.

Algeria also purchased two Romeo-class submarines designed for training crews that were intended to operate modern Kilo-class submarines later in the decade. The latter submarines, fitted with quiet engines, were supplied to Algeria in the late 1980s. Until then, these submarines were supplied only to the navies of the Soviet Union, Poland, Romania, and India. Algeria, however, found it difficult to operate the submarines.

By the early 1990s, the navy also became a victim of Algeria's civil war. Funds were diverted from the navy, and the service began to deteriorate. Still, in 1997, Algeria signed an agreement with Russia for the refitting of the Koni-class frigates and Nanuchka-class corvettes. Under the agreement, Russia will also replace the missiles on these ships with the modern sub-sonic SSN-25, the Russian equivalent to the US Harpoon. These missiles could help revive the offensive potential of the Algerian navy.

### The Moroccan Navy

Like Tunisia, most of Morocco's navy is designed for coastal defense. Substantial portions of Morocco's vessels were procured in Spain, France and Denmark, and entered service only in the last decade. The navy's missile-carrying vessels–procured from Spain in the early 1980s – include four Lazaga-class missile boats and the navy's flagship, a Descubierta-class frigate. All of these vessels are armed with French Exocet missiles.

# The Persian Gulf and the Red Sea

One fifth of the world's oil supply flows through the Straits of Hormuz, a narrow waterway threatened repeatedly by Iran and Iraq. Over the past decades, the regional naval balance has undergone a number of changes as a result of the buildup of regional navies as well as the deployment of Western naval forces.

Three main naval forces are active at present in the Persian Gulf:

The **Iranian Navy.** After a long decline following the 1979 Khomeni revolution and the drawn-out war with Iraq, Tehran's navy has been bolstered in recent years. The service has grown to become an important naval force in the region, and perhaps even beyond.

The **navies of the GCC.** These navies perceive themselves as inferior to those of Iran, the main naval power in the region. Saudi Arabia and the oil-rich sheikdoms address these weaknesses by relying on political and military alliances with the United States and European powers, as well as on massive procurement of Western weaponry. The combination of the naval forces at the disposal of the GCC states appears formidable, but these forces are not sufficiently integrated to meet any threat. Hence, without US support and guidance, these forces are ineffective.

The **United States** naval presence dominates the Persian Gulf. That presence began in the late 1980s after the US Central Command (Centcom) was established in 1983. In 1995, the Fifth Fleet was reconstituted as the command's permanent naval component. A number of other Western navies have also maintained a presence in the Gulf. This presence peaked during the 1991 Gulf War.

In the 1980s, Iraq's navy was a significant factor in the Gulf. But in the wake of the Gulf War and the collapse of the Soviet Union, the Iraqi navy deteriorated rapidly and practically ceased to exist. Should United Nations sanctions be lifted, Iraq will rebuild its navy and attempt to reestablish a presence in the Gulf.

## The Iranian Navy

In the last years of the Pahlavi regime, Iran implemented an ambitious naval buildup program. The Shah sought for his navy a central role in safeguarding the Gulf sea-lanes for oil exports. But his ouster in the wake of the Islamic revolution ended that dream. Plans to acquire six destroyers and three submarines from the United States were canceled, and Germany suspended its sale of submarines.

The end of Iran's ties with the West damaged its navy during the 1980-88 war with Iraq. Toward the end of the decade, it also suffered heavy damage from US forces during the "tanker war." The early 1990s left the navy with only the remnants of Western-supplied ships and weapons systems. These vessels were disabled because of severe maintenance and logistics problems.

After the Iran-Iraq war, Tehran began a military buildup that also included the navy as well as naval units of the Revolutionary Guards. In this framework, Iran procured naval weaponry from China, including Hudong missile boats, C-802 and C-801K anti-ship missiles, and HY2 coastal missiles. Russia sold Tehran Kilo-class submarines and North Korea was said to have helped in an effort to build midget submarines. In addition, the Iranians upgraded old platforms with modern Chinese missiles.

At the same time, Iran developed its capacity to hinder traffic through the Persian Gulf and, particularly, the Straits of Hormuz. This was manifested by the deployment of anti-ship missiles in three small islands conquered from the UAE in 1971. Iran's capacity to disrupt traffic in the Gulf was strengthened by the acquisition of appropriate weapons systems, including submarines and sea mines.

A key component of Iran's naval procurement was the purchase from Russia of three Kilo-class submarines. The acquisition startled Iran's neighbors as well as Western fleets in the Gulf. The Arabs responded with programs to improve submarine detection with ASW capabilities. Saudi Arabia and the United Arab Emirates also announced their intentions to procure submarines but these plans did not materialize.

Subsequently, the Iranian threat appeared to have receded. Iran has encountered difficulties operating and deploying the Kilo submarines. Accidents have already been reported, reflecting poor maintenance. Moreover, these submarines do not appear suited to the bathymetric and bathythermal conditions of the Persian Gulf. By contrast, they may be more effective in the Gulf of Oman and the Indian Ocean. This assessment, fueled by reports that Iran has signed agreements for docking rights in Sudan and Mozambique, leads to concerns that it might project its naval power toward Africa.

## *The Gulf Cooperation Council (GCC) Navies*

The Gulf Cooperation Council was founded in 1981 by six Gulf states: Saudi Arabia, Kuwait, Qatar, Oman, Bahrain, and the United Arab Emirates. Until the 1991 Gulf War, this regional framework had very limited military significance. After the war, the GCC states began to allocate considerable financial resources to enhance their military capabilities. Funding for the GCC navies focused on missile-carrying surface vessels. Lesser priority was attached to the development of ASW and mines countermeasures (MCM) capabilities. In short, the GCC states did not build a balanced collective naval force.

Despite the efforts of Western contractors, Gulf states have made relatively limited purchases of naval platforms in recent years. These states have deferred orders of new platforms; instead, they procured second-hand vessels such as the US Oliver Hazard Perry class (OHP) frigates (by Bahrain), and two Dutch Kortnaer-class frigates (by the UAE).

**Kuwait:** In 1990, Iraq captured all but two vessels of the Kuwaiti navy. Many were later destroyed in Allied bombings during the liberation of the emirate. By the late 1990s, the navy had acquired mostly surface combat vessels. Eight Combattante missile boats have been built in France during 1997-1998.

**Saudi Arabia:** Of the GCC navies, the Saudi navy is the largest, and the only one that possesses modern frigate-size vessels, and that operates in two theaters. The navy's first-line order of battle comprises missile-carrying vessels acquired in the early 1980s in two large arms deals – one with the United States and the other with France.

After the Gulf War, France won a contract for renewing the Saudi surface fleet. The deal (SAWARI II) was signed in late 1994, and included the construction of three modern F-3000 frigates, training facilities, and logistical infrastructure. At the same time, the French also won a contract to refit four of the frigates purchased by the Saudis in an earlier transaction.

The Saudis have also enhanced their MCM capabilities by purchasing three Sandown minesweepers from Britain. In addition, they invested in improving their naval air arm and ASW capabilities. In the 1980s, the Saudis demonstrated an interest in procuring submarines. The plan, however, was shelved and appears unlikely to be revived soon.

The Saudis' modern platforms pose a real challenge to their navy's operational and maintenance capability. The navy continues to depend heavily on foreign technicians, and remains unable to fully exploit the potential of its weapons.

**Bahrain:** In September 1996, the United States delivered an OHP-class missile frigate to Bahrain, the smallest of the GCC navies. This modern, complex vessel, operating alongside the older six missile boats, will demand a considerable portion of the manpower and financial resources of the sheikdom's navy.

**Qatar:** The acquisition of missile-carrying surface vessels is the centerpiece of Qatar's naval buildup. In 1996-97, the sheikdom took delivery of four British Barzan-class (VITA) corvettes.

**The United Arab Emirates:** Until recently, the UAE navy has employed only small vessels, some of them armed with missiles. At the center of the navy's new build-up program is the procurement of larger missile-carrying vessels (corvettes/frigates) that would enhance its operational capabilities on the high seas. In the interim, the navy took delivery of two Kortenaer-class frigates, decommissioned from the Dutch Navy and refitted in Dutch shipyards. The build-up program has also included the acquisition of marine patrol aircraft and ASW capabilities.

**Oman:** Oman's long coast along the Persian Gulf and the Indian Ocean requires the emirate's navy to employ vessels for long-distance operations. Consequently, in the second half of 1996 and early 1997, the navy took delivery of two British-built missile corvettes designed for long-range operations.

Like its neighbors, the Omani navy also plans to enhance its ASW capabilities by installing modern detection systems in its warships.

## *The Red Sea*

**Yemen:** The Yemeni navy, deployed along the straits of Bab-el-Mandeb (at the southern approaches of the Red Sea), operates a variety of vessels manufactured by the former Soviet Union, China and France. These vessels, some of which were inherited from South Yemen, provide very limited capabilities. Yemen's surface force consists of two partially-operational Soviet-supplied Tarantul-class missile boats, in service since the early 1990s, and three Chinese-built missile boats delivered in 1995.

**Sudan:** Sudan's navy is one of the smallest and weakest in the Red Sea. The condition of its patrol boats is poor. Khartoum has obtained several small vessels from Iran, and Tehran has also provided aid in refitting and maintenance.

# Trends in Middle Eastern
# Defense Expenditures

## Shmuel Even

Over the past decade, the Middle East has continued to be one of the areas of the longest-standing tension in the world, despite the Arab-Israeli peace process and the curtailment of Iraqi power. In many of the region's states, the ratio between defense expenditures and the gross domestic product (henceforth– the defense burden) has been at least double that of most countries of the world,[1] while six Middle Eastern states have been among the twenty largest arms buyers in the world.[2]

Nevertheless, the trend of the defense burdens borne by Israel and its Arab neighbors has been downward, and such burdens are currently at their lowest levels in at least twenty-five years. For example, in the years 1973-74, the defense burdens of Israel and Egypt exceeded 30%, while those of Syria and Jordan stood at approximately 15%. These states have reduced their defense burdens, since they could not continue to bear the economic, social, and political prices involved. Realization that this is the case has been among the basic factors that have led Arab leaders to conclude that they could not solve their dispute with Israel by force, and that, consequently, they have no choice but to take part in the peace process. Thus, it was no accident that President Sadat of Egypt came to Jerusalem in November 1977, in the wake of the "Bread Riots," and after the Soviet Union demanded hard currency for continued arms shipments and maintenance. Neither was it entirely a matter of chance that President Assad of Syria and King Hussein of Jordan joined the peace process in October 1991; in the second half of the 1980s, both countries experienced economic crises that threatened their internal stability, and forced them to cut defense expenditures. Other contributing factors include the discontinuation of financial aid from Arab oil-producing states to Syria and Jordan, and the collapse of the Soviet Union, which had supplied Syria with arms at very favorable terms. Likewise, the Palestine Liberation Organization joined the Oslo process in 1993 following a severe economic crisis that reduced its ability to finance the struggle against Israel, and perhaps even threatened its very survival. All these cases illustrate the impact of economics on military and political developments in the Middle East.

This chapter focuses on the significance of developments, which commenced in the 1990s, relating to defense expenditures and the defense burdens of Middle Eastern states. Before presenting the relevant data, it is important to mention the difficulties involved in a comparative study of defense expenditures in the Middle East. Some of the regime's states, among them Syria, Jordan, and Egypt, do not include figures for arms imports in their defense budgets. Some states publish figures only for planned budgets, but not for actual defense spending. Several states, including Syria and Egypt, do not adjust foreign currency exchange rates for inflation; hence, a comparison of nominal defense spending data for such countries has little meaning, even when such data are stated in dollars. Such difficulties notwithstanding, it is possible to outline trends, and to reach important conclusions from an examination of real changes in defense expenditures, and from their relative weight in gross domestic products and national budgets, as well as from an analysis of published information about large arms transactions, and other macro-economic data.

The general trends in defense expenditures and arms burdens in the Middle East[3] have been:

- In the late 1980s, defense expenditures and defense burdens had begun to decline in most of the region's states, mainly due to economic constraints.
- In the early 1990s, defense expenditures and defense burdens rose in a majority of the states of the region. This trend was most salient among states affected by the war with Iraq.
- Around the mid-1990s, another downward trend in defense burdens was discernible in most Middle Eastern states. Yet, while there was a decline in defense expenditures in some states, in others, notably Egypt and Jordan, there was actually an increase in such outlays (see tables 1, 2). This occurred despite the reduction in their defense burden, thanks to a rapid expansion of the gross domestic product (GDP).

## Table 1: The Middle Eastern Defense Burden

Defense expenditures as a percentage of gross domestic product[4]

| Year | 1988 | 1989 | 1990 | 1991 | 1992 | 1993 | 1994 | 1995 | 1996 | 1997 |
|---|---|---|---|---|---|---|---|---|---|---|
| **Arab–Israel** | | | | | | | | | | |
| Syria | 7.9 | 8.0 | 6.9 | 10.4 | 9.0 | 7.2 | 7.4 | 7.3 | 6.7 | 6.5 |
| Lebanon | NK | NK | NK | 3.5 | 11.7 | 6.9 | 8.0 | 7.7 | 6.3 | NK |
| Jordan | 11.4 | 10.6 | 9.5 | 9.4 | 7.8 | 7.9 | 8.3 | 8.4 | 8.7 | NK |
| Egypt | 4.5 | 3.5 | 3.4 | 3.4 | 3.2 | 3.1 | 3.0 | 3.1 | 3.23 | 3.1 |
| Israel | 10.7 | 10.4 | 10.2 | 9.3 | 9.0 | 8.0 | 7.9 | 7.7 | 7.5 | 7.3 |
| **Persian Gulf** | | | | | | | | | | |
| Iran | 3.2 | 3.1 | 2.9 | 2.6 | 2.4 | 2.6 | 3.4 | 2.6 | 2.5 | NK |
| Saudi Arabia | 17.6 | 15.4 | (12.8) | (22.6) | 11.7 | 13.9 | 11.9 | 10.6 | (13.2) | NK |
| Kuwait | 8.2 | 8.5 | 48.5 | 117 | 31.8 | 12.4 | 13.3 | 13.9 | 11.9 | NK |
| **North Africa** | | | | | | | | | | |
| Algeria | 1.9 | 1.7 | (1.5) | 1.2 | (1.9) | 2.6 | 3.2 | 3.0 | 3.4 | NK |
| Morocco | 4.1 | 5.8 | 4.1 | 4.1 | 4.3 | 4.7 | 4.5 | 4.4 | (3.9) | NK |
| Tunisia | 2.7 | 2.8 | 2.7 | 2.6 | 2.3 | 2.4 | 2.3 | 1.9 | 1.8 | NK |

NK  - Not known

( )   - SIPRI estimate

## Figure 1. Arab-Israel – Real changes in defense expenditures (1990 = 100)

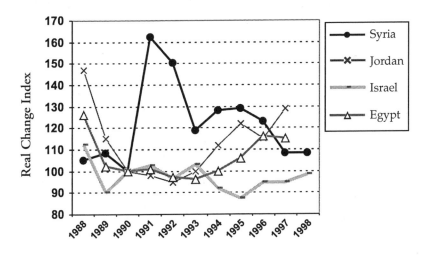

*Figure 2. The Persian Gulf – Real changes in defense expenditures (1990 = 100)*

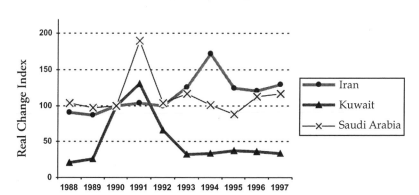

# Factors Affecting Defense Expenditures

During the 1990s, defense expenditures of Middle East states were affected by a number of factors:

## Conflicts in the region

Conflicts in the Middle East have been the main direct reason for heavy defense expenditures in the region. The current decade has been characterized by a certain reduction in the tension of the Israeli-Arab dispute, with progress in the peace process since the 1991 Madrid conference, and expectations for its continuation. Consequently, during the 1990s, the defense expenditures of Israel and its neighbors were no longer characterized by the dynamics that had marked the arms race in the past – a military buildup by one side would lead to an even stronger counter-buildup by others.

In the Gulf region, defense expenditures of all states have been affected by Saddam Hussein's attempts in two wars to make Iraq the major power in the region and control its oil. The 1991 Gulf War, and continued elevated tensions between Iraq and the United States and its allies, were reflected in the defense expenditures of Saudi Arabia and Kuwait throughout the decade. In addition, Iran's efforts to increase its influence in the Gulf area and throughout the Middle East, and the rebuilding of its armed forces after eight years of war with Iraq, induced an increase in its defense expenditures. The defense expenditures of Gulf states that view Iran as a threat experienced similar growth.

In North Africa, the defense expenditures of Algeria, which is experiencing serious internal security problems, have increased significantly. On the other hand, the defense expenditures of Morocco and Tunisia have remained stable.

## Economic resources

A state's economic resources constitute the major constraint on the level of its defense expenditures. States are likely to change the level of their defense expenditures as a direct result of changes in their economic circumstances. Examples abound: the rise in Saudi defense spending in the 1970s, in the wake of rising oil prices, and the sharp decline in the defense spending of Syria, Jordan, and Egypt in the second half of the 1980s, due to economic slumps.

As oil is one of the main national resources of several Arab states and Iran, there is a correlation between the state of the oil market and the level of defense expenditures in these states. Thus, the 1970s boom in the oil market led to a rise in their defense spending, while the fall in prices in the second half of the 1980s led to reduced military outlays. In the past decade, the benchmark Brent type of oil fetched an annual average of $16-21 per barrel on the world market, with the exception of 1998, when it declined to $13.

The state of the oil market affects both the major producing states, such as Saudi Arabia and Iraq, and Arab states that border on Israel. Egyptian and Syrian oil export revenues, and remittances from Syrian, Jordanian, and Egyptian workers in the Persian Gulf, comprise the major part of the hard currency earnings of these states. For example, Egyptian workers overseas send home more than $3 billion every year. And without some $2 billion in annual oil revenues, Syria would have to contend with significantly diminished defense capabilities.

## Foreign aid

Foreign aid constitutes a major source of financing for the arms purchases of a number of states in the region. United States security assistance – $1.8 billion a year to Israel and $1.3 billion a year to Egypt – comprises the principal source of outside military assistance to the Middle East, and the main source of weapons procurement financing for both states. By contrast, Jordan receives only several tens of millions of dollars in US assistance a year.

United States aid contributes significantly to strengthening its allies in the Middle East, especially in comparison to the allies of the former Soviet Union, who no longer have access to similar economic and military assistance. It should be borne in mind that until the 1990s, Syria, Libya, and Iraq had enjoyed large-scale Soviet aid, in the form of long-term credit for arms procurement at easy terms. The dissolution of the Soviet Union in 1991 led to the discontinuation of such credit. In fact, already by the mid-1980s, the Soviet Union had found it difficult to extend aid to its Arab clients. For their part, these clients have been unable to repay their debts to the Soviet Union. The aggregate current military debts of Syria, Iraq, and Libya – mostly now to Russia – are estimated at over $20 billion. It is unlikely, however, that Russia will be able to collect much of this debt. Currently, Russia is unwilling to sell arms to Arab states except on ordinary commercial terms. However, because of the low prices it charges for these weapons, Russia remains an attractive supplier.

Inter-Arab aid also contributed to the military buildups of several Arab states in previous decades. In the 1979-88 period, the oil producing states remitted to Syria, Jordan, and the Palestine Liberation Organization (PLO) some $15 billion, to help finance the armed struggle against Israel. These funds were extended in the framework of the "Baghdad aid," agreed upon in 1979 in response to the peace agreement between Israel and Egypt. In the 1990s, Egypt and Syria also received lump sums of several billion dollars from Saudi Arabia and Kuwait, for their participation in the liberation of Kuwait. Since then, however, the oil producing states have not extended significant assistance to Syria or Egypt.

## *The state of arms suppliers*

The circumstances of arms suppliers have considerable impact on military expenditures of states in the Middle East, all of which import arms from outside the region. While Israel is a world class arms manufacturer and exporter, and Egypt's arms industry is quite developed in comparison to that of other Arab states, both still procure most of their armaments from the United States.

Middle Eastern arms procurements from Russia and Eastern Europe declined drastically in the 1990s. Among the reasons for this have been the international sanctions applied against Iraq and Libya, the economic difficulties experienced by Arab states and Iran, and the fact that exporting states are willing to sell only when doing so is economically profitable.

The United States has thus become the main arms supplier to the Middle East and to the world market in general (in the period 1993-97, US worldwide arms exports totaled $53 billion, while Russian exports totaled only some $15 billion). Other Western suppliers – France, the UK, Italy, and Spain – have exported only limited amounts of armaments to the Middle East. This is due to the sanctions applied against Iraq, the difficulties that importers encounter in attempting to obtain financing at acceptable terms, and the preference several states in the region have for US arms. Nevertheless, armaments supplied in the past by the former Soviet Union and East European countries still comprise the main component in the arsenals of several states, among them Syria, Iraq, Libya, and Iran. These armaments are cheap – as low as a quarter of the price of Western armaments – because of low labor costs in Eastern Europe and Asia, and the high competitiveness of the arms market. The removal of sanctions against Libya, and a future removal of the sanctions applied against Iraq, are likely to increase arms exports by Russia, East European countries, and China to the Middle East.

Economic difficulties experienced by arms suppliers such as North Korea, and Middle Eastern importers, such as Syria and Iran, have not dampened efforts to procure unconventional weapons and surface-to-surface missiles required for delivering these weapons. In fact, such difficulties may have even spurred such procurement. These strategic weapons confer considerable power at relatively low cost, (as compared to massive procurement of conventional arms), while the suppliers enjoy high profits for their willingness to circumvent prohibitions on the supply of such weaponry enshrined in international and global treaties. The states most heavily involved in the export of components required for the development of unconventional weapons to the Middle East over the past decade have been Russia, China, and North Korea, whose imports of Middle Eastern oil over the same period have grown substantially. For their part, a number of Western European states, which are totally dependent on oil imports, have failed to supervise commercial companies engaged in transactions that have contributed to the development of unconventional weapons in Iran, Iraq, and Libya.

## *Competing Civilian Requirements*

Civilian needs, above all the furnishing of at least minimally tolerable living standards, have served to substantially inhibit the growth of defense expenditures over the past 15 years in such Middle Eastern states as Syria, Jordan, Egypt, and Iran. Their requirements have increased rapidly, as the populations of Arab states have been rising at over 3% a year (only Egypt has managed to restrain its population growth to approximately 2% a year). A continued population increase at this rate will lead to a doubling of the Arab world's population in 25 years – half under the age 18. Thus, there is a high proportion of dependents per gainfully employed person. The regimes of the region must furnish the needs of their populations at increasing levels – in the areas of housing, food, water, energy, public transportation, and education. Since civilian consumption (excluding investment) comprises two thirds or more of all economic resources in most states of the region, each year resources allotted to such consumption will have to increase by at least 2% merely to maintain existing standards of living (in terms of per capita civilian consumption). The conflict with the Islamic opposition, along with low standards of living, limits the ability of Arab regimes to undertake the reforms necessary to bring about a sharp economic turnaround. Under such circumstances, it is difficult to increase military spending.

From the standpoint of economic circumstances and living standards, Israel is immeasurably better off than its Arab neighbors. Nevertheless, in Israel as well, the military budget must compete with the rising costs of social benefits demanded by the population.

# The Israeli-Arab Conflict States

In the 1990s, the defense expenditures of Syria, Jordan, and Egypt stabilized, and even rose, after experiencing a sharp decline in real terms – estimated at 20% or more – in the late 1980s. Contraction of their military budgets was the result of economic crises that led to widespread discontent. The governments of these states concluded that the internal threats to their regimes were more serious than the external threats they faced. Other major reasons for the decrease in defense expenditures were the collapse of the Soviet Union and the discontinuation of assistance to Syria and Jordan by other Arab states.

While the peace process, which commenced at the 1991 Madrid Conference, raised expectations for a comprehensive political solution to the Israeli-Arab conflict, the defense expenditures of Syria, Jordan and Egypt rose considerably in the first half of the 1990s. Possible reasons for this were the following: the desire of these states to offset the sharp reductions in defense expenditures they had experienced in the late 1980s; the financial rewards received by Syria and Egypt from the Gulf states in return for their participation in the Gulf War against Iraq; an economic upturn in Syria, Jordan, Egypt, and Lebanon, reflected in rapid expansion of their GDPs during part of the early 1990s; and their desire to improve the balance of forces vis-à-vis Israel.

In contrast, Israeli defense expenditures stabilized and even declined modestly in the early 1990s, in inflation-adjusted terms. This followed Israel's sharp reduction of its defense burden in the 1980s.

## Syrian defense expenditures

Over the past decade, Syrian defense expenditures have fluctuated sharply. The most conspicuous rise was in the 1991-92 period, in the wake of Syrian participation in the Gulf War. This increase was motivated by the desire to offset the steep reductions in defense expenditures implemented by Syria in the late

1980s. The reversal of the downward trend was made possible by an economic upswing, as well as by grants from Saudi Arabia and Kuwait. Nevertheless, no material change took place; during most of the 1990s, the Syrian military did not grow significantly, and its arms procurements remained modest compared to the early 1980s.

According to preliminary data,[5] the 1998 military budget (which does not include military procurement) comprised 16.6% of the total budget and 33.5% of the current account budget (excluding investments). In monetary terms, the value of the major conventional weapons systems obtained by Syria in the 1993-97 period totaled only $321 million[6] (procurements not including such items as ammunition, spare parts, and ancillary systems).

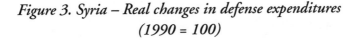

*Figure 3. Syria – Real changes in defense expenditures*
*(1990 = 100)*

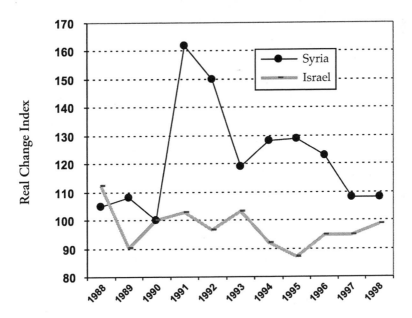

In the next few years, Syria's economic conditions are unlikely to permit a major military buildup without a significant lowering of the Syrian population's standard of living. In turn, such a development could endanger the regime's internal stability (except in the case of an actual national emergency), especially in a delicate period during which Assad is grooming his son Bashar as his successor. Yet, Syria remains capable of allocating several hundred million dollars to procure strategic weapons systems, like the SA-10 anti-aircraft missile or advanced aircraft from Russia.

In light of Syria's difficulties in obtaining external financial assistance, the level of its defense spending depends on the rate of growth of its GDP, which is strongly affected by developments in the oil sector (the major source of Syria's hard currency) and the agricultural sector (which constitutes approximately a fifth of the GDP). It is worth noting that both these sectors are influenced by factors over which Syria has no control, such as world oil prices and changes in the weather – critical to Syria's largely unirrigated agriculture. Thus, forecasting developments in the Syrian economy is difficult. While Syria enjoyed impressive growth rates in the 1993-95 period, these rates have since declined, resulting in an inflation-adjusted decline in defense expenditures in 1997-98. Even with economic improvement, it appears that in the next few years Syria will not be able to build up its military significantly, or to permit replacing its major Eastern weapons systems with Western armaments.

## *Figure 4. Syria – The rate of real growth of GDP*
in percentages

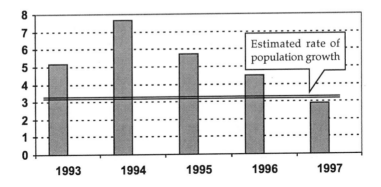

### *Jordan*

The small Jordanian military budget (approximately $600 million in 1997) nevertheless represents a relatively heavy defense burden, comprising approximately 8.7% of the GDP. Jordan's real defense burden is even higher, since these figures include outlays for internal security, but not for arms procurement.

During the 1990s, Jordan increased its military spending, in real terms, partly as a corrective to the sharp decline of the late 1980s, and partly as a result of its improved economy. (In the 1991-97 period, the Jordanian GDP grew at an average annual rate, discounted for inflation, of over 6%.[7] )

Over the past decade, Jordan has reduced the level of its arms acquisitions. The US was the source of most of this procurement, within the framework of a $220 million aid package provided after Jordan signed the peace agreement with Israel. Jordan has ordered, from US surplus military stocks, 12 F-16A aircraft (in 1997, it received 4 F-16Bs), and several helicopters and C-130 transport aircraft (which were delivered in 1997). Major conventional weapons systems delivered to Jordan in the 1995-97 period were worth approximately $160 million.

Jordan's defense expenditures are unlikely to increase significantly over the next few years, unless new tensions develop with its neighbors. In fact, Jordan's dire economic circumstances – reflected in such indicators as 25% unemployment and an external debt of $7 billion (140% of its GDP) – require that defense expenditures be kept low, in favor of economic stability. This is particularly important given that King Abdullah is in his first year on the throne, and that the Jordanian population expects greater prosperity.[8]

*Figure 5. Jordan – Real changes in defense expenditures (1990 = 100)*

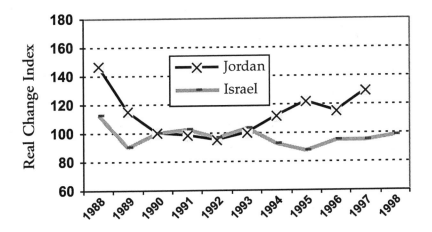

## Egypt

Egypt's military budget does not include US military assistance, which totals $1.3 billion. After an inflation-adjusted decline in the late 1980s, the Egyptian military budget stabilized; toward the mid-1990s it even increased in real terms. In 1997, defense expenditures accounted for 3% of Egypt's GDP[9] and 10.9% of its state budget. The long-term downward trend in the defense burden has been the result of an average annual rise in GDP of 4%[10] in the 1991-97 period. Assistance from the United States has included state-of-the-art weapons systems, such as F-16C aircraft, Apache attack helicopters (a transaction involving 12 helicopters, delivered in 1996-97, was worth $518 million), multiple rocket launchers (MRLS), and M-1A-1 tanks (assembled in Egypt). Egypt also imports military equipment from other states such as Russian MI-17 helicopters, purchased in 1997 at full price.

In the 1993-97 period, Egypt took delivery of major conventional weapons systems valued at $6.6 billion. Some of this weaponry was procured by mortgaging part of future US military assistance. Indeed, during this period, Egypt was ranked the third largest arms importer in the world.[11] Egypt's defense expenditures are unlikely to change in the next few years, barring significant unexpected political or military developments in the region.

*Figure 6. Egypt – Real changes in defense expenditures*
*(1990 = 100)*

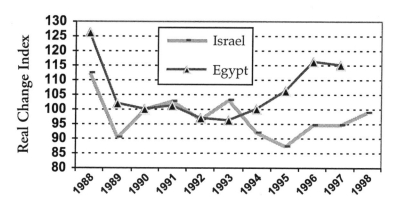

*Figure 7. Egypt – Rate of real growth of GDP[12]*

in percentages

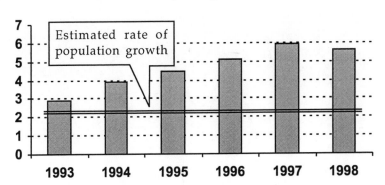

## Lebanon

Lebanon's defense expenditures total $400-500 million a year, representing a defense burden estimated at approximately 7%. Rising defense expenditures reflect increased activity by the Lebanese military in the course of imposing order in the country, under Syrian aegis. This increase was particularly sharp in 1991-92, when the Lebanese military was reconstituted in the wake of the country's internal stabilization. Most Lebanese military procurement in recent years has been within the framework of US military aid, and has included 460 M-113A2 armored personnel carriers and several Bell 205 helicopters from surplus US military stocks. On the budgetary side, there has been considerable similarity between the indices related to Lebanese and Syrian defense expenditures, raising the possibility that both budgets are determined in Damascus.

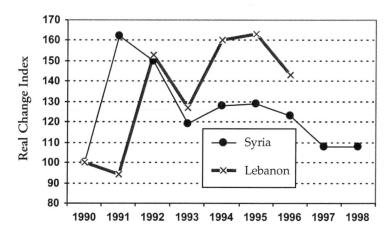

*Figure 8. Lebanon – Real changes in defense expenditures*
*(1990 = 100)*

*Table 2: The defense expenditures of*
*Syria, Jordan, Egypt, and Lebanon*
in millions of 1995 dollars[13]

| Year | 1988 | 1989 | 1990 | 1991 | 1992 | 1993 | 1994 | 1995 | 1996 | 1997 | 1998 |
|---|---|---|---|---|---|---|---|---|---|---|---|
| Syria | 2953 | 3020 | 2801 | 4529 | 4197 | 3322 | 3585 | 3608 | 3435 | 3030 | 3020 |
| Lebanon | NK | NK | 300 | 283 | 458 | 382 | 480 | 490 | 428 | NK | NK |
| Jordan | 669 | 520 | 454 | 444 | 432 | 453 | 508 | 552 | 570 | 585 | NK |
| Egypt | 2487 | 2005 | 1973 | 1987 | 1946 | 1890 | 1968 | (2100) | 2293 | 2271 | NK |

NK - Not known
() - Estimate

## Trends in Israeli defense expenditures

The Israeli military budget for 1999 totaled NIS 34.1 billion ($8.6 billion). This represented 14% of the state budget and 9.2% of the 1998 GDP. Since the mid-1970s, real military consumption in Israel has declined by over one third.[14] Investment and total civilian consumption (civilian public sector and private consumption) increased concurrently. Between 1982 (the war in Lebanon) and 1997, military consumption declined in inflation-adjusted terms by at least 10%.

By contrast, civilian consumption doubled (while the population rose by only approximately 75%), and the rate of inflation-adjusted investment rose by 128%. Consequently, the ratio of military consumption to GDP declined from 20.6% in 1982, to 9.8% in 1998.[15]

### Table 3: Military consumption, civilian consumption, and investment in Israel, 1982-98[16]

NIS millions (1995 prices)

| Year | Civilian Consumption | Military Consumption | | Investments | Total |
|------|------|------|------|------|------|
| | | Total | (Domestic)* | | |
| 1982 | 119,883 | 30,073 | 23,164 | 26,800 | 176,756 |
| 1988 | 153,504 | 31,691 | 22,119 | 28,115 | 213,310 |
| 1992 | 180,211 | 27,233 | 21,794 | 51,436 | 258,880 |
| 1995 | 218,266 | 24,623 | 20,151 | 64,897 | 307,786 |
| 1998 | 246,146 | 28,155 | 20,966 | 61,239 | 335,272 |
| Real change 1982-98 | 105.3% | -6.4% | -9.5% | 128.5% | 89.6% |

* Domestic military consumption = military consumption less overseas purchases

### Figure 9. Israel – Military consumption relative to civilian consumption and to investment

NIS millions (1995 prices)

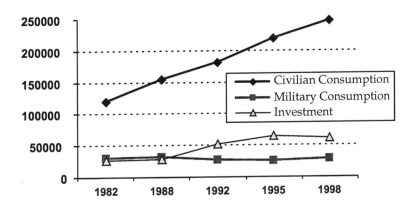

*Table 4: Israel – Resource allocation to military consumption, civilian consumption, and investment*

In percentages[17]

| Year | Civilian consumption | Military consumption Total | (Domestic) | Gross domestic investment |
|------|---------|-------|------------|------------|
| 1980 | 60.3 | 19.9 | 11.9 | 19.7 |
| 1982 | 61.9 | 18.1 | 12.4 | 20.1 |
| 1984 | 62.1 | 18.3 | 12.0 | 19.6 |
| 1986 | 69.1 | 14.0 | 9.7 | 16.9 |
| 1988 | 69.3 | 14.4 | 9.4 | 16.2 |
| 1990 | 69.9 | 12.4 | 9.2 | 17.6 |
| 1992 | 67.6 | 10.5 | 7.9 | 21.9 |
| 1994 | 70.1 | 9.0 | 6.8 | 20.9 |
| 1996 | 70.4 | 8.5 | 6.5 | 21.1 |
| 1998 | 73.2 | 8.9 | 6.6 | 17.9 |

*Figure 10. Defense consumption as percent of national resources*

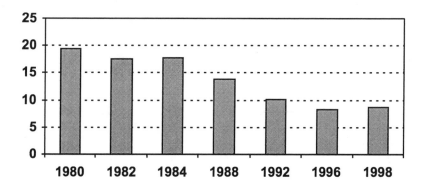

The sharp decline in Israel's defense burden can be partly explained by its altered strategic environment – primarily the evolving Arab-Israeli peace process and the crippling of Iraqi power, as well as by Israel's economic growth. But this cannot by itself explain the reduction in Israel's defense burden, since the peace process has yet to bring about a reduction in Arab military power. Furthermore, the struggle against terrorism continues, and the threats to Israel from surface-to-surface missiles and unconventional weapons have not abated. While the military budgets of the Arab states bordering on Israel declined considerably in the second half of the 1980s, they subsequently rose, and the budgetary cuts they did make did not result in a substantial long-term reduction in the scope of their forces. By contrast, Israel had already significantly reduced its combat forces by the mid-1980s,[18] while diverting a substantial portion of the remaining budget to financing military activities in Lebanon, Judea, Samaria, and the Gaza Strip, at the expense of preparedness for conventional war. This may indicate another reason for a reduction in Israel's defense burden: a shift in priorities from security to social-economic welfare. Thus, defense issues, which in the past had stood unchallenged at the top of the national agenda, have lost a large part of their claim to the national pie, in favor of social issues. This significant trend was already discernible in the 1980s (see table 5).

*Table 5: Defense expenditures relative to social services allocations*
in percentages[19]

| Year | Military | Education | Health | Social benefits and welfare | Religion-related services | Total social services |
|------|----------|-----------|--------|------------------------------|----------------------------|------------------------|
| 1980 | 32.5 | 10.7 | 6.4 | 10.3 | 0.3 | 31.8 |
| 1985 | 28.7 | 10.8 | 6.1 | 13.0 | 0.3 | 33.8 |
| 1992 | 20.1 | 12.6 | 6.1 | 17.6 | 0.6 | 49.3 |
| 1994 | 18.9 | 13.8 | 7.2 | 19.6 | 0.8 | 50.3 |
| 1996 | 17.6 | 14.9 | 10.6 | 20.7 | 0.7 | 54.6 |
| Change* | -54 | 39 | 66 | 101 | 133 | 72 |

* Between 1980 and 1996

Economic policy, which had become paramount since the hyperinflation of the 1980s, probably also contributed to the relative decline in Israel's defense expenditures. A reduction in government expenditures was considered necessary to prevent a continued inflationary explosion; defense expenditures were marked as a prime target for reduction, both because of their relative weight in the national budget, and because some economists tend to view the military as an unproductive sector.

The expectation that a continuation of the Middle East peace process will make possible a further large-scale reallocation of resources from the military to social purposes is liable to prove groundless. First, the transition of the military to a peacetime footing requires heavy investment, to permit adaptation to new circumstances. Second, the states with which Israel has signed peace agreements have thus far not significantly reduced their armed forces. And third, the ratio of domestic military consumption to civilian sector consumption (civilian consumption and investment) is approximately 1:15. Even if half of the Israeli-currency denominated military budget is reallocated toward improving living standards and investment, total civilian expenditures would rise by only less than 4%. Since the contribution that a dramatic reduction in defense expenditures would make to the economy is likely to be so limited, it is doubtful that it would be worthwhile to take the risks involved in such a change.

# *The Persian Gulf*

The Persian Gulf region has experienced the heavy defense expenditures associated with two wars initiated by Saddam Hussein: the eight-year war between Iraq and Iran, and the war between Iraq and the international coalition led by the United States. These wars cost the treasuries of the states in the region tens of billions of dollars, and caused damage estimated at several hundred billion dollars. The main distinguishing characteristic of the region's states is the centrality of oil exports to their economies.

## *Saudi Arabia*

Saudi Arabia's military expenditures are the largest in the Middle East, totaling approximately $18 billion in 1997 (12% of the GDP). This included the expenditures for military procurement and internal security. According to estimates, Saudi defense expenditures rose in 1996 and 1997. Previously, in 1991, Saudi Arabia provided tens of billions of dollars to finance the international coalition confronting Iraq. As the largest arms importer in the world, in 1993-97, Saudi Arabia procured $9.8 billion worth of major conventional weapons systems, mainly from the United States, the United Kingdom, and France.[20]

Subsequent to the Gulf War, Saudi Arabia entered into several huge arms transactions with the United States and the United Kingdom, which were partially implemented during 1995-97. In 1992, an agreement was signed with the United States for the delivery of 72 F-15S aircraft, worth $9.1 billion. At the same time, the Saudis entered into an agreement with the United Kingdom, which included 48 Tornado and 20 Hawk aircraft.

### Figure 11. Saudi Arabia's defense expenditures
billions of 1995 dollars

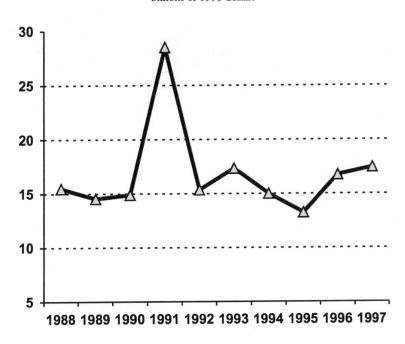

## Iraq

Iraq's military budget is not known; since the war with Iran, it has not published data related to defense expenditures. In 1979, according to its published data, Iraq's defense expenditures totaled approximately $2.7 billion, representing approximately 11% of its GDP. Since then, its defense expenditures and defense burden have increased sharply. In August 1990, an embargo on arms deliveries to Iraq was imposed; since then, most of its defense expenditures have been allocated to maintenance and salaries.

## Kuwait

In the early 1990s, Kuwait's defense expenditures were particularly heavy, in the wake of the Iraqi invasion of August 1990. After the invasion, Kuwait had to completely rebuild its military. Important arms transactions over the past decade have included purchase of 16 advanced anti-tank helicopters and 218 M-1A2 tanks from the United States. Aside from funding its own forces, Kuwait helped to finance the international coalition forces that fought Iraq during the Gulf War.

## Iran

Between the late 1980s and the mid-1990s, Iran's defense expenditures have increased, but this has since been halted, because of economic difficulties. The military budget comprises 2.5-3% of the Iranian GDP, although this does not properly reflect the actual defense burden. The struggle waged within Iran between moderate forces identified with President Khatami and the conservative camp of religious leader Khamenei reflects heavy popular pressure for significant social and economic change. This has caused resources to be reallocated toward raising the standard of living of Iran's population in order to stem dissatisfaction. Still, as the effort to develop the Shihab 3 surface-to-surface missile (which can reach Israel) has shown in 1998, economic difficulties have not prevented allocations to attain strategic capabilities. In fact, such difficulties may have even spurred the unconventional military effort.

### Table 6: The Persian Gulf – Defense expenditures*
in millions of 1995 dollars[21]

| Year | 1988 | 1989 | 1990 | 1991 | 1992 | 1993 | 1994 | 1995 | 1996 | 1997 |
|------|------|------|------|------|------|------|------|------|------|------|
| Iran | 1903 | 1799 | 2089 | 2175 | 2076 | 2635 | 3586 | 2597 | 2504 | 2715 |
| Kuwait | 2075 | 2574 | 9928 | 12933 | 6555 | 3174 | 3369 | 3693 | 3597 | (3325) |
| Saudi Arabia | 15431 | 14580 | (14927) | (28459) | 15382 | 17375 | 15010 | 13218 | (16789) | (17455) |

* Data for Iraq is not available.

# North Africa

The most salient development in North Africa has been the steep increase, after discounting for inflation, in the current defense expenditures of Algeria, which have risen nearly three-fold in the 1988-97 period because of severe internal security problems.[22] Yet, in the first half of the 1990s, Algeria spent only about half a billion dollars on the acquisition of major conventional weapons systems, while in the second half of the 1980s, it spent as much as $3 billion a year on such procurement.

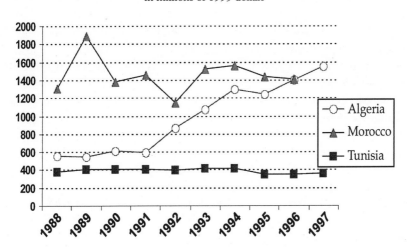

*Figure 12. North Africa – defense expenditures*
in millions of 1995 dollars

Morocco has maintained its defense expenditures at a constant level (adjusted for inflation) during most of the 1990s. These expenditures experienced sharp fluctuations in the late 1980s and early 1990s. Morocco spends approximately 4.5% of its GDP on defense.

Tunisia has maintained a relatively stable level of defense expenditures. At the same time, its defense burden has declined from 2.7% in the late 1980s to 1.8% in 1996.

It is impossible to reflect on Libyan arms expenditures, because data on these expenditures are not available.

## Conclusions

The defense expenditures of the Arab states bordering on Israel have increased somewhat in the 1990s after a sharp reduction in the second half of the 1980s. At this point, Syrian defense expenditures do not point to an accelerated arms race, but rather to fluctuations that apparently derive from changes in Syria's economic resources, and possibly from Syrian uncertainty about the peace process. Egypt's increased defense expenditures indicate that it continues to regard Israel as a threat and that it is committed to maintaining its status as a regional power. Both Egypt and Jordan have taken advantage of growth in their economies to increase their defense expenditures (at least through 1997).

Despite an impressive increase in the GDP of some states, bottlenecks to economic development still exist. Most states of the region suffer large current account deficits, and several of these states are experiencing high unemployment rates. The populations of Arab states continue to rise rapidly and demand substantial resources; the state of the oil market does not yet permit the Arab oil producing states and Iran to significantly increase their defense expenditures; and Russia is not able, or willing, to supply arms on the same terms as the Soviet Union had in the past. Without substantial external aid, military budgets in the Middle East (except for Egypt and Israel) will continue to be limited by growth in GDPs. Thus, in the next few years, barring a deterioration of the political and security situation in the region, it would be difficult for the Arab states and Iran to substantially increase their defense expenditures, without impairing standards of living and investments to a degree liable to have a negative impact on internal stability. Nevertheless, some developments may initiate a new arms race, such as the repeal of sanctions against Libya -- and in the future, possibly those applied against Iraq as well -- changes that could influence the behavior of neighboring states.

Even if, or when, peace agreements are signed between Israel and additional Arab states in the years ahead, large reductions in the defense expenditures in the region cannot be expected, unless verifiable arms control agreements stipulating such reductions are concluded. Existing peace agreements will be put to the test in the next few years; the parties to them are likely to examine the stability of the peace they achieved before reducing their armed forces. Moreover, some of the threats facing the region's states are likely to continue, and in Arab states, the military sector will continue to constitute a major component of the political establishment and, hence, to remain a key to the preservation of existing regimes.

## Notes

1   Middle Eastern states such as Syria, Jordan, Lebanon, Israel, Kuwait, and Saudi Arabia bear defense burdens of 6% (the ratio of defense expenditures to GDP), compared to 2-3% for most of the world.

2   Among the 20 principal arms importers in the world, in the 1991-97 period, were: Saudi Arabia, Egypt, Kuwait, Israel, the United Arab Emirates, and Iran.

3   This is not the case for the states of northern Africa where the trends have been different and are presented in condensed form at the end of the chapter.

4   *SIPRI Yearbook 1998: Armaments, Disarmament and International Security.* Oxford University Press, New York: 1998 p. 228. Henceforth: SIPRI 1998. Figures in parentheses are SIPRI estimates. Figures in boldface are the author's estimates. The figures for Israel relate to domestic military consumption, as a proportion of GDP,

according to the *Bank of Israel Report for 1998*, Bank of Israel, Jerusalem:1998. p. 274. These data have been selected because those for Egypt, Syria, and Jordan are apparently based on domestic military consumption, and because most Israeli military imports are paid for through US assistance. Data for Iraqi and Libyan military spending are not available.

5   *Al Hayat*, London, 7 July 1998.

6   *SIPRI* 1998.

7   *International Financial Statistics*. International Monetary Fund, (IMF), Washington, D.C., December 1998, p. 274.

8   In a CNN interview on May 3, 1999, King Abdullah termed his country's economic difficulties as the greatest problem confronting Jordan. He said he wants to concentrate on putting food on the tables of the Jordanian people, and expressed concern about the low salaries in the Jordanian military.

9   While in many countries with large populations and low standards of living (e.g., Egypt, Iran, or India), the ratio of defense expenditures to GDP is relatively low, that ratio does not reflect the real defense burden. The reason in this flaw is that a significant portion of the population does not participate in financing the state budget. It makes more sense to use other indices of the defense burden, such as the ratio of military to total state expenditures.

10   *International Financial Statistics, IMF*, December 1998, p. 408.

11   *SIPRI* 1998, p. 300.

12.   *Egypt*, Country Report. The Economist Intelligence Unit (EIU), 4th quarter 1997, p. 11.

13   *SIPRI 1998*, p. 222; The author's estimates, on the basis of EIU data from 1998 (for Egypt) and *Al Hayat*, 7 July, 1998 (for Syria).

14   Military consumption reflects public sector defense expenditures, as stated in the national accounting system. Military consumption and the military budget are of similar magnitudes, but not identical. Military consumption data are more appropriate for a study of trends in Israeli defense expenditures than are budgetary data.

15   These data also include military imports. Domestic military consumption (the total less imports) declined from 15% of Israel's GDP in 1982 to 7.4% in 1998 (according to the *Bank of Israel Report 1998*, Bank of Israel, Jerusalem: 1999. p. 274).

16   *Statistical Abstracts of Israel 1998*. Vol. 49, Central Bureau of Statistics, Jerusalem: 1998.

17   Computed on the basis of current data. Sources: The Israeli Central Bureau of Statistics Internet site (http://www.cbs.gov.il/sikron.htm) and *Bank of Israel Report 1998* (http://www.bankisrael.gov.il).

18   In December 1986, Defense Minister Itzhak Rabin stated: "We have reduced the size of the Israel Defense Forces, we are disbanding units, and have decommissioned hundreds of tanks … We have put aside dozens of combat aircraft." *Ma'ariv*, December 30, 1987.

19   *Statistical Abstracts of Israel 1998*. Vol. 49, pp. 15-20.

20   *SIPRI 1998*, p. 300.

21   *SIPRI 1998*, p. 222 (data in parentheses are estimates).

22   The data for Algeria's defense expenditures – recurrent expenditures only.

# Middle East Terrorism:
# The "Afghanistan Alumni"

### Yoram Schweitzer

In recent years, students of political violence in the Middle East and elsewhere have noted the phenomenon of the "Afghanistan alumni." The term refers to veterans of the decade-long war in Afghanistan (1979-89) which was waged between Afghan fighters and the thousands of Muslim volunteers from around the world who came to help them, and the country's Marxist regime and the former Soviet Union. Also included are the hundreds of volunteers, mostly members of Arab Islamic terrorist organizations, who have been sent to Afghanistan since the early 1990s for training in terrorism and guerrilla warfare.

Thus, Afghanistan has become a central training camp for Islamic terrorist organizations around the world, and the Afghanistan alumni have become a significant factor in the development of terrorism in the Middle East and beyond. They comprise a central cadre in the leadership of the main fundamentalist terrorist organizations operating in the Middle East. Their unique standing is based on the legendary quality of their struggle in the "Islamic war" that overcame the power of the "Christian" Soviet Union and led, finally, to its total collapse.

The myth of heroism that attended their status as veterans of the Afghan war conferred on these men, in the eyes of members of their organizations, the moral and professional authority to wage violent struggles against heretical regimes in their home countries. Their return to the ranks of their organizations has led to an escalation of terrorist activity in various countries, threatening the stability of their regimes. Afghanistan alumni have also played major roles in some of the principal terrorist attacks on the international scene during the 1990s.

The war in Afghanistan created a reservoir of violent, extreme individuals, with training and experience in guerrilla warfare and terrorism, animated by radical religious views. After acquiring their training and experience, the Afghanistan alumni have continued their militant activities in a variety of ways:

- Returning to their home countries (including Egypt, Algeria, Tunisia, Morocco, and Jordan), they have reinforced existing Islamic organizations.
- They have established new organizational frameworks, such as the Al-Qaida group, under the leadership of Osama bin Ladn.
- They have built autonomous terrorist cells, without links to defined organizations, but with mutual links to one another and to established fundamentalist organizations.
- They have participated in the fighting in areas where Muslim communities have been involved in conflict, such as Bosnia, Chechnia, Tajikistan, Kosovo, and Kashmir.

The presence of "Afghanistan alumni" has had a noticeable impact on the activities of terrorist organizations and networks. This has been particularly salient in the Egyptian organizations, the Gama'a al-Islamiya and the Egyptian Jihad; the Algerian Armed Islamic Movement (GIA); and the Al-Qaida, under the command of Osama bin Ladn.

## Egypt

Terrorist activity in Egypt has escalated considerably since mid-1992. The return to Egypt of several hundred Afghanistan alumni has served to goad local terrorist organizations, primarily the Gama'a al-Islamiya and the Egyptian Jihad, to greater violence. These groups have mainly operated against public figures and Egyptian government officials, foreign tourists, and the Coptic minority. Since 1995, they have also operated against Egyptian targets abroad.

Since the assassination of President Anwar Sadat in October 1981, senior government officials have been a primary strategic target for the Islamic organizations in Egypt. During the 1990s, these organizations have attempted to assassinate other senior officials of the regime, both inside Egypt and abroad. The most notorious of these attempts was the attack on President Hosni Mubarak during a state visit to Ethiopia in June 1995. Among other attempts by the Egyptian Jihad were those made on the lives of Prime Minister Atif Najib Sidqi (August 1993), the interior minister Hasan Muhammad al-Alfi (November 1993), and the speaker of the National Assembly, Rif'at Mahjub, who was assassinated in October 1990.

Egyptian terrorist organizations have marked tourism as a primary target. Their goal is to inflict damage on two levels: to hurt the economy (tourism is Egypt's second largest source of income, after the Suez Canal), and to damage the standing of the regime, both within Egypt and in the international arena. Spectacular terrorist operations against tourists are meant to undermine confidence in the stability of the regime and to attract new volunteers. These attacks also serve to strike a blow against the "infidel" culture of the West, which threatens to "pollute" the Islamic world.

The tourist seasons of 1992 and 1993 were severely disrupted, with direct damage to state coffers estimated in the billions of dollars. In 1997, the slaughter of 58 tourists and four Egyptians by the Gama'a al-Islamiya at the Tashpatos temple in Luxor did much to undermine Egypt's tourist industry, which was then in the process of recovering from earlier blows. It also caused economic damage estimated at half a billion dollars.

Attacks on the Coptic minority have been motivated by the perception that it is an alien religious, ethnic and cultural presence. In addition, the Islamic organizations have come to envy Christians for their economic success.

The heavy-handed policies of the Egyptian security forces against the Islamic organizations have limited their freedom of action. Some of their activists were forced to flee the country, leading the organizations to conduct operations abroad, as well as inside Egypt. Most overseas terrorist operations were conducted in revenge for arrests and extraditions to Egypt for killings of organization members abroad, carried out in cooperation with local security forces. These overseas operations included an attempt on the life of an Egyptian diplomat in Switzerland and the blowing up of the Egyptian embassy in Pakistan (both by the Egyptian Jihad, in November 1995), and the suicide bombing of a police station in Riaka, Croatia (Gama'a al-Islamiya, in October 1995). As noted earlier, the crowning achievement of overseas terrorism was the unsuccessful attempt on the life of President Mubarak in Ethiopia, by the Gama'a al-Islamiya in June 1995. The perpetrators had hoped to take advantage of the fact that Mubarak was outside the tight security net that guards him in his own country.

The Egyptian organizations, especially the Gama'a al-Islamiya, have also been indirectly involved in international terrorism through Egyptian members of the "Afghanistan alumni" – those trained in Mujahidin camps after the war ended – who operate in autonomous cells abroad. It is worth noting that the blind Egyptian sheikh, Omar Abd al-Rahman – the ultimate spiritual authority for both the Gama'a al-Islamiya and Egyptian Jihad – is the source of the religious sanction for such cells. In recent years, particularly in 1998, the Egyptian organizations have been influenced by their ties with Osama bin Ladn and his Al-Qaida group, which has attracted a considerable number of Egyptians to its ranks. At least one of the suicide bombers involved in Al-Qaida bombings in Nairobi and Dar-al-Salam in August 1998, was Egyptian.

The alliance between bin Ladn and the Egyptian organizations can be observed at the highest levels. Several leading officers of the Egyptian organizations, such as Rif'ai Ta, chief of the political bureau of the Gama'a al-Islamiya; Mustafa Hamza, head of the Gama'a al-Islamiya military wing and above all, Ayman Al-Zawahiri, head of an Egyptian Jihad splinter group, maintain close ties to Osama bin Ladn. The Egyptian Jihad group under Zwahiri has gone so far as to subordinate its terrorist activities to the bin Ladn strategy, which consists of focusing on American, rather than Egyptian, targets. The frontal assault on the Egyptian regime has led to the loss of innocent Egyptian lives, leading in turn to an estrangement of Egypt's Muslim masses from the terrorist movement. On the other hand, assaults on the "infidel Americans" have the potential of bringing the organizations public sympathy. Adoption of this strategy by the Al-Zawahiri faction can be seen in an abortive attack on the US embassy in Albania in June 1998, and the two attacks in East Africa in August 1998.

The Gama'a al-Islamiya, which bin Ladn views as the focal grouping of the military-religious coalition he has forged, has vacillated over the past two years over the issue of conducting terrorism against Egyptian targets versus terrorism against American targets. In July 1997, a declaration by the organization's imprisoned leaders in Egypt of a cease-fire against the Egyptian regime ignited a controversy between the leadership in Egypt and its leadership in exile, over targets and terrorism policy. The slaughter of tourists at Luxor in October 1997 exacerbated the controversy, mainly because of the Egyptian regime's pressure on the organization, both in Egypt and abroad. The declaration of Sheikh al-Rahman from his US prison cell (October 1998), the apparent meaning of which was that the organization's aims should be achieved by peaceful means, is likely to weigh the argument in favor of those who prefer a cessation of violence inside Egypt. Should a formal resolution along such lines be made by the Gama'a al-Islamiya leadership, it would have a moderating influence on the organization's terrorist activity, possibly leading to its disavowal, if only temporarily, of the strategy of international terrorism of bin Ladn's Islamic front.

## Algeria

Terrorist activity in Algeria has become considerably more violent with the return of the "Afghanistan alumni." The cancellation of the results of the 1992 elections, and the outlawing of the Islamic party, provided the excuse for extremist elements in the Islamic movement to adopt terrorism in the struggle against the ruling regime. These elements contend that "stealing" the power won by the Islamic movement in a democratic election was additional proof of the despotic nature of a regime they view as un-Islamic and patently illegitimate.

In the wake of the election, the leadership of the FIS, the leading movement in the Islamic camp, was arrested. The aggravation of the conflict between the Islamic movement and the regime led to a bitter controversy within the movement over the methods of struggle, and the movement split. The dominant and violent faction is the Armed Islamic Movement (GIA), led by Gamal Zeituni, a veteran "Afghanistan alumni" who returned to Algeria after the war in Afghanistan ended. In the beginning, GIA directed its violence against government officials, writers, journalists, and foreign nationals in Algeria. However, beginning in 1994, and especially during 1995-96, GIA has undertaken terrorist operations abroad. All such operations have either taken place in France or have been directed against French citizens abroad. They were justified by citing French support for the Algerian regime. The bitterness of the Franco-GIA confrontation is also explained by GIA in the historical context of the war against France for Algerian independence in the early 1960s.

GIA terrorist effort overseas has included the hijacking of an Air France passenger plane and two waves of sabotage in France (July-October 1995 and December 1996), in which some 20 people were killed and scores were injured.

GIA, like other Islamic terrorist organizations, supports the establishment of a regime based on Islamic religious law, and views the United States, Israel, and Judaism as enemies of Islam. However, the organization has thus far not engaged in terrorist actions directly aimed at US or Israeli targets. Nevertheless, it has staged three attacks against Jewish targets in France as part of its overall effort in that country: the (attempted) car bombing of a synagogue in Lyons, in 1994; the attempted car bombing of a Jewish school in Villerban, near Lyons, in 1995; and the sending of a letter bomb to the editor of a Jewish newspaper, in 1996.

As a result of GIA's overseas attacks, the organization's infrastructure, spread over several countries, but based mainly in France, Belgium, the United Kingdom, Germany, Italy, Sweden, and Spain, has been uncovered. It consisted of terrorist cells of a limited number of members, who shared responsibilities in all spheres: logistics, finances, and operations. The main purpose of the European network was to obtain money and arms, and smuggle them to their comrades in Algeria.

Countermeasures taken by European security forces, at French initiative but with wide international cooperation, crippled the GIA network and led to a cessation of its activities in the international arena.

It is worth noting that unlike Palestinian and Shi'ite terrorist organizations, GIA has not undertaken "blackmail" operations aimed at winning release for the scores of its members imprisoned in various European countries. This policy may derive from the organization's desire to concentrate on its struggle in Algeria, and to avoid arousing European opinion against it to the extent that its ability to use Europe as a vital logistic base for operations inside Algeria would be impaired.

Other terrorist cells linked to GIA were uncovered in Europe in 1998 as well. The involvement of immigrants and the children of immigrants from the Maghreb in acts of terrorism in France, and in terrorist cells in other European countries, points to a widespread network for recruitment of potential volunteers for Islamic terrorist organizations among immigrants of the lower socio-economic strata, who have a grievance and are alienated from their host countries. These immigrant populations have provided pools of new recruits, some of whom were sent to Afghanistan for terrorist training in the early 1990s. In some cases, they went on to volunteer for service in Bosnia.

## *Independent Terrorist Cells*

One of the salient features of international terrorism in recent years has been the activities of "ad hoc organizations" – networks of autonomous, compartmentalized terrorist cells, operating without any defined structural hierarchy. Such cells have maintained reciprocal links with established terrorist organizations. "Afghanistan alumni" have played a central role in the operation of such cells, availing themselves both of the skills they acquired in their Afghanistan training and their ties with Islamic welfare organizations, which have extended them logistical support and financed their activities. Some of the terrorist attacks that such cells have been responsible for are: the World Trade Center explosion in New York in February 1993, which killed six and injured some 1,000 people; the planned attacks on the United Nations headquarters and the Lincoln tunnel, connecting New York to New Jersey, in June 1993 (both of which were thwarted); an attack on a Philippine Air Lines passenger plane, in December 1994; and a series of planned (and thwarted) attacks on US aircraft in Asia in early 1995.

Investigation of these terrorist cells has uncovered links between them and nongovernmental Islamic welfare organizations (NGOs), such as the International Islamic Welfare League, the International Islamic Welfare Organization, and Islamic cultural centers in Europe, most notably that in Milan. Also, widespread connections have been uncovered between these cells and Osama bin Ladn.

## Al-Qaida

Another organization through which "Afghanistan alumni" have played an important role in the international arena in recent years is the Al-Qaida. It was founded in 1988 by Osama bin Ladn, himself an Afghanistan alumnus and scion of an extremely wealthy Saudi family with close ties to the royal family. The Al-Qaida organization was established out of the Service Bureau (the "al-Hadmat letter"), an NGO specializing in recruiting, processing, and sending thousands of Islamic volunteers, from some 50 countries around the world, to Mujahidin bases in Pakistan and Afghanistan.

After the war ended, most of the organization's activities were conducted from Sudan and Afghanistan, through a far-flung network of offices that operated in Afghanistan, Pakistan, the United States (mainly the Al-Kifah center in Brooklyn), and the Philippines. Al-Qaida has extended aid to other terrorist organizations that have maintained links with it, thus contributing to the radicalization of the Islamic movements in Chechnia, Bosnia, Tajikistan, Somalia, Kashmir, Yemen, and Kosovo.

Along with this support, Al-Qaida members have also been involved in acts of terrorism. The organization has been accused of direct complicity in the attack on UN forces in Somalia in October 1993, in which 18 US servicemen lost their lives, as well as in attacks in Kenya and Tanzania in August 1998. Furthermore, there is clear evidence linking the Al-Qaida to terrorist acts perpetrated or planned by terrorist cells under Ramzi Yousouf in New York (1993) and the Philippines (1994). There is also evidence that it was involved in the attack in Riyadh, Saudi Arabia, in November 1995, which claimed the lives of six Americans, five of them servicemen.

In 1998, the "Afghanistan alumni" became part of the international agenda, in the wake of the Al-Qaida's spectacular attacks in East Africa. Bin Ladn, accused by the United States as responsible for these acts, has been portrayed in some of the news media, both in the West and the Arab world, as the embodiment of fundamentalist terrorism. He has contributed to that image by assuming the leading role in what he terms the "religious-cultural-historical struggle between Islam and the 'Judeo-Crusader' alliance, aimed at subduing Islam and conquering its hallowed lands."

In a series of interviews and pronouncements, such as his "Declaration of War," in June 1996, and his *fatwa* (religious ruling) of February 1998, bin Ladn has outlined a Weltanschauung according to which the world, and particularly the Middle East, is seen as the arena of a deterministic struggle for survival between the three monotheistic faiths. A coalition of Christians and Jews, embodied by the United States and Israel (and world Jewry), has formed, with the aim of conquering the most hallowed soil consecrated to Islam – Mecca, Medina, and Jerusalem – and of subduing Islam. Bin Ladn contends that this alliance perpetrates the deliberate, systematic slaughter of Muslims. As examples, he cites such incidents as the "slaughter" of the Muslim Iraqi population by US forces in the 1991 Gulf Crisis, the bombing of Iraq in December 1998, the massacre at the Sabra and Chatilla refugee camps in Lebanon (1982), and the killing of Palestinians in the territories occupied by Israel.

As a vehicle to mobilizing the masses, bin Ladn employs rhetoric laden with historic and religious significance for Muslim believers, such as "Crusaders" and "Jihad." He justifies the violence he preaches as a necessary measure in the defense of what is sacred to Islam; he portrays Muslims as victims.

Bin Ladn employs terrorism as a means of demonstrating to the community of the faithful that even the seemingly most invincible of Islam's foes, like the United States and the Soviet Union, are vulnerable because of the feebleness of their faith. He relies on the ethos of the successful struggle in Afghanistan, which eventually led to the dissolution of the "Christian empire of the Soviet Union." He cites other instances of the weakness of the enemy, especially of the United States, which withdrew from Somalia under the pressure of the guerrilla campaign he supported.

Attacks undertaken by Saudi opposition forces in Riyadh (October 1995) and Bahrain (June 1996), resulting in 24 US dead and scores of wounded, were part of a struggle with a dual purpose: purging the holy places in Mecca and Medina, which bin Laden regards as being under US occupation, and providing moral-psychological victory to the warriors of Islam. He has also prophesied a dire outcome for the Israeli occupation of the hallowed ground of Al-Aqsa.

In the course of 1998, bin Ladn formed an Islamic coalition, with which he aims to oppose the Judeo-Christian alliance. On February 23, 1998, he convened the leaders of several Islamic organizations in Afghanistan and announced the establishment of the International Islamic Front for Jihad Against Crusaders and Jews. The Front published a religious sanction of its aims, signed by bin Ladn himself, on behalf of the Al-Qaida, and the leaders of four other Islamic movements: Ayman Al-Zawahiri, leader of an Egyptian Jihad faction; Ahmed Rif'ai Ta, of Egypt's Gama'a al-Islamiya; Sheikh Mir Hamza, secretary of the Jamiat ul-Ulema e-Pakistani; and Fazlul Rahman, leader of the Jihad in Bangladesh. Bin Ladn needed religious sanction and the support of the heads of other Islamic organizations, since he has neither religious authority nor a significant military or terrorist force. The religious figures, above all Sheikh Mir Hamza, widely respected as an Islamic authority, issued a *fatwa*, thus giving bin Ladn's resolutions an aura of religious sanction, while the heads of the Gama'a al-Islamiya and Egyptian Jihad have provided the necessary military-terrorist backbone.

In their *fatwa*, the Front's leaders called upon Muslims throughout the world to consider the killing of Americans and their allies, both servicemen and civilians, as a personal obligation, aimed at liberating the Holy Mosque in Mecca (and by implication, all of Saudi Arabia), and the Al-Aqsa Mosque (and thus Jerusalem and all Palestine).

In May 1998, bin Ladn said in an interview with ABC that the Front intended to conduct attacks on US citizens around the world, because of their support for the "criminal policy" of the US government. Shortly afterward, in July 1998, three-way cooperation between the United States, Egypt, and Albania thwarted the planned attack by the Egyptian Jihad (Zawahiri Faction) on the US embassy in Tirana, and the perpetrators were extradited to Egypt. Subsequent to that attempt, the Front and Egyptian Jihad sent letters on August 6 to the Egyptian newspaper *Al-Hayat*, explicitly threatening to hit US targets. On the following day, members of the Al-Qaida launched the spectacular attacks on the US embassies in Kenya and Tanzania, with a toll of 291 dead and some 5,000 injured, most of them local people. Twelve US citizens, all employees of the Nairobi embassy, were among the dead.

The attacks in East Africa gave the United States the pretext it needed to take limited military action against the threat that the "Afghanistan alumni" – largely the Egyptian organizations and bin Ladn – had been posing for several years. On August 20, 1998, the United States bombed Al-Qaida bases in Afghanistan and Sudan. The specific targets involved were five Al-Qaida bases in Afghanistan, and a pharmaceuticals factory in Khartoum, Sudan, which, according to the United States, was financed by bin Ladn and used to manufacture chemical weapons. All the explicit evidence of Al-Qaida complicity in the planning and execution of terrorist raids, acquired over the years in interrogation of captured terrorists, was now made public to justify US violation of the territorial sovereignty of the states that had given the Al-Qaida sanctuary.

Concurrently with the US military and intelligence effort, the United States and Britain put diplomatic pressure on Afghanistan's Taliban government. The United States sent Ambassador Bill Richardson to Afghanistan to persuade the Taliban to extradite bin Ladn, or at least to arrest him to prevent his continued inflammatory pronouncements. Britain, for its part, offered the Taliban a deal whereby it would be allowed to open a liaison office in London, and the British government would limit the activities of the exiled leader of the opposition Mujahidin in London, in exchange for limiting bin Ladn's activities (*Al-Hayat*, February 12, 1999).

Thus far, the Taliban has not acceded to the request to extradite bin Ladn to the United States, or to prevent him from threatening acts of terrorism, despite promises by high-ranking Taliban officials that their movement would restrain him. Interviews bin Ladn gave to the Arab and Western media in late 1998, threatening to escalate the struggle against the United States and its allies, demonstrate the limited effectiveness of the pressure brought to bear on the Afghan government.

The United States has continued to work with its Arab and European partners to thwart the operations of the Al-Qaida and the Egyptian organizations, and to apprehend their members. In September 1998, several key men in the bin Ladn network were arrested. One of them, Wadia al-Haj, a Lebanese Christian who converted to Islam, was arrested in Texas. Until 1994, Al-Haj had been bin Ladn's personal secretary in Sudan. He then went to Kenya, where he played an important role in establishing the terrorist infrastructure that was eventually used in the August 1998 attacks in East Africa. In 1997, al-Haj went to Texas, apparently with the aim of establishing a terrorist infrastructure in the United States.

On September 16, Mamduch Mahmad Mahmoud Salem, a senior bin Ladn aide, was arrested in Munich. Salem had responsibility for finances and logistics, as well as for weapons procurement (including possibly unconventional weapons). Salem was extradited to the United States on December 24, 1998, in order to stand trial for his activities in the bin Ladn terrorist network.

Several members of the bin Ladn network have been arrested in London. The most prominent of them is Haled Fuez, bin Ladn's representative in the British capital, a Saudi opposition figure, and head of the organization Advice and Consent. Proceedings for his extradition to the United States were opened.

Throughout the second half of 1998, Egypt also stepped up its operations against the Egyptian organizations overseas. Through US mediation, the Egyptians have obtained the cooperation of a number of states, among them Albania, Azerbaijan, Bulgaria, South Africa, Ecuador, Saudi Arabia, Kuwait, and Oman, which have extradited to Egypt members of the Egyptian Jihad and of bin Ladn's network. These operations have presented bin Ladn and his collaborators with a challenge that threatens the very survival of their Islamic coalition.

The US bombings of Iraq, on December 17-20, 1998, served as a pretext for bin Ladn to renew his threats against US citizens, "because of their support for the slaughter of Iraq's Muslim population." In a series of bellicose interviews in *Time*, *Newsweek*, and on the *BBC*, he urged his Muslim brothers to renew their attacks on the enemies of Islam.

In the future, bin Ladn may make an effort to involve terrorist organizations other than those from Egypt, such as the Indian organization *Harakat al-Ansar*, and the Philippine organization *Abu Saiaf*. In interviews, he has also mentioned his efforts to obtain unconventional weapons. He contends that obtaining such weapons is a religious obligation; any Muslim who abjures their use sins against his faith. Bin Ladn has been purposely vague as to whether such weapons are actually in his arsenal, and as to the circumstances under which he would use them.

The United States had been monitoring bin Ladn's efforts to procure and manufacture unconventional weapons even before he publicly discussed the subject. As has been mentioned, the United States justified the bombing of the pharmaceuticals plant in Khartoum on the grounds that it was used to manufacture components of chemical weapons. The extradition of Mamduh Salem from Germany to the United States on December 24, 1998, has also been linked to the issue of unconventional weapons procurement.

## Conclusions

The "Afghanistan alumni" have had a considerable impact on both the scope and nature of political violence in the Middle East, as well as on the perceived degree of political stability of regimes in the region. Their effect has been most pronounced on terrorism in the international arena.

At present, it does not seem that fundamentalist terrorist organizations have the capability to induce a change in regimes in any of the region's states. However, they do have the capability to exploit changes of regime, or the illness of leaders, or severe economic hardship, to engender political instability. Their desire and ability to cause significant economic damage and loss of life through terrorist operations is clear, and they are expected to continue to constitute a potential threat in the years to come. The frontal clash between bin Ladn, who claims to lead the main cadre of "Afghanistan alumni," and the United States and its allies, has placed these "alumni" on the international agenda.

Efforts by bin Ladn to construct an organic umbrella framework that unites the radical Islamic forces into a common front against the West has not attracted all such organizations. It appears that his vision of an "Islamic International" that would unite under his leadership to provide a comprehensive, coordinated response to the Western-secular challenge, has not been realized. In this context, it should be noted that the dominant Islamic movement in the Arab world, the Muslim Brotherhood, has serious reservations about the path bin Ladn has taken.

Nevertheless, he and the terrorist organizations he supports enjoy a logistic infrastructure, resources and financing that give them the operational capability to wage terrorist campaigns worldwide.

The main danger posed to international relations by Sunni Muslim terrorism is its ability to cause violent friction between the West and Arab Muslim states. Such a clash could result from an escalation of the confrontation between the United States and its allies on the one hand, and the fundamentalist terrorist

## *Terrorist Attacks Attributed to Afghanistan Alumni*

| | |
|---|---|
| September 1992 | Terrorist attacks on two hotels in Aden, where Western tourists were staying. |
| February 1993 | Explosive device detonated in the World Trade Center office building, in New York City. |
| December 1993 | A Philippine Air Lines plane blown up by Ramzi Yousouf. |
| December 1994 | Hijacking of an Air France passenger plane in Algeria, by GIA. |
| June 1995 | Attempt made on the life of Egyptian President Mubarak, by the Gama'a al-Islamiya, in Ethiopia. |
| July-October 1995 | Wave of terrorist attacks in France, by GIA. |
| October 1995 | Car-bombing in Riaka, Croatia, by a Gama'a al-Islamiya suicide attacker. |
| November 1995 | Egyptian diplomat in Switzerland murdered by the Egyptian Jihad. |
| November 1995 | Egyptian embassy in Pakistan blown up by Gama'a al-Islamiya suicide squad. |
| November 1995 | US aid offices to the Saudi Civil Defense were car-bombed. |
| April 1996 | 17 Greek pilgrims shot to death at the Hotel Europa, in Cairo, by the Gama'a al-Islamiya. |
| November 1997 | 58 Western tourists in Luxor murdered in attack by the Gama'a al-Islamiya. |
| August 1998 | US embassies in Tanzania and Kenya car-bombed, by the Al-Qaida. |

organizations in which Afghanistan alumni are active, and perhaps even states that support them, on the other. The desire for revenge against the United States and its allies by bin Ladn and his collaborators may well cause the conflict to escalate into a wave of spectacular acts of terrorism followed by military reactions, mainly by the United States.

The US success in forging international cooperation against terrorism, and the arrest of leading figures in the Al-Qaida and Egyptian organizations around the world, were answered by bin Ladn and his collaborators in late 1998 and early 1999, with threats against the United States, the United Kingdom, and others. In response to the bombing of Iraq, bin Ladn again threatened acts of international terrorism. Corroboration of the seriousness of his threats can be found in declarations by the heads of the US security services, who have publicly warned that a wave of spectacular acts of terrorism may take place in the near future.

Bin Ladn's threats to continue his efforts to procure unconventional "Islamic" weapons are also likely to require a common, coordinated international response. Western states, especially the United States, the United Kingdom, and Israel, are concerned because his personality and methods suggest that he is liable to escalate the level of violence to the point where he would use weapons of mass destruction.

In addition to posing a threat to the democratic way of life in the West, the spectacle of the "Afghanistan alumni" has become the main symbol of the violent struggle of Islamic fundamentalism against the West and its culture, and an expression of the hatred of Western culture prevalent in large parts of the Islamic world. As such, the "Afghanistan alumni," and bin Ladn as their most militant spokesman, are likely to continue to have a substantial impact on economic, political, and military processes in the Middle East and worldwide in the next few years.

# PART II

# MILITARY FORCES

# Introductory Note

This part of the Middle East Military Balance contains data on the arsenals and the order of battle of 20 states and the Palestinian Authority. It also contains information on other security activities of these states – arms procurement, military production and security co-operation.

## Definitions

### Armor

Tanks are divided into two main categories: light tanks (under 25 tons) and main battle tanks (MBTs). High quality MBTs and other MBTs are also differentiated. The criteria for "high quality" are any three of the following attributes:
1. A 120mm (or higher) caliber gun.
2. A power-plant of more than 900hp and\or power-to-weight ratio of 19 hp/ t or better.
3. Reactive or modular armor.
4. A capability to fire barrel launched AT missiles.
5. An advanced fire control system, with tracking capability.

Under this categorization, some versions of the T-72 MBT are categorized as "high quality," although they are not necessarily on par with tanks like the M1A1 or the Merkava Mk III.

### Armored Fighting Vehicles

AFVs are divided into three categories:
1. Armored personnel carriers – armored vehicles designed to carry several infantrymen, armed with light weapons only.
2. Infantry fighting vehicles – armored vehicles built to carry several infantrymen, armed with heavier weapons, like guns or missiles.
3. Reconnaissance vehicles – armored vehicles of various sizes and armament, designed to carry a small crew of weapon operators (but not intended for dismounted infantry fighting).

It should be noted that the dividing lines between the categories are not well defined, and sometimes it is difficult to decide how a certain vehicle should be categorized. For example, heavier reconnaissance vehicles can be categorized as light tanks, especially when they use tracks rather than wheels.

## Air Defense

Some militaries in the region have a separate air defense arm. In other countries, air defense equipment is divided between the air force and the ground forces. In this volume all air defense weapon systems are aggregated into one sub-section in each chapter, regardless of the organizational distribution of the weapons systems.

Air defense equipment is categorized as follows:
- Shoulder-launched missiles
- Light SAMs - with a range up to 12 km, self propelled or towed.
- Mobile medium SAMs - self propelled, with a range of 12 - 30 km.
- Medium to heavy SAMs - stationary or towed systems with a range of 12 - 30 km, or any system with a range of more than 30 km.
- Other systems - AA guns and combined systems.

## Combat Aircraft

Combat aircraft are divided into the following categories:
1. Interceptors.
2. Multi-role (high quality and others).
3. Ground attack.
4. Obsolete.

## Navy

The size and armament of each vessel appear in the tables for each country.

## Note on Symbols

The plus (+) sign, appearing in many of the following tables, represents our estimate that the relevant country probably possesses the noted weapon, but that credible information regarding the exact number of these weapons is not available.

## *Economic data*

The tables on economic data include data about GDP (in current local currency and in current US dollars). Per capita GDP is derived from a simple division of the GDP by the size of the population.

Data on military expenditures in the Middle East are notoriously elusive. Hence they should be regarded primarily, as an indication of prevailing trends.

Yiftah S. Shapir
July 1999

# 1. ALGERIA

## General Data

**Official Name of the State:** Democratic and Popular Republic of Algeria
**Head of State:** President of the High State Council Brigadier General
Abdelaziz Bouteflika (also Minister of Defense)
**Prime Minister:** Smail Hamdani
**Chief of General Staff:** Major General Muhammad Lamari
**Commander of the Staff of the Ground Forces:** Major General
Salih Ahmad Jaid (also Deputy Chief of the General Staff)
**Commander of the Air Force:** Brigadier General Muhammad Ibn Suleiman
**Commander of the Air Defense Force:** Brigadier General Achour Laoudi
**Commander of the Navy:** Admiral Shabane Ghodbane

**Area:** 2,460,500 sq. km.
**Population:** 29,200,000

## Demography

| | | |
|---|---|---|
| *Ethnic groups* | | |
| Arabs | 22,922,000 | 78.5% |
| Berbers | 5,664,800 | 19.4% |
| Europeans | 292,000 | 1.0% |
| Others | 321,200 | 1.1% |
| *Religious groups* | | |
| Sunni Muslims | 28,908,000 | 99.0% |
| Christians and Jews | 292,000 | 1.0% |

## Economic Data

| | | 1993 | 1994 | 1995 | 1996 | 1997 |
|---|---|---|---|---|---|---|
| GDP current price, | | | | | | |
| local currency | AD bn | 1,162.1 | 1,471.4 | 1,961.7 | 2,494.6 | 2,716.4 |
| GDP (US $) | $ bn | 49.46 | 41.97 | 41.16 | 45.56 | 47.08 |
| GDP per capita | $ | 1,838 | 1,526 | 1,465 | 1,593 | 1,612 |
| Real GDP growth | % | -1.9 | -1.1 | 3.9 | 3.8 | 1.3 |
| **Balance of payments** | | | | | | |
| • Exports fob | $ bn | 10.41 | 8.89 | 10.26 | 13.21 | 13.82 |
| • Imports fob | $ bn | 7.99 | 9.15 | 10.10 | 9.09 | 8.13 |
| • Account balance (including services and income) | $ bn | 0.8 | -1.84 | -2.24 | 1.25 | 3.46 |
| • External debt | $ bn | 26.0 | 29.9 | 32.7 | 33.3 | 34.3 |

## Economic Data *(continued)*

|  |  | 1993 | 1994 | 1995 | 1996 | 1997 |
|---|---|---|---|---|---|---|
| Government income and expenditure | | | | | | |
| • Revenue, local currency | AD bn | 320.1 | 434.2 | 600.9 | 824.8 | 926.6 |
| • Expenditure, local currency | AD bn | 390.5 | 461.9 | 589.1 | 724.6 | 845.1 |
| • Defense expenditure | AD bn | 29.81 | 46.80 | 58.84 | 79.52 | 101.12 |
| • Defense expenditure/GDP | % | 2.56 | 3.18 | 3.0 | 3.19 | 3.73 |
| • Defense expenditure/CGE | % | 7.63 | 10.13 | 10.0 | 10.97 | 11.96 |
| • Population | m | 26.9 | 27.5 | 28.1 | 28.6 | 29.2 |
| • Official exchange rate | AD : $1 | 23.35 | 35.06 | 47.66 | 54.75 | 57.7 |

*sources:* EIU quarterly report, EIU country profile, IMF statistical yearbook, SIPRI Yearbook

## Arms Sales and Security Assistance Received

| Country | Type | Details |
|---|---|---|
| Britain | • Arms transfers | naval vessels (1997) |
| Egypt | • Arms transfers | Fahd APCs (1993) |
| France | • Arms transfers | helicopters (1995) |
| PRC | • Arms transfers | patrol craft (1992) |
| Russia | • Arms transfers | helicopters (1995), Kh-35 missiles (1998) |
| South Africa | • Arms transfers | UAV systems (1998) |

## Foreign Military Cooperation

| | Details |
|---|---|
| • Joint maneuvers | USA - joint maritime SAR exercise (1998) |

## Defense Production

|  | M | P | A |
|---|---|---|---|
| **Army equipment** | | | |
| • Trucks (in collaboration with France) | | √ | |
| • Small arms | | √ | |
| **Naval craft** | | | |
| • Tugs | √ | | |
| • Kebir class PBs | | √ | √ |

*note:*　M - manufacture (indigenously developed)
　　　　P - production under license
　　　　A - assembly

## Weapons of Mass Destruction

### Nuclear capabilities

- A 1 MW nuclear research reactor (from Argentina); a second nuclear reactor of 15 MW, probably upgradable to 40 MW (from PRC); basic R&D; known/acknowledged Algerian facilities are subject to IAEA safeguards; Algeria is a signatory to the NPT

### CW capabilities

- No details available

### Biological warfare capabilities

- No details available

# Armed Forces

**Major changes:** No major changes occurred in the Algerian order of battle in 1998.

## Order of Battle

| Year | 1994 | 1995 | 1996 | 1997 | 1998 |
|---|---|---|---|---|---|
| **General data** | | | | | |
| • Personnel (regular) | 155,000 | 152,500 | 152,500 | 124,000 | 127,000 |
| • Divisions | 13 | 5 | 5 | 5 | 5 |
| • Total number of brigades | 69 | 37 | 37 | 26 | 26 |
| **Ground forces** | | | | | |
| • Tanks | 1,060-1,160 | 1,100 | 1,100 | 930 (1,060) | 860 (1,060) |
| • APCs/AFVs | 1,780 | 1,780 | 1,780 | 1,930 | 1,930 |
| • Artillery (incl. MRLs) | 985 | 980 | 980 | 985 | 900 (985) |
| • SSM launchers | 30-35 | 35 | 35 | | |
| **Air Force** | | | | | |
| • Combat aircraft | 305 | 205 | 205 | 205 | 187 (205) |
| • Transport aircraft | 57 | 76 | 76 | 48 | 39 (45) |
| • Helicopters | 84 | 108 | 108 | 116 | 114 |
| **Air defense forces** | | | | | |
| • Heavy SAM batteries | 41 | 30 | 30 | 11 | 11 |
| • Medium SAM batteries | 25 | 23 | 23 | 18 | 18 |
| • Light SAM launchers | + | + | + | 40 | 78 |

## Order of Battle *(continued)*

| Year | 1994 | 1995 | 1996 | 1997 | 1998 |
|---|---|---|---|---|---|
| **Navy** | | | | | |
| • Combat vessels | 31 | 32 | 32 | 29 | 29 |
| • Patrol crafts | 28 | 28 | 28 | 21 | 21 |
| • Submarines | 2 | 2 | 2 | 2 | 2 |

*Note:* Beginning with data for 1997, we refer to quantities in active service. The number in parentheses refers to the total.

### Personnel

| | Regular | Reserves | Total |
|---|---|---|---|
| Ground Forces | 107,000 | 150,000 | 257,000 |
| Air Force | 14,000 | | 14,000 |
| Navy and Coast Guard | 6,000 | | 6,000 |
| Total | 127,000 | 150,000 | 277,000 |
| **Paramilitary** | | | |
| • National security force | 16,000 | | 16,000 |
| • Republican guards brigade | 1,200 | | 1,200 |
| • Gendarmerie | 24,000 | | 24,000 |

*Note:* Air defense personnel are included in the army and air force personnel.

# Ground Forces

### Formations

| | Division | Independent brigade/ group | Independent battalions | Brigades in division |
|---|---|---|---|---|
| Armored | 2 | 1 | | 2 tanks, 2 mech. each |
| Mechanized/ Infantry | 2 | | | 2 mech., 2 tanks each |
| Motorized Infantry | | 5 | | |
| Special forces/ Airborne | 1 | | | |
| Artillery | | | 7 | |
| Air Defense | | | 5 | |
| Engineering | | | 4 | |
| Total | 5 | 13 | 9 | |

## Tanks

| Model | Quantity | In service | Since | Notes |
|-------|----------|-----------|-------|-------|
| **MBTs** | | | | |
| **High quality** | | | | |
| • T-72 | 300 | 285 | 1980 | |
| **Medium and low quality** | | | | |
| • T-62 | 330 | 300 | 1978 | |
| • T-55/T-54 | 310 | 275 | 1964 | Some in storage |
| Subtotal | 640 | 575 | | |
| **Light tanks** | | | | |
| • AMX-13 | 50 | | 1962 | Possibly phased out |
| • PT-76 | 70 | | 1985 | Possibly phased out |
| Subtotal | 120 | 0 | | |
| **Total** | **1,060** | **860** | | |

## APCs/AFVs

| Model | Quantity | In service | Since | Notes |
|-------|----------|-----------|-------|-------|
| **APCs** | | | | |
| • BTR-50/60 | 445 | 445 | 1975 | |
| • BTR-152 | 100 | 100 | 1965 | |
| • Fahd | 200 | 200 | 1992 | |
| • M-3 (panhard) | 50 | 50 | 1983 | |
| Subtotal | 795 | 795 | | |
| **IFVs** | | | | |
| • BMP-2 | 230 | 230 | | |
| • BMP-1 | 685 | 685 | 1981 | |
| Subtotal | 915 | 915 | | |
| **Reconnaissance** | | | | |
| • Engesa EE-9 | 50 | 50 | 1981 | |
| • AML-60 | 55 | 55 | 1963 | |
| • BRDM-2 | 115 | 115 | 1980 | |
| Subtotal | 220 | 220 | | |
| **Total** | **1,930** | **1,930** | | |
| **On order** | | | | |
| • Akrep | 700 | | | Unconfirmed |
| • Fahd | 100 | | | |

## Artillery

| Model | Quantity | In service | Since | Notes |
|---|---|---|---|---|
| **Self-propelled guns and howitzers** | | | | |
| • 152mm 2S3 | 35 | + | 1966 | |
| • 122mm 2S1 | 150 | + | 1977 | |
| Subtotal | 185 | 100 | | |
| **Towed guns and howitzers** | | | | |
| • 152mm ML-20 | 20 | 20 | 1966 | |
| • 130mm M-46/Type-59 | 10 | 10 | | |
| • 122mm D-74          } | | | 1966 | Refers to all types |
| • 122mm M-1931/37  } 180-190 | | 180-190 | 1984 | Refers to all types |
| • 122mm M-30          } | | | 1983 | Refers to all types |
| (M-1938) | | | | |
| • 122mm D-30 | 190 | 190 | 1984 | |
| • 85 mm M-1945/ | 80 | 80 | 1976 | |
| D-44 field/AT | | | | |
| Subtotal | 490 | 490 | | |
| **Mortars, over 160mm** | | | | |
| • 160mm M-43 | 60 | 60 | 1978 | |
| **Mortars, under 160mm** | | | | |
| • 120mm M-43 | 120 | 120 | 1974 | |
| **MRLs** | | | | |
| • 240mm BM-24 | 30 | 30 | 1962 | |
| • 140mm BM-14-16 | 50 | 50 | 1962 | |
| • 122mm BM-21 | 50 | 50 | 1980 | |
| Subtotal | 130 | 130 | | |
| **Total** | **985** | **900** | | |

## Anti-tank Weapons

| Model | Quantity | In service | Since | Notes |
|---|---|---|---|---|
| **Missiles** | | | | |
| • AT-1 (Snapper) | | | | |
| • AT-2 | | | | |
| • AT-3 (Sagger) | | | 1980 | Some mounted on BRDM-2 APCs |
| • AT-4 (Spigot) | | | | |
| • AT-5 (Spandrel) | | | | Mounted on BMP-2 APCs |
| • Milan | approx. 200 | approx. 200 | | |
| **Total** | **approx. 1,400** | **approx. 1,400** | | |
| **Guns** | | | | |
| • 76mm AT gun | 50 | 0 | | Possibly phased out |
| • 107mm B-11 recoilless rifle | 40 | 40 | | Unconfirmed |
| **Total** | **90** | **40** | | |

# Air Force

## Order of Battle

| Model | Quantity | In service | Notes |
|---|---|---|---|
| • Combat | 205 | 187 | |
| • Transport | 45 | 39 | |
| • Helicopters | 114 | 114 | |

## Combat Aircraft

| Model | Quantity | In service | Since | Notes |
|---|---|---|---|---|
| **Interceptors** | | | | |
| • MiG-25 A/B/U (Foxbat) | 20 | 12 | 1979 | |
| • MiG-23MF/MS (Flogger G) | 30 | 30 | 1978 | |
| Subtotal | 50 | 42 | | |
| **Ground attack** | | | | |
| • Su-24 (Fencer C) | 10 | 10 | | |
| • MiG-23BN (Flogger B/D) | 40 | 40 | 1978 | |
| • Su-20/22 (Fitter C) | 15 | 15 | 1978 | |
| Subtotal | 65 | 65 | | |
| **Obsolete** | | | | |
| • MiG-21 MF/bis/U (Fishbed) | 90 | 80 | 1970 | |
| **Total** | **205** | **187** | | |

## Transport Aircraft

| Model | Quantity | In service | Since | Notes |
|---|---|---|---|---|
| • An-12 (Cub) | 4 | 0 | 1964 | |
| • Beechcraft Queen Air/ Beechcraft King Air/ Beechcraft Super King Air T-200T | 12 | 12 | 1977 | 2 employed in maritime patrol role |
| • C-130H and L-100-30 Hercules | 17 | 17 | 1981 | |
| • Fokker F-27 Mk 400/ Mk 600 | 3 | 1 | 1973 | Employed in maritime patrol role |
| • Gulfstream III | 3 | 3 | 1983 | |
| • IL-76 (Candid) | 4 | 4 | 1994 | |
| • Mystère-Falcon 900 | 2 | 2 | 1990 | Unconfirmed |
| **Total** | **45** | **39** | | |

## Training and Liaison Aircraft

| Model | Quantity | In service | Since | Notes |
|---|---|---|---|---|
| With ground attack/close air support capability | | | | Not all serviceable |
| • CM-170 Fouga Magister | 20 | 20 | 1971 | |
| • L-39 Albatross | 30 | 24 | 1987 | |
| Subtotal | 50 | 44 | | |
| **Others** | | | | |
| • Beechcraft Sierra 200 | 18 | 18 | 1976 | |
| • Zlin 142 | 30 | 30 | | |
| • Beechcraft T-34C (Turbine Mentor) | 6 | | 1978 | Possibly phased out |
| Subtotal | 54 | 48 | | |
| Total | **104** | **92** | | |

## Helicopters

| Model | Quantity | In service | Since | Notes |
|---|---|---|---|---|
| **Attack** | | | | |
| • Mi-24/Mi-25 (Hind) | 36 | 36 | 1978 | Number unconfirmed |
| **Medium transport** | | | | |
| • Mi-8/Mi-17 (Hip) | 56 | 56 | 1975 | |
| • SA-330 Puma | 5 | 5 | 1971 | |
| Subtotal | 61 | 61 | | |
| **Light transport** | | | | |
| • Alouette II/III | 6 | 6 | 1983 | |
| • Bell 206 | 3 | 3 | 1988 | |
| • AS-350 Ecureuil | 8 | 8 | 1995 | |
| Subtotal | 17 | 17 | | |
| Total | **114** | **114** | | |
| **On order** | | | | |
| • Rooivalk | | | | Under negotiations |
| • Mi-8/17 | 47 | | | From Russia |

## Miscellaneous Aircraft

| Model | Quantity | Notes |
|---|---|---|
| **Maritime surveillance aircraft** | | |
| • Fokker F-27 and Super King Air T-200T | | Listed under transport a/c |
| **On order** | | |
| • Seeker UAVs | | |

## Advanced Armament

**Air-to-air missiles**
AA-2 (Atoll), AA-6 (Acrid), AA-7 (Apex), AA-11 (Archer)
**Air-to-ground missiles**
AT-2 (Swatter), AT-6 (Spiral), AS-10 (Karen), AS-14 (Kedge)

## Air Force Infrastructure

**Military airfields:**     16
Ain Ousira, Algiers, Amanas, Balida, Bechar, Biskra, Boufarik, Bousfear, Laghuat, Oran, Ouargla, Tafa Aoui, Tindouf, 3 additional

# Air Defense Forces

## Surface-to-Air Missiles

| Model | Batteries | Launchers | Since | Notes |
|---|---|---|---|---|
| **Heavy missiles** | | | | |
| • SA-2 (Guideline) | 6 | 30 | 1970 | |
| • SA-3 (Goa) | 5 | 20 | 1982 | |
| Total | **11** | **50** | | |
| **Medium missiles** | | | | |
| • SA-6 (Gainful) | 10 | 40 | 1979 | |
| • SA-8 (Gecko) | 8 | 24 | | |
| Total | **18** | **64** | | |
| **Light missiles** | | | | |
| • SA-9 (Gaskin) | | 46 | 1980 | |
| • SA-13 (Gopher) | | 32 | | Unconfirmed |
| Total | | **78** | | |
| **Shoulder-launched missiles** | | | | |
| • SA-7 (Grail) | | 180 | 1978 | |

## Other Air Defense Systems

| Model | Quantity | In service | Since | Notes |
|---|---|---|---|---|
| **Short-range guns** | | | | |
| • 57mm ZSU 57x2 SP | | | 1980 | |
| • 57mm S-60 | 50 | 50 | 1974 | |
| • 23mm ZSU 23x4 SP (Gun Dish) | 30 | 30 | 1980 | |
| • 23mm ZU 23x2 | 50 | 50 | | |
| • 37mm M-1939 | 145 | 145 | | |
| • 20mm | 100 | 100 | | |
| Total | **375** | **375** | | |

# Navy

## Combat Vessels

| Type | Original class name | Quantity | Length (m.)/ Displacement (t.) | Armament/ special equipment |
|---|---|---|---|---|
| **Submarines** | | | | |
| • K class | Kilo | 2 | 73.8/3,076 (dived) | 6 x 533mm torpedoes or 24 mines |
| Total | | 2 | | |
| **MFPBs** | | | | |
| • Ossa I | | 2 | 38.6/171 | 4 x SS-N-2A (Styx) |
| • Ossa II | | 9 | 38.6/171 | 4 x SS-N-2B (Styx) |
| Subtotal | | 11 | | |
| **ASW frigates** | | | | |
| • Mourad rais | Koni | 3 | 96.4/1,440 | RBU 6000 a/s mortars 2 x SA-N-4 (Gecko) |
| **Missile corvettes** | | | | |
| • Nanuchka II | | 3 | 59.3/660 | 4 x SS-N-2B (Styx) 2 x SA-N-4 (Gecko) |
| **Gun corvettes** | | | | |
| • Djebel chinoise (C-58) | Type 802 | 2 | 58.4/496 | 76mm guns 40mm guns |
| **Gunboats/MBTs** | | | | |
| • Kebir class Marine | Brooke | 9 | 37.5/166 | 1 x 76mm gun 4 x 25mm guns |
| **Mine warfare** | | | | |
| • T 43 | | 1 | 58.0/500 | 2 a/s mortars 16 mines 2 x 45mm guns |
| Total | | 29 | | |
| **Patrol craft** | | | | |
| • El muderib | Chui-E | 7 | 58.8/388 | 2 x twin 14.5mm MG |
| • Baglietto mangusta | | 6 | 30/91 | 1 x 40mm gun 1 x 20mm gun |
| • Baglietto 20 GC | | 8 | 20.4/44 | 1 x 20mm gun |
| Total | | 21 | | |
| **On order** | | | | |
| • Djebel Chinoise | | 1 | | |
| • Kebir class | | 3 | | |
| • Kh-35 missiles | | 48 | | |

## Landing Craft

| Type | Original class name | Quantity | Length (m.)/ Displacement (t.) | Armament/ special equipment |
|---|---|---|---|---|
| • Polnochny class | | 1 | 75/760 | 2 x 140mm MRLs 2 x 30mm guns |
| • Kalaat Beni Hammad | Brooke Marine | 2 | 93/2,450 | 2 x 40mm guns 2 x 25mm guns |
| Total | | 3 | | |

## Auxiliary Vessels

| Type | Original class name | Quantity | Length (m.)/ Displacement (t.) | Armament/ special equipment |
|---|---|---|---|---|
| • Poluchat I | | 1 | 29.6/70 | |

## Coastal Defense

| Type | Batteries | Notes |
|---|---|---|
| • SS-N-2 Styx | 4 | |

## Naval Infrastructure

**Naval bases:**     5

Algiers, Annaba, Mers al-Kebir, Oran, Skikda

**Ship maintenance and repair facilities**

3 slipways belonging to Chantier Naval de Mers al-Kebir at Oran; 4,000-ton dry docks at Algiers; 3 small graving docks at Annaba; small dry dock at Beni Saf

# Non-governmental Para-military Forces

## Personnel

| | Regular | Total |
|---|---|---|
| • Islamic Salvation Army (AIS) | | |
| • Armed Islamic Group (GIA) | | |
| Total | 1,000 - 1,500 | 1,000 - 1,500 |

# 2. BAHRAIN

## General Data

**Official Name of the State:** State of Bahrain
**Head of State:** Amir Shaykh Hamad bin Isa al-Khalifa
**Prime Minister:** Khalifa ibn Salman al-Khalifa
**Minister of Defense:** Lieutenant General Khalifa ibn Ahmad al-Khalifa
  (also Commander in Chief of the Armed Forces)
**Chief of Staff of the Bahraini Defense Forces:** Major General Abdallah ibn
  Salman al-Khalifa
**Commander of the Air Force:** Hamad Ibn Abdallah al-Khalifa
**Commander of the Navy:** Lieutenant Commander Yusuf al-Maluallah

**Area:** 620 sq. km. (estimate, including 32 small islands)
**Population:** 630,000

## Demography

| | | |
|---|---|---|
| *Ethnic groups* | | |
| Arabs | 460,000 | 73.0% |
| Persians | 50,000 | 8.0% |
| Southeast Asians | 82,000 | 13.0% |
| Others | 38,000 | 6.0% |
| *Religious groups* | | |
| Shi'ite Muslims | 472,500 | 75.0% |
| Sunni Muslims | 157,500 | 25.0% |
| *National groups* | | |
| Bahrainis | 397,000 | 63.0% |
| Alien Arabs | 63,000 | 10.0% |
| *Alien non-Arabs* | | |
| Southeast Asians | 82,000 | 13.0% |
| Iranians | 50,000 | 8.0% |
| Others | 38,000 | 6.0% |

## Economic Data

| | | 1993 | 1994 | 1995 | 1996 | 1997 |
|---|---|---|---|---|---|---|
| GDP current price, local currency | BD bn | 1.88 | 2.00 | 2.06 | 2.18 | 2.29 |
| GDP (US $) | $ bn | 5 | 5.319 | 5.478 | 5.797 | 6.090 |
| GDP per capita | $ | 9,260 | 9,498 | 9,285 | 9,503 | 9,666 |
| Real GDP growth | % | 12.6 | -0.5 | 4 | 4.1 | 3.1 |

## Economic Data *(continued)*

|  |  | 1993 | 1994 | 1995 | 1996 | 1997 |
|---|---|---|---|---|---|---|
| **Balance of payments** | | | | | | |
| • Exports fob | $ bn | 3.72 | 3.62 | 4.11 | 4.70 | 4.16 |
| • Imports fob | $ bn | 3.47 | 3.37 | 3.34 | 3.90 | 3.46 |
| • Account balance (including services and income) | $ bn | 0.035 | 0.198 | 0.557 | 0.573 | 0.577 |
| • External debt | $ bn | 1.97 | 2.57 | 2.80 | 2.53 | 2.39 |
| **Government income and expenditure** | | | | | | |
| • Revenue, local currency | BD bn | 0.564 | 0.514 | 0.668 | 0.616 | 0.706 |
| • Expenditure, local currency | BD bn | 0.566 | 0.572 | 0.596 | 0.689 | 0.704 |
| • Defense expenditure | BD bn | 0.094 | 0.096 | 0.103 | 0.106 | 0.135 |
| • Defense expenditure/GDP | % | 5 | 4.8 | 5 | 4.9 | 5.9 |
| • Defense expenditure/CGE | % | 16.60 | 16.78 | 17.28 | 15.38 | 19.17 |
| • Population | m | 0.54 | 0.56 | 0.59 | 0.61 | 0.63 |
| • Official exchange rate | BD: $1 | 0.376 | 0.376 | 0.376 | 0.376 | 0.376 |

*Sources:* EIU quarterly report, EIU country profile, IMF statistical yearbook, SIPRI Yearbook

## Arms Procurement and Security Assistance Received

| Country | Type | Details |
|---|---|---|
| Britain | • Arms transfers | Patrol craft (1993), electronics |
| | • Military training | Number of retired British officers hold senior positions in Bahraini force, training the new National Guard |
| Germany | • Arms transfers | Missile corvettes, missile boats, helicopters |
| Netherlands | • Arms transfers | 203mm SP howitzers, AIFVs (1996) armored CP, ARVs |
| | • Military training | Foreign advisers |
| Saudi Arabia | • Military training | Trainees abroad |
| Sweden | • Arms transfers | Early warning system (1997) |

## Arms Procurement and Security Assistance Received *(continued)*

| Country | Type | Details |
|---------|------|---------|
| USA | • Arms transfers | ATGMs, APCs, combat aircraft, SAMs, helicopters (1994), tanks, artillery pieces(1992), MLRS, a missile frigate (1997), landing craft |
| | • Military training | Foreign advisers/instructors; Trainees abroad |
| | • Maintenance | Foreign technicians |

## Arms Sales and Security Assistance Extended

| Country | Type | Details |
|---------|------|---------|
| UK | • Facilities | Air force facilities |
| USA | • Facilities | Naval facilities, storage facilities, prepositioning of army equipment & intelligence installations, HQ facilities for the US forces in the Gulf at Mina Salman |

## Foreign Military Cooperation

| | Details |
|---|---------|
| • Foreign forces | About 1,500 US soldiers |
| • Forces deployed abroad | Saudi Arabia (part of GCC Rapid Deployment Force) |
| • Joint maneuvers | USA--joint air force, navy and special forces exercises |
| • Security agreements | USA, Britain, GCC countries |

# Armed Forces

**Major Changes:** Additional M-60 A3 main battle tanks entered service in 1998, as well as some more APCs. A new deal for 10 more F-16 combat aircraft was signed. These will be equipped with AMRAAM AA missiles.

## Order of Battle

| Year | 1994 | 1995 | 1996 | 1997 | 1998 |
|------|------|------|------|------|------|
| **General data** | | | | | |
| • Personnel (regular) | 6,050 | 7,100 | 7,400 | 7,400 | 7,400 |
| • Total number of battalions | 6 | 6 | 6 | 7 | 7 |
| **Ground forces** | | | | | |
| • Tanks | 81 | 81 | 81 | 110 | 180 |
| • APCs/AFVs | 195 | 192 | 192 | 217 (237) | 277 (297) |
| • Artillery (including MRLs) | 29 | 44 | 44 | 44 (50) | 48 (50) |

## Order of Battle *(continued)*

| Year | 1994 | 1995 | 1996 | 1997 | 1998 |
|------|------|------|------|------|------|
| **Air Force** | | | | | |
| • Combat aircraft | 24 | 24 | 24 | 24 | 24 |
| • Transport aircraft | 3-4 | 3-4 | 3-4 | 2 | 2 |
| • Helicopters | 28 | 23 | 23 | 41 | 41 |
| **Air Defense forces** | | | | | |
| • Heavy SAM batteries | 1 | 1 | 1 | 1 | 1 |
| • Medium SAM batteries | - | 7 | 7 | 2 | 2 |
| • Light SAM launchers | 160 | 160 | 160 | 40* | 40 |
| **Navy** | | | | | |
| • Combat vessels | 8 | 8 | 11 | 11 | 11 |
| • Patrol boats | 26 | 26 | 19 | 19 | 19 |

*Note:* beginning with data for 1997, we refer to quantities in active service. The numbers in parentheses refer to the total.

* Due to change in estimate.

## Personnel

| | Regular | Reserves | Total |
|------|---------|----------|-------|
| Ground Forces | 6,000 | | 6,000 |
| Air Force | 700 | | 700 |
| Navy | 700 | | 700 |
| **Total** | **7,400** | | **7,400** |
| **Paramilitary** | | | |
| • Coast Guard and National Guard | 2,000 | | 2,000 |

# Ground Forces

## Formations

| Independent battalions | |
|------|------|
| Armored | 2 |
| Mechanized | 2 |
| Infantry | 2 |
| Artillery | 1 |
| Air defense | 1 |
| Special forces | 1 |
| Total | 9 |

## Tanks

| Model | Quantity | In service | Since | Notes |
|---|---|---|---|---|
| Medium and low quality | | | | |
| • M-60 A3 | 180 | 180 | 1987 | |
| Total | **180** | **180** | | |

## APCs/AFVs

| Model | Quantity | In service | Since | Notes |
|---|---|---|---|---|
| APCs | | | | |
| • M-113 | 110 | 110 | 1990 | |
| • M-3 (Panhard) | 110 | 110 | 1979 | |
| • AT-105 Saxon | 10 | 10 | 1981 | |
| Subtotal | 230 | 230 | | |
| IFVs | | | | |
| • YPR-765 | 25 | 25 | 1996 | |
| Reconnaissance | | | | |
| • Saladin | 10 | 0 | 1973 | Possibly phased out |
| • AML-90 | 22 | 22 | 1979 | |
| • Ferret | 10 | 0 | 1972 | Possibly phased out |
| Subtotal | 42 | 22 | | |
| Total | **297** | **277** | | |

## Artillery

| Model | Quantity | In service | Since | Notes |
|---|---|---|---|---|
| Self-propelled guns and howitzers | | | | |
| • 203mm M-110 | 13 | 13 | 1994 | |
| Towed guns and howitzers | | | | |
| • 155mm M-198 A1 | 20 | 18 | 1984 | |
| • 105mm L-118 | 8 | 8 | | |
| Subtotal | 28 | 26 | | |
| MRLs | | | | |
| • 227mm MLRS | 9 | 9 | 1992 | |
| Total | **50** | **48** | | |

## Anti-tank weapons

| Model | Quantity | In service | Since | Notes |
|---|---|---|---|---|
| Missile launchers | | | | |
| • BGM-71C Improved TOW | 15 | | | |
| On order | | | | |
| • BGM-71E (TOW 2A) | | | | |

# Air Force

## Order of Battle

| Model | Quantity | In service | Notes |
|---|---|---|---|
| • Combat | 24 | 24 | |
| • Transport | 2 | 2 | |
| • Helicopters | 41 | 41 | |

## Combat Aircraft

| Model | Quantity | In service | Since | Notes |
|---|---|---|---|---|
| **Advanced multi-role** | | | | |
| • F-16C/D | 12 | 12 | 1990 | |
| **Multi-role** | | | | |
| • F-5E/F | 12 | 12 | 1985 | |
| Total | **24** | **24** | | |
| **On order** | | | | |
| • 14 F-16 C/D | | | | Scheduled delivery: 2000 |

## Transport Aircraft

| Model | Quantity | In service | Since | Notes |
|---|---|---|---|---|
| • Gulfstream II | 2 | 2 | 1977 | |

## Helicopters

| Model | Quantity | In service | Since | Notes |
|---|---|---|---|---|
| **Ground Attack** | | | | |
| • AH-1E | 14 | 14 | 1996 | |
| • 500MD | 2 | 2 | | |
| • MBB BO-105 | 5 | 5 | 1976 | |
| Subtotal | 21 | 21 | | |
| **Medium Transport** | | | | |
| • UH-60A Black Hawk | 2 | 2 | 1996 | executive a/c |
| • S-70L | 1 | 1 | | |
| • AB-212 | 12 | 12 | | |
| • Bell 412 | 3 | 3 | 1982 | with police |
| Subtotal | 18 | 18 | | |
| **Naval combat** | | | | |
| • SA-365 Dauphin | 2 | 2 | | |
| Total | **41** | **41** | | |

## Advanced armaments

**Air-to-air-missiles**
AIM-9P Sidewinder
**Air-to-ground missiles**
AS-15TT anti-ship missile
**On order**
Three Sharpshooter pods (for F-16 a/c); AIM-120 AMRAAM

# Air Defense Forces

## Surface-to-Air Missiles

| Model | Batteries | Launchers | Since | Notes |
|---|---|---|---|---|
| **Heavy missiles** | | | | |
| • MIM-23B Improved HAWK | 1 | | 1994 | |
| **Medium missiles** | | | | |
| • Crotale | 2 | 7 | 1995 | Number unconfirmed |
| **Light missiles** | | | | |
| • RBS-70 | | 40 | 1980 | |
| **Shoulder-launched missiles** | | | | |
| • FIM-92A Stinger | | 18 | 1987 | 400 missiles (number unconfirmed) |

## Other Air Defense Systems

**Short-range guns**
• 35mm Oerlikon
**On order**
• Air defense command and control system from Britain (Ferranti)

## Air Force Infrastructure

**Military airfields:**     1
• Shaykh Isa

# Navy

## Combat vessels

| Type | Original class name | Quantity | Length (m.)/ Displacement (t.) | Armament/ special equipment |
|---|---|---|---|---|
| **Missile frigates** | | | | |
| • Sabha | Oliver Hazard Perry class | 1 | 135.6/3,638 | 1 x SH-2G helicopter<br>1 x missile launcher for 4x Harpoon SSM<br>36 x Standard SM-1<br>6 x 324mm torpedo tube<br>1 x 76mm gun<br>1 x Vulcan Phalanx 20mm gun |
| **Missile corvettes** | | | | |
| • Al Manama | Lürssen | 2 | 63.0/632 | 4 x Exocet MM-40<br>1 x 76mm gun<br>1 x twin 40mm gun |
| **MFPBs** | | | | |
| • Ahmad al-Fateh | Lürssen FPB-45 | 4 | 44.9/259 | 4 x Exocet MM-40<br>1 x 76mm gun<br>1 x twin 40mm gun |
| **Gunboat/MTBs** | | | | |
| • Al-Riffa | Lürssen FPB-38 | 2 | 38.5/205 | 2 x twin 40mm guns<br>1 x 57mm rocket launcher |
| • Al-Jarim | Swift FPB-20 | 2 | 19.2/33 | 1 x 20mm gun |
| Subtotal | | 4 | | |
| Total | | 11 | | |

## Combat vessels *(continued)*

| Type | Original class name | Quantity | Length (m.)/ Displacement (t.) | Armament/ special equipment |
|---|---|---|---|---|
| **Patrol craft** | | | | |
| (mostly with Coast Guard) | | | | |
| • Al-Muharraq | Wasp | 1 | 30/90 | 1 x 30mm gun |
| • Dera'a | Tracker | 2 | 19.5/31 | |
| • Dera'a | Halmatic | 4 | 20.1/31.5 | |
| • Dera'a | Wasp | 2 | 20/36.3 | |
| • Saif | Halmatic | 6 | 14.4/17 | |
| • Saif | Fairey Marine Sword | 4 | 13.7/15 | |
| Total | | 19 | | |

## Landing Craft

| Type | Original class name | Quantity | Length (m.)/ Displacement (t.) | Armament/ special equipment |
|---|---|---|---|---|
| • 150 ton Fairey Marine LCM | 150 ton Fairey Marine LCM | 1 | 22.5/150 | |
| • Tiger class hovercraft | Tiger class hovercraft | 1 | 7.97/4.5 | |
| Total | | 2 | | |

## Naval Infrastructure

**Naval bases:**            1

Mina Salman

### Ship maintenance and repair facilities

Arab Shipbuilding and Repair Yard (ASRY), a 500,000 dwt drydock engaged in
   repairs and construction (mainly supertankers; jointly owned by Bahrain,
   Kuwait, Qatar, Saudi Arabia, UAE each 18.84%;Iraq--4.7%; and Libya--1.1%)

# 3. EGYPT

## General Data

**Official Name of the State:** The Arab Republic of Egypt
**Head of State:** President Mohammad Hosni Mubarak
**Prime Minister:** Kamal Ahmad al-Ganzuri
**Minister of Defense and War Production:** Field Marshal Mohammad
Hussayn Tantawi
**Chief of General Staff:** General Magdi Hatata
**Commander of the Air Force:** Lieutenant General Ahmad Abd al-Rahman
Nasser
**Commander of the Navy:** Vice Admiral Ahmad Ali Fadil

**Area:** 1,000,258 sq. km. (dispute with Sudan over "Halaib triangle" area)
**Population:** 62,010,000

## Demography

| | | |
|---|---|---|
| *Ethnic groups* | | |
| Arabs | 61,018,000 | 98.4% |
| Nubians | 62,000 | 0.1% |
| Greeks, Italians, Armenians | 620,000 | 1.0% |
| Others | 310,000 | 0.5% |
| *Religious groups* | | |
| Sunni Muslims | 58,289,000 | 94.0% |
| Copts, other Christians | 3,721,000 | 6.0% |

## Economic data

| | | 1993 | 1994 | 1995 | 1996 | 1997 |
|---|---|---|---|---|---|---|
| GDP current price, local currency | E£ bn | 157.30 | 175.00 | 205.00 | 228.30 | 255.80 |
| GDP (US $) | $ bn | 46.676 | 51.622 | 60.472 | 67.345 | 75.457 |
| GDP per capita | $ | 826 | 892 | 1,029 | 1,111 | 1,217 |
| Real GDP growth | % | 3.0 | 3.8 | 4.6 | 5.1 | 5.9 |
| **Balance of payments** | | | | | | |
| • Exports fob | $ bn | 3.55 | 4.04 | 4.67 | 4.78 | 5.53 |
| • Imports fob | $ bn | 9.92 | 10.00 | 12.27 | 13.17 | 14.16 |
| • Account balance (including services and income) | $ bn | 2.30 | 0.03 | -0.25 | -0.19 | -0.71 |
| • External debt | $ bn | 30.6 | 32.4 | 33.4 | 31.4 | 28.6 |

## Economic data *(continued)*

|  |  | 1993 | 1994 | 1995 | 1996 | 1997 |
|---|---|---|---|---|---|---|
| **Government income and expenditure** | | | | | | |
| • Revenue, local currency | E£ bn | 56.33 | 60.443 | 66.195 | 71.147 | 73.521 |
| • Expenditure, local currency | E£ bn | 65.314 | 65.047 | 71.632 | 77.451 | 76.016 |
| • Defense expenditure | E£ bn | 5.413 | 5.724 | 9.119 | 9.153 | NA |
| • Defense expenditure/GDP | % | 3.44 | 3.27 | 4.44 | 4.00 | NA |
| • Defense expenditure/CGE | % | 8.29 | 8.80 | 12.73 | 11.81 | NA |
| • Population | m | 56.49 | 57.85 | 59.23 | 60.60 | 62.01 |
| • Official exchange rate | E£: $1 | 3.37 | 3.39 | 3.39 | 3.39 | 3.39 |

*Sources:* EIU quarterly report, EIU country profile, IMF statistical yearbook, SIPRI Yearbook

## Arms Procurement and Security Assistance Received

| Country | Type | Details |
|---|---|---|
| Britain | • Military training | Trainees abroad |
|  | • Arms transfers | Naval radars(1996), mortar locating radar upgrade (1997) |
| Czech Republic | • Arms transfers | L-59 jet trainer aircraft |
| France | • Military training | Trainees abroad |
|  | • Cooperation in | Electronics, components of arms production, SP AA systems assembly, R&D |
| Germany | • Military training | Trainees abroad |
|  | • Maintenance of equipment | Transport aircraft, Anti-mine equipment (1998) |
| India | • Arms transfers | Spare parts for Soviet made aircraft (1998) |
| Italy | • Arms transfers | Terminally guided aerial bombs |
| Netherlands | • Arms transfers | AIFVs (1996) |
| North Korea | • Arms transfers | Assistance to Egyptian production of SSMs (1996 - alleged) |
| PRC | • Arms transfers | Spare parts for F-7 combat aircraft |
| Russia | • Arms transfers | BMP turrets for Egyptian Fahd APCs |

## Arms Procurement and Security Assistance Received *(continued)*

| Country | Type | Details |
|---------|------|---------|
| Turkey | • Arms transfers | US-designed F-16 fighter a/c, assembled in Turkey |
| USA | • Financial | $1.3 billion grant (1998), and a few items from US drawdown, worth several hundred million dollars |
| | • Military training | Foreign advisers/instructors, trainees abroad (1998) |
| | • Arms transfers | M-88 armored recovery vehicles (1998), APCs, artillery, ATGMs, combat aircraft (1996), helicopters including AH-64 (1995), SH-2G (1997), CH-47D (1999), AAMs, early warning aircraft, radars, SAMs (1998), upgrading kits for SAMs and tanks, UAVs and mini-UAVs, missile frigates (1998), Harpoon anti-ship missiles (1998), torpedoes, fire control systems for submarines, sonars, communication and ECCM equipment, F-16 simulators (1998) |
| | • Cooperation in | Upgrading M-113 APCs, AIFVs, arms production, ammunition, electronics including assembly, R&D radars and radio transceivers, M-1 A1 tank assembly, upgrading of PRC-made submarines |
| | • Construction aid | Upgrading of airfields and dry docks |
| | • Maintenance aid | Aircraft |

## Arms Sales and Security Assistance Extended

| Country | Type | Details |
|---------|------|---------|
| Algeria | • Arms transfers | Fahd APCs |
| Bahrain | • Military training | Advisers/instructors, foreign trainees |
| Bosnia | • Arms transfers | 10 T-55 tanks and spare parts (1997), artillery |
| Brazil | • Cooperation in | Trainer aircraft arms production, assembly, R&D |
| Greece | • Military training | Foreign trainees |
| Iraq | • Facilities | Naval vessels anchored in Egypt since the Iran-Iraq war |
| Jordan | • Military training | Foreign trainees |
| Kuwait | • Military training | Advisers/instructors |
| | • Arms transfers | Skyguard AA systems, optronics, gas masks, surveillance radar (AN-TPS/63) |

## Arms Sales and Security Assistance Extended *(continued)*

| Country | Type | Details |
|---|---|---|
| Lebanon | • Military training | Foreign trainees |
| Libya | • Military training | Foreign trainees |
| Mali | • Arms transfers | Fahd APCs |
| Oman | • Arms transfers | Optronics |
| | • Military training | Advisers/instructors |
| Palestinians | • Military training | Foreign trainees |
| Qatar | • Arms transfers | Optronics, gas masks |
| Rwanda | • Arms transfers | 6 artillery pieces |
| Saudi Arabia | • Arms transfers | Engineering equipment |
| Singapore | • Arms transfers | Optronics |
| Sweden | • Cooperation in arms production assembly, R&D | Radio transceivers |
| Turkey | • Military training | Foreign trainees |
| Uganda | • Arms transfers | Optronics |
| USA | • Facilities | Airfields at Cairo West, Qena, Inshas, Hurghada |
| Yemen | • Military training | Foreign trainees |
| Zaire | • Military training | Advisers/instructors |
| | • Arms transfers | Optronics |
| Zimbabwe | • Military training | Foreign trainees |

## Foreign Military Cooperation

| | Details |
|---|---|
| • Forces deployed abroad | Troops with UN forces in Angola, Croatia, Georgia and Liberia |
| • Joint maneuvers | France, Britain, Italy, USA |

## Defense Production

| | M | P | A |
|---|---|---|---|
| **Army equipment** | | | |
| • 130mm artillery pieces | | √ | |
| • 122mm Saqr 18/30/36 MRLs | √ | | |
| • Conversion of 122mm D-30 howitzers to 122mm AR SP howitzers | √ | | |
| • British tank guns | | √ | |
| • Upgrading of Soviet tanks (with British assistance) | | √ | |
| • M-1 A1 tanks, with cooperation from USA (some parts will be produced in Egypt) | | | √ |
| • Conversion of 23mm AAGs to Sinai 23 SP AA systems | √ | | |
| • Add-on armor to M-113 APCs | √ | | |

## Defense Production *(continued)*

| | M | P | A |
|---|:-:|:-:|:-:|
| • Upgraded Scud B SSMs (with North Korean cooperation) | √ | | |
| • Fahd APCs (with FRG components and assistance) | | √ | |
| • MRLs (copy of Soviet models) | | √ | |
| • Short-range SAMs | | | √ |
| • AAGs | | | √ |
| • Tank tracks | | √ | |
| • Trucks and jeeps (with USA) | | √ | |
| • Soviet design AAGs and small arms | | √ | |
| • Minefield crossing systems (similar to Viper) | | √ | |
| • Mines, including scatterable | √ | √ | |
| • Ammunition for artillery, tanks, and small arms | √ | | |
| • Rifles (Hakim 7.92mm, Rashid 7.62mm) | √ | | |
| • Chemical agents (unconfirmed) | √ | | |
| **Aircraft and air ammunition** | | | |
| • CBUs (US design) | | √ | |
| • Anti-runway bombs | | √ | |
| • A few parts for F-16 | | √ | |
| • Parts for Mirage 2000 | | √ | |
| • Parts for Mystère-Falcon 50 executive aircraft | | √ | |
| • Aircraft fuel pods | | √ | |
| • Aerial bombs | | √ | |
| **Electronics** | | | |
| • Bassal artillery fire control system | √ | | |
| • Simulators for rifle firing | √ | | |
| • AN/TPS-63 radars (assembly, with 30% of components locally produced) | | √ | |
| • Radio transceivers (in collaboration with France, Germany, Sweden and Britain) | | √ | |
| • SAM electronics (in collaboration with Britain) | | √ | |
| • Fire control system | | √ | |
| **Optronics** | | | |
| • Night vision devices | | √ | |

*Note:*   M - manufacture (indigenously developed)
P - production under license
A - assembly

## Weapons of Mass Destruction

### Nuclear capabilities

- R&D; a declared policy not to produce nuclear weapons; NPT signatory, all declared installations under IAEA safeguards; a 2 MW Soviet-made nuclear research reactor in operation since 1961; a 22 MW research reactor from Argentina, completed 1997

### CW capabilities

- Alleged continued research and possible production of chemical warfare agents
- Egypt refused to sign the chemical weapons convention (CWC)
- Personal protective equipment. Soviet type decontamination units. Stockpile of chemical agents (mustard and nerve agents)
- Fuchs (Fox) ABC detection vehicle (12)
- SPW-40 P2Ch ABC detection vehicle (small numbers)

### Biological warfare capabilities

- Suspected biological warfare program; no details available

### Surface-to-surface missiles

- Egypt is probably producing or assembling Scud missiles (possibly of an upgraded, extended range version) and their lauchers

| Model | Launchers | Missiles | Since | Notes |
|---|---|---|---|---|
| • FROG-7 | 12 | | | |
| • SS-1 (Scud B) | 24 | 100 | 1973 | Possibly some upgraded |
| • Saqr 80 | | | | Delivery unconfirmed |
| Total | 36 | 100+ | | |

On order
- Upgraded SS-1 Scud B, locally produced; Scud C (unconfirmed)

# Armed Forces

**Major Changes:** Egypt has increased its defense budget in recent years. In 1998 Egypt concluded the production of 555 M1A1 Abrams main battle tanks. The Egyptian navy received its fourth and last Oliver Hazard Perry class frigate. Please note that we have reassessed the number of Scud SSM launchers in Egypt's possession, and increased it to 24 launchers.

## Order of Battle

| Year | 1994 | 1995 | 1996 | 1997 | 1998 |
|---|---|---|---|---|---|
| **General data** | | | | | |
| • Personnel (regular) | 428,000 | 426,000 | 424,000 | 421,000 | 455,000 |
| • Divisions | 12 | 12 | 12 | 12 | 12 |
| • Number of brigades | 14 | 14 | 14 | 18 | 12+ |
| **Ground forces** | | | | | |
| • Tanks | 2,750 | 2,800 | 2,900 | 2,662 (3,162) | 2,685 - 2,785 (3,462) |
| • APCs/AFVs | 4,400 | 4,400 | 5,180 | 3,025 (4,995) | 3,160 - 3,210 (5,030 - 5,080) |
| • Artillery (including MRLs) | 2,200 | 2,200 | 3,046 | 3,146 | 3,146 |
| • SSM launchers | 24 | 24 | 24 | 21 | 36 |
| **Air Force** | | | | | |
| • Combat aircraft | 457 | 497 | 497 | 505 | 498 (505) |
| • Transport aircraft | 47 | 47 | 43 | 35 | 38 |
| • Helicopters | 197 | 211 | 211 | 223 | 224 (234) |
| **Air Defense Forces** | | | | | |
| • Heavy SAM batteries | 122 | 122 | 122 | 105 | 105 |
| • Medium SAM batteries | 48 | 48 | 48 | 48 | 44 |
| • Light SAM launchers | 50 | 50 | 50 | 50 | 50 |
| **Navy** | | | | | |
| • Submarines | 8 | 8 | 8 | 6 | 6 |
| • Combat vessels | 56 | 58 | 59 | 64 | 66 |
| • Patrol crafts | 69 | 69 | 70 | 83 | 83 |

*Note:* beginning with data for 1997, we refer to quantities in active service. The numbers in parentheses refer to the total.

## Personnel

| | Regular | Reserves | Total |
|---|---|---|---|
| Ground Forces | 320,000 | 150,000 | 470,000 |
| Air Force | 35,000 | 20,000 | 55,000 |
| Air Defense | 80,000 | 60,000 | 140,000 |
| Navy | 20,000 | 14,000 | 34,000 |
| **Total** | **455,000** | **244,000** | **699,000** |

## Personnel *(continued)*

|  | Regular | Reserves | Total |
|---|---|---|---|
| **Paramilitary** | | | |
| • Coast Guard | | | 2,000 |
| • Frontier Corps | | | 6,000 |
| • Central Security Forces | | | 325,000 |
| • National Guard | | | 60,000 |
| • Border Guard | | | 12,000 |

# Ground Forces

## Formations

|  | Corps/ Armies | Divisions | Independent brigades/ groups | Brigades in divisions |
|---|---|---|---|---|
| All arms | 2 | | | |
| Armored | | 4 | 4 | 2 armd., 1 mech., 1 arty. each |
| Mechanized | | 7 | 4 | 2 mech., 1 tank, 1 arty. each |
| Infantry | | 1 | 2 | |
| Airborne | | | 1 | |
| Paratroopers | | | 1 | |
| Special forces | | | several | |
| Artillery | | | 15 | |
| SSM | | | 2 | |
| **Total** | **2** | **12** | **29+** | |

## Tanks

| Model | Quantity | In service | Since | Notes |
|---|---|---|---|---|
| **MBTs** | | | | |
| **High Quality** | | | | |
| • M-1 A1 | 512 | 250 | 1992 | |
| **Medium and low quality** | | | | |
| • M-60 A3 | 850 | 835 | 1981 | |
| • M-60 A1 | 700 | 600 | 1990 | |
| • T-62 | 600 | 500-600 | 1972 | |
| • T-55 | 800 | 500+ | | Most in storage |

## Tanks *(continued)*

| Model | Quantity | In service | Since | Notes |
|---|---|---|---|---|
| Subtotal | 2,950 | 2,435-2,535 | | |
| Total | 3,462 | 2,685-2,785 | | |

**On Order**
- additional 200 M-1 A1, under negotiation
- 340 M-60 A3, out of US drawdown (under negotiation), upgrading M-60 A1 to A3 standard contemplated

## APCs/AFVs

| Model | Quantity | In service | Since | Notes |
|---|---|---|---|---|
| **APCs** | | | | |
| • M-113 A2 | 1,768 | 1,000 | 1980 | Additional 52 M-901 ITV |
| • BMR-600 | 250 | 250 | 1983 | |
| • Fahd | 165 | 160 | 1986 | |
| • OT-62/BTR-50 | 1,100 | + | | Older models possibly phased out |
| Subtotal | 3,283 | 1,410 | | |
| **IFVs** | | | | |
| • BMP-1 | 220 | 220 | | |
| • YPR-765 | 400 | 400 | 1996 | Additional 200 with TOW under armor |
| • V-150/V-300 commando | approx. 180 | approx. 180 | | |
| Subtotal | 800 | 800 | | |
| **Reconnaissance** | | | | |
| • BRDM-2 | 300 | 300 | 1968 | Storage/phased out |
| • BTR-40/152 | 650 - 700 | 650 - 700 | | |
| Subtotal | 950 - 1,000 | 950 - 1,000 | | |
| Total | 5,033 - 5,083 | 3,160 - 3,210 | | |

**On order**
- Fahd

## Artillery

| Model | Quantity | In service | Since | Notes |
|---|---|---|---|---|
| **Self-propelled guns and howitzers** | | | | |
| • 155mm M-109 A2 | 200 | 200 | 1984 | |
| • 122mm SP122 | 80 | 80 | | |
| Subtotal | 280 | 280 | | |

## Artillery *(continued)*

| Model | Quantity | In service | Since | Notes |
|---|---|---|---|---|
| **Towed guns and howitzers** | | | | |
| • 130mm M-46 gun/ Type-59 | + | + | | |
| • 122mm D-30 | + | + | | |
| Subtotal | 970 | 970 | | |
| **Mortars, over 160mm** | | | | |
| • 240mm | + | + | | |
| • 160mm | 60 | 60 | | |
| **Mortars, under 160mm** | | | | |
| • 120mm M-43 | 1,800 | 1,800 | | |
| • 107mm (4.2") M-30 SP | 100 | 100 | | On M-106 A2 carrier |
| Subtotal | 1,900 | 1,900 | | |
| **MRLs** | | | | |
| • 122mm BM-11 | 100 | 100 | | |
| • 122mm BM-21 | | | | |
| • 122mm Saqr 18/30/36 } | 200 | 200 | | |
| Subtotal | 300 | 300 | | |
| **Total** | **3,510** | **3,510** | | |

**Artillery/mortar-locating radars**
• AN/TPQ-37

**On order**
• AN/TPQ-37 artillery and mortar-locating radar

## Logistic and Engineering Equipment

• Bar mine-laying system, EWK pontoon bridges, GSP self-propelled ferries, M-123 Viper minefield crossing system/ Egyptian Viper-like system, designated al-Fatah, MT-55 bridging tanks, MTU-55 bridging tanks, Egyptian bridging tanks (on T-34 chassis), mine-clearing rollers, PMP folding pontoon bridges, PRP motorized bridges, M-88 armored recovery vehicles

## Anti-Tank Weapons

| Model | Quantity | In service | Since | Notes |
|---|---|---|---|---|
| **Missiles** | | | | |
| • AT-3 (Sagger) | 1,400 | 1,400 | 1972 | |
| • BGM-71C Improved TOW/BGM-71D TOW II | 530-630 | 530-630 | | |
| • M-901 ITV SP (TOW under armor) | 52 | 40 | | |

### Anti-Tank Weapons *(continued)*

| Model | Quantity | In service | Since | Notes |
|---|---|---|---|---|
| • YPR-765 (TOW under armor) | 200 | 200 | 1996 | |
| • Milan | 250 | 200 | 1978 | |
| • Swingfire | 200 | 200 | 1976 | |
| Total | **2,950** | **2,500** | | |
| On order | | | | |
| • Tow 2B | 540 | | | |

# Air Force

### Order of Battle

| Model | Quantity | In service | Notes |
|---|---|---|---|
| • Combat | 505 | 498 | |
| • Transport | 38 | 38 | |
| • Helicopters | 234 | 224 | |

### Combat aircraft

| Model | Quantity | In service | Since | Notes |
|---|---|---|---|---|
| **Advanced multi-role** | | | | |
| • F-16A/B | 30 | 30 | 1982 | |
| • F-16C/D | approx. 130 | approx. 130 | 1986 | |
| • Mirage 2000 | 18 | 18 | 1986 | |
| **Multi-role** | | | | |
| • F-4E Phantom | 32 | 25 | 1980 | |
| **Ground attack** | | | | |
| • Alpha Jet and Alpha Jet MS-2 | 42 | 42 | 1983 | Normally an advanced trainer; defined in Egypt as CAS a/c (originally 30 MS-1, 15 MS-2) |
| **Obsolete** | | | | |
| • F-7 Shenyang/ MiG-21 MF | 150 | 150 | 1981 | Partly used as strike a/c. 14 additional under reconnaissance |
| • F-6 Shenyang/FT-6 | 44 | 44 | | |

## Combat aircraft *(continued)*

| Model | Quantity | In service | Since | Notes |
|---|---|---|---|---|
| • Mirage 5 | 59 | 59 | 1974 | Including 6 Mirage 5DR |
| Subtotal | 253 | 253 | | |
| **Total** | **505** | **498** | | |

On order
• 21 F-16C from US drawdown

## Transport Aircraft

| Model | Quantity | In service | Since | Notes |
|---|---|---|---|---|
| • Beechcraft 1900C (executive a/c) | 2 | 2 | 1988 | |
| • Boeing 707 | 1 | 1 | 1974 | |
| • C-130H/C-130H-30 Hercules | 19 | 19 | 1978/1990 | |
| • DHC-5D Buffalo | 9 | 9 | 1982 | |
| • Gulfstream III/V | 4 | 4 | 1985/1996 | |
| • Mystère-Falcon 20 | 3 | 3 | | |
| **Total** | **38** | **38** | | |

## Training and Liaison Aircraft

| Model | Quantity | In service | Since | Notes |
|---|---|---|---|---|
| With ground attack/close air support capability | | | | |
| • Alpha Jet and Alpha Jet MS-2 | | | 1983 | Listed as ground attack a/c, above |
| • L-29 (Delfin) | 40 | 40 | | |
| • L-39 (Albatross) | 48 | 48 | 1990 | |
| • L-59 | 25 | 25 | 1993 | |
| Subtotal | 113 | 113 | | |
| Others | | | | |
| • al-Gumhuriya | 36 | 36 | | |
| • Embraer EMB-312 (Tucano) | 54 | 54 | 1984 | |
| Subtotal | 90 | 90 | | |
| **Total** | **203** | **203** | | |

## Helicopters

| Model | Quantity | In service | Since | Notes |
|---|---|---|---|---|
| Attack | | | | |
| • AH-64A Apache | 36 | 36 | 1995 | |
| • SA-342 L/M Gazelle | 65 | 65 | 1983 | |
| Subtotal | 101 | 101 | | |

## Helicopters *(continued)*

| Model | Quantity | In service | Since | Notes |
|---|---|---|---|---|
| **Heavy transport** | | | | |
| • CH-47C Chinook | 25 | 15 | 1981 | |
| **Medium transport** | | | | |
| • Mi-8 (Hip) | approx. 40 | approx. 40 | 1972 | Some may be armed |
| • UH-60A Black Hawk | 2 | 2 | | VIP service |
| • Westland Commando Mk 2 | 25 | 25 | 1974 | |
| Subtotal | 67 | 67 | | |
| **Light transport** | | | | |
| • UH-12E Hiller | 17 | 17 | 1982 | |
| **Naval combat** | | | | |
| • Westland Sea King Mk 47 | 5 | 5 | 1976 | |
| • SH-2G | 10 | 10 | 1997 | |
| • SA-342L Gazelle | 9 | 9 | 1983 | |
| Subtotal | 24 | 24 | | |
| **Total** | **234** | **224** | | |
| **on order** | | | | |
| • CH-47D Chinook | 4 | | | (to be delivered in 1999) |

## Miscellaneous Aircraft

| Model | Quantity | In service | Since | Notes |
|---|---|---|---|---|
| **Reconnaissance** | | | | |
| • MiG-21R | 14 | 14 | | |
| • Mirage 5DR | 6 | 6 | 1974 | |
| **AEW/AWACS aircraft** | | | | |
| • E-2C Hawkeye AEW | 5 | 5 | 1986 | |
| **ELINT/maritime surveillance/ASW** | | | | |
| • Beechcraft 1900C | 4 | 4 | 1992 | |
| • C-130H | 2 | 2 | 1978 | |
| **UAVs and mini-UAVs** | | | | |
| • Kader | | | | |
| • R4E-50 Skyeye mini-UAVs | 48 | 48 | | |
| • Teledyne Ryan model 324 Scarab | 50 | 50 | | |

## Miscellaneous Aircraft *(continued)*

| Model | Quantity | In service | Since | Notes |
|---|---|---|---|---|
| **Target drones** | | | | |
| • Aerospatiale CT-20 target drone | | | | |
| • Beech AQM-37A target drone | | | | |
| • Beech MQM-107B target drone | | | | |
| • TTL BTT-3 Banshe target drone | Several dozen | Several dozen | | |

## Advanced Armament

**Air-to-air-missiles**
• AIM-7F/7M Sparrow, AIM-9 Sidewinder; AIM-9L; AIM-9P, R-550 Magic, R-530D Super
**Air-to-ground missiles**
• AGM-65 Maverick (1,100),  AS-30L, Hellfire (AGM-114), HOT
**Avionics**
• LANTIRN          (30 units)

## Air Force Infrastructure

**Aircraft shelters**
In all operational airfields, for combat aircraft
**Military airfields:**      29
Abu Hammad, Abu Suweir, Alexandria, Aswan, Beni Suef, Bilbeis, Cairo
International, Cairo West, Fayid, Hurghada, Inshas, Janaklis, Jebel al-Basour,
Kabrit, Kom Awshim, Luxor, al-Maza, al-Minya, Mansura, Marsah Matruh,
Qena, al-Qutamiya, Saqqara, Sidi Barani, Ras Banas, Salahiya, Tanta,
al-Zaqaziq, one additional airfield

# Air Defense Forces

## Surface-to-Air Missiles

| Model | Batteries | Launchers | Since | Notes |
|---|---|---|---|---|
| **Heavy missiles** | | | | |
| • MIM-23B | | | | |
| Improved HAWK | 12 | 78 | 1981 | |
| • SA-2 (Guideline) | 40 | 282 | 1965 | |
| • SA-3 (Goa) | 53 | 212 | 1965 | |
| Subtotal | 105 | 572 | | |
| **Medium missiles** | | | | |
| • Crotale | 12 | 24 | 1977 | |
| • SA-6 (Gainful) | 14 | 52 | 1972 | |
| • Sparrow | 18 | 18 | | |
| Subtotal | 44 | 94 | | |
| **Light missiles** | | | | |
| • MIM72A | 12 | 50 | | |
| **Shoulder-launched missiles** | | | | |
| • Ain al-Saqr (Saqr Eye) | | | | |
| • SA-7 (Grail) | | Some 2,000 | 1972 | |
| **On order** | | | | |
| • 1,000 FIM-92A Stinger; AdSAMs, under negotiations, 50 Avenger systems with 1,000 missiles | | | | |

## Other Air Defense Systems

| Model | Quantity | In service | Since | Notes |
|---|---|---|---|---|
| **Air defense systems (missiles, radars and guns)** | | | | |
| • Skyguard AA system (Egyptian designation: Amoun) | | | | (18) included in SAM |
| • Sinai 23mm AA system | | | | |
| **Short-range guns** | | | | |
| • 57mm ZSU 57x2 SP | 40 | 40 | | |
| • 35mm Oerlikon-Buhrle 35x2 GDF-002 | 36 | 36 | | Integral part of Skyguard systems |
| • 23mm ZSU 23x4 SP (Gun Dish) | 550 | 550 | | |
| • 23mm ZU 23x2 | 117 | 117 | | |
| Total | 743 | 743 | | |

## Other Air Defense Systems *(continued)*

| Model | Quantity | In service | Since | Notes |
|---|---|---|---|---|
| Radars | | | | |
| • AN/TPS-59 | | | | |
| • AN/TPS-63 | 42 | 42 | | |
| • P-15 Flat Face | | | | |
| • P-12 Spoon Rest | | | | |
| • Tiger S (TRS-2100) | 15 | 15 | | |
| On order | | | | |
| • Trackstar L-band acquisition radar; Skyguard AA systems | | | | |

# Navy

### Combat vessels

| Type | Original class name | Quantity | Length (m.)/ Displacement (t.) | Armament/ special equipment |
|---|---|---|---|---|
| Submarines | | | | |
| • R class (Romeo ex-Soviet) | | 2 | | 2 non operational |
| • R class (Romeo ex-Chinese) | | 4 | 76.6/1,830 | sub-Harpoon SSM 8x533mm torpedo tubes 14xMk.37F Mod 2 torpedoes or 28 mines |
| Total | | 6 | | |
| Missile frigates | | | | |
| • Descubierta class | | 2 | 88.8/1,233 | 8xHarpoon SSMs 24xAspide SAMs 6x324mm torpedoes 1x375mm ASW launcher 1x76mm gun 2x40mm guns |
| • Jianghu class | | 2 | 103.2/1,425 | 4xHai Ying-II SSMs 4x57mm guns 12x37mm guns 2 RBU 1200 ASW mortars |

## Combat vessels (continued)

| Type | Original class name | Quantity | Length (m.)/ Displacement (t.) | Armament/ special equipment |
|---|---|---|---|---|
| • Knox class | | 2 | 134/3,011 | 1x Seasprite helicopter 8xHarpoon SSMs 1x127mm gun 1x20mm phalanx 4x324mm torpedoes |
| • Oliver Hazard Perry | | 4 | 135.6/2,750 | 2xSeasprite helicopters 4xHarpoon SSMs 36xStandard SAM 1x76mm gun 1x20mm Phalanx 6x324mm torpedoes |
| Subtotal | | 10 | | |
| **MFPBs** | | | | |
| • Hegu class | | 6 | 27.0/88 | 2xSY -1 SSMs or 2xSS-N-2 Styx 2x23mm gun |
| • October | Komar | 6 | 25.5/82.0 | 2xOtomat SSMs 4x30mm gun |
| • Ossa I | | 4 | 38.6/171 | 4x SS-N-2A Styx SA-N-5 Grail 4x30mm gun (plus 1 non-operational) |
| • Ramadan | Vosper Thornycroft | 6 | 52.0/307 | 4xOtomat SSMs 1x76mm gun 2x40mm gun SA-N-5 portable SAMs |
| Subtotal | | 22 | | |
| **Gun destroyers** | | | | |
| • El Fateh | Zenith, Wessex | 1 | 110.6/1730 | 2xSA-N-5 SAMs 4x115mm guns 6x37mm guns 2x40mm guns 8x533mm torpedo tubes |

## Combat vessels *(continued)*

| Type | Original class name | Quantity | Length (m.)/ Displacement (t.) | Armament/ special equipment |
|------|---------------------|----------|-------------------------------|-----------------------------|
| **Mine warfare vessels** | | | | |
| • T-43 class minesweeper | | 6 | 58.0/580 | 4x37mm guns 20 mines (plus 2 non - operational) |
| • Swiftships coastal minesweep | | 3 | 33.8/203 | |
| • Yurka class minesweeper | | 4 | 52.4/540 | 4x30mm guns 10 mines |
| • Swiftships route survey | | 2 | 27.4/165 | |
| Subtotal | | 15 | | |
| **Gunboat/MTBs** | | | | |
| • Hainan class | | 8 | 58.8/375 | 4x57mm guns 4x23mm guns (3 possibly non operational) |
| • Shanghai II | | 4 | 38.8/113 | 4x37mm guns 4x23mm guns |
| • Shershen class MTB | | 6 | 34.7/145 | SA-N-5 portable SAM 4x30mm guns 2x122mm MRL |
| Subtotal | | 18 | | |
| **Total** | | **66** | | |
| **Patrol craft** | | | | |
| (Mostly with Coast Guard) | | | | |
| • Spectre | | 12 | 13.8/37 | |
| • Peterson | | 9 | 13.9/18 | replaced older Bertram type |
| • Crestitalia | | 6 | 21.0/36 | 2x30mm guns 1x20mm gun |
| • DC 35 type | | 29 | 10.7/4 | |
| • Nisr class | de Castro | 5 | 31.0/110 | 2-4x25mm guns 1x122mm RL |
| • Swiftships (93-ft.) | | 10 | 28.4/102 | 2x23mm gun 1x20mm gun |
| • Timsah class | | 12 | 30.5/106 | 2x30mm gun or 2x20mm guns |
| Total | | 83 | | |

## Landing Craft

| Type | Original class name | Quantity | Length (m.)/ Displacement (t.) | Armament/ special equipment |
|------|------|------|------|------|
| • LCM | | 5 | | |
| • Polnochny class LSM | | 3 | 73.0/800 | 2x30mm guns 2x140mm MRL 6 tanks or 350 tons |
| • Vydra class LCU | | 9 | 54.8/425 | 4x37mm guns 200 troops or 250 tons |
| Total | | 17 | | |

On order
• US-made landing ship

## Auxiliary Vessels

| Type | Original class name | Quantity | Length (m.)/ Displacement (t.) | Armament/ special equipment |
|------|------|------|------|------|
| • Black Swan class frigate (training) | | 1 | 91.2/1,925 | 6x102mm guns 4x37mm guns possibly no longer serviceable |
| • Niryat diving support | | 1 | | |
| • Okhtensky (tug) | | 6 | 47.6/930 | |
| • Poluchat II torpedo recovery | | 2 | 29.6/100 | |
| • Toplivo 2 class tanker | | 8 | 53.7/1,029 | 500 tons diesel |
| • training (1 Sekstan, 1 4,650-ton, 1 3,008-ton and 1 other) | | 5 | | |

## Coastal Defense

| Type | Quantity | Notes |
|------|------|------|
| • OTOMAT coastal defense missile | 3 batteries | |
| • HY-2 in coastal defense role | | |
| Total | 30 | Unconfirmed |

## Naval infrastructure

Naval bases:    8
Abu Qir (naval academy), Alexandria, Hurghada, Marsa Matruh, Port Said, Safaga, Suez, Berenice (Ras Banas)

### Ship maintenance and repair facilities
Alexandria (including construction up to 20,000dwt), Port Said, Ismailiya

# 4. IRAN

## General Data

**Official Name of the State:** Islamic Republic of Iran
**Supreme Religious and Political National Leader (Rahbar):** Hojatolislam Ali Hoseini Khamenei
**Head of State (formally subordinate to national leader):** President Hojatolislam Seyyed Mohammed Khatami
**Minister of Defense:** Rear Admiral Ali Shamkhani
**Chief of Staff of the Armed Forces (including IRGC):** Major General Hassan Firuzabadi
**Chief of Staff of the Army:** Major General Ali Shabazi
**Commander of the Air Force:** Assad Abadi Habiballah Baqa'i
**Commander of the Navy:** Rear Admiral Abbas Mohtaj
**Commander-in-Chief of the Islamic Revolution Guards Corps (IRGC):** Major General Yahya Rahim Safavi
**Commander of the IRGC Ground Forces:** Brigadier General Shahbazi
**Commander of the IRGC Air Wing:** Brigadier General Muhammad Baqr Ghalibaf
**Commander of the IRGC Naval Wing:** General Ali Akbar Ahmadian

**Area:** 1,647,240 sq. km. (not including Abu Musa Island and two Tunb islands; control disputed)
**Population:** approx. 60,700,000

## Demography

| | | |
|---|---|---|
| *Ethnic groups* | | |
| Persians | 30,950,000 | 51.0% |
| Azeris | 14,560,000 | 24.0% |
| Gilaki and Mazandarani | 4,860,000 | 8.0% |
| Kurds | 4,250,000 | 7.0% |
| Arabs | 1,820,000 | 3.0% |
| Balouchis | 1,215,000 | 2.0% |
| Turkmens | 1,215,000 | 2.0% |
| Lurs | 1,215,000 | 2.0% |
| Others | 607,000 | 1.0% |
| *Religious groups* | | |
| Shi'ite Muslims | 54,023,000 | 89.0% |
| Sunni Muslims | 6,070,000 | 10.0% |
| Christians, Zoroastrians, Jews, Bahais and others | 607,000 | 1.0% |

## Economic Data

|  |  | 1993 | 1994 | 1995 | 1996 | 1997 |
|---|---|---|---|---|---|---|
| GDP current price, local currency | IR tr | 93.80 | 128.4 | 178.9 | 232.7 | 279.4 |
| GDP (US $) | $ bn | 80.161 | 73.42 | 59.63 | 77.56 | 159.65 |
| GDP per capita | $ | 1,370 | 1,228 | 971 | 1,269 | 2,630 |
| Real GDP growth | % | 2.6 | 1.2 | 2.7 | 5.0 | 2.9 |
| **Balance of payments** | | | | | | |
| • Exports fob | $ bn | 18.08 | 19.43 | 18.36 | 22.39 | 18.51 |
| • Imports fob | $ bn | 19.29 | 12.62 | 12.77 | 14.99 | 15.00 |
| • Account balance (including services and income) | $ bn | -3.90 | 4.96 | 3.36 | 5.23 | 1.24 |
| • External debt | $ bn | 20.55 | 22.71 | 21.94 | 21.18 | 15.00 |
| **Government income and expenditure** | | | | | | |
| • Revenue, local currency | IR tr | 29 | 20.25 | 29.24 | 41.57 | 57.28 |
| • Expenditure, local currency | IR tr | 34.9 | 20.88 | 28.91 | 41.33 | 57.88 |
| • Defense expenditure | IR tr | 2.32 | 2.86 | 4.21 | 5.59 | 7.11 |
| • Defense expenditure/GDP | % | 2.4 | 2.2 | 2.4 | 2.4 | 2.5 |
| • Defense expenditure/CGE | % | 6.6 | 13.7 | 14.6 | 13.5 | 12.3 |
| • Population | m | 58.5 | 59.8 | 61.4 | 61.1 | 60.7 |
| • Official exchange rate | IR: $ | 1,170.14 | 1,748.75 | 3,000 | 3,000 | 1,750 |

## Arms Procurement and Security Assistance Received

| Country | Type | Details |
|---|---|---|
| France | • Arms transfers | Socata training aircraft, assistance in satellite launch (1998) |
| Germany | • Arms transfers | Aircraft, missile parts, chemical and nuclear technology (unauthorized by government) |
| Israel | • Arms transfers | Decontamination equipment, trucks (1992) (unauthorized by government) |
| North Korea | • Arms transfers | SSMs (1992) , SSM technology (1997) |
| Poland | • Arms transfers | T-72 tanks (1995) |

## Arms Procurement and Security Assistance Received *(continued)*

| Country | Type | Details |
|---|---|---|
| PRC | • Arms transfers | C-802 naval SSMs (1995), F-7 aircraft (1992), SAMs (1992), Houdong MFPBs (1995), missile technology (1996), Transport aircraft (1997); chemical weapon precursors, alleged (1998) |
| | • Foreign advisers | Nuclear technicians |
| Russia | • Arms transfers | SSM technology (1997), tanks (1992), APCs and AIFVs (1994), Kilo submarines (1997), MiG 29 aircraft(1992), SAMs (1998); satellite technology (1998) |
| | • Foreign advisers | A large group of nuclear technicians |
| Singapore | • Arms transfers | Spare parts for American weapons |
| Taiwan | • Arms transfers | Spare parts for American aircraft |
| Ukraine | • Arms transfers | SAMs (1993), Naval SSMs (1993), tanks (1996) |
| USA | • Arms transfers | Shoulder-launched SAMs originally supplied to Afghan rebels. |

## Arms Sales and Security Assistance Extended

| Country | Type | Details |
|---|---|---|
| Afghanistan | • Arms transfers | Ammunition and small arms (1998) |
| Bosnia | • Advisers | Several hundred IRGC fighters (1997) |
| | • Arms transfers | Chinese ATGMs, artillery shells (1996) |
| Kurds | • Arms transfers | Shoulder-launched SAMs |
| | • Facilities provided | To PKK by IRGC, unconfirmed |
| Lebanon | • Advisers | Some IRGC instructors with Hizbullah militia in Syrian-held Beka' |
| | • Arms transfers | Artillery, MRLs, small arms, ATGMs, engineering equipment, SAMs, night vision equipment (1997) |
| | • Financial aid | Hizbullah militia in Lebanon--grant estimated at tens of millions of dollars per annum |
| | • Military training | Hizbullah militia |
| North Korea | • Financial aid | Funding for development of long-range missiles (No-Dong-2) (1996) |
| Palestinians | • Financial aid | $ 20 million annually for Hamas (1997) |
| | • Military training | Palestinian Hamas and Islamic Jihad; PFLP-GC |
| Sri Lanka | • Arms transfers | Small arms |

## Arms Sales and Security Assistance Extended *(continued)*

| Country | Type | Details |
|---|---|---|
| Sudan | • Advisers | A few IRGC personnel in the Sudanese Army and with People's Defense Forces (1996) |
| | • Arms transfers | Small arms, tanks (1996), combat aircraft (1996) |
| | • Financial aid | (1998) |
| Syria | • Cooperation in | Joint development of SSMs arms production/ assembly/R&D |

## Foreign Military Cooperation

| | Details |
|---|---|
| • Joint maneuvers with | India, Pakistan (naval maneuvers), Kuwait (proposed naval maneuvers), Oman (observations) |

## Defense Production

*Note:* Some of the alleged manufactured goods might well be upgraded existing items, presented as indigenously manufactured for propaganda purposes

| | M | P | A |
|---|---|---|---|
| **Army equipment** | | | |
| • Zulfikar and Towsan tanks, upgrading of T-55 tanks to Iranian T-72Z | √ | √ | |
| • Production of Russian T-72S tanks | | √ | |
| • Boragh, Cobra and BMT-2 APCs | √ | | |
| • Assembly and production of SSMs (with North Korea, Russia, and possibly also Pakistan) | √ | | √ |
| • 122, 160, and 240mm MRLs | √ | | |
| • 122mm and 155mm SP guns | √ | | |
| • 81, 120, and 320mm mortar ,and artillery ammunition | √ | | |
| • 120mm Russian artillery guns | | √ | |
| • Laser-guided AT missiles | √ | | |
| • RPG-7, Nafez and Saegheh ATRLs | √ | √ | |
| • Raad ATGM | √ | | |
| • Improvment of RPG warheads | √ | | |
| • ERA for various tanks | √ | | |
| • Chemical agents (mustard, attempts to produce nerve agents) | √ | | |
| • Gas masks | √ | | |
| • Spare parts, trucks | √ | | |
| • Heckler & Koch G-3 AR rifles | | √ | |
| • MG-1A1 machine guns | | √ | |

## Defense Production *(continued)*

| | M | P | A |
|---|---|---|---|
| **Aircraft and air ammunition** | | | |
| • Tondar and Dorneh training aircraft | √ | | |
| • Azarakhsh and Owaz fighter aircraft | √ | | |
| • Zafar 300 attack helicopter, Sanjack light helicopter | √ | | |
| • RPVs and UAVs | √ | | |
| • An-140 and IL 114 transport aircraft | | √ | |
| • Parasto light aircraft (probably still under development) | √ | | |
| • Conversion of HAWK and Standard missiles to be carried on aircraft | √ | | |
| • ZU-23mm anti-aircraft guns | | √ | |
| • SAMs (assembly of Chinese HN-5A and HQ-2, unconfirmed) | | | √ |
| • TV guided missile | √ | | |
| • Spare parts for aircraft | √ | | |
| **Electronics** | | | |
| • Radio transceivers (copy of USA model) | √ | | |
| **Naval craft and ammunition** | | | |
| • Tareq patrol craft | √ | | |
| • MiG-S-1800 and MiG-S-1900 patrol crafts | √ | | |
| • 250-ton LCU (Foque 101) | √ | | |
| • Hendijan auxiliary vessels | √ | | |
| **Space** | | | |
| • Telecommunication satellite under development, to be launched with French cooperation | √ | | |

*Note:* M - manufacture (indigenously developed)
P - production under license
A - assembly

## Weapons of Mass Destruction

### Nuclear capabilities
• A 5 MW research reactor acquired from the USA in the 1960s (in Tehran) and a small 27 Kw miniature neutron source reactor (in Esfahan). A 1,000 MW VVER reactor under construction, under a contract with Russia, in Bushehr.

### CW capabilities
• Iran admitted recently that it possessed chemical weapons in the past. Iran is a CWC signatory, but nevertheless suspected of still producing and stockpiling chemical agents and munitions decontamination units
• Personal protective equipment for part of the armed forces
• Assistance in CW technology and precursors is allegedly given by PRC

## Weapons of Mass Destruction *(continued)*

### Biological warfare capabilities

• Suspected biological warfare program; no details available

### Surface-to-Surface missiles

| Model | Launchers | Missiles | Notes |
|---|---|---|---|
| • SS-1 (Scud B/Scud C) | 10-20 | 300 Scud B, 100 Scud C | |
| • Shahab-3 | 1-3 | | |
| • CSS-8 | 16 | | |
| Total | 27 - 39 | | |
| On order | | | |
| • Shahab-4 | | | Under development |

# Armed Forces

**Major Changes:** No major change has been recorded in Iran's regular forces in 1998. The Iranian army is in a slow process of receiving the indigenously built Boragh APC and Zulfikar MBT. Iran tested and probably deployed its first Shahab-3 IRBM.

## Order of Battle

| Year | 1994 | 1995 | 1996 | 1997 | 1998 |
|---|---|---|---|---|---|
| **General data** | | | | | |
| • Personnel (regular) | 435,000 | 413,000 | 410,000 | 518,000 | 518,000 |
| • Divisions | 40 | 32 | 32 | 32 | 32 |
| • Total number of brigades | 100 | 87 | 87 | 87 | 87 |
| **Ground forces** | | | | | |
| • Tanks | 1,000 | 1,500 | 1,500 | 1,500 | 1,520 |
| • APCs/AFVs | 800 | 1,000 | 1,300 | 1,200 | 1,235 |
| • Artillery (Incl. MRLs) | 1,500-2,000 | 1,500-2,000 | 1,500-2,000 | 2,640 (2,930) | 2,640 (2,930) |
| • SSM launchers | 10 | 15 | 15 | 26 - 36 | 27 - 39 |
| **Air force** | | | | | |
| • Combat aircraft | 214 | 214 | 214 | 226 (318) | 205 (297) |
| • Transport aircraft | 120 | 119 | 119 | 93 (114) | 91 (112) |
| • Helicopters | 275 | 275 | 275 | 310 (553) | 293 (555) |
| **Air defense forces** | | | | | |
| • Heavy SAM batteries | 30-35 | 30-35 | 30-35 | 30-35 | 30-35 |
| • Medium SAM batteries | + | + | + | + | + |
| • Light SAM launchers | 110 | 110 | 110 | 95 | 95 |

## Order of Battle *(continued)*

| Year | 1994 | 1995 | 1996 | 1997 | 1998 |
|---|---|---|---|---|---|
| **Navy** | | | | | |
| • Combat vessels | 24 | 34 | 33 | 33 | 31 |
| • Patrol crafts | 177 | 177 | 176 | 136 | 139 |
| • Submarines | 2 | 2 | 2 | 3 | 3 |

*Note:* Beginning with data for 1997, we refer to quantities in active service. The numbers in parentheses refer to the total.

## Personnel

| | Regular | Reserves | Total |
|---|---|---|---|
| Ground Forces | approx. 350,000 | 350,000 | 700,000 |
| Air Force | 18,000 | | 18,000 |
| Air Defense | 12,000 | | 12,000 |
| Navy | approx. 18,000 | | 18,000 |
| IRGC - Ground Forces | 100,000 | | 100,000 |
| IRGC - Navy | 20,000 | | 20,000 |
| **Total** | **518,000** | **350,000** | **868,000** |
| **Paramilitary** | | | |
| • Baseej | | 2,000,000 | |

# Ground Forces

## Formations

| | Corps | Divisions | Independent brigade/ group | Brigades in division |
|---|---|---|---|---|
| All arms | 4 | | | |
| Armored | | 4 | 1 | 3 armd., 1 mech., 1 arty. each |
| Infantry/Mechanized | | 6 | 1 | 4 inf., 1 arty. each |
| Airborne | | | 1 | |
| Special forces | | 2 | 5 | 3 commando each |
| Artillery | | | 6 | |
| **Total** | **4** | **12** | **14** | |

## IRGC Formation

| | Divisions | Independent brigades | Brigades in division |
|---|---|---|---|
| Armored | 4 | | |
| Infantry/ Mechanized | 16 | | |
| Special forces | | 3 | |
| Artillery | | 6 | |
| SSMs | | 1 - 2 | |
| Total | 20 | 10-11 | |

*Note:* The IRGC has possibly reorganized as 26 divisions without independent brigades. IRGC divisions are smaller in size than army divisions, sometimes equivalent to the strength of one brigade.

## Tanks

| Model | Quantity | In service | Since | Notes |
|---|---|---|---|---|
| **MBTs** | | | | |
| **High quality** | | | | |
| • T-72 S/M1 | approx. 200 | approx. 200 | 1990 | |
| • Zulfikar | approx. 40 | approx. 40 | 1996 | Based on estimated production rate of 20 per year |
| Subtotal | 240 | 240 | | |
| **Medium and low quality** | | | | |
| • Chieftain MK 3/MK 5 | approx. 100 | approx. 100 | 1973 | |
| • T-62 | 150 | 150 | | |
| • T-55/Type 69/ Type 59 | 550-700 | 550-700 | 1985 | |
| • M-60 A1 | 150 | 150 | 1972 | |
| • M-48/M-47 | 150 | 150 | 1958 | |
| Subtotal | 1,200 | 1,200 | | |
| **Light tanks** | | | | |
| • Scorpion | 50-80 | 50-80 | | |
| Subtotal | 80 | 80 | | |
| **Total** | 1,520 | 1,520 | | |
| **On order** | | | | |
| • Zulfikar | | | | being produced |
| • T-72S | several hundred | | | |

## APCs/AFVs

| Model | Quantity | In service | Since | Notes |
|---|---|---|---|---|
| **APCs** | | | | |
| • M-113 | 200 | 200 | 1968 | |
| • Boragh | 50 | 50 | 1996 | |
| • BTR-50/60 | 500 | 500 | 1967 | |
| • MT-LB | scores | scores | | |
| Subtotal | 800 | 800 | | |
| **IFVs** | | | | |
| • BMP-1 | 300 | 300 | 1977 | |
| • BMP-2 | 100 | 100 | | |
| Subtotal | 400 | 400 | | |
| **Reconnaissance** | | | | |
| • Engesa EE-9 Cascavel | 35 | 35 | 1982 | |
| **Total** | **1,235** | **1,235** | | |

## Artillery

| Model | Quantity | In service | Since | Notes |
|---|---|---|---|---|
| **Self-propelled guns and howitzers** | | | | |
| • 203mm M-110 | 20-30 | 20-30 | 1976 | |
| • 175mm/170mm Koksan M-1978 | 10-30 | 10-30 | | |
| • 175mm M-107 | 25 | 25 | 1975 | |
| • 155mm M-109 | 440 | 120-150 | 1978 | |
| • 122mm 2S1 | 60 | 30-60 | | |
| Subtotal | 585 | 290 | | |
| **Towed guns and howitzers** | | | | |
| • 203mm (8") M-115 | 20-30 | 20-30 | 1974 | |
| • 155mm G-5 | 30 | 30 | | |
| • 155mm GHN-45 | 100 | 100 | | |
| • 155mm M-114 | 80-120 | 80-120 | 1970 | |
| • 152mm (PRC) | 30 | 30 | | |
| • 130mm M-46/ Type 59 | 500-1,000 | 500-1,000 | 1973 | |
| • 122mm D-30 | 400-500 | 400-500 | 1982 | |
| • 122mm Type 54/60 | 80-100 | 80-100 | | |
| • 105mm M-101 | 150-200 | 150-200 | 1966 | |
| Subtotal | 1,390 - 2,100 | 1,390 - 2,100 | | |
| **Mortars, over 160mm** | | | | |
| • 320 mm | some | some | | |

### Artillery *(continued)*

| Model | Quantity | In service | Since | Notes |
|-------|----------|------------|-------|-------|
| **Mortars, under 160mm** | | | | |
| • 120mm M-65 | | | 1980 | |
| • 107mm (4.2") M-30 | | | | |
| **MRLs** | | | | |
| • 355mm Nazeat | | | | |
| • 333mm Shahin 2 | | | | |
| • 240mm Fajr-3 | | | | |
| • 230mm Oghab | | | | |
| • 122mm BM-21 | 50-100 | 50-100 | 1978 | |
| • 122mm Hadid/ Azrash/Nur | 50 | 50 | | |
| • 107mm Type 63 | 100 | 100 | | |
| Subtotal | 250 | 250 | | |
| **Total** | **2,930** Approx. | **2,640** Approx. | | |

### Logistic and Engineering Equipment

Pontoon bridges, light infantry assault boats, self-propelled pontoons,
   AFV transporters (several hundred)

### Anti-tank Weapons

**Missiles**
AT-11 (Spandrel), AT-4 (Spigot), AT-3 (Sagger), BGM-71A TOW, SS-11/SS-12
**Guns**
106mm M-40 A1C recoilless rifle (200)

# Air Force

### Order of Battle

| Model | Quantity | In service | Notes |
|-------|----------|------------|-------|
| • Combat | 297 | 205 | |
| • Transport | 112 | 91 | |
| • Helicopters | 555 | 293 | |

*Note:* about 60% serviceable, not counting most of the 115 combat aircraft, and the transport and civilian aircraft brought from Iraq during the 1991 Gulf War; the only Iraqi a/c integrated into the Iranian force are 24 Su-24s and a few MiG-29s ; all figures include aircraft with army aviation and navy.

## Combat Aircraft

| Model | Quantity | In service | Since | Notes |
|---|---|---|---|---|
| **Interceptors** | | | | |
| • F-14A Tomcat | 60 | 25 | 1972 | |
| • MiG-29 | 35 | 35 | 1990 | |
| Subtotal | 95 | 60 | | |
| **Multi role** | | | | |
| • F-4 D/E/RF Phantom | 70 | 40 | 1968 | |
| • Mirage F1E | 24 | 12 | 1991 | |
| Subtotal | 94 | 52 | | |
| **Ground attack** | | | | |
| • Su-24 | 24 | 24 | 1991 | |
| **Obsolete** | | | | |
| • F-7 | 24 | 24 | 1987 | |
| • F-5 A/B/E | 60 | 45 | 1974 | |
| Subtotal | 84 | 69 | | |
| **Total** | **297** | **205** | | |
| **On order** | | | | |
| • MiG-29 | | | | Unconfirmed |
| • Su-24 | | | | Unconfirmed |
| • Su-25 | | | | Negotiations with Georgia |
| • Su-27 | | | | Negotiations |
| • F-1 | | | | Plans to integrate into air force |

## Transport Aircraft

| Model | Quantity | In service | Since | Notes |
|---|---|---|---|---|
| • Aero Commander 690 | 3 | 3 | 1978 | |
| • Boeing 747 | 9 | 9 | 1976 | |
| • Boeing 707 and KC-707 tanker -refueling | 14-15 | 14-15 | 1973 | Including Boeing 707s in electronic surveillance/ EW/CEW role |
| • C-130 E/H Hercules | 49 | 25-35 | 1970 | Including 2-3 in electronic surveillance role |
| • Dornier Do-228 | 4 | 4 | | Possibly civilian, or employed in maritime surveillance role |

### Transport Aircraft *(continued)*

| Model | Quantity | In service | Since | Notes |
|-------|----------|------------|-------|-------|
| • Fokker F-27 400M/600 | 18 | 18 | 1972 | |
| • Mystère-Falcon 20 | 13 | 13 | 1991 | |
| • Jetstar | 1 | 1 | | |
| Total | 112 | approx. 91 | | |

### Training and Liaison Aircraft

| Model | Quantity | In service | Since | Notes |
|-------|----------|------------|-------|-------|
| With Light Attack/Close Air Support capability | | | | |
| • Mushshak (PAC Mushshak) | 25 | 25 | 1991 | |
| • Embraer EMB-312 (Tucano) | 25 | 25 | 1989 | |
| • T-33 | 9 | 9 | 1968 | |
| Subtotal | 59 | 59 | | |
| Others | | | | |
| • Beechcraft Bonanza F-33 | 20-25 | 20-25 | 1974 | |
| • Cessna 185/180/150 | 45 | 45 | 1978 | |
| • Socata TB 21/TB 200 (Trinidad/Tobago) | 12 | 12 | | |
| • Pilatus PC-7 Turbo-trainer | 45 | 45 | 1983 | |
| • Pilatus PC-6 | 15 | 15 | 1982 | |
| Subtotal | 142 | 142 | | |
| Total | 201 | 201 | | |

On order
• EMB-312

### Helicopters

| Model | Quantity | In service | Since | Notes |
|-------|----------|------------|-------|-------|
| Attack | | | | |
| • AH-1J Cobra | 100 | 70 | 1974 | |
| Heavy transport | | | | |
| • CH-47C Chinook | 45 | 35 | 1973 | |
| • RH-53D/SH-53D | 20-25 | 10 | 1976 | |
| Subtotal | approx. 70 | 45 | | |
| Medium transport | | | | |
| • AB-214A | 180-200 | 50-70 | 1974 | |
| • AB-205 | 50 | 50 | 1969 | |
| • AB-212 | 28 | 28 | 1971 | |

## Helicopters *(continued)*

| Model | Quantity | In service | Since | Notes |
|---|---|---|---|---|
| • SA-330/ IAR-330 Puma | small number | small number | | |
| • AS-61 | 2 | 2 | 1978 | |
| Subtotal | 280 | 150 | | |
| **Light transport** | | | | |
| • AB-206 Jetranger | 90 | small number | 1969 | |
| • IAR-316 | 12 | 12 | | |
| • IAR-317 | | | | |
| Subtotal | 102 | Approx. 25 | | |
| **Naval combat** | | | | |
| • SH-3D | 3 | small number | 1977 | |
| Total | 555 | approx. 293 | | |

## Miscellaneous Aircraft

| Model | Quantity | In service | Since | Notes |
|---|---|---|---|---|
| **Maritime surveillance aircraft** | | | | |
| • P-3 Orion | 5 | 2 | 1984 | |
| **Electronic surveillance** | | | | |
| • RC-130 | | | | Listed under Transport |

## Advanced Armament

**Air-to-air missiles**
AA-10 (Alamo), AA-11 (Archer), AIM-54A Phoenix, AIM-9 Sidewinder,
   AIM-7 Sparrow
**Air-to-ground missiles**
AGM-65 Maverick, AS 10 (Karen), AS-12, C-801 anti-ship missile
**On order**
AS-1, AS-5, AS-6, AA-11 (Archer AAM), AA-12

## Air Force Infrastructure

**Aircraft shelters:** In all operational airfields
**Military airfields:** 20
Bandar Abbas, Birjand, Bushehr, Ghaleh-Marghi, Isfahan, Kerman, Kharg Island,
   Mehrabad, Mashhad, Qeshm, Shiraz, Tabriz, Tehran, at least 7 additional

# Air Defense Forces

## Surface-to-Air Missiles (SAM)

| Model | Batteries | Launchers | Since | Notes |
|---|---|---|---|---|
| **Heavy missiles** | | | | |
| • HAWK/MIM-23B Improved HAWK | 12-15 | | 1964 | |
| • SA-2 (Guideline)/ HQ-2J | 8-10 | 45-60 | | May be under control of IRGC |
| • SA-5 (Gammon) | | | | |
| Total | 30-35 | | | |
| **Medium missiles** | | | | |
| • SA-6 (Gainful) | + | | 1974 | |
| **Light missiles** | | | | |
| • Rapier | | 30 | 1971 | |
| • RBS-70 | | 50 | 1984 | |
| • Tigercat | | 15 | 1968 | |
| Total | | 95 | | |
| **Shoulder-launched missiles** | | | | |
| • FIM-92A Stinger (with IRGC) | | small number | 1987 | |
| • SA-7 (Grail)/ HN-5A/SA-14 | | hundreds | 1974 | |
| **On order** | | | | |
| • SA-10/(S-300-P) | 6 | | | |
| • SA-5 (Gammon) | | | | |
| • SA-6 | | | | |
| • C³I system | | | | Upgrading air defense C³I by Russia (unconfirmed) |

## Other Air Defense Systems

| Model | Quantity | In service | Since | Notes |
|---|---|---|---|---|
| **Air defense systems (including radars, missiles, and guns)** | | | | |
| • 35mm Contraves Skyguard ADS | 100 | 24 | | |
| **Short-range guns** | | | | |
| • 57mm ZSU 57x2 SP | 100 | 100 | 1974 | |
| • 57mm S-60 | 50 | 50 | 1966 | |

## Other Air Defense Systems *(continued)*

| Model | Quantity | In service | Since | Notes |
|-------|----------|------------|-------|-------|
| • 40mm L-70 | 95 | 95 | | |
| • 40mm M1 | 20 | 20 | 1968 | |
| • 23mm ZSU 23x4 SP (Gun Dish) | 75 | 75 | 1974 | |
| • 23mm ZU 23x2 | 500 | 500 | 1977 | |
| Total | 840 | 840 | | |
| Radars | | | | |
| • AR-3D | | | | |

# Navy

## Combat Vessels

| Type | Original class name | Quantity | Length (m.)/ Displacement (t.) | Armament/ special equipment |
|------|---------------------|----------|-------------------------------|------------------------------|
| **Submarines** | | | | |
| • K class (Kilo) | Type 877 | 3 | 73.8/3,076 | 6 x 533 torpedoes 24 mines |
| • Iranian midget submarines | | 3 | 9.2/90 | |
| Total | | 6 | | |
| **MFPBs** | | | | |
| • Kaman class | Combattante II | 10 | 47.0/249 | 4 x C-802/ Harpoon SSMs (several without SSMs) 1 x 76mm gun 1 x 40mm gun |
| • Ossa II (ex-Iraqi) | | 1 | 38.6/245 | 4 x SS-N-2B (Styx) SSMs (probably has no SSMs) 4 x 30mm guns |
| • Houdong | | 10 | 36.6/171 | 4 x C-802 SSMs 2 x 30mm guns |
| Subtotal | | 21 | | |

## Combat Vessels *(continued)*

| Type | Original class name | Quantity | Length (m.)/ Displacement (t.) | Armament/ special equipment |
|---|---|---|---|---|
| **Missile frigates** | | | | |
| • Alvand class | Vosper Mk 5 | 3 | 94.5/1,100 | 4 x C-802 SSM/ 1 Seakiller II SSM 1 MK- 10 a/s mortar 1 x 114mm gun 2 x 35mm guns 3 x 20mm guns |
| **Gun corvettes** | | | | |
| • Bayandor class | PF-103 | 2 | 84/900 | 2 x 76mm guns 2 x 40mm guns 2 x 20mm guns |
| **Mine warfare vessels** | | | | |
| • MSC 292 and MSC 268 class | | 3 | 44.5/384 | Acoustic and magnetic sweep 2 x 20mm guns |
| • Cape class | | 2 | 33.9/239 | Mechanical, acoustic and magnetic sweep 1 x 12.7mm MG |
| Subtotal | | 5 | | |
| **Total** | | **31** | | |
| **Patrol craft** | | | | |
| • Parvin class | PGM-71 | 3 | 30.8/98 | 4 depth charges 1 x 40mm gun 2 x 20mm guns 2 x 12.7mm MGs |
| • Zafar class | Chaho | 3 | 26/70 | 1 BM-21 122mm MRL 2 x 20mm guns |
| • PBI | Peterson | 60 | 15.2/20.1 | 1 Tigercat SSM 2 x 12.7mm MGs |
| • Peterson—Mk IIs | | 6 | 15.2/22.9 | 2 x 12.7mm MGs |
| • US Mk III coastal patrol craft | | 9 | 19.8/41.6 | 1 x 20mm gun 1 x 12.7mm MG |
| • MIG-S-1800 | | 6 | 18.7/60 | 1 x 20mm gun 1 x 12.7mm MG |
| • MIG-G-1900 | | 8 | 19.5/30 | 2 x 23mm guns |

## Combat Vessels *(continued)*

| Type | Original class name | Quantity | Length (m.)/ Displacement (t.) | Armament/ special equipment |
|---|---|---|---|---|
| • Boghammar | | 24 | 13/6.4 | 1 x 107mm MRL 1 x 106mm RCL 3 x 12.7mm MGs RPG 7 (with IRGC) |
| • Boston Whaler craft type 1 | | 20 | 6.7/1.3 | 1 x 107mm MRL 1 x 12.7mm MG |
| • Bertram Enforcer and various other small craft | | numerous | 5 - 7 m | Some with 12.7mm MGs |
| Total | | 139 | | |
| On order | | | | |
| • EM-52 mines | | | | |

## Landing Craft

| Type | Original class name | Quantity | Length (m.)/ Displacement (t.) | Armament/ special equipment |
|---|---|---|---|---|
| • Wellington class hovercraft | BH-7 class | 6 | 23.9/53.6 | |
| • Winchester class hovercraft | SRN-6 class | 4 | 14.8/10.9 | 50 troops & 5 tons |
| • Hengam class landing ship | | 4 | 93/2,540 | Up to 9 tanks or 227 troops 4 x 40mm guns 8 x 23mm guns 2 x 12.7mm MGs |
| • Iran Ajr class | | 2 | 53.7/2,274 | 65 tons 2 x 12.7mm MGs |
| • Iran Hormuz 24 class | | 3 | 73.1/2,014 | 9 tanks or 140 troops |
| • Iran Hormuz 21 class | | 3 | 65/1,280 | 600 tons |
| • Fouque class | MIG-S-3700 | 2 | 37/276 | 140 tons |
| Total | | 24 | | |

## Auxiliary Vessels

| Type | Original Class name | Quantity | Length (m.)/ Displacement (t.) | Armament/ special equipment |
|---|---|---|---|---|
| • Delvar class support ship | | 7 | 64/890 | 765 dwt<br>2 x 23mm guns |
| • Luhring Yard-supply ship | | 2 | 108/4,673 | 3,250 dwt<br>1 AB 212 helicopter<br>3 x 20mm guns |
| • Kangan class water tanker | Mazagon | 4 | 148/12,000 | 9,430 dwt<br>2 x 23mm guns |
| • Swan Hunter replenishment ship | | 1 | 207.2/33,014 | 9,367 dwt<br>3 Seaking helicopter<br>1 x 76mm gun |
| • Hendijan | MIG-S-4700 | 13 | 50.8/460 | 40 ton on deck and 95m³ liquid |
| • Damen 1550 | | 10 | 16/25 | |

## Coastal Defense

| Type | Batteries | Missiles | Notes |
|---|---|---|---|
| • HY-2 (Silkworm) | approx. 12 | 300 | |
| • C-802 | 15 - 25 | approx. 100 | |
| • SS-N-22 (Sunburn) | | | Alleged. Probably not extant |
| Total | approx. 25-30 | approx. 400 | |

## Naval Infrastructure

**Naval bases:** 9

Bandar Abbas, Bandar Anzelli, Bandar Khomeini, Bandar Lengeh, Bushehr, Chah Bahar, Farsi island, Jask, Kharg Island, Abu Musa island (under construction)

**IRGC naval bases:** 10

Abadan oil terminal, Abu Musa island, al-Fayisiyah island, Cyrus oilfield, Halul Island platform (unconfirmed), Larak island, Qeshm island, Rostam island oilfield, Sir Abu Nuair, Sirri island

**Ship maintenance and repair facilities:** 2

MAN Nordhaman 28,000-ton floating dock

# Non-governmental Paramilitary Forces

## Personnel

| | regular |
|---|---|
| Ismael khan (Afghans) | 1,000 - 2,000 |
| Democratic Party of Iranian Kurdistan (DPIK) | 10,000 |

# 5. IRAQ

## General data

**Official Name of the State:** The Republic of Iraq
**Head of State:** President Saddam Hussein (also Prime Minister and Supreme Commander of the Armed Forces)
**Minister of Defense:** Lieutenant General Sultan Hashim Ahmad Al - Jabburi Tai
**Chief of Staff of the Ground Forces:** General Abd Alwahed Shenan Al Rubatt
**Commander of the Air Force:** Lieutenant General Khaldoun Khatab Bakr
**Commander of the Navy:** Rear Admiral Khalid Baqer Khadar
**Commander of the Republican Guard:** General Ibrahim Abdul al-Sattar Mohammad al-Takriti

**Area:** 432,162 sq. km. (no effective control over autonomous Kurdish region in northern Iraq)
**Population:** (Estimate) 22,000,000

## Demography

| | | |
|---|---|---|
| *Ethnic groups* | | |
| Arabs | 16,170,000 | 73.5% |
| Kurds | 4,752,000 | 21.6% |
| Turkmens | 528,000 | 2.4% |
| Assyrians and others | 550,000 | 2.5% |
| *Religious groups* | | |
| Shi'ite Muslims | 12,100,000 | 55.0% |
| Sunni Muslims | 9,240,000 | 42.0% |
| Christians, Yazidis, and others | 660,000 | 3.0% |

## Economic Data

| | | 1993 | 1994 | 1995 | 1996 | 1997 |
|---|---|---|---|---|---|---|
| GDP current price, local currency | ID bn | NA | NA | NA | NA | NA |
| GDP (US $) | $ bn | NA | NA | NA | NA | NA |
| GDP per capita | $ | NA | NA | NA | NA | NA |
| Real GDP growth | % | NA | NA | NA | NA | NA |

## Economic Data *(continued)*

|  |  | 1993 | 1994 | 1995 | 1996 | 1997 |
|---|---|---|---|---|---|---|
| **Balance of payments** | | | | | | |
| • Exports fob | $ bn | 0.75 | 0.77 | 0.81 | 1.48 | 5.63 |
| • Imports cif | $ bn | 1.00 | 1.20 | 1.38 | 2.15 | 4.68 |
| • Account balance (including services and income) | $ m | -250 | -229 | -438 | -332 | -574 |
| • External debt | $ bn | 97 | 101 | 107 | 113 | 119 |
| **Government income and expenditure** | | | | | | |
| • Revenue, local currency | ID bn | NA | NA | NA | NA | NA |
| • Expenditure, local currency | ID bn | NA | NA | NA | NA | NA |
| • Defense expenditure | ID bn | NA | NA | NA | NA | NA |
| • Defense expenditure/GDP | % | NA | NA | NA | NA | NA |
| • Defense expenditure/CGE | % | NA | NA | NA | NA | NA |
| • Population | m | 19.5 | 19.9 | 20.5 | 21.3 | 22.0 |
| • Official exchange rate | ID: $ | 0.311 | 0.311 | 0.311 | 0.311 | 0.311 |

## Arms Procurement and Security Assistance Received

| Country | Type | Details |
|---|---|---|
| No data is available on the last 7 years. | | |

## Arms Sales and Security Assistance Extended

| Country | Type | Details |
|---|---|---|
| No data available | | |

## Defense Production

|  | M | P | A |
|---|---|---|---|
| **Army equipment** | | | |
| • Small arms and artillery ammunition | √ | | |
| • Electronics | √ | | |
| • Chemical agents | √ | | |
| • Biological weapons | √ | | |
| • SSMs under development | √ | | |
| • Land mines, including scatterable | √ | | |

## Defense Production (continued)

| | M | P | A |
|---|:---:|:---:|:---:|
| • ATRLs | | √ | |
| • Artillery | | √ | |
| • MRLs | | √ | |
| • Tanks | | √ | |
| **Aircraft and air ammunition** | | | |
| • Aerial bombs | √ | √ | |
| • Conversion of aircraft to UAVs | √ | | |
| **Naval craft and ammunition** | | | |
| • Small PBs | √ | | |
| • Rubber boats | √ | | |
| • Copy of Soviet-designed naval mines | | √ | |

*Note:* All information is outdated
M - manufacture (indigenously developed)
P - production under license
A - assembly

## Weapons of Mass Destruction

### Nuclear capabilities
• Since the Gulf War, all known Iraqi efforts have been stalled by UN's and IAEA's facility-destruction and monitoring regimes. Though inspections were suspended in 1998, renewal of nuclear weapons' activities still unlikely.

### CW capabilities
• Production of chemical agents could have been renewed due to suspension of UNSCOM inspections in Iraq.
• Personal protective equipment. Soviet-type unit decontamination equipment
• Stockpile of chemical agents: until 1991 Iraq had Mustard (sulfur Mustard and purified Mustard), Sarin, Tabun; Soman, VX, Hydrogen Cyanide (unconfirmed); a large portion of chemical agents were destroyed by UN missions, though Iraq has the know-how to renew CW production.
• Delivery systems (SSM warheads, thousands of artillery shells, mortar bombs, MRL rockets, aerial bombs and land mines)

### Biological warfare capabilities
• Production and development of biological agents could have been renewed due to suspension of UNSCOM inspections in Iraq.
• Toxins and other biological weapons, specifically Anthrax and Typhoid; Botulinium; BW capability largely unaffected by UN observer activity, Iraq now admits having had BW, but claims it destroyed it in October 1990; there are claims BW still exists in large quantities

## Surface-to-Surface Missiles and Rockets

| Model | Launchers | Missiles | Notes |
|-------|-----------|----------|-------|
| • FROG-7 | 29 | | |
| • Al-Hussein mobile | up to 5 | 20-30 | Concealed |
| • Laith 90 | | | |
| Total | up to 34 | | |

# Armed Forces

**Major Changes:** No changes have been recorded in the Order of Battle of the Iraqi forces, due to the embargo on Iraq, and lack of information. UNSCOM inspections were suspended in 1998, which enables Iraq to renew production of various WMDs. Number of Navy fighting vessels were reduced considerably due to change in estimate.

## Order of Battle

| Year | 1994 | 1995 | 1996 | 1997 | 1998 |
|------|------|------|------|------|------|
| **General data** | | | | | |
| • Personnel (regular) | 500,000 | 450,000 | 400,000 | 391,800 | 432,500* |
| • Divisions | 28 | 26 | 23 | 23 | 23 |
| **Ground forces** | | | | | |
| • Tanks | 2,200 | 2,100 | 2,100 | 2,000 | 2,000 (2,300) |
| • APCs/AFVs | 3,500 | 3,300 | 3,300 | 2,000 (3,300) | 2,000 (2,900) |
| • Artillery (incl. MRLs) | 1,650 | 1,800 | 1,800 | 2,050 | 2,050 |
| • SSM launchers | small number | 34 | 34 | 34 | 34 |
| **Air Force** | | | | | |
| • Combat aircraft | 400 | 380 | 380 | 210 (333) | 210 (333) |
| • Transport aircraft | small number | small number | small number | small number | small number |
| • Helicopters | 400 | 400 | 400 | 370 (460) | 370 (460) |
| **Air defense forces** | | | | | |
| • Heavy SAM batteries | NA | NA | NA | 60 | 60 |
| • Medium SAM batteries | NA | NA | NA | NA | NA |
| • Light SAM launchers | NA | NA | NA | NA | NA |
| **Navy** | | | | | |
| • Combat vessels | 7 | 7 | 7 | 5 | 2* |
| • Patrol crafts | 9 | 9 | 9 | 9 | 0 |

*Note:* Beginning with data for 1997, we refer to quantities in active service. The numbers in parentheses refer to the total.

* Change in estimate

## Personnel

|  | Regular | Reserves | Total |
|---|---|---|---|
| Ground Forces | 400,000 | 650,000 | 1,050,000 |
| Air Force | 15,000 |  | 15,000 |
| Air Defense | 15,000 |  | 15,000 |
| Navy | 2,500 |  | 2,500 |
| Total | 432,500 | 650,000 | 1,082,500 |
| **Paramilitary** |  |  |  |
| • Border guards | 20,000 |  |  |
| • Security forces | 25,000 - 45,000 |  |  |
| • Special Republican Guard | 26,000 |  |  |
| • Security troops | 4,800 |  |  |

# Ground Forces

## Formations

|  | Corps | Divisions | Independent brigade/ group | Brigades in division |
|---|---|---|---|---|
| All arms | 5+2 |  |  |  |
| Armored |  | 6 |  |  |
| Mechanized |  | 4 |  |  |
| Infantry |  | 13 |  |  |
| Special forces |  |  | 2 |  |
| Total | 5 | 23 | 2 |  |

*Note:* 4 armored/mechanized divisions and 2 infantry divisions constitute the elite Republican Guard.

## Tanks

| Model | Quantity | In service | Since | Notes |
|---|---|---|---|---|
| **MBTs** |  |  |  |  |
| **High quality** |  |  |  |  |
| • T-72/T-72M | 700 | 700 | 1982 |  |
| • Assad Babil (T-72 M1) | small number | small number | 1989 |  |
| Subtotal | approx. 800 | approx. 800 |  |  |
| **Medium and low quality** |  |  |  |  |
| • T-62 |  |  | 1973 |  |

## Tanks *(continued)*

| Model | Quantity | In service | Since | Notes |
|---|---|---|---|---|
| • T-55/Type 59/ Type 69/M-77 | | | 1962/1982 | Some upgraded |
| Subtotal | 1,500-1,600 | 1,200 | | |
| **Total** | **2,300-2,400** | **approx. 2,000** | | |

## APCs/AFVs

| Model | Quantity | In service | Since | Notes |
|---|---|---|---|---|
| **APCs** | | | | |
| • YW-531 | | | | |
| • MT-LB | | | | An artillery prime-mover, employed also as APC |
| • M-60P | | | 1988 | |
| • Engesa EE-11 | | | 1979 | |
| • BTR-40/50/60 | | | 1974 | |
| • FUG-70/PSZH-IV | | | 1981 | |
| • M-3 (Panhard) | | | 1981 | |
| • OT-62/OT-64 | | | 1978 | |
| **IFVs** | | | | |
| • BMP-1 } | 900 | | 1988 | |
| • BMP-2 } | | | | |
| • BMD | | | 1978 | |
| **REECs** | | | | |
| • Engesa EE-9 | | | 1979 | |
| • AML-90/60 | | | 1969 | |
| • BRDM-2 | | | 1982 | |
| **Total** | **2,900** | **2,000** | | |

## Artillery

| Model | Quantity | In service | Since | Notes |
|---|---|---|---|---|
| **Self-propelled guns and howitzers** | | | | |
| • 155mm M-109 | | | 1984 | |
| • 155mm GCT | | | 1982 | |
| • 155mm Majnoon | | | 1982 | |
| • 152mm M-1973 | | | 1975 | |
| • 122mm M-1974 | | | 1977 | |
| Subtotal | 150 | 150 | | |

## Artillery *(continued)*

| Model | Quantity | In service | Since | Notes |
|---|---|---|---|---|
| **Towed guns and howitzers** | | | | |
| • 180mm S-23 | | | 1974 | |
| • 155mm G-5 | | | 1986 | |
| • 155mm GHN-45 | | | 1984 | |
| • 155mm M-114 A1 | | | 1983 | |
| • 152mm D-20 | | | 1977 | |
| • 152mm M-1976 (2A36) | | | | |
| • 152mm M-1943 (D-1) | | | 1974 | |
| • 130mm M-46/130mm Type 59 | | | 1962 | |
| • 122mm D-30/Saddam | | | 1984 | |
| • 122mm M-1938 | | | 1977 | |
| • 105mm M-56 | | | 1982 | |
| • 105mm M-102 | | | 1984 | |
| • 85mm field/AT | | | | |
| Subtotal | 1,800 | 1,800 | | |
| **Mortars, over 160mm** | | | | |
| • 160mm mortar | | | 1975 | |
| **Mortars, under 160mm** | | | | |
| • 120mm x 4 SP | | | | |
| • 120mm M-43 | | | 1975 | |
| Total | approx. 1,950 | approx. 1,950 | | |
| **Artillery/mortar-locating radars** | | | | |
| • Rasit | | | | |
| • Cymbeline | | | | |
| **MRLs** | | | | |
| • Arbil (262mm Ababil-50, 400mm Ababil-100) | | | | |
| • Astros II (127mm SS-30, 180mm SS-40, 300mm SS-60) | | | 1986 | |
| • 132mm BM-13 | | | | |
| • 130mm | | | | |
| • 128mm M-63 | | | | |
| • 122mm BM-21/BM-11 | | | 1977 | |
| • 122mm Firos-25 | | | | |
| • 107mm | | | | |
| Total | 100 | 100 | | |

## Logistic and Engineering Equipment

BLG-60, MTU-55 bridging tanks, GSP self-propelled ferries, mine-clearing rollers, minefield crossing system, PMP pontoon bridges, TPP pontoon bridges, Soviet-model tank-towed bridges, AFV transporters (1,500-2,000).

## Anti-tank Weapons

### Missiles

AT-3 (Sagger), AT-4 (Spigot), BGM-71A TOW , Milan, AT-5 (Spandrel) mounted
on BMP-2, BRDM-2 (carrying AT-3 Sagger) SP, M-3 (carrying HOT) SP, VCR/
TH (carrying HOT) SP, M-901 ITV (TOW under armor).

Total                                      1,500

### Guns

107mm B-11

# Air Force

## Order of Battle

| Model | Quantity | In service | Notes |
|---|---|---|---|
| Combat | 331 | 180-230 | 119 additional planes flown to Iran during the Gulf War (1991) |
| Transport | small number | small number | |
| Helicopters | 460 | 370 | |

## Combat Aircraft

| Model | Quantity | In service | Since | Notes |
|---|---|---|---|---|
| Interceptors | | | | |
| • MiG-25 (Foxbat) | 15 | 8-10 | 1982 | Additional 4 in Iran |
| • MiG-29 (Fulcrum) | 15 | 8-10 | 1988 | Additional 4 in Iran |
| • MiG-23 MF/ML | 30 | approx. 20 | 1976 | |
| Subtotal | 60 | 36-40 | | |
| **Multi-Role** | | | | |
| • Mirage F-1B/EQ5/ EQ2/EQ4 | 30 | 30 | 1980 | Additional 24 in Iran |
| **Ground Attack** | | | | |
| • Su-24 (Fencer C) | 6 | 0 | 1989 | Not serviceable, Additional 24 in Iran |
| • MiG-23 B (Flogger)/ MiG-27 | 30 | 25 | 1976 | Additional 12 in Iran |
| • Su-20/22 (Fitter C/H) | 45 | 30 | 1974 | Additional 24 in Iran |
| • Su-25 (Frogfoot) | 25 | 10-20 | 1985 | Additional 7 in Iran |
| Subtotal | 106 | 65-75 | | |

## Combat Aircraft *(continued)*

| Model | Quantity | In service | Since | Notes |
|---|---|---|---|---|
| **Obsolete** | | | | |
| • MiG-21 MF/BIS/U (Fishbed)/F-7 | 130 | 40-80 | 1974 | |
| • Su-7B (Fitter A) | | | 1969 | Possibly not serviceable |
| Subtotal | 130 | 40-80 | | |
| **Bombers** | | | | |
| • Tu-22 (Blinder) | 6 | approx. 4 | 1973 | Additional 20 in Iran |
| • Tu-16 (Badger)/ An-6 (B-6D) | 1 | 1 | 1987 | |
| Subtotal | 7 | 5 | | |
| **Total** | **333** | **180-230** | | |

## Transport Aircraft

| Model | Quantity | In service | Since | Notes |
|---|---|---|---|---|
| • An-12 (Cub) | 5 | 5 | 1966 | |
| • An-24 (Coke) | | | 1967 | |
| • An-26 (Curl) | | | 1977 | |
| • Il-76 (Candid) | | | 1989 | Some tankers |
| • Mystère-Falcon 20/Falcon 50 | | | | |
| • Tu-124A/Tu-134 (Crusty) | | | 1962 | |
| **Total** | **small number** | **small number** | | |

*Note:* Additional 15 aircraft in Iran, 6 in Kuwait and 8 in Jordan

## Training and Liaison Aircraft

| Model | Quantity | In service | Since | Notes |
|---|---|---|---|---|
| **With ground attack/close air support capability** | | | | |
| • L-29 (Delfin) | approx. 20 | approx. 20 | 1974 | |
| • L-39 (Albatross) | approx. 30 | approx. 30 | 1975 | |
| • Embraer EMB-312 (Tucano) | 50-80 | 50-80 | 1985 | |
| Subtotal | 120 | 120 | | |
| **Others** | | | | |
| • MBB-223 Flamingo/ AS 202 Braud/Zlin 326 | 20-50 | 20-50 | 1979 | |
| • Pilatus PC-7 | 25 | 25 | 1980 | |

## Training and Liaison Aircraft *(continued)*

| Model | Quantity | In service | Since | Notes |
|---|---|---|---|---|
| • Pilatus PC-9 | 30 | 30 | 1987 | |
| Subtotal | 90 | 90 | | |
| Total | approx. 210 | approx. 210 | | |

## Helicopters

| Model | Quantity | In service | Since | Notes |
|---|---|---|---|---|
| **Attack** | | | | |
| • Alouette III (armed) | 30 | 30 | 1971 | |
| • Mi-24/Mi-25 (Hind) | 30 | 30 | 1982 | |
| • SA-342 Gazelle | 50 | 50 | 1977 | |
| • MBB BO-105 | 40 | 40 | 1979 | Number unconfirmed |
| Subtotal | 150 | 150 | | |
| **Heavy transport** | | | | |
| • Mi-6 (Hook) | 15 | 10-15 | 1974 | |
| **Medium transport** | | | | |
| • AS-332 Super Puma | small number | small number | | |
| • AS-61 | 5 | 3 | 1982 | |
| • Mi-8/Mi-17 (Hip) | 100 | 100 | 1974 | |
| • SA-330 Puma | 20 | 10 | 1977 | |
| • Bell 214 | 40 | 10-20 | 1985 | |
| • Mi-2 (Hoplite) | small number | small number | | |
| • SA-321 Super Frelon | 10 | 10 | 1976 | Also employed in naval combat role |
| Subtotal | approx. 185 | approx. 150 | | |
| **Light transport** | | | | |
| • BK-117 | 20-25 | 10-20 | 1988 | |
| • Hughes 500D | 30 | 10 | 1983 | |
| • Hughes 300C | 30 | 10 | 1983 | |
| • Hughes 530F | 25 | 16 | 1985 | |
| Subtotal | 110 | 56 | | |
| Total | approx. 460 | approx. 370 | | |

## Miscellaneous Aircraft

| Model | Quantity | In service | Notes |
|---|---|---|---|
| **AEW/AWACS aircraft** | | | |
| • Adnan 1/Adnan 2 AEW | 2 | 1-2 | 2 Adnan 2 flown to Iran |
| **UAVs and mini-UAVs** | | | |
| • Mirach 100 | | | |

## Advanced Armament

**Air-to-air missiles**

AA-2 (Atoll), AA-6 (Acrid), AA-7 (Apex), AA-8 (Aphid), R-530, R-550 Magic, Super 530D/F.

**Air-to-ground missiles**

AM-39 Exocet, Armat (anti-radar), AS-2 (Kipper), AS-4 (Kitchen), AS-5 (Kelt), AS-6 (Kingfish), AS-7 (Kerry), AS-9 (Kyle), AS-10 laser-guided, AS-12, AS-14 (Kedge), AS-15TT anti-ship missile, AS-20, AS-30L laser-guided, AT-2 (Swatter), C-601, HOT, LX anti-ship missile, X-23 anti-radiation missile

**Bombs**

Belouga CBU, Cardoen CBU, fuel-air explosive (FAE)

## Air Force Infrastructure

**Aircraft shelters**

For all combat aircraft (some damaged)

**Military airfields:** 38

Abu-Ajal, al-Assad, al Bakr, Balad, Basra, H-2, H-3, Habbaniyah, Irbil, Jalibah, Khalid, Kirkuk, Kut al-Amarah, Kut al-Amarah new field, Mosul, Mudaysis, Muthanah, al-Nasiriyah, al-Qadisiyah, al-Rashid, al-Rumaylah, Saddam, Salman, al-Shuaiba, al-Tallil, al-Taqaddum, al-Tuz, Wadi al-Khir, 10 additional

# Air Defense Forces

## Surface-to-Air Missiles (SAMs)

| Model | Batteries | Launchers | Since | Notes |
|---|---|---|---|---|
| **Heavy missiles** | | | | |
| • SA-2 (Guideline)/ SA-3 (Goa) | 60 | | 1972 | |
| Total | 60 | | | |
| **Medium missiles** | | | | |
| • SA-6 (Gainful) | | | 1974 | |
| • SA-8 (Gecko) | | 20 | 1987 | |
| Total | | | | |

## Surface-to-Air Missiles (SAMs) *(continued)*

| Model | Batteries | Launchers | Since | Notes |
|-------|-----------|-----------|-------|-------|
| **Light missiles** | | | | |
| • Roland I/II | | 100 | 1981 | |
| • SA-9 (Gaskin) | | | 1981 | |
| • SA-13 (Gopher) | | 30 | 1985 | |
| Total | | | | |
| **Shoulder-launched missiles** | | | | |
| • SA-7 (Grail) | | 400 | | |
| • SA-14 (Gremlin) | | | | |
| • SA-16 (Gimlet) | | | | |
| Total | | | | |

*Note:* Serviceability of missile batteries is uncertain due to American bombing (approx. 40% were damaged).

## Other Air Defense Systems

| Model | Quantity | In service | Since | Notes |
|-------|----------|------------|-------|-------|
| **Short-range guns** | | | | |
| • 57mm ZSU 57x2 SP | | | 1977 | |
| • 57mm S-60 | | | 1982 | |
| • 37mm M-1939 | | | 1972 | |
| • 23mm ZSU 23x4 SP (Gun Dish) | | | 1977 | |
| • 23mm ZU 23x2 | | | 1972 | |
| Total | | 2,000-3,000 | | |
| **Radars** | | | | |
| • P-35/37 Barlock | | | | |
| • P-15/P-18 Flat Face | | | | |
| • P-15M Squat Eye | | | | |
| • P-14 Tall King | | | | |
| • P-12 Spoon Rest | | | | |
| • TRS-2215 | | | | |
| • TRS-2230 | | | | |

# Navy

## Combat Vessels

| Type | Original class name | Quantity | Length (m.)/ Displacement (t.) | Armament/ special equipment |
|---|---|---|---|---|
| Corvettes | | | | |
| • Assad | | 2 | 62.3/658 | 2 x Otomat Mk 2 SSMs, 1 x Aspide SAM launcher, 1 x AB 212 helicopter, 1 x 76mm gun (Weapon systems not serviceable) |
| Total | | 2 | | |

## Auxiliary Vessels

| Type | Original class name | Quantity | Length (m.)/ Displacement (t.) | Armament/ special equipment |
|---|---|---|---|---|
| • Stromboli class support ship | | 1 | 129/3,556 | 3,000 ton cargo 1 x 76mm gun |

## Advanced Armament

**Surface-to-surface missiles**
SS-N-2 Styx
**Naval mines**
Soviet models, Italian Manta mines

## Coastal Defense

**HY-2 (Silkworm):** 5 Batteries

## Naval Infrastructure

| | |
|---|---|
| Naval bases: | 4 |

Basra, Umm Qasr, Faw, al-Zubayir

| | |
|---|---|
| Ship maintenance and repair facilities: | 1 |

6,000-ton capacity floating dock, held in Egypt

# Non-governmental Paramilitary Forces

## Personnel

| | Active | Reserves | Total |
|---|---|---|---|
| Kurdish Democratic Party (KDP) | 25,000 | 30,000 | 55,000 |
| Kurdish Workers Party (PKK) | 20,000 | | 20,000 |
| Patriotic Union Of Kurdistan (PUK) | 18,000 | | 18,000 |
| Supreme Assembly of the Islamic Revolution (SAIRI) | 2,000 | | 2,000 |
| National Liberation Army (NLA - Mujahedin Khalq) | 15,000 | | 15,000 |
| Total | 80,000 | 30,000 | 110,000 |

## Equipment

| Organization | System | Model | Notes |
|---|---|---|---|
| NLA | Helicopters | • MI 17 | |
| | | • MD 530 | |
| | Tanks | • Chieftain | |
| PUK | Tanks | • T - 54/55 | |

# 6. ISRAEL

## General Data

**Official Name of the State:** State of Israel
**Head of State:** President Ezer Weizman
**Prime Minister:** Ehud Barak
**Defense Minister:** Ehud Barak
**Chief of General Staff:** Lieutenant General Shaul Mofaz
**Commander of the Air Force:** Major General Eytan Ben-Eliyahu
**Commander of Field Forces HQ:** Major General Moshe Ivri- Sukenik
**Commander of the Navy:** Rear Admiral Alex Tal

**Area:** 20,770 sq. km., including East Jerusalem and vicinity, annexed in 1967 (not including Golan Heights, 1,176 sq. km., to which Israeli law was applied in 1981)
**Population:** 5,830,000

## Demography

| | | |
|---|---|---|
| *Ethnic groups* | | |
| Jews | 4,746,000 | 81.4% |
| Arabs, Druzee, and others | 1,084,000 | 18.6% |
| *Religious groups* | | |
| Jews | 4,746,000 | 81.4% |
| Muslims | 822,000 | 14.1% |
| Christians | 163,000 | 2.8% |
| Druze and others | 99,000 | 1.7% |

## Economic Data

| | | 1993 | 1994 | 1995 | 1996 | 1997 |
|---|---|---|---|---|---|---|
| GDP current price, local currency | Nis bn | 186.6 | 224.8 | 260.7 | 303.6 | 338.3 |
| GDP (US $) | $ Bn | 62.40 | 74.43 | 83.02 | 93.41 | 95.56 |
| GDP per capita | $ | 11,863 | 13,783 | 14,985 | 16,387 | 16,391 |
| Real GDP growth | % | 3.4 | 6.8 | 7.1 | 4.4 | 2.2 |
| **Balance of payments** | | | | | | |
| • Exports fob | $ Bn | 14.722 | 17.179 | 19.237 | 20.758 | 21.894 |
| • Imports fob | $ Bn | 20.533 | 22.753 | 26.834 | 28.404 | 27.742 |
| • Account balance (including services and income) | $ Bn | -2.74 | -3.75 | -6.20 | -6.64 | -5.01 |
| • External debt | $ Bn | 25.35 | 28.08 | 30.00 | 32.13 | 34.26 |

## Economic Data *(continued)*

|  |  | 1993 | 1994 | 1995 | 1996 | 1997 |
|---|---|---|---|---|---|---|
| **Government income and expenditure** | | | | | | |
| • Revenue, local currency | Nis bn | 105.309 | 130.871 | 145.227 | 177.029 | 183.742 |
| • Expenditure, local currency | Nis bn | 105.309 | 130.871 | 145.227 | 177.029 | 191.685 |
| • Defense expenditure | Nis bn | 17.539 | 19.836 | 22.216 | 26.489 | 30.000 |
| • Defense expenditure/GDP | % | 9.40 | 8.82 | 8.52 | 8.72 | 8.86 |
| • Defense expenditure/CGE | % | 16.65 | 15.15 | 15.30 | 14.96 | 15.65 |
| • Population | m | 5.26 | 5.40 | 5.54 | 5.70 | 5.83 |
| • Official exchange rate | Nis: $1 | 2.99 | 3.02 | 3.14 | 3.25 | 3.54 |

## Arms Procurement and Security Assistance Received

| Country | Type | Details |
|---|---|---|
| Belgium | • Arms transfers | LMGs (1993) |
| France | • Arms transfers | Spare parts, Socata training aircraft, CW detectors (1998) |
|  | • Military training | Trainees abroad |
| Germany | • Arms transfers | ABC detection vehicles, CW personal protection gear (1998), submarines on order (1998) |
|  | • Financial | A commitment for approx. $140 million per year over five years (since 1991) to cover the cost of a MIM-104 battery and current construction of 2 submarines in Germany, and part of the cost of a third submarine |
|  | • Military training | trainees abroad |
| Netherlands | • Arms transfers | CW personal protection gear (1998) |
|  | • Cooperation in arms production, assembly, R&D | Cooperation in builiding patrol boats (1998) |
| South Africa | • Arms transfers | Patrol boats (1997) |
| Turkey | • Arms transfers | Otokar Scorpion (1998) |
|  | • Facilities | Use of airfields and airspace for training (1998) |

## Arms Procurement and Security Assistance Received *(continued)*

| Country | Type | Details |
|---------|------|---------|
| USA | • Arms transfers | SP artillery, naval SSMs (1998), SAMs, F-15I combat aircraft (1998), MLRS (1998), upgrading of MLRS (1998), helicopters (1998), tank transporters (1997), missile corvettes, ATGMs, AAMs |
| | • Financial aid | $1.8 billion grant (1998), will be gradually increased up to $2.4 billion in 2008; a gift of surplus weapons from European drawdown arsenal worth approximately $700 million spread over several years; special funding for various projects - $200 million |
| | • Cooperation in arms production, assembly, R&D | Finance and assistance for Arrow TMD and Nautilus laser defense |
| | • Military training | Trainees abroad |

## Arms Sales and Security Assistance Extended

| Country | Type | Details |
|---------|------|---------|
| Argentina * | • Arms transfers | Upgrading Boeing 707 transport a/c, HUD for Pampas trainers (1997), radars and electronic reconnaissance systems for naval surveillance a/c (1998) |
| Australia | • Arms transfers | Radars for upgraded P-3C, jointly with a US company; ESM for Australian C-130 aircraft, Popeye AGMs, ESM for helicopters (1998) |
| Belgium | • Arms transfers | Hunter UAVs (1998) |
| Brazil * | • Arms transfers | HUD and avionics for trainer a/c (1997), avionics suit for ALX attack aircraft and upgrading of F-5 fighter (1998) |
| Britain | • Arms transfers | Artillery and infantry ammunition (1996), CATS & ACE simulators, ESM for Nimrod 2000, EHUD air combat debriefing systems (1998) |
| Cambodia | • Arms transfers | Upgrading of MiG-21 a/c (1997); avionics for L-39 trainer a/c |
| Chile * | • Arms transfers | Patrol boats (1996), AAMs, AAGs(1998), artillery, Barak shipborne anti-missile missile, mini-UAVs, components for upgrading of F-5 combat a/c (1998), AEW a/c (1995), tanker a/c (1996) |

* *Note:* According to foreign publications, as cited by Israeli publications.

## Arms Sales and Security Assistance Extended *(continued)*

| Country | Type | Details |
|---|---|---|
| Colombia * | • Arms transfers | Radio transceivers |
| | • Military training | Advisers/instructors/technicians, foreign trainees |
| | • Cooperation in arms production, assembly, R&D | Assistance in upgrading combat aircraft in Colombia, co-production of Galil assault rifle |
| Cyprus | • Arms transfers | Torpedo boats |
| Czech Republic | • Arms transfers | Avionics for L-39 trainer aircraft, ground forces radar, jointly produced |
| | • Cooperation in arms production, assembly, R&D | Cooperation in upgrading T-72 tanks |
| Ecuador* | • Arms transfers | Kfir combat aircraft (1997), AAMs, naval SSMs |
| | • Military training | Advisers/instructors/technicians |
| Eritrea * | • Arms transfers | Fast patrol boats (1997), landing craft (1993) |
| Estonia | • Arms transfers | Small arms, AAGs |
| Ethiopia | • Arms transfers | Upgrading Mig-21 combat a/c |
| Finland | • Arms transfers | AD command and control system (1996) |
| France | • Arms transfers | Protective vests, Hunter UAVs, hand-held SAR systems (1997) |
| | • Cooperation in arm production, assembly, R&D | Cooperation with ALCATEL in military communications (1997) |
| Germany | • Arms transfers | Electronic equipment, ECMs, a/c warning systems, protective vests, Litening designators for combat a/c, EHUD air combat debriefing system (1996), upgrading of CH-53 helicopters (1998) |
| | • Cooperation in arms production, assembly, R&D | Joint production of EW systems for Tornado a/c (1998), joint production of Litening pods for NATO (1998), joint production in Germany of mini-UAVs, joint development of an anti-radiation attack drone, joint production of Panzerfaust 3LR light ATRL, joint development of a satellite, joint production of NT series AT missiles (1998) |
| Greece | • Arms transfers | Ground radar (1996) |

* *Note:* According to foreign publications, as cited by Israeli publications.

## Arms Sales and Security Assistance Extended *(continued)*

| Country | Type | Details |
|---|---|---|
| India* | • Arms transfers | Avionics for upgrade of fighter aircraft (1998), upgrading of artillery, UAVs, ammunition; on order: early warning technology, Harpy anti-radiation drone*, upgrading of tanks, executive jets, EL/M-2032 radar for Jaguar a/c, Litening pods, Super-Dvora patrol boats, communication equipment (1998) |
| Indonesia | • Arms transfers | Mini UAVs (1996) |
| Italy | • Arms transfers | Enhanced add-on armor kit for some Italian M-113 family APCs, Opher guiding kit for bombs (1997), airborne SAR system |
| Lebanese Militia (SLA) | • Arms transfers | Small arms, tanks, artillery pieces |
| | • Military training | Advisers/instructors/technicians, foreign trainees |
| | • Financial aid | $23 million for infrastructure (1997), and approx. $70 million for salaries of SLA personnel |
| Lithuania | • Arms transfers | Submachine guns |
| Myanmar (Burma) | • Arms transfers | Upgrading of F-7 fighter a/c (1998), AA missiles (1998) |
| Nepal | • Arms transfers | Galil assault rifles |
| Netherlands | • Arms transfers | Aircraft warning systems, Ranger mini-UAVs, under negotiation, artillery C&C systems, aircraft debriefing system |
| | • Cooperation in arms production, assembly, R&D | |
| Nicaragua | • Arms transfers | Dabur patrol boats (1997) |
| Poland | • Cooperation in | Night vision for tanks, tank arms production, upgrading, upgrading Huzar assembly, R&D attack helicopters & supply of AT missiles (1998- currently suspended) |
| Portugal | • Arms transfers | EHUD air combat debriefing systems |

---

\* *Note:* According to foreign publications, as cited by Israeli publications.

## Arms Sales and Security Assistance Extended *(continued)*

| Country | Type | Details |
|---------|------|---------|
| PRC* | • Arms transfers | Python-3 AAMs; radio sets; night vision systems; additional items; a/c radars; thermal imaging tank-sights, IL-76 AEW aircraft with Russia |
| | • Military training | Advisers/instructors/technicians |
| | • Cooperation in | Contribution to Chinese combat arms production, a/c avionics, joint development of assembly, R&D * an AGM/cruise missile; thermal imaging tank sights |
| Romania | • Arms transfers | OWS-25 weapon system for APCs |
| | • Cooperation in arms production, assembly, R&D | Joint production of night vision equipment for Romanian IAR-330 Puma helicopters, upgrading Dracula attack helicopters, cooperation on ATGM production in Romania, cooperation in upgrading 100 MiG-21s in Romania, cooperation in upgrading IAR-99/109 trainer a/c (1998), cooperation in production of avionics (1998) |
| Russia | • Cooperation in arms production, assembly, R&D | IL-76 AEW for China, joint development and marketing of KA-50/52 attack helicopter (1998) |
| Singapore* | • Arms transfers | Electronic warfare systems, Searcher UAVs, aerial refueling aircraft, electronic components for F-5 combat a/c (1998), Barak shipborne anti-missile missile, AAMs, naval tactical training center, air combat debriefing system |
| | • Military training | Advisers/instructors/technicians |
| | • Cooperation in arms production, assembly, R&D | Cooperation in upgrading Turkish F-5 combat a/c |
| Slovakia | • Cooperation in arms production, assembly, R&D | Upgrading T-72 tanks, developing Strop light air defense system |
| Slovenia | • Arms transfers | 155mm canons, 120 mm mortars, upgrading of PC-9 training a/c (1998) |
| South Africa | • Arms transfers | Avionics for upgrading Cheetah combat a/c; upgrading Boeing 707 to SIGINT configuration |

* *Note:* According to foreign publications, as cited by Israeli publications.

## Arms Sales and Security Assistance Extended *(continued)*

| Country | Type | Details |
|---|---|---|
| South Korea * | • Arms transfers | Popeye-2 ASM, Harpy anti radar drones (1997), night vision systems |
| | • Cooperation in arms production, assembly, R&D | A joint venture civilian aircraft; upgrading Korean F-4 and F-5 under negotiation |
| Spain* | • Arms transfers | Griffin guided bombs; upgrading tanks and aircraft; upgrading Boeing 707 to SIGINT configuration, UAVs, military communications (1995) |
| Sri Lanka | • Arms transfers | Kfir aircraft, Superhawk UAVs, mine detection radar |
| Sweden | • Arms transfers | 120mm ammunition for tanks, ground penetrating radar |
| | • Cooperation in arms production, assembly, R&D | Joint development of NBC protection for civilians |
| Switzerland | • Arms transfers | Communication intelligence systems |
| | • Cooperation in arms production, assembly, R&D * | Ranger UAVs and ADS-95 systems (1998-2000), C$^3$I simulators |
| Taiwan * | • Arms transfers | Naval SSMs |
| Thailand | • Arms transfers | Searcher mini-UAVs (1998), Python 3 AAMs, naval SSMs, upgrading avionics in Czech L-39 trainer aircraft, VHF tactical radios, Popeye AGM (1998-temp. suspended), F-5 (1998- temp. suspended), conversion of transport a/c to tanker (1998-temp. suspended) |
| Turkey | • Arms transfers | Upgrading F-4 and F-5 a/c (1998), AGMs (1998), EHUD debriefing system for air combat training (1998), ARS-700 airborne search and rescue systems for Cougar helicopters (1998), mine detection and ground penetrating radar |
| | • Cooperation in arms production, assembly, R&D | Joint production of Popeye AGMs, production of Delila antiradar air launched drone, possible cooperation on ATBM system |
| Ukraine | • Cooperation in arms production, assembly, R&D | Joint upgrading of AN-72P maritime surveillance aircraft, joint upgrading of MiG-21 a/c for Ethiopia |

*Note:* According to foreign publications, as cited by Israeli publications.

## Arms Sales and Security Assistance Extended *(continued)*

| Country | Type | Details |
|---|---|---|
| USA | • Arms transfers | Python 4 AAMs (1998), F-15I fuselage parts (1998), image processing technology (1998), digital mapping systems for V-22 a/c (1998), Litening pods for F-16 a/c (1998), engine parts for F-15/F-16 a/c (1998), ARS-700 airborne search and rescue systems (1998), Pioneer and Hunter UAVs (being phased out), tactical air-launched decoys, AGMs jointly produced, 120mm mortars, tactical communication, crashworthy troop seats for helicopters (1998), Astra SPX a/c, central computer for Bradley AFV's, LASER designators for the Comanche helicopter (1998), |
| | • Cooperation in arms production, assembly, R&D | Enhanced applique armor kits for APCs (1998), electronics, aircraft components, Helmet Mounted Cueing-system for US Air Force (1998), terminal guidance bombs, tactical airlaunched decoys, UAVs, upgrading UH-1 helicopters, joint production of Popeye AGMs (1998), joint research on Arrow ATBM (1998), joint research on Nautilus laser weapon (1998), production and marketing of satellite launchers (1998) remote sensing satellites, BPI ATBM systems (1998), upgrading of T-38 a/c (1998), naval vessels |
| Venezuela | • Arms transfers | MRLs, aerial tanker a/c, EW and command and control systems for frigates(1998), Litening pods (1998) |
| Zambia | • Military training | Advisers/instructors/technicians, foreign trainees |
| | • Arms transfers | Upgrading MiG-21 a/c (1997) |

\* *Note:* According to foreign publications, as cited by Israeli publications.

## Foreign Military Cooperation

| | Details |
|---|---|
| • Forces deployed in Lebanon | Units in the southern Lebanese security zone |
| • Joint maneuvers | With the USA, joint naval exercise with Turkey, joint naval SAR exercise with Jordan, Air Force training in Turkey |

## Defense Production

|  | M | P | A |
|---|---|---|---|
| **Ground forces equipment** | | | |
| • Overhead weapon systems for IFVs | √ | | |
| • Artillery pieces | √ | | |
| • Small arms | √ | | |
| • ATGMs: NT-G, NT-S, NT-D, Lahat (barrel-launched AT missile) | √ | | |
| • ATRLs | √ | | |
| • Artillery, mortar and small arms ammunition | √ | | |
| • Mines | √ | | |
| • Mine-clearing rollers | √ | | |
| • Tanks | √ | | |
| • Tank guns | √ | | |
| • Tread width mine plows for tanks (TWMP) | √ | | |
| • SP AAGs (Soviet gun, USA carrier) | | | √ |
| • Tank-towed bridges (TAB) | √ | | |
| • Upgrading of tanks | √ | | |
| **Aircraft and air ammunition** | | | |
| **(some joint ventures with US companies)** | | | |
| • AAMs : Python 4/5 | √ | | |
| • AGMs | √ | | |
| • CBUs | √ | | |
| • TV and laser terminal guidance bombs | √ | | |
| • UAVs and mini-UAVs | √ | | |
| • Operational flight trainer systems | √ | | |
| • Radars | √ | | |
| • Upgrading of combat aircraft | √ | | |
| • Arrow ATBM | √ | | |
| • Cruise missiles | √ | | |
| • Refueling system for aircraft | √ | | |
| • Helicopter parts | | √ | |
| • Combat aircraft parts | | √ | |
| **Naval craft and ammunition** | | | |
| • LCTs | √ | | |
| • MFPBs | √ | √ | |
| • PBs | √ | | |
| • SSMs | √ | | |
| • Torpedo components | | √ | |

## Defense Production *(continued)*

|  | M | P | A |
|---|---|---|---|
| **Electronics** | | | |
| • Radars | √ | | |
| • Direction finders | √ | | |
| • Pilot rescue radio sets | √ | | |
| • ELINT equipment | √ | | |
| • EW jammers | √ | | |
| • Radio transceivers | √ | | |
| • Audio/video microwave transceivers | √ | | |
| • Radio voice scramblers and encryption units | √ | | |
| • Air-launched decoys | √ | | |
| • AEW a/c conversion | √ | | |
| • Aircraft warning systems | √ | | |
| **Optronics** | | | |
| • Night vision devices | √ | | |
| • Laser rangefinders and target designators | √ | | |
| **Space** | | | |
| • Military satellites including launching capability | √ | | |
| • Amos communications satellite (launched in May 1996) | √ | | |

*Note:* M - manufacture (indigenously developed)
P - production under license
A - assembly

## Weapons of Mass Destruction

**Nuclear capabilities**
• Two nuclear research reactors

**CW capabilities**
• Personal protective equipment
• Unit decontamination equipment
• Fuchs (Fox) ABC detection vehicles (8 vehicles )
• SPW-40 P2Ch ABC detection vehicles (50 vehicles)
• AP-2C CW detectors

**Surface-to-surface missiles**

| Model | Launchers | Missiles | Since | Notes |
|---|---|---|---|---|
| • MGM-52C (Lance) | 12 | | 1976 | |
| • Jericho Mk 1/2/3* SSM* | + | | | |
| Total | 12 | | | |

*Note:* According to foreign publications, as cited by Israeli publications

# Armed Forces

**Major Changes:** There has been no major change in the order of battle of the IDF in 1998. In January 1999, a major reorganization in the force structure was declared. The land forces HQ will be now equal in status to those of the navy and the air force. The land forces introduced the Gil anti-tank missile into its combat units. The air force received all its F-15Is, combat aircraft and 15 new UH-60L helicopters. The navy received (in early 1999) its first Dolphin submarine. The third submarine was launched, and will be delivered in 2000. The navy also received its fourth missile patrol boat upgraded to the Sa'ar 4.5 standard. Two more boats will be upgraded in the future.

## Order of battle

| Year | 1994 | 1995 | 1996 | 1997 | 1998 |
|---|---|---|---|---|---|
| **General data** | | | | | |
| • Personnel (regular) | 177,500 | 177,500 | 187,000 | 187,000 | 186,500 |
| • Divisions | 16 | 16 | 16 | 16 | 16 |
| • Total number of brigades | 13 | 13 | 13 | 13 | 13 |
| **Ground forces** | | | | | |
| • Tanks | 3,850 | 3,845 | 3,870 | 3,900 | 3,895 |
| • APCs/AFVs | 8,100 | 8,000 | 8,010 | 8,010 | 8,040 |
| • Artillery | 1,300 | 1,300 | 1,292 | 1,312 | 1,348 |
| (including MRLs) | | | | (1,912) | (1,948) |
| • SSM launchers | 12 | 12 | 12 | 12 | |
| **Air Force** | | | | | |
| • Combat aircraft | 742 | 677 | 640 | 613 (780) | 624 (801) |
| • Transport aircraft | 93 | 83 | 83 | 83 (93) | 77 (87) |
| • Helicopters | 253 | 269 | 285 | 278 (288) | 289 (299) |
| **Air Defense Forces** | | | | | |
| • Heavy SAM batteries | 4+ | 4+ | 4+ | 21 | 22 |
| • Light SAM launchers | 50 | 50 | 50 | 50 | 70 |
| **Navy** | | | | | |
| • Submarines | 3 | 3 | 3 | 4 | 4 |
| • Combat vessels | 19 | 22 | 22 | 21 | 21 |
| • Patrol crafts | 40 | 36 | 36 | 35 | 35 |

*Note:* beginning with data for 1997, we refer to quantities in active service. The numbers in parentheses refer to the total.

## Personnel

|  | Regular | Reserves | Total |
|---|---|---|---|
| Ground Forces | 141,000 | 380,000 | 521,000 |
| Air Force | 36,000 | 55,000 | 91,000 |
| Navy | 9,500 | 10,000 | 19,500 |
| **Total** | **186,500** | **445,000** | **631,500** |
| **Paramilitary** | | | |
| • Border Police | 6,000 | | 6,000 |

# Ground Forces

## Formations (including reserves)

|  | Corps/ HQ | Divisions | Independent brigades/ groups | Brigades in divisions |
|---|---|---|---|---|
| All arms | 3* | | | |
| Armored | | 12 | | 2-3 armd. 1 mech. 1 arty. each |
| Mechanized/ Infantry/ Territorial | | 4 | 8 | |
| Airborne | | | 5 | |
| **Total** | | **16** | **13** | |

Anti-guerrilla HQ: 3 divisional HQ for control of units engaged in anti-guerrilla activities in Samaria and Gaza (after May 1994—Gaza HQ stationed in Jewish settlements) and on the Lebanese border. In emergency, the HQ will be reinforced by armor, infantry, engineering and anti-tank forces.

* *Note:* According to foreign publications, as cited by Israeli publications.

## Tanks

| Model | Quantity | In service | Since | Notes |
|---|---|---|---|---|
| **MBTs** | | | | |
| **High quality** | | | | |
| • Merkava Mk 1/Mk 2/Mk 3 | 1,210 | 1,210 | 1979/ 1983/1989 | |

## Tanks *(continued)*

| Model | Quantity | In service | Since | Notes |
|---|---|---|---|---|
| **Medium and low quality** | | | | |
| • Centurion/ upgraded Centurion | 1,000 | 1,000 | 1965 | |
| • M-60A3/upgraded M-60/Magach 7 | 1,020 | 1,020 | 1980 | |
| • M-60/M-60 A1 | 380 | 380 | 1970 | |
| • M-48 A5 | 235 | 235 | | |
| • T-62 | 50 | 50 | 1974 | |
| Subtotal | 2,685 | 2,685 | | |
| **Total** | **3,895** | **3,895** | | |
| **On Order** | | | | |
| • Merkava Mk 3/Mk4 | | | | |

## APCs/AFVs

| Model | Quantity | In service | Since | Notes |
|---|---|---|---|---|
| **APCs** | | | | |
| • Achzarit, Israeli APC | + | + | 1994 | |
| • M-113 (various marks) | | + | + | |
| • Nagmashot* | 100 | 100 | 1989 | |
| • Nagmachon | + | + | | |
| • Nakpadon | 15 | 15 | | |
| • M-2 and M-3 halftrack | 2,685 | 2,685 | | Some phased out |
| • Otokar Scorpion (Akrep) | 30 | 30 | 1998 | |
| • RBY | + | + | | |
| **Total** | **8,040** | **8,040** | | |

* *Note:* According to foreign publications, as cited by Israeli publications.

## Artillery

| Model | Quantity | In service | Since | Notes |
|---|---|---|---|---|
| **Self-propelled guns and howitzers** | | | | |
| • 203mm M-110 SP | + | + | 1975 | |
| • 175mm M-107 SP | + | + | 1974 | |
| • 155mm M-109 A1 and } M-109 A2 } | | | | |
| • 155mm M-109 Doher } | 600 | 600 | | |
| • 155mm M-50 | + | + | | |
| • 155mm L-33 SP | + | + | | |
| Subtotal | 900 | 900 | | |

## Artillery *(continued)*

| Model | Quantity | In service | Since | Notes |
|---|---|---|---|---|
| **Towed guns and howitzers** | | | | |
| • 155mm M-71 | + | + | | |
| • 130mm M-46 | + | + | | |
| • 122mm D-30 | + | + | | |
| **mortars, over 160mm** | | | | |
| • 160mm SP | + | + | | |
| **mortars, under 160mm** | | | | |
| • 120mm | 250 | 250 | | |
| **MRLs** | | | | |
| • 290mm MAR 290 | + | + | | |
| • 240mm | + | + | 1974 | |
| • 140mm | + | + | | |
| • 122mm BM-21 | + | + | | |
| • Keres anti-radar missile | + | + | | |
| • Kachlilit anti-radar missile | + | + | | |
| • 227mm MLRS | 48 | 48 | | |
| **Total** | **1,948** | **1,348** | | |
| **Artillery/mortar-locating radars** | | | | |
| • AN/TPQ-37 | + | + | | |
| • AN/PPS-15 | + | + | | |
| • Elta Shilem artillery ranging radar | + | + | | |

## Logistic and Engineering Equipment

Gilois motorized bridges, M-123 Viper minefield crossing system, M-60 AVLB, mine-clearing rollers, mine layers, Pomins II portable mine neutralization system*, Puma vehicle, TAB (towed assault bridge, towed by tanks), TLB (trailer launched bridge), TWMP (tread width mine ploughs), M-1000 heavy equipment transporters

* *Note:* According to foreign publications, as cited by Israeli publications.

## Anti-tank weapons

### Missiles
• AT-3 (Sagger), BGM-71A TOW and BGM-71C Improved TOW, M-47 Dragon (1980), Mapats SP, Nimrod, Israeli BGM-71C Improved TOW SP; Spike, Gil and Dandy* AT missiles (NT-S, NT-G, NT-D)

### On order
• BGM-71E (TOW 2A)

* *Note:* According to foreign publications, as cited by Israeli publications.

# Air Force

## Order of Battle

| Model | Quantity | In service | Notes |
|---|---|---|---|
| • Combat | 801 | 624 | Including aircraft in operational storage |
| • Transport | 87 | 77 | |
| • Helicopters | 299 | 289 | |

## Combat Aircraft

| Model | Quantity | In service | Since | Notes |
|---|---|---|---|---|
| **Advanced multi-role** | | | | |
| • F-15I | 25 | 25 | 1998 | |
| • F-15 Eagle | 72 | 72 | 1976 | |
| • F-16A/B/C/D | 243 | 243 | 1980/1986 | Most F-16A/C may be employed as interceptors |
| Subtotal | 340 | 340 | | |
| **Multi-role** | | | | |
| • F-4E/RF-4E Phantom and Phantom 2000 | 140 | 140 | 1969 | |
| • A-4 Skyhawk | 176 | 119 | 1967 | 57 in operational storage, for sale/ emergency |
| • Kfir C-2/TC-2/C-7/TC-7 | 145 | 25 | 1976 | 120 in operational storage, for sale/ emergency |
| Subtotal | 461 | 284 | | |
| **Total** | **801** | **624** | | |

## Transport Aircraft

| Model | Quantity | In service | Since | Notes |
|---|---|---|---|---|
| • Arava | 10 | 10 | 1984 | |
| • Beechcraft Queen Air | 6 | 6 | 1990 | |
| • Boeing 707 | 10 | 10 | 1973 | |
| • Boeing 707 tanker (refueling) | 3 | 3 | | |
| • C-130H Hercules | 22 | 22 | 1970 | |
| • DC-3 Dakota (C-47) | 18 | 8 | 1948 | 10 in storage for sale |

## Transport Aircraft *(continued)*

| Model | Quantity | In service | Since | Notes |
|---|---|---|---|---|
| • Dornier Do-28 | 15 | 15 | 1971 | |
| • KC-130 tanker (refueling) | 3 | 3 | 1976 | |
| Total | 87 | 77 | | |
| On order | | | | |
| • Beechcraft King Air | | | | Delivery 1999 |

## Training and Liaison Aircraft

| Model | Quantity | In service | Since | Notes |
|---|---|---|---|---|
| With ground attack/close air support capability | | | | |
| • CM-170 Fouga Magister/Tzukit | 80 | 80 | 1960 | Some in storage |
| Subtotal | 80 | 80 | | |
| Others | | | | |
| • Socata Trinidad TB-21 | 22 | 22 | 1995 | |
| • Cessna U-206 (Stationair-6) | 21 | 0 | | In storage, for sale |
| • Piper Cub | 35 | 35 | | |
| Subtotal | 78 | 57 | | |
| Total | 158 | 137 | | |

## Helicopters

| Model | Quantity | In service | Since | Notes |
|---|---|---|---|---|
| Attack | | | | |
| • AH-64A Apache | 42 | 42 | 1990 | |
| • AH-1G/1S Cobra | 64 | 64 | 1981 | |
| • 500MD Defender | 30 | 30 | 1979 | |
| Subtotal | 136 | 136 | | |
| Heavy transport | | | | |
| • CH-53 | 39 | 39 | 1970 | Including CH-53-2000 |
| Medium transport | | | | |
| • Bell 212 | 55 | 45 | | 10 in storage for sale |
| • UH-60L Black Hawk | 15 | 15 | 1998 | |
| • UH-60A Black Hawk | 10 | 10 | 1994 | |
| Subtotal | 80 | 70 | | |
| Light transport | | | | |
| • AB-206 JetRanger/ Bell 206L | 39 | 39 | | |
| Naval attack/search & rescue | | | | |
| • AS 536 Panther | 5 | 5 | 1995 | |
| Total | 299 | 289 | | |

228

## Miscellaneous Aircraft

| Model | Quantity | In service | Since | Notes |
|-------|----------|------------|-------|-------|
| **AEW/AWACS aircraft** | | | | |
| • E-2C Hawkeye AEW | 4 | 4 | 1978 | |
| • Boeing 707 AEW * | Several | | | |
| **ELINT and EW** | | | | |
| • Boeing 707 ELINT* | | | | |
| • Boeing 707 EW* | | | | |
| • Beechcraft King Air | 6 | 6 | 1990 | |
| **Maritime surveillance aircraft** | | | | |
| • Seascan (Westwind 1124N) | 3 | 3 | | |
| **UAVs and mini-UAVs** | | | | |

**UAVs and mini-UAVs**
• Hermes 450S, Hermes 450 High Altitude*, Mastif, Pioneer mini-UAV, Scout, Searcher, MQM-74C Chuckar II, Teledyne Ryan 1241

**Target drones**
• Beech AQM-37A; Beech BQM-107B

**On order**
• Hunter UAV; Heron UAV

*Note:* According to foreign publications, as cited by Israeli publications

## Advanced Armament

**Air-to-air-missiles**
• AIM-9 Sidewinder, AIM-9L, AIM-7 Sparrow, Python 3, Python 4, Shafrir, AMRAAM AIM-120

**Air-to-ground missiles**
• AGM-78D Standard ARM, AGM-65 Maverick, AGM-62A Walleye, AGM-45 A/B Shrike, Hellfire, Hellfire II, Delilah anti-radar air-launched drone/cruise missile, Popeye (equivalent to AGM-142)*, NT-D AT missile*

**Bombs**
• CBU (including Tal-1, ATA-1000, ATA-500), runway-penetration bombs, Pyramid TV terminal-guidance bombs, Griffin laser-guided bomb, Harpy antiradar drone*, Guillotine laser terminal-guidance bombs, Opher terminal-guidance bombs

**On order**
• AIM-9M AAM, Hellfire 2, Star-1 AGM/cruise missile (under development)

## Advanced Armament *(continued)*

### EW and CEW

- Chaff and flare dispensers for combat aircraft, Samson AN/ADM-141 TALD, EL/L-8202 ECM pod, EL/L-8230 ECM system, EL/L-8231 ECM system, EL/L-8240 ECM system, EL/M-2160 warning system, LWS-20 system, SRS-25 airborne receiver, SPS-20 self protection system, SPS-65 self protection system, SPS-200 airborne self protection system, SPS-1000 EW system, SPS-2000 self protection system, Sky-Jam 200 jammer

### On order

- AN/ALQ 131 electronic countermeasure systems (20)

*Note:* According to foreign publications, as cited by Israeli publications.

### Air Force Infrastructure

**Aircraft shelters**
In all operational airfields, for combat aircraft
**Military airfields:**       11
Haifa, Hatzerim, Hatzor, Lod, Nevatim, Palmachim, Ramat David, Ramon, Tel Aviv, Tel Nof, Uvda
**Aircraft maintenance and repair capability**
Maintenance on all models in service, partly in airfields, partly at Israel Aircraft Industries facilities

# Air Defense Forces

### Surface-to-Air Missiles

| Model | Batteries | Launchers | Since | Notes |
|---|---|---|---|---|
| **Heavy missiles** | | | | |
| • MIM-23B Improved HAWK | 17 | | 1965 | |
| • MIM-104 Patriot | 4 | | 1991 | |
| • Hetz (Arrow) | 1 | | 1998 | Including Green Pine radar and Citrus Tree command post |
| Total | **22** | | | |
| **Light missiles** | | | | |
| • MIM-72A Chaparral | | Approx. 50 | | |
| • Mahbet SP | | Approx. 20 | | M-163 Vulcan with Stinger SAMs |

## Surface-to-Air Missiles *(continued)*

| Model | Batteries | Launchers | Since | Notes |
|---|---|---|---|---|
| **Shoulder-launched missiles** | | | | |
| • FIM-92C Stinger | | 500 missiles | | |
| • MIM-43A Redeye | | | 1975 | |
| **on order** | | | | |
| • MIM-104 Patriot | 3 | | | Under negotiation |
| • Arrow ATBMs | 3 | | | Total order - 3 |

## Other Air Defense Systems

| Model | Quantity | In service | Since | Notes |
|---|---|---|---|---|
| **Short-range guns** | | | | |
| • 40mm Bofors L-70 | | | | |
| • 23mm ZU 23x2 | | | | |
| • 20mm M-163 SP A1 Vulcan | 20 | 20 | | Being converted to Mahbet |
| • 20mm TCM-20 Hispano Suiza SP | | | | |
| • 20mm Hispano Suiza | | | | |
| Total | 900 | 900 | | |

**Radars**
- Elta-Ramit, FPS-100, AN/TPS-43, Oren Yarok (Green Pine), Alufa-3

**Aerostats with airborne radars**
- "Status"

**On order**
- ADAMS system; 20mm M-163 from US drawdown

# Navy

### Combat vessels

| Type | Original class name | Quantity | Length (m.)/ Displacement (t.) | Armament/ special equipment |
|---|---|---|---|---|
| **Submarines** | | | | |
| • GAL | IKL/Vickers Type 540 | 3 | 45/600 | sub-Harpoon SSMs 8 x 533mm torpedoes (to be sold) |

## Combat vessels *(continued)*

| Type | Original class name | Quantity | Length (m.)/ Displacement (t.) | Armament/ special equipment |
|------|---------------------|----------|-------------------------------|-----------------------------|
| • Dolphin (Thyssen) | | 1 | 57.3/1,900 | sub-Harpoon SSMs<br>6 x 533mm torpedoes |
| **Total** | | **4** | | |
| **Missile corvettes** | | | | |
| • Eilat class | Sa'ar 5 | 3 | 86.4/1,075 | 1 x SA-536 helicopter<br>8 x Harpoon SSMs<br>8 x Gabriel II SSMs<br>64 x Barak-1 SAM launchers<br>1 x 76mm gun<br>2 x 25mm Sea Vulcans<br>6 x 324mm torpedoes |
| **MFPBs** | | | | |
| • Aliya class | Sa'ar 4.5 | 2 | 61.7/498 | 1 x SA 536 helicopter<br>8 x Harpoon SSMs<br>4 x Gabriel II SSMs<br>2 x 20mm guns<br>1 x Vulcan Phalanx<br>2 x 12.7mm MGs |
| • Hetz class | Sa'ar 4.5 | 9 | 61.7/488 | 8 x Harpoon SSMs<br>6 x Gabriel II SSMs<br>32 x Barak I SAMs<br>1 x 76mm<br>1 x Vulcan Phalanx<br>2 x 12.7mm MGs |
| • Reshef class | Sa'ar 4 | 5 | 58/415 | 4 x Harpoon SSMs<br>4-6 x Gabriel II SSMs<br>1-2 x 76mm guns<br>1 x Vulcan Phalanx<br>2 x 20mm guns<br>2 x 12.7mm MGs<br>used for ASW with<br>2x3x324 torpedoes<br>with sonar |
| • Mivtach class | Sa'ar 2 | 2 | 45/250 | 5xGabriel II SSMs<br>2x3x324mm torpedoes<br>Sonar used for ASW |
| Subtotal | | 18 | | |

## Combat vessels *(continued)*

| Type | Original class name | Quantity | Length (m.)/ Displacement (t.) | Armament/ special equipment |
|---|---|---|---|---|
| **Patrol craft** | | | | |
| • Super Dvora | | 14 | 21.6/54 | 2 x 20mm guns or 2 x 25mm guns 2 x 12.7mm MGs 1 x 84mm MRL depth charges |
| • Dabur | | 18 | 19.8/39 | 2 x 20mm guns 2 x 12.7mm MGs 2 x 324mm torpedoes 1 x 84mm MRL depth charges |
| • Nahshol | | 3 | | 2x12.7mm MGs |
| Subtotal | | 35 | | |
| Total | | 56 | | |
| **On order** | | | | |
| • Dolphin submarines | | 2 | | delivery 1999-2000 |
| • upgrading of Sa'ar 4 class to improved Sa'ar 4.5/Nirit level | | | | |
| • Super Dvora | | 2 | | |

## Landing Craft

| Type | Original class name | Quantity | Length (m.)/ Displacement (t.) | Armament/ special equipment |
|---|---|---|---|---|
| • Ashdod class LCT | | 3 | 62.7/400 | In reserve |
| • LCM type | | 2 | | |
| Total | | 5 | | |

## Auxiliary Vessels

| Type | Original class name | Quantity | Length (m.)/ Displacement (t.) | Armament/ special equipment |
|---|---|---|---|---|
| • Ro-Ro | | 1 | | |
| • Bat Sheva support ship | | 1 | 95.1/1,150 | 4 x 20mm guns 4 x 12.7 MGs |

## Special Maritime Forces

Midget submarines; Zaharon fast boats

## Naval infrastructure

Naval bases:          3
- Ashdod, Eilat, Haifa

### Ship maintenance and repair facilities
- Repair and maintenance of all naval vessels at Haifa,
  partly in conjunction with Israel Dockyards

# 7. JORDAN

## General Data

**Official Name of the State:** The Hashemite Kingdom of Jordan
**Head of State:** King Abdullah bin Hussein al-Hashimi
**Prime Minister:** Abd al-Rauf al-Rawabidah (also Minister of Defense)
**Chief of the Joint Staff of the Armed Forces:** General Mohammad Malkawi
**Chief of Staff of Ground Forces:**
**Commander of the Air Force:** Major General Muhammad Khair al-Ababna (to be replaced)
**Commander of the Navy/Coast guard:** Commodore Ali Mahmoud al-Khasawna

**Area:** 90,700 sq. km.
**Population:** 5,720,000

## Demography

| | | |
|---|---|---|
| *Ethnic groups* | | |
| Arabs | 5,602,600 | 98.0% |
| Circassians and Armenians | 144,400 | 2.0% |
| *Religious groups* | | |
| Sunni Muslims | 5,491,200 | 96.0% |
| Greek Orthodox and other Christians | 228,800 | 4.0% |

## Economic Data

| | | 1993 | 1994 | 1995 | 1996 | 1997 |
|---|---|---|---|---|---|---|
| GDP current price, local currency | JD bn | 3.802 | 4.219 | 4.616 | 4.762 | 4.999 |
| GDP (US $) | $ bn | 5.487 | 6.036 | 6.595 | 6.716 | 7.051 |
| GDP per capita | $ | 1,110 | 1,160 | 1,212 | 1,203 | 1,233 |
| Real GDP growth | % | 5.6 | 8.5 | 5.9 | 0.6 | 1.2 |
| **Balance of payments** | | | | | | |
| • Exports fob | $ bn | 1.246 | 1.425 | 1.770 | 1.817 | 1.836 |
| • Imports fob | $ bn | 3.145 | 3.004 | 3.288 | 3.818 | 3.644 |

## Economic Data *(continued)*

|  |  | 1993 | 1994 | 1995 | 1996 | 1997 |
|---|---|---|---|---|---|---|
| • Account balance (including services and income) | $ bn | -0.628 | -0.398 | -0.259 | -0.222 | 0.029 |
| • External debt | $ bn | 7.609 | 7.708 | 8.11 | 8.118 | 8.053 |
| **Government income and expenditure** | | | | | | |
| • Revenue, local currency | JD bn | 1.404 | 1.477 | 1.609 | 1.703 | 1.651 |
| • Expenditure, local currency | JD bn | 1.466 | 1.560 | 1.746 | 1.851 | 1.763 |
| • Defense expenditure | JD bn | 0.3 | 0.348 | 0.387 | 0.417 | 0.444 |
| • Defense expenditure/GDP | % | 7.9 | 8.2 | 8.3 | 8.7 | 8.9 |
| • Defense expenditure/CGE | % | 20.5 | 22.3 | 22.2 | 22.5 | 25.1 |
| • Population | M | 4.94 | 5.2 | 5.44 | 5.58 | 5.72 |
| • Official exchange rate | JD : 1$ | 0.693 | 0.699 | 0.7 | 0.709 | 0.709 |

*Sources:* EIU quarterly report, EIU country profile, IMF statistical yearbook, SIPRI Yearbook

## Arms Procurement and Security Assistance Received

| Country | Type | Details |
|---|---|---|
| Canada | • Arms transfers | Avionics upgrade for C-130 (1998) |
| Germany | • Arms transfers | Ex-GDR PBs for Coast Guard/police |
| Iraq | • Financial aid | Oil purchase subsidies (1997) |
| Turkey | • Arms transfers | CN-235 aircraft (1998) |
|  | • Facilities provided | Training facilities for Jordanian aircraft (1998) |
|  | • Military training | Flight simulation (1998) |
| USA | • Arms transfers | F-16 combat aircraft (1997), M-60 MBTs (1998), helicopters (1996), M-110 SP guns (1998) |
|  | • Financial aid | $75 million in military aid out of $225 million total aid (1998-1999) |
|  | • Military training | Advisers |

## Arms Sales and Security Assistance Extended

| Country | Type | Details |
|---------|------|---------|
| Palestinians | • Facilities | Camp for Badr unit; PLO and other organizations (offices) |
| Philippines | • Arms transfers | F-5s aircraft (1997) |
| Singapur | • Arms transfers | F-5s aircraft (1994) |
| Turkey | • Facilities provided | Training facilities for Turkish aircraft (1998) |
| USA | • Facilities | Deployment of combat aircraft |

## Foreign Military Cooperation

| | Details |
|---|---------|
| Forces deployed abroad | Small contingency force in Bosnia and Croatia; observers in Angola, Georgia and Tajikistan; 20 troops in Liberia; a military police company in Cambodia |
| Joint maneuvers | USA, Britain, France, Oman, Qatar, Turkey |
| Security agreements | USA, Turkey |

## Defense Production

| | M | P | A |
|---|---|---|---|
| **Army equipment** | | | |
| • A plant to produce high explosives under construction (with assistance from India) | √ | | |
| • Conversion of M-47 tanks to ARVs | √ | | |
| • Badia's APCs and Sangyong vehicles | √ | | |
| **Electronics** | | | |
| • Assembly and production of computers (joint venture with companies from USA, Britain and Singapore) | | √ | √ |
| • Upgrading of avionics (joint venture) | √ | | |
| **Optronics** | | | |
| • Night vision devices | | √ | |

*Note:* M - manufacture (indigenously developed)
P - production under license
A - assembly

## Weapons of Mass Destruction

### CW capabilities
• Personal protective and decontamination equipment

# Armed Forces

**Major Changes:** A major package of military equipment from United States, which was announced in 1996, arrived in late 1997 and early 1998. It includes 50 M-60 A3 MBT's, 18 transport helicopters, 5 transport aircraft, 16 F-16 combat aircraft, and 18 M-110 203mm SP artillery.

## Order of Battle

| Year | 1994 | 1995 | 1996 | 1997 | 1998 |
|---|---|---|---|---|---|
| **General data** | | | | | |
| • Personnel (regular) | 90,000 - 100,000 | 94,000 | 94,000 | 94,200 | 94,200 |
| • Divisions | 4 | 4 | 4 | 4 | 4 |
| • Total number of brigades | 15 | 15 | 15 | 14 | 14 |
| **Ground forces** | | | | | |
| • Tanks | 765 | 765 | 815 | 834 (1,226) | 872 (1,174) |
| • APCs/AFVs | 1,480 | 1,480 | 1,480 | 1,475 (1,575) | 1,475 (1,575) |
| • Artillery | 450 | 450 | 450 | 770 (795) | 788 (813) |
| **Air force** | | | | | |
| • Combat aircraft | 103 | 85 | 85 | 91 | 91 |
| • Transport aircraft | 18 | 12 | 12 | 11 (13) | 12 (14) |
| • Helicopters | 53 | 70 | 60 | 68 | 68 |
| **Air defense forces** | | | | | |
| • Heavy SAM batteries | 14 | 14 | 14 | 14 | 14 |
| • Medium SAM batteries | 50 | 50 | 50 | 50 | 50 |
| • Light SAM launchers | + | + | + | 50 | 50 |
| **Navy** | | | | | |
| • Patrol Craft | 12 | 12 | 12 | 10 | 13 |

*Note:* Beginning with data for 1997, we refer to quantities in active service. The numbers in parentheses refer to the total.

## Personnel

| | Regular | Reserves | Total |
|---|---|---|---|
| Ground Forces | 85,000 | 60,000 | 145,000 |
| Air Force | 8,500 | | 8,500 |
| Navy | 700 | | 700 |
| **Total** | **94,200** | **60,000** | **154,200** |

## Personnel *(continued)*

|  | Regular | Reserves | Total |
|---|---|---|---|
| **Paramilitary** | | | |
| • General security forces (including Desert Patrol) | 25,000 | | |
| • Popular Army | | 200,000 – 250,000 | |

*Note:* The Popular Army is not regarded as a fighting force.

# Ground Forces

## Formations

|  | Division | Independent brigade/ group | Brigades in division |
|---|---|---|---|
| Armored | 2 | | 3 Armd. ,1 Arty., 1 AD each |
| Mechanized | 2 | | 1 Inf. , 2 Mech. , 1 Arty. ,1 AD each |
| Infantry/Royal guard | | 1 | |
| Special forces | | 1 | |
| Artillery | | 5 | |
| **Total** | 4 | 7 | |

## Tanks

| Model | Quantity | In service | Since | Notes |
|---|---|---|---|---|
| **MBTs** | | | | |
| **High Quality** | | | | |
| • Khalid (Chieftain) | 275 | 275 | 1984 | |
| **Medium and low quality** | | | | |
| • Centurion (Tariq) | 290 | 290 | 1955 | Improved |
| • M-60 A1/A3 | 288 | 288 | 1980 | |
| • Chieftain | 90 | 0 | | From Iran, captured by Iraq, in storage, not serviceable |
| • M-48 A1 | 212 | 0 | 1966 | In storage, not operational |
| Subtotal | 880 | 578 | | |
| **Light Tanks** | | | | |
| • Scorpion | 19 | 19 | | With desert patrol |
| **Total** | **1,174** | **872** | | |

## APCs/AFVs

| Model | Quantity | In service | Since | Notes |
|-------|----------|------------|-------|-------|
| **APCs** | | | | |
| • M-113 A1/A2 | 1,240 | 1,240 | 1968 | |
| • Engesa EE-11 | 100 | 100 | 1986 | With general security forces |
| • Saracen | + | 0 | 1963 | Obsolete, in storage. Quantity includes both Saracen and Saladin |
| Subtotal | 1,340 | 1,340 | | |
| **IFVs** | | | | |
| • BMP-2 | 35 | 35 | | |
| **Reconnaissance vehicles** | | | | |
| • Saladin | 60 | 0 | 1963 | Obsolete, in storage. Quantity includes both Saracen and Saladin |
| • Ferret | 140 | approx. 100 | 1955 | Some in storage |
| Subtotal | 200 | 100 | | |
| **Total** | **1,575** | **1,475** | | |

## Artillery

| Model | Quantity | In service | Since | Notes |
|-------|----------|------------|-------|-------|
| **Self-propelled guns and howitzers** | | | | |
| • 203mm M-110 A2 | 128 | 128 | 1980 | |
| • 155mm M-109 A2 | 220 | 220 | 1980 | |
| Subtotal | 348 | 348 | | |
| **Towed guns and howitzers** | | | | |
| • 203mm (8") M-115 | 25 | 0 | 1965 | Not in service |
| • 155mm M-59 (Long Tom) | 10 | 10 | 1965 | |
| • 155mm M-114 | 30 | 30 | 1970 | |
| • 105mm M-102 A1 | 50 | 50 | 1970 | |
| Subtotal | 115 | 90 | | |
| **Mortars, under 160mm** | | | | |
| • 120mm | 300 | 300 | 1975 | |
| • 107mm | 50 | 50 | 1975 | |
| Subtotal | 350 | 350 | | |
| **Total** | **813** | **788** | | |

## Artillery *(continued)*

| Model | Quantity | In service | Since | Notes |
|---|---|---|---|---|
| Artillery/mortar-locating radars | | | | |
| • AN/TPQ 36/37 | | | 1984 | |
| PGMs | | | | |
| • 155mm Copperhead projectiles (CLGP) | 100 | 100 | | |

## Logistic and Engineering Equipment

Mk 2 (D) flail, bridges, mine-clearing plows and bulldozers, UDK-1, AFV transporters (200)

## Anti-tank Weapons

| Model | Quantity | In service | Since | Notes |
|---|---|---|---|---|
| Missiles | | | | |
| • BGM-71A TOW/ BGM-71C improved TOW | 260 | 260 | 1974 | |
| • M-47 Dragon | 310 | 310 | 1976 | |
| • M-901 ITV SP (TOW under armor) | 70 | 70 | | |
| Total | 640 | 640 | | |
| Guns | | | | |
| • 106mm M40 | 330 | 330 | | |

# Air Force

## Order of Battle

| Model | Quantity | In service | Notes |
|---|---|---|---|
| • Combat | 91 | 91 | |
| • Transport | 14 | 12 | |
| • Helicopters | 68 | 68 | |

## Combat Aircraft

| Model | Quantity | In service | Since | Notes |
|---|---|---|---|---|
| Multi role aircraft | | | | |
| • F-16 (A/B) | 16 | 16 | 1997 | |
| • Mirage F-1 C/E | 30 | 30 | 1981 | |
| • F-5 E/F | 55 | 55 | 1975 | |
| Total | 91 | 91 | | |
| On order | | | | |
| • A-10 | | | | Under negotiations |

## Transport Aircraft

| Model | Quantity | In service | Since | Notes |
|---|---|---|---|---|
| • C-130 Hercules | 7 | 5 | 1972 | Some grounded |
| • CASA C-212 | 2 | 2 | 1975 | |
| • Dove | 1 | 1 | 1965 | |
| • Gulfstream III/IV | 3 | 3 | 1986 | |
| • L-1011-500 | 1 | 1 | 1984 | |
| Total | **14** | **12** | | |
| On order | | | | |
| • CN-235 | 2 | | | |

## Training and Liaison Aircraft

| Model | Quantity | In service | Since | Notes |
|---|---|---|---|---|
| With ground attack/close air support capability | | | | |
| • CASA C-101 | 13 | 13 | 1987 | |
| • Cessna 318 (T-37) | 10 | 10 | 1975 | |
| Subtotal | 23 | 23 | | |
| **Others** | | | | |
| • AS-202 Bravo | 20 | 20 | | |
| • BAe-SA-3-125 Bulldog | 15 | 15 | 1978 | |
| Subtotal | 35 | 35 | | |
| Total | **58** | **58** | | |

## Helicopters

| Model | Quantity | In service | Since | Notes |
|---|---|---|---|---|
| **Attack** | | | | |
| • AH-1G/1S Cobra | 22 | 22 | 1985 | |
| **Medium transport** | | | | |
| • UH-60A Black Hawk | 3 | 3 | 1987 | |
| • AS-332 Super Puma | 10 | 10 | 1986 | |
| • Bell 205/UH - 1H | 18 | 18 | 1995 | |
| Subtotal | 31 | 31 | | |
| **Light transport** | | | | |
| • Alouette III | 1 | 1 | 1977 | |
| • MD 500D | 8 | 8 | 1980 | |
| • MBB BO-105 | 3 | 3 | | With police |
| • BK-117 | 3 | 3 | | |
| Subtotal | 15 | 15 | | |
| Total | **68** | **68** | | |
| **On order** | | | | |
| • UH-60A Black Hawk | 4 | | | Under negotiations |

## Miscellaneous Aircraft

**On order**
TTL BTT-3 Banshee target drones (82), 2 launchers

## Advanced Armament

**Air-to-air missiles**
AIM-9B/E/J/M/P Sidewinder, R-550 Magic, AIM-7M Sparrow

**Air-to-ground missiles**
AS-30L

**Bombs**
Belouga CBU, Durandal anti-runway bombs

## Air Force Infrastructure

**Aircraft shelters**
For all combat aircraft
**Military airfields:** 6
Amman (Marka), Azrak, H-4, H-5, Jaafar, Mafraq

# Air Defense Forces

## Surface-to-Air Missiles

| Model | Batteries | Launchers | Since | Notes |
|---|---|---|---|---|
| **Heavy missiles** | | | | |
| • MIM-23B | 14 | | 1976 | |
| Improved HAWK | | | | |
| **Medium missiles** | | | | |
| • SA-8 (Gecko) | | 50 | 1982 | |
| **Light missiles** | | | | |
| • SA-13 (Gopher) | | 50 | 1986 | |
| **Shoulder-launched missiles** | | | | |
| • Javelin | | | | |
| • MIM-43A Redeye | | 250 | 1977 | |
| • SA-14 (Gremlin) | | 300 | 1987 | |
| • SA- 16 (Igla) | | 240 | | |
| Total | | 800 | | |

## Other Air Defense Systems

| Model | Quantity | In service | Since | Notes |
|---|---|---|---|---|
| **Short-range guns** | | | | |
| • 40mm M-42 SP | 218 | 0 | 1966 | To be phased out |
| • 23mm ZSU 23x4 SP (Gun Dish) | 45 | 45 | 1983 | |
| • 20mm M-163 A1 Vulcan SP | 100 | 100 | 1976 | |
| Total | 363 | 145 | | |
| **Radars** | | | | |
| • AN/TPS-43 | 2 | 2 | | |
| • AN/TPS-63 | 5 | 5 | | |
| • S-711 | 5 | 5 | | |

# Navy

## Combat Vessels

| Type | Original class name | Quantity | Length (m.)/ Displacement (t.) | Armament/ special equipment |
|---|---|---|---|---|
| **Patrol craft** | | | | |
| • Feysal class | Bertram | 4 | 11.6/8 | 1 x 12.7mm MGs |
| • Al Hussein class | VT Hawk | 3 | 30.5/124 | 2 x 30mm guns<br>1 x 20mm gun<br>2 x 12.7mm MGs |
| • ARB 65 | | 1 | 19.8/ | 2 x 12.7mm MGs |
| • Al Hashim class | Rotork type 412 | 3 | 12.7/9 | In Dead Sea<br>1 x 12.7mm MG |
| • Patrol boat | Mk-5 | 2 | 12.2/ | |
| Total | | 13 | | |

## Naval Infrastructure

| Naval bases | Aqaba, Hingat al-Ramat |
|---|---|

# 8. KUWAIT

## General Data

**Official Name of the State:** State of Kuwait
**Head of State:** Jabir al-Ahmad al-Jabir al-Sabah
**Prime Minister:** Saad Abdallah al-Salim al-Sabah (also Crown Prince)
**Minister of Defense:** Salim al Sabah al Salim al Sabah
**Chief of General Staff:** Major General Ali al-Mumin
**Commander of the Air Force and Air Defense Forces:** Brigadier General Sabir al-Suwaidan
**Commander of the Navy:** Commodore Ahmad Yousuf al-Mualla

**Area:** 17,820 sq. km., including 2,590 sq. km. of the Neutral Zone
**Population:** 2,210,000

## Demography

| | | |
|---|---|---|
| *Ethnic groups* | | |
| Kuwaitis | 994,500 | 45.0% |
| Other Arabs | 773,500 | 35.0% |
| Southeast Asians | 199,000 | 9.0% |
| Persians/Iranians | 88,500 | 4.0% |
| Others | 154,500 | 7.0% |
| *Religious groups* | | |
| Sunni Muslims | 994,500 | 45.0% |
| Shi'ite Muslims | 884,000 | 40.0% |
| Christians, Parsis, Hindus, and others | 331,500 | 15.0% |

## Economic data

| | | 1993 | 1994 | 1995 | 1996 | 1997 |
|---|---|---|---|---|---|---|
| GDP current price, local currency | KD bn | 7.23 | 7.38 | 7.93 | 9.31 | 9.21 |
| GDP (US $) | $ bn | 23.94 | 24.76 | 26.61 | 31.13 | 30.39 |
| GDP per capita | $ | 14,597 | 13,530 | 13,576 | 14,894 | 13,751 |
| Real GDP growth (1984 prices) | % | 34.2 | 8.4 | 1.0 | 3.3 | -2.8 |
| **Balance of payments** | | | | | | |
| • Exports fob | $ bn | 10.26 | 11.28 | 12.83 | 14.95 | 14.28 |
| • Imports fob | $ bn | 6.94 | 6.61 | 7.25 | 7.95 | 7.76 |

## Economic data (continued)

| | | 1993 | 1994 | 1995 | 1996 | 1997 |
|---|---|---|---|---|---|---|
| • Account balance (including services and income) | $ bn | 2.49 | 3.23 | 5.02 | 7.11 | 7.82 |
| • External debt | $ bn | 10.03 | 9.93 | 10.19 | 7.63 | 7.31 |
| **Government income and expenditure** | | | | | | |
| • Revenue, local currency | KD bn | 2.775 | 3.101 | 3.473 | 4.391 | 3.105 |
| • Expenditure, local currency | KD bn | 4.241 | 4.193 | 4.127 | 3.889 | 4.378 |
| • Defense expenditure | KD bn | 0.900 | 0.979 | 1.102 | 1.108 | 1.037 |
| • Defense expenditure/GDP | % | 12.45 | 13.26 | 13.89 | 11.90 | 11.26 |
| • Defense expenditure/CGE | % | 21.22 | 23.34 | 26.70 | 28.49 | 23.68 |
| • Population | m | 1.64 | 1.83 | 1.96 | 2.09 | 2.21 |
| • Official exchange rate | KD: $1 | 0.302 | 0.298 | 0.298 | 0.299 | 0.303 |

*Sources:* EIU quarterly report, EIU country profile, IMF statistical yearbook, SIPRI Yearbook

## Arms Procurement and Security Assistance Received

| Country | Type | Details |
|---|---|---|
| Australia | • Arms transfers | Patrol craft, APCs |
| Austria | • Arms transfers | Small arms |
| Belgium | • Arms transfers | 90mm ammunition (1998) |
| Britain | • Arms transfers | APCs (1997), trainer aircraft, shoulder-launched SAMs, anti-ship missiles on order |
| | • Military training | Foreign advisers/instructors, trainees abroad |
| Finland | • Arms transfers | CW protective equipment (1998) |
| France | • Arms transfers | Radars (1996), SAMs, MFPBs (1998), anti-ship missiles |
| PRC | • Arms transfers | SP artillery |
| Russia | • Arms transfers | Spare parts for APCs, MRLs, ATGMs, AIFVs |
| Singapore | • Arms transfers | Two landing craft |
| South Africa | • Arms transfers | Mortars, laser rangefinders, light armament |
| USA | • Arms transfers | APCs, SAMs, combat aircraft, command and control systems, M-1A2 tanks, ARVs, ATGMs |
| | • Maintenance aid | SP artillery |

## Arms Sales and Security Assistance Extended

| Country | Type | Details |
|---|---|---|
| USA | • Financial aid | Annual grant to US ($215 million in 1992) for US force in Kuwait |
| | • Facilities | Facilities for US forces |

## Foreign Military Cooperation

| | Details |
|---|---|
| • Forces deployed abroad | 138 troops in UN forces in Somalia, 1993-1995 |
| • Forces deployed in country | 1,200 US army soldiers, 1,000 US navy personnel and 4 batteries of MIM-104 Patriot SAMs, prepositioning of US tanks (110), APCs (110) and artillery pieces (equipment for one brigade); 24 US A-10 attack a/c stationed in Kuwait; 12 UK Tornado GR1/1A a/c; 900 UNIKOM troops and 200 observers |
| • Joint maneuvers | USA (amphibious, command post and naval exercises) (1998); Britain (marines); GCC countries; France, Egypt, Syria |
| • Security agreements | USA, Britain, France, Russia, China, Italy |

## Weapons of Mass Destruction

**CW capabilities**
• Personal protective equipment; decontamination units

# Armed forces

**Major Changes:** The Kuwaiti ground forces are still negotiating acquisition of M-109 A6 Paladin SP howitzers. The US agreed to supply AH-64D Apache attack helicopters. The navy received 4 out of 8 P-37 BRL (Combattante) patrol boats.

## Order of Battle

| Year | 1994 | 1995 | 1996 | 1997 | 1998 |
|---|---|---|---|---|---|
| General data | | | | | |
| • Personnel (regular) | 24,100 | 32,500 | 32,500 | 15,500 | 19,500 |
| • Number of brigades | 6 | 6 | 6 | 6 | 6 |
| • Number of batallions | 1 | 1 | 1 | 1 | 1 |
| Ground forces | | | | | |
| • Tanks | 340 | 472 | 700 | 320 (455) | 320 (483) |
| • APCs/AFVs | + | 50 | 50 | 455 (515) | 436(715) |
| • Artillery (including MRLs) | 24 | 24 | 24 | 75 (128) | 75 (128) |

## Order of Battle *(continued)*

| Year | 1994 | 1995 | 1996 | 1997 | 1998 |
|---|---|---|---|---|---|
| **Air Force** | | | | | |
| • Combat aircraft | 78 | 78 | 59 | 40 (59) | 40 (59) |
| • Transport aircraft | 4 | 4 | 6 | 5 | 5 |
| • Helicopters | 22 | 22 | 18-21 | 24-27 | 24-27 |
| **Air Defense Forces** | | | | | |
| • Heavy SAM batteries | 6 | 6 | 6 | 6 | 6 |
| **Navy** | | | | | |
| • Combat vessels | 2 | 2 | 2 | 4 | 6 |
| • Patrol craft | 33 | 33 | 33 | 54 | 21 |

*Note:* Beginning with data for 1997, we refer to quantities in active service. The numbers in parentheses refer to the total. The number of tanks in 1997 has been changed, due to reassessment of the status of older models. The number of patrol craft has been changed, due to reassessment.

## Personnel

| | Regular | Reserves | Total |
|---|---|---|---|
| Ground Forces | 15,000 | 24,000 | 39,000 |
| Air Force | 2,500 | | 2,500 |
| Navy | 2,000 | | 2,000 |
| **Total** | **19,500** | **24,000** | **43,500** |
| **Paramilitary** | | | |
| • National Guard | 5,000 | | 5,000 |
| • Civil Defense | 2,000 | | 2,000 |

# Ground Forces

## Formations

| | Independent brigades/groups | Independent battalions |
|---|---|---|
| Armored | 2 | |
| Mechanized | 2 | |
| Artillery | 1 | |
| Border defense | 1 | |
| Royal guard | 1 | |
| Commando | | 1 |
| Total | 7 | 1 |

## Tanks

| Model | Quantity | In service | Since | Notes |
|---|---|---|---|---|
| **MBTs** | | | | |
| **High quality** | | | | |
| • M1A2 Abrams | 218 | 218 | 1994 | |
| • M-84 | 200 | 100 | 1990 | |
| Subtotal | 418 | 318 | | |
| **Medium and low quality** | | | | |
| • Chieftain | 45 | 0 | 1977 | In storage |
| • Vickers Mk 1 | 20 | 0 | 1970 | |
| Subtotal | 65 | 0 | | |
| Total | **483** | **318** | | |

## APCs/AFVs

| Model | Quantity | In service | Since | Notes |
|---|---|---|---|---|
| **APCs** | | | | |
| • M-113 | 230 | 52 | | Additional 8 M-901 ITV (TOW under armor) |
| • Fahd | 60 | + | 1994 | |
| Subtotal | 290 | 52 | | |
| **IFVs** | | | | |
| • BMP-3 | 55 | 20 | 1995 | |
| • BMP-2 | 46 | 40 | 1988 | |
| • Pandur | approx. 30 | approx. 30 | 1998 | Being delivered; of various models, incl. mortars |
| • Desert Warrior | 254 | 254 | 1994 | |
| • M-577 artillery command post vehicle | 40 | 40 | | |
| Subtotal | 425 | 384 | | |
| Total | **715** | **436** | | |
| **On order** | | | | |
| • Pandur | 70 | | | Being delivered, different models, option for up to 200 vehicles |

## Artillery

| Model | Quantity | In service | Since | Notes |
|---|---|---|---|---|
| **Self-propelled guns and howitzers** | | | | |
| • 155mm M-109 A3 SP howitzer | 24 | 24 | | |
| • M-109A2 | 23 | 0 | 1986 | Were damaged during the Gulf War, being overhauled |
| • 155mm AMX-13 F-3 | 18 | 0 | | In storage, offered for sale |
| • 155mm GCT AuF-1 | 12 | 0 | 1992 | In storage, offered for sale |
| Subtotal | 77 | 24 | | |
| **Mortars, under 160mm** | | | | |
| • 120mm RTF-1 | 12-18 | 12-18 | | |
| • 107mm | 6 | 6 | | |
| Subtotal | 18-24 | 18-24 | | |
| **MRLs** | | | | |
| • 300mm Smerch (BM-9A52-2) | 27 | 27 | 1995 | |
| Total | **122-128** | **69-75** | | |
| **On order** | | | | |
| • 155mm Norinco 45 calibre | 27 | | | Ordered 1997, Total requirement for 75 |
| • 120mm SP mortars | 30-100 | | | |
| • M-109A6 Paladin | 48 | | | Under negotiation |

## Logistic and Engineering Equipment

| Model | Quantity | In service | Since | Notes |
|---|---|---|---|---|
| • Mk 3 (D) flail | | | | |
| • M88 ARVs | 14 | 14 | 1996 | |

## Anti-tank Weapons

| Model | Quantity | In service | Since | Notes |
|---|---|---|---|---|
| **Missiles** | | | | |
| • AT-4 Spigot | | | | Unconfirmed |
| • BGM-71A/B Improved TOW | 82 | 82 | | |
| • HOT | | | | |

## Anti-tank Weapons *(continued)*

| Model | Quantity | In service | Since | Notes |
|-------|----------|------------|-------|-------|
| • M-901 ITV (TOW under armor) | 8 | 8 | | |
| • M-47 Dragon | | | | |
| **On order** | | | | |
| • HOT; BGM-71F (TOW 2B) | | | | |

# Air Force

### Order of Battle

| Model | Quantity | In service | Notes |
|-------|----------|------------|-------|
| • Combat | 59 | 40 | |
| • Transport | 5 | 5 | |
| • Helicopters | 24-27 | 24-27 | |

### Combat Aircraft

| Model | Quantity | In service | Since | Notes |
|-------|----------|------------|-------|-------|
| **Advanced multi-role** | | | | |
| • F/A-18C/D | 40 | 40 | 1992 | Number of pilots less than a/c |
| **Multi-role** | | | | |
| • Mirage F-1B/C | 19 | 0 | 1976 | Not in service |
| Total | 59 | 40 | | |
| **On order** | | | | |
| • F/A-18C/D | 10-20 | | | Under negotiation |

### Transport Aircraft

| Model | Quantity | In service | Since | Notes |
|-------|----------|------------|-------|-------|
| • Boeing 737-200 | 1 | 1 | | |
| • C-130-30 Hercules/L-100-30 | 3 | 3 | 1971 | |
| • DC-9 | 1 | 1 | 1976 | |
| Total | 5 | 5 | | |

## Training and Liaison Aircraft

| Model | Quantity | In service | Since | Notes |
|---|---|---|---|---|
| **With ground attack/close air support capability** | | | | |
| • BAC-167 Strikemaster Mk 83 | 8 | 0 | 1969 | |
| • Hawk | 12 | 0 | 1985 | |
| Subtotal | 20 | 0 | | |
| **Others** | | | | |
| • S-312 (Shorts Tucano) | 18 | 18 | 1995 | |
| Total | **38** | **18** | | |

## Helicopters

| Model | Quantity | In service | Since | Notes |
|---|---|---|---|---|
| **Attack** | | | | |
| • SA-342K Gazelle | 16 | 16 | 1974 | |
| **Medium transport** | | | | |
| • SA-330 Puma | 5-8 | 5-8 | 1975 | |
| **Naval combat** | | | | |
| • AS-332 Super Puma | 3 | 3 | 1985 | |
| Total | **24-27** | **24-27** | | |
| **On order** | | | | |
| • SA-365N maritime attack | | | | |
| • AH-64D Apache Longbow | 16 | | | |
| • UH-60A/L Blackhawk | 20 | | | Under negotiation |
| • Cougar (SA-532) | 20 | | | Under negotiation |

## Miscellaneous Aircraft

| Model | Quantity | In service | Since | Notes |
|---|---|---|---|---|
| **on order** | | | | |
| • Skyeye UAVs | | | | 3 systems, 12 UAVs under negotiation |

## Advanced Armament

**Air-to-air-missiles**
• AIM-9M Sidewinder, AIM-7F Sparrow, R-550 Magic, Super R-530D/F

**Air-to-ground missiles**
• AGM-65G Maverick, AS-11, AS-12, HOT

**Bombs**
• Paveway II laser-guided

## Advanced Armament *(continued)*

### On order
- AM-39 Exocet air-to-ship missiles
- AGM-65G Maverick AGMs (300 missiles) - some delivered
- AIM-7 Sparrow AAMs (200 missiles) - some delivered
- AIM-9 Sidewinder AAMs (120 missiles) - some delivered
- AGM-84 Harpoon air–launched anti-ship missiles

## Air Force Infrastructure

### Aircraft shelters
In airfields; for combat aircraft; under reconstruction
**Military airfields:**    3
al-Ahmadi, al-Jahra (Ali al-Salam AFB), Kuwait International Airport

# Air Defense Forces

## Surface to Air Missiles

| Model | Batteries | Launchers | Since | Notes |
|---|---|---|---|---|
| **Heavy missiles** | | | | |
| • MIM-23B Improved Hawk | 6 | 18 | 1977 | |
| • Aspide | | 12 | | With Skyguard - see below |
| Total | 6 | 30 | | |
| **Shoulder-launched missiles** | | | | |
| • FIM-92A Stinger | | | | |
| • Starburst | | 48 | | approx. 250 missiles |
| Total | | 48+ | | |

## Other Air Defense Systems

| Model | Quantity | In service | Since | Notes |
|---|---|---|---|---|
| **Air defense systems (missiles, radars and guns)** | | | | |
| • Skyguard AA system (Egyptian Amoun) | 6 | 6 | | Each battery with 2 x Aspide launchers, 2 x Oerlikon 35mm |
| **Short-range guns** | | | | |
| • 40mm Bofors L-70/L-60 | | | | Unconfirmed |

### Other Air Defense Systems *(continued)*

| Model | Quantity | In service | Since | Notes |
|---|---|---|---|---|
| • Oerlikon-Buhrle 2x35 GDF-002 | | | | With Skyguard |
| • 23mm ZSU 23x4 SP (Shilka) | | | | |
| • 20mm Oerlikon GAI | | | | |
| **Radars** | | | | |
| • AN/FPS-117 (Seek Igloo) | 1 | | | |
| • AN/TPS-32 | 1 | | | |
| • Tiger (TRS-2100) | 1 | | | |
| • AD command and control unit (ADGE) | | | | |
| **On order** | | | | |
| • MIM-104 Patriot | 5 | | | |
| • SA-10/SA-12 | 5 | | | Under negotiation |
| • ADSAMS | | | | Under negotiation |
| • AN/TPS-63 radars | 2 | | | |
| • Thomson CSF radar | 1 | | | |
| • Crotale SAMs | | | | Unconfirmed |
| • ZSU 23x4 | | | | |
| • SA-15 (Gauntlet, Tor) | | | | Under negotiation |

# Navy

### Combat Vessels

| Type | Original class name | Quantity | Length (m.)/ Displacement (t.) | Armament/ special equipment |
|---|---|---|---|---|
| **MFPBs** | | | | |
| • Lurssen FPB-57 | | 1 | 58.1/410 | 4 x Exocet MM 40 SSMs 1 x 76mm gun 2 x 40mm guns mines |
| • Lurssen TNC-45 | | 1 | 44.9/255 | 4 x Exocet MM 40 SSMs 1 x 76mm gun 2 x 40mm guns |
| • Um almaradim | P-37 BRL | 4 | 42/245 | 4 x Sea Skua SSMs 1 x 40mm gun 1 x 20mm gun |
| **Total** | | 6 | | |

## Combat Vessels *(continued)*

| Type | Original class name | Quantity | Length (m.)/ Displacement (t.) | Armament/ special equipment |
|---|---|---|---|---|
| **Patrol craft (mostly with Coast Guard)** | | | | |
| • Cougar 1300 | | 4 | 10-12m | 12.7mm MG |
| • Cougar 1200 | | 4 | 10-12m | 12.7mm MG |
| • Predator 1100 | | 3 | 10-12m | |
| • Cougar 1000 | | 3 | 10-12m | 12.7mm MG |
| • Cougar 900 (CAT-900) | | 3 | 10-12m | 12.7mm MG |
| • OPV-310 class | | 4 | 31.5/150 | 1 x 22mm gun 1 x 12.7mm MG |
| Total | | 21 | | |
| On order | | | | |
| • Magnum Sedan PBs | | 20 | | |
| • 2,000 ton OMV corvettes | | 4 | | |
| • P-37 BRL MFPBs | | 8 | 42/245 | Delivery 1999-2000; 4 were delivered of a Total order of 8 |

## Landing Craft

| Type | Original class name | Quantity | Length (m.)/ Displacement (t.) | Armament/ special equipment |
|---|---|---|---|---|
| • Al Tahaddy landing craft | | 2 | 45/215 | 80 tonnes |
| • RTK Sea Truck | | 1 | 12.7/9 | |
| Total | | 3 | | |

## Auxiliary Vessels

| Type | Original class name | Quantity | Length (m.)/ Displacement (t.) | Armament/ special equipment |
|---|---|---|---|---|
| • Logistic support ship | | 2 | 32.3/320 | 170 tonnes |
| • Logistic support ship | | 1 | 27/170 | 40 tonnes equip. |
| • Support ship | | 1 | 55.4/545 | 2 x 12.7mm MGs |

## Naval Infrastructure

Naval bases (including Coast Guard):          3
• Kuwait City (Shuwaikh), al-Qulaya (Ras al-Qalaya), Umm al-Hainam

Ship maintenance and repair facilities
• Kuwait City (Shuwaikh harbor) - 190 meter floating dock,
  repair capacity 35,000 dwt

# 9. LEBANON

## General Data

**Official Name of the State:** Republic of Lebanon
**Head of State:** President Emile Lahoud
**Prime Minister:** Salim al-Huss
**Minister of Defense:** Ghazi Zaitar
**Commander-in-Chief of the Armed Forces:** Lieutenant General Michel Sulayman
**Chief of General Staff:** Brigadier General Samir al-Kadi
**Commander of the Air Force:** Brigadier General George Sha'aban
**Commander of the Navy:** Rear Admiral George Ma'alouf

**Area:** 10,452 sq. km.
**Population:** 4,010,000

## Demography

| | | |
|---|---|---|
| *Ethnic groups* | | |
| Arabs | 3,810,000 | 95.0% |
| Armenians | 160,000 | 4.0% |
| Others | 40,000 | 1.0% |
| *Religious groups* | | |
| Shi'ite Muslims | 1,283,000 | 32.0% |
| Sunni Muslims | 842,000 | 21.0% |
| Druze | 241,000 | 6.0% |
| Alawis | 40,000 | 1.0% |
| Christians | | |
| Maronites | 842,000 | 21.0% |
| Greek Orthodox | 321,000 | 8.0% |
| Greek Catholic | 201,000 | 5.0% |
| Armenians | 160,000 | 4.0% |
| (Orthodox and Catholic) | | |
| Others | 80,000 | 2.0% |

## Economic Data

|  |  | 1993 | 1994 | 1995 | 1996 | 1997 |
|---|---|---|---|---|---|---|
| GDP current price, local currency | L£ bn | 13,118.4 | 15,304.8 | 18,022.3 | 20,412 | 22,758.7 |
| GDP (US $) | $ bn | 7.535 | 9.110 | 11.118 | 12.993 | 14.788 |
| GDP per capita | $ | 2,283 | 3,131 | 3,610 | 4,219 | 3,688 |
| Real GDP growth | % | 7.1 | 8.0 | 6.5 | 4.0 | 3.5 |
| **Balance of payments** |  |  |  |  |  |  |
| • Exports fob | $ bn | 0.686 | 0.544 | 0.825 | 1.017 | 0.642 |
| • Imports fob | $ bn | 4.939 | 5.541 | 6.722 | 6.992 | 6.876 |
| • Account Balance (including services and income) | $ bn | -3.724 | -3.279 | -3.587 | -3.405 | -2.862 |
| • External debt | $ bn | 1.347 | 2.118 | 2.966 | 3.996 | 4.744 |
| **Government income and expenditure** |  |  |  |  |  |  |
| • Revenue, local currency | L£ bn |  | 2,246 | 3,280 | 3,532 | 3,752 |
| • Expenditure, local currency | L£ bn | 2,640 | 4,106 | 5,630 | 7,225 | 9,161 |
| • Defense expenditure | L£ bn | 518.482 | 703.981 | 795.168 | 759.944 | 702.181 |
| • Defense expenditure/GDP | % | 3.9 | 4.6 | 4.4 | 3.7 | 3.1 |
| • Defense expenditure/CGE | % | 19.6 | 17.1 | 14.1 | 10.5 | 7.7 |
| • Population | m | 3.3 | 2.91 | 3.08 | 3.08 | 4.01 |
| • Official exchange rate | L£ :$1 | 1,741 | 1,680 | 1,621 | 1,571 | 1,539 |

*Sources:* EIU quarterly report, EIU country profile, IMF statistical yearbook, SIPRI Yearbook

## Arms Procurement and Security Assistance Received

| Country | Type | Details |
|---|---|---|
| Arab countries | • Financial aid | $500 million ($274 million in cash, of which $100 million are from Kuwait; this aid program followed Israel's Operation Accountability, July 1993. Only part is defense-related) |
| France | • Maintenance of equipment | Helicopters |
| Qatar | • Financial aid | $1 million grant, possibly for civilian purpose |
| Saudi Arabia | • Financial aid | $60 million grant (1991) |

## Arms Procurement and Security Assistance Received *(continued)*

| Country | Type | Details |
|---------|------|---------|
| South Africa | • Military training | Ex-South African officers training the Hizballah |
| Syria | • Advisers | |
| | • Military training | Approx. 50 trainees annually (1997) |
| USA | • Advisers | |
| | • Arms transfers | Jeeps, trucks, M-113 APCs (1996), helicopters (1996) |
| | • Financial aid | Approx. $400,000 in 1995 for training |
| | • Military training | Few dozen trainees in USA |

### Foreign Military Cooperation

| | Details |
|---|---------|
| • Foreign forces in country | Syria (25,000 in Biqa', Tripoli area, and Beirut); Palestinian organizations; Israeli units (in the security zone in South Lebanon); some Iranian Islamic Revolution Guards Corps (IRGC), several instructors in the Syrian-held Biqa', with Hizbullah non-government militia; UNIFIL force in South Lebanon (from Fiji, Finland, Ghana, Ireland, Italy, India and Poland) |

# Armed Forces

**Major Changes:** No major changes have been recorded in the Lebanese armed forces in 1998.

### Order of Battle

| Year | 1994 | 1995 | 1996 | 1997 | 1998 |
|------|------|------|------|------|------|
| **General data** | | | | | |
| • Personnel (regular) | 45,000 | 52,000 | 52,000 | 51,400 | 51,400 |
| • Number of brigades | 12 | 17 | 17 | 17 | 13 |
| **Ground forces** | | | | | |
| • Tanks | 350 | 350 | 350 | 320 (350) | 280 (350) |
| • APCs/AFVs | 500 | 670 | 670 | 730 (875) | 730 (875) |
| • Artillery (incl. MRLs) | 190 | 190 | 190 | 328 (331) | 333 |
| **Air Force** | | | | | |
| • Combat aircraft | 16 | 16 | 16 | (16) | (16) |
| • Transport aircraft | 1 | 1 | 1 | (2) | (2) |
| • Helicopters | 22 | 40 | 40 | 16 (34) | 16 (34) |

## Order of Battle *(continued)*

| Year | 1994 | 1995 | 1996 | 1997 | 1998 |
|---|---|---|---|---|---|
| **Navy** | | | | | |
| • Patrol craft | 36 | 36 | 36 | 39 (43) | 39 (41) |

*Note:* Beginning with data for 1997, we refer to quantities in active service. The numbers in parentheses refer to the total.

### Personnel

| | **Regular** | **Total** |
|---|---|---|
| Ground Forces | approx. 50,000 | approx. 50,000 |
| Air Force | 1,000 | 1,000 |
| Navy | 400 | 400 |
| Total | **51,400** | **51,400** |
| **Paramilitary** | | |
| • Gendarmerie/ internal security | 13,000 | |

# Ground Forces

### Formations

| | **Independent brigade/group** | **Independent battalions** |
|---|---|---|
| Mechanized/Infantry | 11 | |
| Presidential guard | 1 | |
| Special forces/Airborne/Intervention | 1 | 6 |
| Artillery | 2 | |
| Support/Logistics/Medical | 3 | |
| Total | **18** | **6** |

### Tanks

| Model | Quantity | In service | Since | Notes |
|---|---|---|---|---|
| **MBTs** | | | | |
| **Medium and low quality** | | | | |
| • M-48 A1/M-48 A5 | 130 | 60 | 1983 | Not all serviceable |
| • T-55/upgraded T-54 | 180 | 180 | 1985 | |
| Subtotal | 310 | 240 | | |

## Tanks *(continued)*

| Model | Quantity | In service | Since | Notes |
|---|---|---|---|---|
| **Light Tanks** | | | | |
| • AMX-13/105mm gun | 20 | 20 | 1982 | |
| • AMX-13/75mm gun | 20 | 20 | 1981 | |
| Subtotal | 40 | 40 | | |
| Total | **350** | **280** | | |

## APCs/AFVs

| Model | Quantity | In service | Since | Notes |
|---|---|---|---|---|
| **APCs** | | | | |
| • M-113 A1/A2 | 595 | 595 | 1980 | |
| • M-3 (Panhard VIT) | 15 | 15 | 1975 | |
| Subtotal | 610 | 610 | | |
| **IFVs** | | | | |
| • V-150 Commando | 50 | 0 | | |
| • VAB - VCI/VTT | 75 | 75 | 1984 | |
| Subtotal | 125 | 75 | | |
| **Reconnaissance** | | | | |
| • Saracen/Saladin | 60 | 0 | 1979 | Probably not serviceable |
| • AML-90 | 80 | 45 | | |
| Subtotal | 140 | 45 | | |
| Total | **875** | **730** | | |
| **On order** | | | | |
| • M-113 A1/A2 | 500 | | | |

## Artillery

| Model | Quantity | In service | Since | Notes |
|---|---|---|---|---|
| **Towed guns and howitzers** | | | | |
| • 155mm M-198 | 36 | 36 | 1984 | |
| • 155mm M-114 | 20 | 20 | 1980 | |
| • 155mm M-50 | 12 | 12 | 1970 | |
| • 130mm M-46 | 20 | 20 | | |
| • 122mm D-30 | 24 | 24 | 1985 | |
| • 122mm M-1938 | 36 | 36 | 1973 | |
| • 105mm M 101A1 | 15 | 15 | 1982 | |
| • 105mm M 102 | 10 | 10 | | |
| Subtotal | 173 | 173 | | |

### Artillery *(continued)*

| Model | Quantity | In service | Since | Notes |
|---|---|---|---|---|
| **Mortars, under 160mm** | | | | |
| • 120mm Brandt M-50 and M-60 | 130 | 130 | 1973 | |
| **MRLs** | | | | |
| • 122mm BM-21/BM-11 | 30 | approx. 30 | | |
| Total | 333 | 333 | | |

### Anti-tank Weapons

| Model | Quantity | In service | Since | Notes |
|---|---|---|---|---|
| **Missiles** | | | | |
| • BGM-71A TOW | 24 | 24 | 1975 | |
| • Milan | | | 1979 | |
| Total | approx. 80 | approx. 80 | | |
| **Guns** | | | | |
| • 106mm M-40 A2 recoilless rifle | | | 1977 | |
| • 85mm M-1945/D-44 | small number | small number | | |
| • Others | small number | small number | | |

# Air Force

### Order of Battle

| Model | Quantity | In service | Notes |
|---|---|---|---|
| • Combat | 16 | 0 | |
| • Transport | 2 | 0 | |
| • Helicopters | 34 | 16 | |

### Combat Aircraft

| Model | Quantity | In service | Since | Notes |
|---|---|---|---|---|
| **Obsolete** | | | | |
| • Mirage III BL/EL | 10 | 0 | 1963 | Grounded |
| • Hawker Hunter F-70/T-66 | 6 | 0 | 1965 | Some grounded |
| Total | 16 | 0 | | |

## Transport Aircraft

| Model | Quantity | In service | Since | Notes |
|---|---|---|---|---|
| • Falcon 20 | 1 | 0 | 1979 | |
| • Dove | 1 | 0 | | |
| Total | 2 | 0 | | |

## Training and Liaison Aircraft

| Model | Quantity | In service | Since | Notes |
|---|---|---|---|---|
| With ground attack/close air support capability | | | | |
| • CM-170 Fouga Magister | 4 | 0 | 1966 | |
| Others | | | | |
| • BAe SA-3-120/126 Bulldog | 4 | 0 | 1975 | |
| Total | 8 | 0 | | |

## Helicopters

| Model | Number | In service | Since | Notes |
|---|---|---|---|---|
| Attack | | | | |
| • SA-342 Gazelle | 3-4 | 0 | 1980 | In flying condition |
| Medium transport | | | | |
| • AB-212 | 5 | 0 | 1973 | Questionable serviceability |
| • SA-330 Puma (possibly IAR-330) | 5 | 0 | 1980 | |
| • UH-1 (Bell 205) | 16 | 16 | 1995 | |
| Subtotal | 26 | 16 | | |
| Light transport | | | | |
| • Alouette II/III | 6-8 | 0 | 1960 | |
| Total | approx. 34 | 16 | | |
| On order | | | | |
| • UH-1 | 16 - 36 | | | |

## Advanced Armament

| Air-to-air-missiles: | Matra R-530 |
|---|---|

## Air Force Infrastructure

Military airfields:   3
Rayaq, Kleiat, Beirut

# Air Defense Forces

### Surface-to-Air Missiles

| Model | Launchers | Since | Notes |
|---|---|---|---|
| Shoulder-launched missiles | | | |
| • SA-7 (Grail) | small number | | |

### Other Air Defense Systems

| Model | Quantity | In service | Since | Notes |
|---|---|---|---|---|
| Short-range guns | | | | |
| • 40mm M-42 SP | 10-12 | 10-12 | 1968 | Probably in storage |
| • 23mm ZU 23x2 | | | 1981 | |
| • 23mm ZU 23x2 SP | | | 1985 | On M-113 |
| • 20mm | | | 1984 | Probably in storage |
| Total | approx. 75 | approx. 75 | | |

# Navy

### Combat Vessels

| Type | Original class name | Quantity | Length (m.)/ Displacement (t.) | Armament/ special equipment |
|---|---|---|---|---|
| Patrol craft | | | | |
| • Tracker II class | | 0 | 19.3/31 | 2 x 23mm guns 2 Unserviceable |
| • Attacker | | 7 | 20/38 | 2 x 23mm guns |
| • Aztec class | | 5 | 9/5.2 | |
| • Fairey Marine small patrol craft | | 27 | 8.2/6 | |
| Total | | 39 | | |

### Landing Craft

| Type | Original class name | Quantity | Length (m.)/ Displacement (t.) | Armament/ special equipment |
|---|---|---|---|---|
| • EDIC class LCT | | 2 | 59/670 | 33 Troops 8 APCs 1x 81mm MRL 2x 20mm guns 2x 12.7mm MGs |

## Naval Infrastructure

**Naval bases:**         5
Beirut, Junieh, Sidon, Tripoli, Tyre
**Ship maintenance and repair facilities**
55-meter slipway for light craft repairs in Junieh

# Non-governmental Para-military Forces

## Personnel

|                                      | Active    | Reserves        |
| ------------------------------------ | --------- | --------------- |
| • Hizbullah                          | 600 - 800 | 3,000 - 5,000   |
| • Popular Liberation Army (Druze)    |           | 10,000          |
| • Lebanese Forces                    |           |                 |
| • Amal                               |           | 10,000          |
| • Army of South Lebanon (SLA)        | 2,600     |                 |

## Equipment

| Organiztion | Category | System | Number | Notes |
| ----------- | -------- | ------ | ------ | ----- |
| Army of South Lebanon | | | | |
| | Tanks | • Sherman & T-54 | 45 | |
| | APCs | • M-113 | few | |
| | MRLs | • 107mm | | |
| | Artillery guns | • 155mm (SP) | | |
| | | • 130mm | | |
| | Mortars | • 120mm | | |
| | Air defense | • SA-7 | | |
| | | • ZU 23x2 | scores | |

## Equipment *(continued)*

| Organiztion | Category | System | Number | Notes |
|---|---|---|---|---|
| Hizbullah | | | | |
| | APCs | • M-113 | several | |
| | Aircraft | • Ultra-light aircraft | | |
| | Air defense | • SA-7 | | |
| | | • Stinger | | |
| | | • 23mm | | |
| | | • 57mm | | |
| | ATGMs | • AT-3 Sagger | | |
| | | • AT-4 Fagot | | |
| | | • TOW | | |
| | Mortars | • 120mm | | |
| | | • 81mm | | |
| | Artillery guns | • 106mm | | |
| | MRLs | • 240mm | | |
| | | • 122mm BM-21 | | |

# 10. LIBYA

## General Data

**Official Name of the State:** The Great Socialist People's Libyan Arab Jamahiriya (Jamahiriya is an Arabic term meaning "public" or "polity of the masses")

**Head of State:** Colonel Muammar al-Qaddafi (leader, does not hold any other title; in practice also in charge of the Defense Ministry and Commander-in-Chief of the Armed Forces)

**Prime Minister:** Mohammad Ahmad al Manqush (official title: Secretary-General of the General People's Committee)

**Commander-in-Chief of the Armed Forces:** Colonel Abu-Bakr Yunis Jaber

**Inspector General of the Armed Forces:** Colonel Mustapha al-Kharrubi

**Commander of the Air Force and Air Defense Forces:** Brigadier General Ali Riffi al-Sharif

**Area:** 1,759,540 sq. km
**Population:** 5,560,000

## Demography

| | | |
|---|---|---|
| *Ethnic groups* | | |
| Arabs and Berbers | 5,393,000 | 97.0% |
| Others: | | |
| Greeks, Maltese, Italians, | | |
| Egyptians, Pakistanis, Indians, | | |
| Tunisians, Turks | 167,000 | 3.0% |
| *Religious groups* | | |
| Sunni Muslims | 5,393,000 | 97.0% |
| Christians and others | 167,000 | 3.0% |

## Economic data

| | | 1993 | 1994 | 1995 | 1996 | 1997 |
|---|---|---|---|---|---|---|
| GDP current price, local currency | LD bn | 9.5 | 9.2 | 10.7 | 8.4 | 8.6 |
| GDP (US $) | $ bn | 31.147 | 28.660 | 30.924 | 23.204 | 22.513 |
| GDP per capita | $ | 6,627 | 5,848 | 6,051 | 4,353 | 4,049 |
| Real GDP growth | % | -4.6 | -4.5 | 2.0 | 1.1 | 0.5 |
| **Balance of payments** | | | | | | |
| • Exports fob | $ bn | 8.59 | 7.79 | 8.47 | 10.03 | 9.32 |
| • Imports fob | $ bn | 8.48 | 7.36 | 6.21 | 6.96 | 6.75 |

## Economic data *(continued)*

|  |  | 1993 | 1994 | 1995 | 1996 | 1997 |
|---|---|---|---|---|---|---|
| • Account balance (including services and income) | $ bn | -1.373 | -1.412 | 0.173 | 0.861 | -0.235 |
| • External debt | $ bn | NA | NA | NA | 3.768 | 3.363 |
| **Government income and expenditure** |  |  |  |  |  |  |
| • Revenue, local currency | LD bn | NA | NA | 4.59 | 4.51 | 5.38 |
| • Expenditure, local currency | LD bn | NA | NA | 5.27 | 4.51 | 5.38 |
| • Defense expenditure | LD bn | 0.468 | 0.433 | NA | NA | NA |
| • Defense expenditure/GDP | % | 6.51 | 6.31 | NA | NA | NA |
| • Defense expenditure/CGE | % | NA | NA | NA | NA | NA |
| • Population | m | 4.70 | 4.90 | 5.11 | 5.33 | 5.56 |
| • Official exchange rate | LD: $1 | 0.305 | 0.321 | 0.346 | 0.362 | 0.382 |

*Sources:* EIU quarterly report, EIU country profile, IMF statistical yearbook, SIPRI Yearbook

## Arms Procurement and Security Assistance Received

| Country | Type | Details |
|---|---|---|
| North Korea | • Arms transfers | Alleged sale of SSMs |
| PRC | • Arms transfers | Alleged sale of SSM technology |
| Ukraine | • Arms transfers | Alleged sale of SSMs |

*Note:* foreign advisers/instructors/serving personnel --300-500 on individual contracts.

## Arms Sales and Security Assistance Extended

| Country | Type | Details |
|---|---|---|
| Niger | • Arms transfers | Antonov cargo aircraft |

## Defense Production

|  | M | P | A |
|---|---|---|---|
| **Army equipment** |  |  |  |
| • Toxic chemical agent | √ |  |  |
| • Plans to upgrade SSMs, with assistance by foreign experts, and efforts to produce an indigenous SSM, al-Fatah, not yet operational | √ |  |  |

## Defense Production

| | M | P | A |
|---|---|---|---|
| • Tank upgrading facility, with assistance of Czech Republic | | √ | |

*Note:*  M - manufacture (indigenously developed)
P - production under license
A - assembly

## Weapons of Mass Destruction

### Nuclear capabilities
• Basic R&D; a 5 MW Soviet-made research reactor at Tadjoura

### CW capabilities
• Personal protective equipment; Soviet type decontamination units; ABC protection of SSM sites; stockpile of chemical agents (mustard)

### Biological warfare capabilities
• Toxins and other biological weapons (unconfirmed)

### Surface-to-Surface Missiles and Rockets

| Model | Launchers | Missiles | Since | Notes |
|---|---|---|---|---|
| • FROG-7 | 48 | | | |
| • SS-1 (Scud B) | 80 | 500 | 1976 | |
| Total | **128** | | | |

### On order
• Scud C (possibly delivered)

# Armed Forces

**Major Changes:** No major change has been recorded in the Libyan armed forces in 1998.

## Order of Battle

| Year | 1994 | 1995 | 1996 | 1997 | 1998 |
|---|---|---|---|---|---|
| **General data** | | | | | |
| • Personnel | 110,000 | 76,000 | 76,000 | 76,000 | 76,000 |
| • Number of brigades | 17 | + | + | 5 | 1 |
| • Number of battalions | + | + | + | 46 | 46 |
| **Ground Forces** | | | | | |
| • Tanks | 2,660-2,760 | 2,700 | 2,700 | 950 (2,700) | 600-700 (2,210) |

## Order of Battle *(continued)*

| Year | 1994 | 1995 | 1996 | 1997 | 1998 |
|---|---|---|---|---|---|
| • APCs/AFVs | 3,000 | 3,000 | 3,000 | 2,750 | 2,720-2,770 |
| | | | | (2,970) | (2,970) |
| • Artillery | 2,600 - | 2,600 - | 2,600 - | 2,245 | 2,220 |
| (including MRLs) | 3,000 | 3,000 | 3,000 | (2,325) | (2,300) |
| • SSM launchers | 110 | 110 | 110 | 110 | 128 |
| **Air Force** | | | | | |
| • Combat aircraft | 528-533 | 483 | 483 | 361-376 | 351-366 |
| | | | | (478-483) | (443) |
| • Transport aircraft | 141 | 106 | 106 | 85 (90) | 85 (90) |
| • Helicopters | 204 | 210 | 210 | 164 (212) | 127 (204) |
| **Air Defense Forces** | | | | | |
| • Heavy SAM batteries | 99 | 90 | 90 | 25-31 | 25-31 |
| • Medium SAM batteries | 35 | 35 | 35 | 6+ | 6+ |
| • Light SAM launchers | 70 | 55 | 55 | 55 | 55 |
| **Navy** | | | | | |
| • Submarines | 6 | 6 | 6 | 4 | 0 |
| • Combat vessels | 43 | 43 | 43 | 34 | 34 |
| • Patrol craft | 9 | 9 | 9 | 2 | 2 |

*Note:* Beginning with data for 1997, we refer to quantities in active service. The numbers in parentheses refer to the total. The numbers of brigades, SSM launchers and tanks have been changed, due to changes in estimates.

## Personnel

| | Regular | Reserves | Total |
|---|---|---|---|
| Ground Forces | 50,000 | | 50,000 |
| Air Force and Air Defense | 18,000 | | 18,000 |
| Navy | 8,000 | | 8,000 |
| **Total** | **76,000** | | **76,000** |
| **Paramilitary** | | | |
| • Coast Guard | | | Included in navy |
| • People's Militia | | 40,000 | 40,000 |
| • Revolutionary Guards | | | |
| (part of the People's Militia) | 3,000 | | 3,000 |
| • Islamic Pan African Legion | | | |
| (part of the People's Militia) | 2,500 | | 2,500 |

# Ground Forces

## Formations

|  | Independent brigade/group | Independent battalion |
|---|---|---|
| Presidential Security Force | 1 | |
| Armored | | 10 |
| Mechanized/Infantry | | 21 |
| Artillery | | 22 |
| Paratroops | | 15 |
| Air Defense | | 8 |
| SSM | 5 | |
| Total | 6 | 76 |

## Tanks

| Model | Quantity | In service | Since | Notes |
|---|---|---|---|---|
| **MBTs** | | | | |
| **High Quality** | | | | |
| • T-72/T-72M | 360 | 150 | 1979 | |
| **Medium and low quality** | | | | |
| • T-62 | 600 | | | |
| • T-55 | 1,250 | | 1974 | |
| Subtotal | 1,850 | 450-550 | | |
| **Total** | **2,210** | **600-700** | | |

## APCs/AFVs

| Model | Quantity | In service | Since | Notes |
|---|---|---|---|---|
| **APC** | | | | |
| • BTR-50/60 | 750 | 750 | 1970 | |
| • Engesa EE-9/11 | 300 | 200 | 1977 | |
| • M-113 A1 | 50 | 0-50 | 1972 | |
| • OT-62/OT-64 | 200 | 100 | 1975 | |
| • Oto-Breda 6614/6616 | 400 | 400 | | |
| Subtotal | 1,700 | 1,450 - 1,500 | | |
| **IFV** | | | | |
| • BMP-1/BMP-2 | 1,050 | 1,050 | 1972 | |
| **Reconnaissance** | | | | |
| • BRDM-2 | 220 | 220 | | |
| • Oto-Breda 6616 | | | 1980 | Listed under APCs |
| • Engesa EE-9 | | | 1975 | Listed under APCs |
| **Total** | **2,970** | **2,720 - 2,770** | | |

## Artillery

| Model | Quantity | In service | Since | Notes |
|---|---|---|---|---|
| **Self-propelled guns and howitzers** | | | | |
| • 155mm M-109 | 20 | 0 | 1973 | |
| • 155mm Palmaria | 160 | 160 | 1983 | |
| • 152mm M-1973 | 60 | 60 | 1982 | |
| • 152mm ZTS Dana | 80 | 80 | 1986 | |
| • 122mm M-1974 | 130 | 130 | 1980 | |
| Subtotal | 450 | 430 | | |
| **Towed guns and howitzers** | | | | |
| • 130mm M-46 gun | 330 | 330 | 1978 | |
| • 122mm D-30 | 245 | 245 | | |
| • 122mm M-1974 | 60 | 60 | | |
| • 105mm M-101 | 60 | 0 | 1970 | |
| Subtotal | 695 | 635 | | |
| **Mortars, over 160mm** | | | | |
| • 240mm | 120 | 120 | | |
| • 160mm | 24 | 24 | | |
| Subtotal | 144 | 144 | | |
| **Mortars, under 160mm** | | | | |
| • 120mm | 48 | 48 | | |
| • 107mm | 64 | 64 | | |
| Subtotal | 112 | 112 | | |
| **MRLs** | | | | |
| • 140mm | | | | |
| • 130mm M-51 | | | 1980 | |
| • 122mm BM-21/ RM-70/BM-11 | 600 | 600 | 1980 | |
| • 107mm Type 63 | 300 | 300 | 1979 | |
| Subtotal | 900 | 900 | | |
| **Total** | **2,300** | **2,220** | | Partly in storage |

## Anti-tank Weapons

| Model | Quantity | In service | Since | Notes |
|---|---|---|---|---|
| **Missiles** | | | | |
| • AT-3 (Sagger) | 620 | 620 | 1977 | |
| • AT-4 (Spigot) | + | + | 1990 | |
| • AT-5 (Spandrel) | + | + | | |
| • BRDM-2 carrying AT-3 (Sagger) SP | 40 | 40 | | |
| • Milan | 400 | 400 | 1981 | |
| Total | **3,000** | **3,000** | | Partly in storage |

## Anti-tank Weapons *(continued)*

| Model | Quantity | In service | Since | Notes |
|---|---|---|---|---|
| **Guns** | | | | |
| • 106mm recoilless rifle | 220 | 220 | | |
| • 84mm Carl Gustav | 400 | 400 | | |

# Air Force

## Order of Battle

| Model | Quantity | In service | Notes |
|---|---|---|---|
| • Combat | 443 | 351-366 | |
| • Transport | 90 | 85 | |
| • Helicopters | 204 | 127 | |

## Combat Aircraft

| Model | Quantity | In service | Since | Notes |
|---|---|---|---|---|
| **Interceptors** | | | | |
| • MiG-25 and MiG-25R (Foxbat) | 80 | 65-70 | 1980 | |
| • MiG-23 (Flogger G) | 170 | 120-130 | 1976 | |
| Subtotal | 250 | 185-200 | | |
| **Multi-role** | | | | |
| • Mirage F-1 | 30 | 30 | 1979 | |
| **Ground attack** | | | | |
| • Su-24 (Fencer C) | 6 | 6 | 1989 | |
| • Su-20/22 (Fitter C) | 40 | 40 | | |
| • MiG-23/27 (Flogger) | | | | Number included in interceptors |
| Subtotal | 46 | 46 | | |
| **Bombers** | | | | |
| • Tu-22 (Blinder) | 7 | 5 | 1974 | |
| **Obsolete** | | | | |
| • MiG-21 bis (Fishbed) | 70 | 45 | | |
| • Mirage 5 | 40 | 40 | 1971 | |
| Subtotal | 110 | 85 | | |
| **Total** | **443** | **351-366** | | |

## Transport Aircraft

| Model | Quantity | In service | Since | Notes |
|---|---|---|---|---|
| • An-26 (Curl) | 15 | 10 | 1983 | |
| • C-130H Hercules/ | | | | |
| L-100-20/L-100-30 | 10 | 10 | 1970 | |
| • C-140 Jetstar | 1 | 1 | | |
| • Fokker F-27-600/F-27-400 | 9 | 9 | 1981 | |
| • G-222L | 19 | 19 | 1980 | |
| • IL-76 (Candid) | 19 | 19 | 1979 | Including about 4 tankers |
| • IL-78 | | | | Tanker, unconfirmed |
| • L-410 UVP | 15 | 15 | | |
| • Mystère-Falcon 20/50 | 2 | 2 | 1981 | |
| Total | 90 | 85 | | |

## Training and Liaison Aircraft

| Model | Quantity | In service | Since | Notes |
|---|---|---|---|---|
| With ground attack/close air support capability | | | | |
| • G-2AE Galeb/ | | | | |
| J-1E Jastreb | 120 | 80 | 1975 | |
| • L-39 Albatross | 177 | 110 | 1978 | |
| Subtotal | 297 | 190 | | |
| Others | | | | |
| • SIAI--Marchetti | | | | |
| SF-260 M/L/W | 70 | 20 | 1977 | |
| • Fouga Magister | 12 | 0 | 1971 | |
| Subtotal | 82 | 20 | | |
| Total | 379 | 210 | | |

## Helicopters

| Model | Quantity | In service | Since | Notes |
|---|---|---|---|---|
| Attack | | | | |
| • Mi-24/Mi-25 | 56 | 30 | 1978 | Hind, number unconfirmed |
| • Mi-35 | 13 | 13 | 1990 | |
| Subtotal | 69 | 43 | | |
| Heavy transport | | | | |
| • CH-47C Chinook | 15 | 15 | 1976 | |

## Helicopters *(continued)*

| Model | Quantity | In service | Since | Notes |
|---|---|---|---|---|
| **Medium transport** | | | | |
| • AB-212/205 | 2 | 2 | 1974 | |
| • Mi-8/Mi-17 (Hip) | 25 | 25 | 1975 | |
| • SA-321 Super Frelon | 10 | 10 | 1971 | Also employed in naval combat role |
| Subtotal | 37 | 37 | | |
| **Light transport** | | | | |
| • Alouette III | 14 | 14 | 1971 | Possibly with police |
| • Mi-2 (Hoplite) | 35 | 0 | | |
| • AB-206 | 4 | 4 | 1970 | |
| • A-109 | 2 | 2 | | |
| Subtotal | 55 | 20 | | |
| **Naval combat** | | | | |
| • Mi-14 (Haze) | 28 | 12 | 1983 | |
| **Total** | **204** | **127** | | |

## Advanced Armament

**Air-to-air-missiles**
• AA-2 (Atoll), AA-6 (Acrid), AA-7 (Apex), AA-8 (Aphid), AA-11 (Archer), R-530, R-550 Magic, Super 530D/F

**Air-to-ground missiles**
• AS-9 (Kyle), AS-10 (Karen), AS-14 (Kedge), AT-2 (Swatter), AT-6 (Spiral) (unconfirmed)

## Air Force Infrastructure

**Military airfields:** 16
al-Adem (Tobruk), Benghazi (Baninah), Beni Walid, al-Bumbah, Ghurdabiyah (Surt), Jufra, Kufra, Maatan al-Sarra, Misratha, Ouqba ben Nafi (Al-Watiya), Sabhah, Tripoli International (Idriss), Umm al-Tika, 3 additional

# Air Defense Forces

## Surface-to-Air Missiles

| Model | Batteries | Launchers | Since | Notes |
|---|---|---|---|---|
| **Heavy missiles** | | | | Some in storage |
| • SA-2 (Guideline) | 15-18 | 90-108 | | |
| • SA-3 (Goa) | 6-9 | 24-36 | | |

### Surface-to-Air Missiles *(continued)*

| Model | Batteries | Launchers | Since | Notes |
|---|---|---|---|---|
| • SA-5 (Gammon) | 4 | 48 | 1985 | |
| Total | **25-31** | **162-192** | | |
| **Medium missiles** | | | | Serviceability not clear |
| • Crotale | | 10 | 1974 | |
| • SA-6 (Gainful) | 6 | 24 | 1975 | |
| • SA-8 (Gecko) | + | 20 | | |
| Total | **6+** | **54** | | |
| **Light missiles** | | | | |
| • SA-9 (Gaskin)/ | | 55 | | |
| SA-13 (Gopher) | | | | |
| **Shoulder-launched missiles** | | | | |
| • SA-7 (Grail) | | 400 | 1979 | |
| • SA-14 (Gremlin) | | + | | |
| Total | | **400** | | |

### Other Air Defense Systems

| Model | Quantity | In service | Since | Notes |
|---|---|---|---|---|
| **Short-range guns** | | | | |
| • 57mm S-60 | 90 | 90 | | |
| • 40mm Bofors L-70 | 50 | 0 | | Possibly phased out |
| • 30mm 30x2 M-53/59 SP | 240 | 0 | | In storage |
| • 23mm ZSU 23x4 SP (Shilka) | 250 | 250 | | |
| • 23mm ZU 23x2 | 100 | 100 | | |
| Total | **730** | **440** | | |

# Navy

### Combat Vessels

| Type | Original class name | Quantity | Length (m.)/ Displacement (t.) | Armament/ special equipment |
|---|---|---|---|---|
| **Submarines** | | | | |
| • F class (Foxtrot) | Type 641 | 0 | 91/2,475 | 10 x 533mm torpedoes 44 mines 4 non-operational submarines |
| Total | | **0** | | |

## Combat Vessels *(continued)*

| Type | Original class name | Quantity | Length (m.)/ Displacement (t.) | Armament/ special equipment |
|------|---------------------|----------|-------------------------------|------------------------------|
| **Missile frigates** | | | | |
| • Koni | Type 1159 | 2 | 96.4/1,440 | 4 x SS-N-2C Styx SSMs<br>2 x SA-N-4 SAMs<br>4 x 76mm guns<br>4 x 30mm guns<br>4 x 406mm torpedoes<br>1 x RBU 6000<br>A/S mortar<br>20 mines |
| **Missile corvettes** | | | | |
| • Nanuchka class | | 3 | 59.3/660 | 4 x SS-N-2C Styx SSMs<br>2 x SA-N-4 SAMs<br>2 x 57mm guns |
| **MFPBs** | | | | |
| • Combattante II | | 9 | 49.0/311 | 4 x Otomat SSMs<br>1 x 76mm gun<br>2 x 40mm guns<br>questionable operability |
| • Ossa II | | 12 | 38.6/245 | 4 x SS-N-2C Styx SSMs<br>4 x 30mm guns |
| Subtotal | | 21 | | |
| **Mine warfare vessels** | | | | |
| • Natya class minesweepers | Type 266ME | 8 | 61.0/804 | 4 x 30mm guns<br>4 x 25mm guns<br>2 x RBU 1200 A/S mortars<br>10 mines<br>Acoustic and Magnetic sweep |
| Total | | 34 | | |
| **Patrol craft**<br>(mostly with Coast Guard) | | | | |
| • Poluchat | | 1 | 29.6/70 | 2 x 14.5mm MGs<br>used for torpedo recovery |
| • Thornycroft | | 1 | 23.5m | |
| Total | | 2 | | |

## Landing Craft

| Type | Original class name | Quantity | Length (m.)/ Displacement (t.) | Armament/ special equipment |
|---|---|---|---|---|
| • Turkish type | | 3 | 56.0/280 | 100 troops; 350 tons |
| • PS-700 class LST | | 2 | 99.5/2,800 | 240 troops; 11 tanks; 6 x 40mm guns helicopter platform |
| • Polnochny class LCT | Type 773U | 3 | 83.9/1,305 | 4 x 30mm guns 2 x 140mm MRLs 100 mines |
| Total | | 8 | | |

## Auxiliary Vessels

| Type | Original class name | Quantity | Length (m.)/ Displacement (t.) | Armament/ special equipment |
|---|---|---|---|---|
| • Vosper (Tobruk) | | 1 | 54.0/500 | 1 x 102mm gun 2 x 40mm guns used for training |
| • Maintenance and repair craft | LSD type | 1 | 98.8/2,200 | 2 x 40mm guns |
| • Yelva | | 1 | 40.9/300 | Diving-support ship |
| • Spasilac class | | 1 | 55.5/1,590 | Yugoslav salvage ship 4 x 12.7mm MGs |
| • Transporters (Ro-Ro) | | 10 | 166.5/2,412 | |

## Coastal Defense

| Type | Quantity | Notes |
|---|---|---|
| • SS-2C Styx | | In 3 sites |

## Naval Infrastructure

Naval bases:    6
- al-Khums, Benghazi, Misratah, Tobruk, Tripoli, Derna

### Ship maintenance and repair facilities
- Facilities at Tripoli with foreign technicians for repair of vessels of up to 6,000dwt; a 3,200-ton lift floating dock; floating docks at Benghazi and Tobruk

# 11. MOROCCO

## General Data

**Official Name of the State:** Kingdom of Morocco
**Head of State:** King Mohammed VI (also Minister of Defense,
    Commander-in-Chief of the Armed Forces and Chief of the General Staff)
**Prime Minister:** Abd al-Rahmane Youssoufi
**Inspector General of the Armed Forces:** General Abd al-Kader Loubarisi
**Commander of the Air Force:** Ali Abd al-Aziz al-Omrani
**Commander of the Navy:** Captain Muhammad al-Tariqi

**Area:** 622,012 sq. km., including the former Spanish Sahara (409,200 sq. km.
    excluding this territory)
**Population:** 28,100,000

## Demography

| | | |
|---|---|---|
| *Ethnic groups* | | |
| Arabs | 16,747,000 | 59.6% |
| Berbers | 11,100,000 | 39.5% |
| Europeans and others | 253,000 | 0.9% |
| *Religious groups* | | |
| Sunni Muslims | 27,734,000 | 98.7% |
| Christians | 310,000 | 1.1% |
| Jews | 56,000 | 0.2% |

## Economic Data

| | | 1993 | 1994 | 1995 | 1996 | 1997 |
|---|---|---|---|---|---|---|
| GDP current price, local currency | Dh bn | 249.8 | 279.3 | 281.7 | 319.6 | 319.3 |
| GDP (US $) | $ bn | 26.86 | 30.36 | 32.98 | 36.66 | 33.52 |
| GDP per capita | $ bn | 1,029 | 1,141 | 1,217 | 1,328 | 1,193 |
| Real GDP growth | % | -1 | 11.1 | -6.3 | 11.5 | -2.2 |
| **Balance of payments** | | | | | | |
| • Exports fob | $ bn | 4.936 | 4.00 | 6.87 | 6.885 | 7.039 |
| • Imports fob | $ bn | 7.16 | 7.185 | 10.011 | 9.708 | 9.521 |
| • Account balance (including services and income) | $ bn | -0.52 | -0.724 | -1.187 | 0.035 | -0.088 |
| • External debt | $ bn | 20.7 | 21.6 | 23.0 | 21.8 | 21.2 |

## Economic Data *(continued)*

|  |  | 1993 | 1994 | 1995 | 1996 | 1997 |
|---|---|---|---|---|---|---|
| **Government income and expenditure** | | | | | | |
| • Revenue, local currency | Dh bn | 91.2 | 105.37 | 106.21 | 107.7 | 114.3 |
| • Expenditure, local currency | Dh bn | 95.06 | 110.65 | 109.81 | 117.2 | 126.7 |
| • Defense expenditure | Dh bn | 11.64 | 12.565 | 12.246 | 12.350 | NA |
| • Defense expenditure/GDP | % | 4.65 | 4.5 | 4.35 | 3.86 | NA |
| • Defense expenditure/CGE | % | 12.2 | 11.35 | 11.15 | 10.5 | NA |
| • Population | m | 26.1 | 26.6 | 27.1 | 27.6 | 28.1 |
| • Official exchange rate | Dh: $1 | 9.3 | 9.2 | 8.54 | 8.716 | 9.527 |

*Sources:* EIU quarterly report, EIU country profile, IMF statistical yearbook, SIPRI Yearbook

## Arms Procurement and Security Assistance Received

| Country | Type | Details |
|---|---|---|
| Britain | • Arms transfers | Aircraft (1994) |
| Denmark | • Arms transfers | Patrol craft (1995) |
| France | • Arms transfers | OPV 64 patrol ships (1997) |
| USA | • Arms transfers | Tanks (1994), T-37 aircraft (1996), supply ship (1994) |
|  | • Financial aid | $95 million grant (1993, and a smaller grant in 1994, approx. $34 million) |

## Arms Sales and Security Assistance Extended

| Country | Type | Details |
|---|---|---|
| USA | • Facilities provided | Use of Sidi Slimane, Marrakech and Casablanca airfields in emergencies; permission for space shuttle to land at Marrakech AFB; use of communications center at Kenitra; storage and use of naval facilities at Mohammedia |

## Foreign Military Cooperation

| | Details |
|---|---|
| • Forces deployed abroad | Small contingency force in Bosnia and Croatia (1998) |
| • Joint maneuvers with | France, USA |

## Defense Production

| | M | P | A |
|---|---|---|---|
| **Army equipment** | | | |
| • Small arms ammunition | √ | | |
| • Assembly of trucks | | | √ |
| **Aircraft and air ammunition** | | | |
| • Trainer aircraft, with foreign aid (Portugal) | √ | | |

Note:  M - manufacture (indigenously developed)
P - production under license
A - assembly

# Armed Forces

**Major Changes:** No major change has been recorded in the Moroccan armed forces in 1998.

## Order of Battle

| Year | 1994 | 1995 | 1996 | 1997* | 1998 |
|---|---|---|---|---|---|
| **General data** | | | | | |
| • Personnel | 138,500 | 141,000 | 141,000 | 196,500 | 196,500 |
| • Number of brigades | 12 | 12 | 12 | 7 | 6 |
| • Number of battalions | 23 | 23 | 23 | 64 | 75 |
| **Ground forces** | | | | | |
| • Tanks | 415 | 415 | 415 | 364 | 379 |
| • APCs/AFVs | 1,450 - 1,550 | 1,500 | 1,500 | 1,200 (1,537) | 1,074 (1,374) |
| • Artillery (Incl. MRLs) | 336 | 386 | 386 | 970 (1,020) | 967 (1,017) |
| **Air force** | | | | | |
| • Combat aircraft | 65 | 74 | 74 | 70 | 70 |
| • Transport aircraft | 54 | 48 | 48 | 45 | 43 |
| • Helicopters | 142 | 127 | 127 | 129 | 130 |
| **Air defense forces** | | | | | |
| • Light SAM launchers | 36 | + | + | 37 | 37 |

## Order of Battle *(continued)*

| Year | 1994 | 1995 | 1996 | 1997 | 1998* |
|---|---|---|---|---|---|
| **Navy** | | | | | |
| • Combat vessels | 14 | 14 | 13 | 13 | 13 |
| • Patrol craft | 34 | 32 | 52 | 49 | 48 |

*Note:* Beginning with data for 1997, we refer to quantities in active service. The numbers in parentheses refer to the total.

\* - Change in estimate.

## Personnel

| | Regular | Reserves | Total |
|---|---|---|---|
| Ground forces | 125,000 | 150,000 | 275,000 |
| Air Force | 13,500 | | 13,500 |
| Navy and Marines | 7,000 | | 7,000 |
| **Total** | **145,500** | **150,000** | **295,500** |
| **Paramilitary** | | | |
| • Gendarmerie Royale | 10,000 | | |
| • Force Auxiliere | 25,000 | | |
| • Mobile intervention corps | 5,000 | | |

Note: Customs and Coast Guard are included in Gendarmerie and Navy.

# Ground Forces

## Formations

| | Independent brigade/group | Independent battalion | |
|---|---|---|---|
| Armored | 10 | | |
| Mechanized | 3 | 19 | |
| Infantry | | 35 | |
| Light Security | 1 | | |
| Camel Corps | | 5 | |
| Paratroops | 2 | | |
| Airborne/Commando | | 2+4 | |
| Artillery | | 12 | |
| Air Defense | | 1 | |
| **Total** | **6** | **88** | |

## Tanks

| Model | Quantity | In service | Since | Notes |
|-------|----------|------------|-------|-------|
| **MBTs** | | | | |
| **Medium and low Quality** | | | | |
| • M-60 A1/A3 | 90 | 90 | 1981 | |
| • M-48 A5 | 184 | 184 | 1974 | |
| Subtotal | 274 | 274 | | |
| **Light tanks** | | | | |
| • SK-105 (Kurassier) | 105 | 105 | 1985 | |
| Total | **379** | **379** | | |

## APCs/AFVs

| Model | Quantity | In service | Since | Notes |
|-------|----------|------------|-------|-------|
| **APCs** | | | | |
| • M-113 A1/A2 | 360 | 360 | 1979 | |
| • OT-62 | 150 | 0 | 1968 | |
| • M-3 half-track | 50 | 0 | 1966 | |
| • M-3 (Panhard) | 30 | 30 | 1981 | Unconfirmed |
| • UR-416 | 13 | 13 | 1977 | Additional 42 equipped with Cobra ATGMs (listed under anti-tank) |
| Subtotal | 603 | 403 | | |
| **IFVs** | | | | |
| • Ratel 20/90 | 60 | 60 | 1981 | |
| • VAB -VCI/VTT | 290 | 290 | 1979 | |
| • Engesa EE-11 | | | 1981 | In storage, included with Engesa EE-9 |
| Subtotal | 370 | 370 | | |
| **Reconnaissance** | | | | |
| • AMX-10 R/CM | 110 | 110 | 1981 | |
| • Engesa EE-9 | 50 | 0 | 1981 | In storage |
| • BRDM-2 | 50 | 0 | | In storage, 36 carrying AT-3 |
| • EBR-75 | 16 | 16 | 1956 | |
| • AML-90/AML-60 | 175 | 175 | 1966 | |
| Subtotal | 401 | 301 | | |
| Total | **1,374** | **1,074** | | |

## Artillery

| Model | Quantity | In service | Since | Notes |
|---|---|---|---|---|
| **Self-propelled guns and howitzers** | | | | |
| • 155mm M-109 A1 | 40 | 40 | 1978 | |
| • 155mm Mk F-3 (AMX) | 100 | 100 | 1980 | |
| • 105mm Mk 61 | 5 | 5 | 1963 | |
| Subtotal | 145 | 145 | | |
| **Towed guns and howitzers** | | | | |
| • 155mm M-114 | 20 | 20 | 1976 | |
| • 155mm M-198 | 35 | 35 | | |
| • 155mm FH-70 | 30 | 30 | | |
| • 130mm M-46 | 18 | 18 | 1981 | |
| • 122mm D-30 | 50 | | | |
| • 105mm L-118 light gun | 30 | 30 | 1980 | |
| • 105mm M-1950 | 35 | 35 | 1972 | |
| • 105mm M-101/M-101A1 | 18 | 18 | 1970 | |
| Subtotal | 236 | 186 | | |
| **Mortars, under 160mm** | | | | |
| • 120mm | 600 | 600 | 1972 | 20 SP mounted on VAB |
| **MRLs** | | | | |
| • 122mm BM-21 | 36 | 36 | 1980 | |
| **Total** | **1,017** | **967** | | |

## Anti-tank Weapons

| Model | Quantity | In service | Since | Notes |
|---|---|---|---|---|
| **Missiles** | | | | |
| • BGM-71A TOW | 150 | 150 | 1978 | |
| • Cobra SP | 42 | 42 | | Mounted on UR- 416 |
| • AT-3 (Sagger) SP | 36 | 0 | | Mounted on BRDM-2, in storage |
| • M-47 Dragon | 480 | 480 | 1978 | |
| • Milan | 80 | 80 | 1982 | |
| **Total** | **788** | **750** | | |
| **Guns** | | | | |
| • 106mm M-40 A2 | 350 | 350 | | |
| • 90mm M-56 | 28 | 28 | 1975 | |
| **Total** | **378** | **378** | | |

# Air Force

## Order of Battle

| Model | Quantity | In service |
|---|---|---|
| • Combat | 70 | 70 |
| • Transport | 43 | 43 |
| • Helicopters | 130 | 130 |

## Combat Aircraft

| Model | Quantity | In service | Since | Notes |
|---|---|---|---|---|
| **Multi-role** | | | | |
| • F-5E/F | 20 | 20 | 1981 | |
| • Mirage F-1 | 34 | 34 | 1979 | |
| Subtotal | 54 | 54 | | |
| **Ground attack** | | | | |
| • OV-10 Bronco | 3 | 3 | 1981 | |
| **Obsolete** | | | | |
| • F-5A/B | 13 | 13 | 1967 | |
| Total | 70 | 70 | | |

## Transport Aircraft

| Model | Quantity | In service | Since | Notes |
|---|---|---|---|---|
| • Beechcraft King Air 100 | 5 | 5 | 1975 | |
| • Beechcraft Super King Air 200 | 5 | 5 | 1983 | |
| • Beechcraft Super King Air 300 | 1 | 1 | 1991 | |
| • Boeing 707 | 2 | 2 | 1982 | |
| • C-130H Hercules | 15 | 15 | 1974 | Including 2 with SLAR employed for electronic surveillance and 2 tankers |
| • CN-235 | 7 | 7 | 1990 | |
| • Dornier DO-28 D-2 | 3 | 3 | 1981 | |
| • Gulfstream II/III | 2 | 2 | 1976 | |
| • Mystère-Falcon 50 | 1 | 1 | 1980 | |
| • Mystère- Falcon 20 | 2 | 2 | 1968 | Electronic counter measures |
| Total | 43 | 43 | | |

## Training and Liaison Aircraft

| Model | Quantity | In service | Since | Notes |
|---|---|---|---|---|
| With ground attack/close air support capability | | | | |
| • Cessna 318 (T-37) | 14 | 14 | 1996 | |
| • Alpha jet | 22 | 22 | 1979 | |
| • Beechcraft T-34C | 12 | 10 | 1977 | |
| • CM-170 Fouga Magister | 22 | 22 | 1964 | |
| Subtotal | 70 | 68 | | |
| **Others** | | | | |
| • AS-202/18A Bravo | 10 | 10 | 1978 | |
| • CAP 10/232 | 9 | 9 | 1983 | Aerobatic team |
| Subtotal | 19 | 19 | | |
| Total | 89 | 87 | | |

## Helicopters

| Model | Quantity | In service | Since | Notes |
|---|---|---|---|---|
| **Attack** | | | | |
| • SA-342 Gazelle | 22 | 22 | 1976 | Of which 6 with gendarmerie |
| **Heavy transport** | | | | |
| • CH-47C Chinook | 7 | 7 | 1979 | |
| **Medium transport** | | | | |
| • AB-212 | 5 | 5 | 1973 | |
| • AB-205 | 32 | 32 | 1969 | |
| • AS - 365 Dauphin II | 2 | 2 | 1983 | With gendarmerie |
| • SA-330 Puma | 28 | 28 | 1976 | Of which 6 with gendarmerie |
| Subtotal | 67 | 67 | | |
| **Light transport** | | | | |
| • Alouette II/III | 5 | 5 | | With gendarmerie |
| • AB-206 JetRanger | 26 | 26 | 1975 | |
| • SA-315B Lama | 3 | 3 | | With gendarmerie |
| Subtotal | 34 | 34 | | |
| Total | 130 | 130 | | |

## Miscellaneous Aircraft

| Model | Quantity | In service | Since | Notes |
|-------|----------|------------|-------|-------|
| **Tankers** | | | | |
| • KC-130 | | | | 2 listed under Transport |
| **Standoff ECM** | | | | |
| • Mystère 20F | | | | 2 listed under Transport |
| **Surveillance aircraft** | | | | |
| • C-130H | | | | 2 listed under Transport |
| **UAVs and mini-UAVs** | | | | |
| • Skyeye R4E-50 | | | | |
| **Maritime surveillance aircraft** | | | | |
| • BN-2T Defender | | 7 | 1993 | Possibly fishery protection |

## Advanced Armament

**Air-to-air-missiles**
AIM-9J Sidewinder (320), R-530, R-550 Magic, Super 530D
**Air-to-ground missiles**
AGM-65 Maverick (380), HOT

## Air Force Infrastructure

**Military airfields:** 10
Agadir, Casablanca (Nouasseur), Fez, Kenitra, Larache, L'Ayoun, Marrakech, Meknes, Rabat, Sidi Slimane, + additional

# Air Defense Forces

## Surface-to-Air Missiles

| Model | Batteries | Launchers | Since | Notes |
|-------|-----------|-----------|-------|-------|
| **Light missiles** | | | | |
| • MIM-72A Chaparral | | 37 | 1977 | |
| **Shoulder-launched missiles** | | | | |
| • SA-7 (Grail) | | 70 | 1978 | |

## Other Air Defense Systems

| Model | Quantity | In service | Since | Notes |
|---|---|---|---|---|
| **Short-range guns** | | | | |
| • 37mm M-1939 | 100 | 14 | 1972 | |
| • 23mm ZU 23x2 | 90 | 30 | 1986 | |
| • 20mm M-163 Vulcan SP | 60 | 60 | 1983 | |
| • 20mm M-167 SP | 40 | 40 | | |
| Total | **290** | **144** | | |
| **Radars** | | | | |
| • AN/TPS-43 | | 8 | | |
| • AN/TPS-63 | | 8 | | Upgraded |

# Navy

## Combat Vessels

| Type | Original class name | Quantity | Length (m.)/ Displacement (t.) | Armament/ special equipment |
|---|---|---|---|---|
| **Missile frigates** | | | | |
| • Descubierta | | 1 | 88.8/1,233 | 4 x MM38 Exocet SSMs<br>1 x 8 Aspide SAMs<br>6 x 324mm torpedoes<br>1 x SR 375 ASW mortar<br>1 x 76mm gun<br>1 x 40mm gun |
| **MFPBs** | | | | |
| • Lazaga | | 4 | 58.1/524 | 4 x MM38 Exocet SSMs<br>1 x 76mm gun<br>1 x 40mm gun<br>2 x 20mm guns |
| **Gunboats/MTBs** | | | | |
| • Okba class | PR-72 | 2 | 57.5/375 | 1 x 76mm gun<br>1 x 40mm gun |
| • Cormoran class | P-200D Vigilance | 6 | 58.1/425 | 1 x 40mm gun |
| Subtotal | | 8 | | |
| Total | | **13** | | |

## Combat Vessels *(continued)*

| Type | Original class name | Quantity | Length (m.)/ Displacement (t.) | Armament/ special equipment |
|---|---|---|---|---|
| **Patrol craft** | | | | |
| • El Wacil class | P-32 | 6 | 32/74 | 6 Elwacil class, 4 Erraid class. 4 with customs/ Coast Guard 1 x 20mm gun |
| • Rais Bargech class | OPV 64 | 5 | 64/580 | |
| • Osprey mk II | | 4 | 54.8/475 | 2 x 20mm guns |
| • Arcor 46 | | 18 | 14.5/15 | With customs/ Coast Guard 2 x 12.7mm MGs |
| • Arcor 53 | | 15 | 16/17 | With customs/ Coast Guard 1 x 12.7mm MG |
| **Total** | | 48 | | |
| **On order** | | | | |
| • Floreal frigates | | 2 | 93/ | To be delivered in 2001 |

## Landing Craft

| Type | Original class name | Quantity | Length (m.)/ Displacement (t.) | Armament/ special equipment |
|---|---|---|---|---|
| • Batral LSL | | 3 | 80/750 | 140 troops, 12 vehicles Helicopter pod. 2 x 81mm mortars 4 x 40mm guns |
| • EDIC LCT | | 1 | 59/250 | 11 vehicles 1 x 120mm mortar 2 x 20mm guns |
| • Newport class LST | | 1 | 159.2/8,450 | 400 troops, 500-ton. vehicles 4 x LCVP/LCPL boats 1 x 20mm Phalanx gun |
| **Total** | | 5 | | |
| **On order** | | | | |
| • Batral LSL | | 3 | | |

## Auxiliary Vessels

| Type | Original class name | Quantity | Length (m.)/ Displacement (t.) | Armament/ special equipment |
|---|---|---|---|---|
| • Cargo ship | | 2 | 77/1,500 | 2 x 14.5mm MGs |
| • Transport ship | | 1 | 784 dwt | |
| • Agor survey ship | Robert D. Conrad class | 1 | 67.3/1,370 | |
| • Dakhla support ship | | 1 | 69/800 | |
| • SAR craft | | 3 | 19.4/40 | With Coast Guard |
| Total | | 8 | | |

## Naval Infrastructure

**Naval bases:**          7

Agadir, al-Hoceima, Casablanca, Kenitra, Dakhla, Safi, Tangier

**Ship maintenance and repair facilities:**

156-meter dry-dock at Casablanca, repair ships of up to 10,000 dwt,
   facility for minor repairs at Agadir

# 12. OMAN

## General Data

**Official Name of the State:** Sultanate of Oman
**Head of State:** Sultan Qabus ibn Said (also Prime Minister and
    Minister of Defense)
**Minister of Defense Affairs:** Badr bin Saud bin Harib Al Busaidi
**Chief of General Staff:** General Khamis al-Kalabani
**Commander of the Ground Forces:** Major General Ali ibn
    Rashid al-Kalabani
**Commander of the Air Force:** Major General Mohammad Ibn
    Mahfoodh al Ardhi
**Commander of the Navy:** Rear Admiral Shihab al-Said

**Area:** 212,000 sq. km.
**Population:** 2,260,000 (including 17% aliens)

## Demography

| | | |
|---|---|---|
| *Ethnic groups* | | |
| Arabs | 2,048,000 | 90.6% |
| Others (Africans, Persians, | | |
| Southeast Asians) | 212,000 | 9.4% |
| *Religious groups* | | |
| Ibadi Muslims | 1,695,000 | 75.0% |
| Sunni Muslims | 425,000 | 18.8% |
| Shi'ite Muslims, Hindus | 140,000 | 6.2% |

## Economic data

| | | 1993 | 1994 | 1995 | 1996 | 1997 |
|---|---|---|---|---|---|---|
| GDP current price, local currency | OR bn | 4.804 | 4.967 | 5.307 | 5.874 | 6.075 |
| GDP (US $) | $ bn | 12.478 | 12.901 | 13.784 | 15.257 | 15.779 |
| GDP per capita | $ | 6,177 | 6,293 | 6,441 | 6,903 | 6,981 |
| Real GDP growth | % | 6.1 | 3.8 | 4.8 | 2.9 | 2.0 |
| **Balance of payments** | | | | | | |
| • Exports fob | $ bn | 5.370 | 5.540 | 6.070 | 7.340 | 7.630 |
| • Imports fob | $ bn | 4.030 | 3.690 | 4.050 | 4.390 | 4.650 |
| • Account balance (including services and income) | $ bn | -1.190 | -0.805 | -0.801 | -0.180 | -0.057 |
| • External debt | $ bn | 2.657 | 3.085 | 3.181 | 3.415 | 3.443 |

## Economic data *(continued)*

|  |  | 1993 | 1994 | 1995 | 1996 | 1997 |
|---|---|---|---|---|---|---|
| **Government income and expenditure** | | | | | | |
| • Revenue, local currency | OR bn | 1.723 | 1.757 | 1.851 | 1.990 | 2.270 |
| • Expenditure, local currency | OR bn | 2.242 | 2.252 | 2.331 | 2.253 | 2.292 |
| • Defense expenditure | OR bn | 0.738 | 0.779 | 0.776 | 0.737 | 0.698 |
| • Defense expenditure/GDP | % | 15.36 | 15.68 | 14.62 | 12.54 | 11.48 |
| • Defense expenditure/CGE | % | 32.91 | 34.59 | 33.29 | 32.71 | 30.45 |
| • Population | m | 2.02 | 2.09 | 2.16 | 2.21 | 2.26 |
| • Official exchange rate | OR:$1 | 0.385 | 0.385 | 0.385 | 0.385 | 0.385 |

*Sources:* EIU quarterly report, EIU country profile, IMF statistical yearbook, SIPRI Yearbook

## Arms Procurement and Security Assistance Received

| Country | Type | Details |
|---|---|---|
| Britain | • Arms transfers | Tanks, Swiss-model MOWAG Piranha APCs (1998), combat aircraft, training aircraft, aircraft radars and navigation systems, upgrade kits for Rapier SAMs, missile corvettes (1997), upgrading Jaguar aircraft |
| France | • Arms transfers | ATGMs, AAMs, naval SSMs, fire control radar, patrol craft (1995) |
| Netherlands | • Arms transfers | Surveillance radar, fire control radar |
| Pakistan | • Arms transfers | Light trainer a/c |
| South Africa | • Arms transfers | Artillery |
| Switzerland | • Arms transfers | AA artillery, fire control radar |
| USA | • Arms transfers | AT guided missiles, AAMs, tanks, SP artillery, a missile frigate |
|  | • Military training | Foreign advisors/instructors/ serving personnel |

## Arms Sales and Security Assistance Extended

| Country | Type | Details |
|---------|------|---------|
| Britain | • Facilities | Use of airfields |
| USA | • Facilities | Airfields at Masira, Seeb, al-Khasb, Thamarit; storage facilities and prepositioning of US Army and Air Force support equipment; naval facilities at Masira and Ghanam Peninsula; communications center |

## Foreign Military Cooperation

| | Details |
|---|---------|
| • Joint maneuvers | Britain, Egypt, GCC countries, USA |
| • Security agreement | USA |

# Armed forces

**Major changes:** The Omani forces are assimilating the new Challenger II MBTs and the Piranha APCs acquired since late 1995. The Omani navy is in the process of deploying its new Qahir class corvettes. No major changes recorded in 1998.

## Order of Battle

| Year | 1994 | 1995 | 1996 | 1997 | 1998 |
|------|------|------|------|------|------|
| **General data** | | | | | |
| • Personnel (regular) | 28,500 | 29,600 | 29,600 | 34,000 | 34,000 |
| • Number of brigades | 3 | 4 | 4 | 4 | 4 |
| • Number of independent battalions | 18 | 22 | 22 | 18 | 18 |
| **Ground forces** | | | | | |
| • Tanks | 106 | 106 | 156 | 178 | 131 (181) |
| • APCs/AFVs | 62 | 62 | 142 | 135 (166) | 135 (166) |
| • Artillery | 153 | 177 | 177 | 148 (154) | 148 (154) |
| **Air force** | | | | | |
| • Combat aircraft | 37 | 37 | 37 | 31 (47) | 31 (47) |
| • Transport aircraft | 44 | 44 | 44 | 38 (42) | 38 (42) |
| • Helicopters | 37 | 37 | 37 | 37 | 37 |
| **Air defense forces** | | | | | |
| • Light SAM launchers | 52 | 54 | 54 | 58 | 58 |

## Order of Battle *(continued)*

| Year | 1994 | 1995 | 1996 | 1997 | 1998 |
|---|---|---|---|---|---|
| **Navy** | | | | | |
| • Combat vessels | 8 | 8 | 14 | 9 | 9 |
| • Patrol craft | 18 | 18 | 18 | 23 | 23 |

*Note:* Beginning with data for 1997, we refer to quantities in active service. The numbers in parentheses refer to the total.

## Personnel

| | Regular | Reserves | Total |
|---|---|---|---|
| Ground Forces | 25,000 | | 25,000 |
| Air Force | 5,000 | | 5,000 |
| Navy | 4,000 | | 4,000 |
| **Total** | **34,000** | | **34,000** |
| **Paramilitary** | | | |
| • Tribal force (Firqat) | 3,500 | | 3,500 |
| • Police/border police (operating aircraft, helicopters and PBs) | | | 7,000 |
| • Royal Household (including Royal Guard, Royal Yachts and Royal Flight) | | | 6,500 |

# Ground Forces

## Formations

| | Independent brigade/group | Independent battalion/regiment |
|---|---|---|
| Royal guard | 1HQ | |
| Armored | 1 HQ | 2+1 royal guard |
| Infantry (partly mechanized) | 2HQ | 8+2 royal guard |
| Reconnaissance | | 2 (1 inf. + 1 armd.) |
| Paratroops/ Special forces | | 1 + 2 royal guard |
| Artillery | | 4 |
| Air Defense | | 1 |
| **Total** | **4** | **23** |

## Tanks

| Model | Quantity | In service | Since | Notes |
|---|---|---|---|---|
| **MBTs** | | | | |
| **High Quality** | | | | |
| • Challenger 2 | 18 | 18 | 1995 | |
| **Medium and low quality** | | | | |
| • M-60 A3 | 93 | 43 | 1990 | |
| • M-60 A1 | 6 | 6 | 1980 | |
| • Chieftain | 27 | 27 | 1982 | |
| • Scorpion | 37 | 37 | 1980 | |
| Subtotal | 163 | 113 | | |
| Total | **181** | **131** | | |
| **On order** | | | | |
| • Challenger 2 | 18 | | | Option for 18 more |

## APCs/AFVs

| Model | Quantity | In service | Since | Notes |
|---|---|---|---|---|
| **APCs** | | | | |
| • GKN-Defense Piranha | 80 | 80 | 1995 | |
| • BTR-80 | small number | small number | 1994 | |
| • AT-105 Saxon | 15 | 15 | 1986 | |
| • Fahd | 31 | + | | Unconfirmed |
| • VAB | 14 | 14 | 1986 | Number unconfirmed |
| Subtotal | 140 | 109 | | |
| **IFVs** | | | | |
| • V-150 Commando | 20 | 20 | 1982 | |
| **Reconnaissance** | | | | |
| • VBC-90 | 6 | 6 | 1986 | |
| Total | **166** | **135** | | |
| **On order** | | | | |
| • Option for 46 more Piranha 8 x 8 | | | | |

## Artillery

| Model | Quantity | In service | Since | Notes |
|---|---|---|---|---|
| **Self-propelled guns and howitzers** | | | | |
| • 155mm M-109 A2 | 15 | 15 | 1986 | |
| • 155mm G-6 | 24 | 24 | 1995 | |
| Subtotal | 39 | 39 | | |

### Artillery *(continued)*

| Model | Quantity | In service | Since | Notes |
|---|---|---|---|---|
| **Towed guns and howitzers** | | | | |
| • 155mm FH-70 | 12 | 12 | 1986 | |
| • 130mm Type 59 | 12 | 12 | 1981 | |
| • 122mm D-30 | 25 | 25 | | |
| • 105mm light gun | 42 | 36 | 1976 | |
| Subtotal | 91 | 85 | | |
| **Mortars, under 160mm** | | | | |
| • 120mm | 12 | 12 | 1976 | |
| • 107mm (4.2") M-30 SP | 12 | 12 | 1986 | |
| Subtotal | 24 | 24 | | |
| Total | **154** | **148** | | |

### Logistic and Engineering Equipment

| Model | Quantity | In service | Since | Notes |
|---|---|---|---|---|
| • Challenger RV | 4 | 4 | 1995 | |

### Anti-tank weapons

| Model | Quantity | In service | Since | Notes |
|---|---|---|---|---|
| **Missiles** | | | | |
| • BGM-71A Improved TOW | 18 | 18 | | |
| • Milan | 32 | 32 | 1984 | |

# Air Force

### Order of Battle

| Model | Quantity | In service | Notes |
|---|---|---|---|
| • Combat | 47 | 31 | |
| • Transport | 42 | 38 | |
| • Helicopters | 37 | 37 | |

### Combat Aircraft

| Model | Quantity | In service | Since | Notes |
|---|---|---|---|---|
| **Multi-role** | | | | |
| • SEPECAT Jaguar S(O) Mk 1/Mk 2/T2 | 19 | 19 | 1977 | To be upgraded to Jaguar 97 standard |
| • Hawk Mk-203 | 12 | 12 | 1994 | |
| Subtotal | 31 | 31 | | |

## Combat Aircraft *(continued)*

| Model | Quantity | In service | Since | Notes |
|---|---|---|---|---|
| **Obsolete** | | | | |
| • Hawker Hunter FGA-6/FR-10/T-67 | 16 | 0 | | Not in service |
| Total | 47 | 31 | | |
| **On order** | | | | |
| • F-16 | 4 | | | From US drawdown (under negotiation) |

## Transport Aircraft

| Model | Quantity | In service | Since | Notes |
|---|---|---|---|---|
| • BAe-111 | 3 | 3 | 1974 | |
| • Britten-Norman BN-2 Defender/Islander | 4 | 0 | 1974 | |
| • C-130H Hercules | 3 | 3 | 1981 | |
| • CN-235 | 3 | 3 | 1993 | With police |
| • DC-8 | 1 | 1 | | |
| • DC-10 | 1 | 1 | 1982 | |
| • DHC-5D Buffalo | 4 | 4 | 1982 | |
| • Dornier Do-228-100 | 2 | 2 | 1984 | Used by police air wing for maritime surveillance & border patrol |
| • Gulfstream | 1 | 1 | 1992 | |
| • Learjet | 1 | 1 | 1981 | In police service |
| • Mystère-Falcon 20 | 1 | 1 | 1983 | |
| • Mystère-Falcon 10 | 1 | 1 | 1980 | |
| • Mystère-Falcon 900 | 2 | 2 | | |
| • Short Skyvan Srs 3M | 15 | 15 | 1970 | Seven employed in maritime patrol role |
| Total | 42 | 38 | | |
| **On order** | | | | |
| • CN-235 | | | | Unconfirmed |

## Training and Liaison Aircraft

| Model | Quantity | In service | Since | Notes |
|---|---|---|---|---|
| **With ground attack/close air support capability** | | | | |
| • BAC-167 Strikemaster Mk 82 | 12 | 12 | 1967 | |
| • Hawk Mk-103 | 4 | 4 | 1993 | |

## Training and Liaison Aircraft *(continued)*

| Model | Quantity | In service | Since | Notes |
|---|---|---|---|---|
| • Mushshak | 3 | 3 | 1994 | |
| Subtotal | 19 | 19 | | |
| Others | | | | |
| • AS-202 Bravo | 4 | 4 | 1976 | |
| Total | 23 | 23 | | |

## Helicopters

| Model | Quantity | In service | Since | Notes |
|---|---|---|---|---|
| Medium transport | | | | |
| • AB-205 | 19 | 19 | 1970 | |
| • AB-212B/Bell 212 | 3 | 3 | 1976 | |
| • AB-214 | 10 | 10 | 1974 | |
| • AS-332 Super Puma/ SA-330 Puma | 2 | 2 | 1982 | |
| Subtotal | 34 | 34 | | |
| Light transport | | | | |
| • AB-206 JetRanger | 3 | 3 | 1970 | |
| Total | 37 | 37 | | |

## Miscellaneous Aircraft

| Model | Quantity | In service | Since | Notes |
|---|---|---|---|---|
| Maritime surveillance aircraft | | | | |
| • Short Skyvan Srs 3M | | | 1970 | 7 listed under transport |
| Target drones | | | | |
| • TTL BTT-3 Banshee | 53 | | | Original number supplied (53) |

## Advanced Armament

Air-to-air-missiles
• R-550 Magic, AIM-9P/AIM-9J Sidewinder
Bombs
• BL-755 CBU

## Air Force Infrastructure

Aircraft shelters
• For all combat aircraft, at Masira and Thamarit
Military airfields:  6
• Bureimi, Dukha, Masira, Muscat (Seeb), Salala, Thamarit

# Air Defense Forces

## Surface-to-Air Missiles

| Model | Batteries | Launchers | Since | Notes |
|---|---|---|---|---|
| **Light missiles** | | | | |
| • Rapier, upgraded to Mk 2/Jernas | | 28 | | |
| • Javelin | | 30 | 1989 | |
| • Tigercat | | | | Unconfirmed |
| Total | | **58** | | |
| **Shoulder-launched missiles** | | | | |
| • Blowpipe | | + | 1982 | |
| • SA-7 (Grail) | | 34 | | |
| Total | | **34** | | |

## Other Air Defense Systems

| Model | Quantity | In service | Since | Notes |
|---|---|---|---|---|
| **Short-range guns** | | | | |
| • 40mm Bofors L-60 | 12 | 12 | 1987 | |
| • 35mm Oerlikon Contraves | + | + | | |
| • 23mm ZU 23x2 | 4 | 4 | 1980 | |
| • 20mm 20x2 VDAA SP | 9 | 9 | | |
| Total | **25** | **25** | | |
| **Radars** | | | | |
| • AR-15 | | | | |
| • S-713 Martello 3D | 2 | 2 | | |
| • S-600 | | | | |
| • Watchman | | | | |
| **On order** | | | | |
| • Javelin | | | | Unconfirmed |

# Navy

**Combat Vessels**

| Type | Original class name | Quantity | Length (m.)/ Displacement (t.) | Armament/ special equipment |
|---|---|---|---|---|
| **Missile corvettes** | | | | |
| • Qahir class | Vosper Thornycroft | 2 | 83.7/1,450 | 1 x helicopter<br>8 x Exocet MM-40 SSMs<br>1 x 8 Crotale-NG<br>1 x 76mm gun<br>2 x 20mm guns<br>6 x 324mm torpedoes |
| **MFPBs** | | | | |
| • Dhofar class | Province class | 4 | 56.7/394 | 6-8 Exocet MM 40 SSMs<br>1 x 76mm gun<br>2 x 40mm guns<br>2 x 12.7mm MGs |
| **Gunboat/MTBs** | | | | |
| • Al-Bushra | P-400 | 3 | 54.5/475 | 1 x 76mm gun<br>1 x 40mm gun<br>2 x 20mm guns<br>2 x 12.7mm MGs<br>4 x 406mm torpedoes<br>to be upgraded to MFPB by addition of MM-38 missiles (unconfirmed) |
| **Total** | | 9 | | |
| **Patrol craft** (some in police service) | | | | |
| • CG-29 | | 3 | 28.9/84 | 2 x 20mm guns with police |
| • CG-27 | | 1 | 24/53 | 1 x 20mm gun with police |
| • Seeb | Vosper Thornycroft | 4 | 25/60.7 | 1 x 20mm gun<br>2 x 7.62mm MGs |
| • Emsworth type | | 2 | 16.0/18 | 2 x 7.62mm MGs with police |

## Combat Vessels *(continued)*

| Type | Original class name | Quantity | Length (m.)/ Displacement (t.) | Armament/ special equipment |
|---|---|---|---|---|
| • Watercraft type | | 3 | 13.9/16 | 2 x 7.62mm MG with police |
| • P-2000 | | 1 | 20.8/80 | 1 x 12.7mm MG with police |
| • P-1903 | | 1 | 19.2/26 | 2 x 12.7mm MGs with police |
| • Tyler-Vortex | | 1 | 13m | |
| • Vosper Thornycroft | | 5 | 22.9/50 | 1 x 20mm gun with police |
| • D-59116 | | 2 | 23/65 | 1 x 12.7mm MG with police |
| Total | | 23 | | |
| On order | | | | |
| • Oliver Hazard Perry class missile frigate | | 1 | | |
| • Al Waffi class | | 2 | | |
| • Vosper Thornycroft Type 83 (Vigilance) missile corvette | | 1 | | |

## Landing Craft

| Type | Original class name | Quantity | Length (m.)/ Displacement (t.) | Armament/ special equipment |
|---|---|---|---|---|
| • Brooke Marine 2,000-ton LST | | 1 | 84.1/2,000 | 550 tonnes; 188 troops; 2 LCVP armament removed |
| • Brooke Marine 2,500-ton LST | | 1 | 93/2,500 | 4 x 40mm guns 2 x 20mm guns 2 x 12.7mm MGs 400 tonnes; 240 troops; 2 LCVP armament removed |
| • LCU | | 1 | 25.5/30 | |
| • Vosper 230-ton LCM | | 3 | 33.0/230 | 100 tonnes |
| Total | | 6 | | |
| On order | | | | |
| • Skima 12 hovercr. | | | | Unconfirmed |

## Auxiliary Vessels

| Type | Original class name | Quantity | Length (m.)/ Displacement (t.) | Armament/ special equipment |
|---|---|---|---|---|
| • Brooke Marine training ship | | | 1 | 62/900 1 x 40mm gun 2 x 20mm guns helicopter deck ex-royal yacht |
| • Conoship, Groningen | | | 1 | 65.7m 1,380dwt |
| • Coastal freighter | | 1 | | |
| • Survey craft | | | 1 | 15.5/23.6 |
| • Diving craft | | | 1 | |
| • Harbor craft | | | 2 | 15m |

## Naval Infrastructure

**Naval bases:**    4
• Mina Raysut (Salala), al-Khasb, Muscat, Wuddam
**Ship maintenance and repair facilities**
• Muscat

# 13. PALESTINIAN AUTHORITY

## General Data

This section includes information on the Palestinian Authority and Palestinian military organizations inside the Palestinian Authority. It does not cover Palestinians living elsewhere.

**Official Name:** Palestinian Authority (PA)
**Chairman:** Yasir Arafat (also Chairman of the PLO)
**Chief of Security Forces:** Formally General Abd al Rizak al Majaida

**Area:** 400 sq. km. (Gaza). By the terms of the Interim Agreement, the West Bank is divided into three areas, designated A, B, and C. The PA has civilian responsibility for Palestinians in all three areas, exclusive security responsibility for Area A, and shared security responsibility for Area B. The size of areas A and B is 1,950 square kilometers; Area C covers 3,850 square kilometers.
**Population:** Gaza - about 1,000,000; West Bank - 1,600,000

### Demography

| Religious groups | | |
|---|---|---|
| Sunni Muslims | 2,340,000 | 90% |
| Christians | 260,000 | 10% |

### Economic Data

| | | 1993 | 1994 | 1995 | 1996 | 1997 |
|---|---|---|---|---|---|---|
| GDP at market prices | Nis bn | 7.763 | 10.044 | 11.132 | 12.383 | 14.500 |
| GDP (US $) (estimate) | $m | 2,745 | 3,336 | 3,574 | 3,897 | 4,170 |
| GDP per capita | $ | 1,236.4 | 1,401.6 | 1,495.3 | 1,540.3 | 1,603.8 |
| Real GDP growth | % | -1.3 | 10.8 | -5.6 | -1.7 | -0.8 |
| **Balance of payments** | | | | | | |
| • Merchandise exports fob | $m | 236 | 423 | 467 | 511 | 520 |
| • Merchandise Imports cif | $m | 1,138 | 2,017 | 2,232 | 2,534 | 2,600 |
| • Account balance | $m | -90 | -614 | -704 | -897 | -955 |
| • External debt | $m | NA | NA | NA | NA | NA |

## Economic Data *(continued)*

|                              |        | 1993  | 1994   | 1995   | 1996   | 1997   |
|------------------------------|--------|-------|--------|--------|--------|--------|
| Government income and expenditure |   |       |        |        |        |        |
| • Revenue, local currency    | Nis bn | 0.789 | 0.809  | 1.538  | 2.183  | 2.845  |
| • Expenditure, local currency | Nis bn | 0.730 | 1.005  | 1.740  | 2.489  | 2.976  |
| • Defense expenditure        | Nis m  | NA    | NA     | 511.8  | 790.6  | 862.2  |
| • Defense expenditure/GDP    | %      | NA    | NA     | 4.59   | 6.38   | 5.94   |
| • Defense expenditure/CGE    | %      | NA    | NA     | 29.41  | 31.76  | 28.97  |
| • Population                 | m      | 2.22  | 2.38*  | 2.39*  | 2.53*  | 2.60   |
| • Official exchange rate (AV) | NIS:$1 | 2.830 | 3.011  | 3.011  | 3.192  | 3.449  |

*Sources:* EIU quarterly report, EIU country profile, IMF statistical yearbook, SIPRI
Yearbook, Palestinian Central Bureau of Statistics
\* Estimate

## Arms Procurement and Security Assistance Received

| Country | Type | Details |
|---------|------|---------|
| Egypt | • Military training | Trainees abroad, police, and civil defense (1997) |
| European Countries | • Financial | |
| | • Military training | Trainees (police) (1998) |
| Israel | • Financial aid | $30 million, plus "non-security assistance," as payment for income tax withheld from Palestinian laborers, and now given the Palestinian Authority - about $200 million (1997) |
| Jordan | • Military training | Trainees (police) |
| Netherlands | • Arms transfers | Light arms (1998) |
| Russia | • Arms transfers | Scout cars (BRDM - 2) |
| Saudi Arabia | • Military training | Trainees (police) |
| USA | • Financial aid | $75 million in FY97 |

## Defense Production

| | M | P | A |
|---|---|---|---|
| **Army equipment** | | | |
| • Possibly clandestine manufacture of small arms | √ | | |

Note: M= manufacture (indigenously developed)
P= production under license
A= assembly

# Armed Forces

**Major Changes:** No major change has been recorded in 1998.

## Order of Battle

| Year | 1994 | 1995 | 1996 | 1997 | 1998 |
|---|---|---|---|---|---|
| **General data** | | | | | |
| • Personnel (regular) | - | 21,000-24,000 | 30,000 | 34,000+ | 34,000+ |
| **Ground forces** | | | | | |
| • APCs/AFVs | - | 45 | 45 | 45 | 45 |
| **Air Force** | | | | | |
| • Transport aircraft* | - | 2 | 2 | 2 (3) | 2 (3) |
| • Helicopters | - | 2 | 2 | 2 (4) | 2 (4) |
| **Navy** | | | | | |
| • Patrol craft | - | - | - | 7 | 7 |

*Note:* Beginning with data for 1997, we refer to quantities in active service. The numbers in parentheses refer to the total.
* Aircraft are not stationed in PA-controlled areas.

## Personnel

| | Gaza | West Bank | Total |
|---|---|---|---|
| Public Security | + | + | + |
| Preventive Security | + | + | + |
| General Intelligence | + | + | + |
| Military Intelligence | + | + | + |
| Presidential Security (including "Force 17") | + | + | + |
| Total | 20,000+ | 14,000+ | 34,000+ |

# Ground Forces

### APCs/AFVs

| Model | Quantity | In service | Since | Notes |
|-------|----------|------------|-------|-------|
| Reconnaissance | | | | |
| • BRDM-2 | 45 | 45 | 1995 | |

### Artillery

| Model | Quantity | In service | Since | Notes |
|-------|----------|------------|-------|-------|
| MRLs | | | | |
| • | | | | Unknown quantity of rocket launchers |

# Air Force

The PLO-affiliated organizations have no air force. The Fatah air arm is designated Force 14. About 200 Palestinians have reportedly undergone training as fighter and helicopter pilots in Libya, Yemen, Romania, Pakistan, Cuba, North Korea and the USSR (until 1991); much of this training took place several years ago, and the number of Palestinians at the disposal of the air units is considerably less than 200. Other PLO members learned to fly commercial aircraft several years ago in civilian flight schools in Romania, Yugoslavia and several Western countries, and have been flying a wide variety of aircraft. In recent years, a concentration of Palestinian pilots and ancillary personnel has reportedly been located in Yemen.

### Order of Battle

| Model | Quantity | In service | Notes |
|-------|----------|------------|-------|
| • Transport | 3 | 2 | |
| • Helicopters | 4 | 2 | |

### Transport Aircraft

| Model | Quantity | In service | Since | Notes |
|-------|----------|------------|-------|-------|
| • Lockheed Jet Star | 1 | 1 | 1996 | |
| • Fokker 50 | 2 | 1 | 1996 | |
| Total | 3 | 2 | | |

*Note:* Aircraft are not stationed in PA-controlled areas.

## Helicopters

| Model | Quantity | In service | Since | Notes |
|---|---|---|---|---|
| Medium transport | | | | |
| • Mi-8 | 2 | 0 | 1996 | |
| • Mi-17 | 2 | 2 | 1996 | |
| Total | 4 | 2 | | |

## Air Force Infrastructure

Airfields:     1
• Dahaniya

# Air Defense Forces

## Air Defense Systems

| Model | Quantity | In service | Since | Notes |
|---|---|---|---|---|
| Short-range guns | | | | |
| • 23mm AA guns | | | | Unknown quantity |

# Navy

The naval force is concentrated in Yemen, Libya, and Algeria; some were in Lebanon until January 1994, then moved to Yemen. The Fatah naval force is to be the Coast Guard of the Palestinian Authority in Gaza.

## Combat Vessels

| Type | Original class name | Quantity | Length (m.)/ Displacement (t.) | Armament/ special equipment |
|---|---|---|---|---|
| Patrol craft | | | | |
| • Volvo | | 2 | 8.0/5 | 7.62 MG |
| • Zodiak mk 5 | | 11 | 5.8m | 7.62 MG |
| Total | | 13 | | |

# Non-governmental Organizations

• Hamas - Several hundred members
• Islamic Jihad - Several hundred members

# 14. QATAR

## General Data

**Official Name of the State:** State of Qatar
**Head of State:** Shaykh Hamad ibn Khalifa al-Thani (also Minister of Defense and Commander in Chief of the Armed Forces)
**Prime Minister:** Abdallah Ibn Khalifa al-Thani
**Chief of General Staff:** Brigadier General Hamad bin Ali al-Attiyah
**Commander of Ground Forces:** Colonel Saif Ali al-Hajiri
**Commander of the Air Force:** General Ali Saeed al-Hawal al-Marri
**Commander of the Navy:** Captain Said al-Suwaydi

**Area:** 11,437 sq. km.
**Population:** 600,000

## Demography

| | | |
|---|---|---|
| *Ethnic groups* | | |
| Arabs | 240,000 | 40.0% |
| Pakistanis | 108,000 | 18.0% |
| Indians | 108,000 | 18.0% |
| Persians | 60,000 | 10.0% |
| Others | | |
| (mostly Southeast Asians) | 84,000 | 14.0% |
| *Religious groups* | | |
| Sunni Muslims | 421,800 | 70.3% |
| Shi'ite Muslims | 145,800 | 24.3% |
| Others | 32,400 | 5.4% |

## Economic Data

| | | 1993 | 1994 | 1995 | 1996 | 1997 |
|---|---|---|---|---|---|---|
| GDP current price, local currency | QR bn | 26.0 | 26.8 | 27.4 | 33.0 | 34.0 |
| GDP (US $) | $ bn | 7.14 | 7.36 | 7.53 | 9.06 | 9.34 |
| GDP per capita | $ | 12,753 | 12,480 | 13,686 | 15,631 | 15,568 |
| Real GDP growth | % | -0.6 | 2.4 | -1.2 | 5.0 | 10.0 |
| **Balance of payments** | | | | | | |
| • Exports fob | $ bn | 3.26 | 2.980 | 3.09 | 3.83 | 5.36 |
| • Imports fob | $ bn | 1.680 | 2.28 | 3.31 | 3.8 | 4.71 |
| • Account balance (including services and income) | $ bn | -0.617 | -1.268 | -2.326 | -2.667 | -2.616 |
| • External debt | $ bn | 2.07 | 4.51 | 6.25 | 6.23 | 10.25 |

## Economic Data *(continued)*

|  |  | 1993 | 1994 | 1995 | 1996 | 1997 |
|---|---|---|---|---|---|---|
| **Government income and expenditure** | | | | | | |
| • Revenue, local currency | QR bn | 10.892 | 9.614 | 12.068 | 11.159 | 15.856 |
| • Expenditure, local currency | QR bn | 12.268 | 11.679 | 14.088 | 14.22 | 16.572 |
| • Defense expenditure | QR bn | 1.2 | 1.1 | 1.2 | NA | NA |
| • Defense expenditure/GDP | % | 4.58 | 4.21 | 4.36 | NA | NA |
| • Defense expenditure/CGE | % | 9.78 | 9.42 | 9.43 | NA | NA |
| • Population | m | 0.56 | 0.59 | 0.55 | 0.58 | 0.6 |
| • Official exchange rate | QR :$1 | 3.64 | 3.64 | 3.64 | 3.64 | 3.64 |

*Sources:* EIU quarterly report, EIU country profile, IMF statistical yearbook, SIPRI Yearbook

## Arms Procurement and Security Assistance Received

| Country | Type | Details |
|---|---|---|
| Brazil | • Arms transfer | MRLs (1993) |
| Britain | • Arms transfer | SAMs (1996), Combat vessels (1996), Aircrafts (1996), APCs (1996) |
| France | • Military training | Advisers (1999) |
|  | • Arms transfer | APCs (1996), combat aircraft (1997), AMX-30 MBTs (1998), SAMs (1996), Mica and Magic II AAMs (1997) |
| USA | • Military training | Advisers, Trainees Abroad |

## Arms Sales and Security Assistance Extended

| Country | Type | Details |
|---|---|---|
| France | • Facilities provided | Training facilities, deployment of equipment (1999) |
| Lebanon | • Financial aid | $1 million grant |
| Spain | • Arms transfer | F-5 aircraft (1996) |
| Syria | • Financial aid |  |
| USA | • Facilities provided | Transportation equipment, deployment of maritime patrol aircraft (1998) |

## Foreign Military Cooperation

| | Details |
|---|---|
| Joint maneuvers with | USA, GCC countries , Yemen, Britain, France. |

# Armed Forces

**Major Changes:** The Qatari ground forces received 10 additional AMX-30 MBTs, and the first batch of Piranha II IFVs, of which it had ordered 40. The Qatari air force received the second batch of its 12 Mirage 2000-5 combat aircraft. The navy is assimilating four Vosper Thornycroft "Barzan class " missile patrol boats, which were received in 1996-97, and placed an order for two additional boats.

## Order of Battle

| Year | 1994 | 1995 | 1996 | 1997 | 1998 |
|---|---|---|---|---|---|
| **General data** | | | | | |
| • Personnel (regular) | 8,200 | 10,300 | 10,300 | 11,800 | 11,800 |
| • Number of brigades | | | | 1 | 1 |
| • Number of regiments | 6 | 1 | 1 | 1 | 1 |
| • Total number of battalions | 7 | 7 | 7 | 10 | 10 |
| **Ground forces** | | | | | |
| • Tanks | 24 | 24 | 24 | 24 | 44 |
| • APCs/AFVs | 245 | 310 | 310 | 230 (310) | 222 (302) |
| • Artillery (incl. MRLs) | 30 | 37 | 37 | 56 | 56 |
| **Air force** | | | | | |
| • Combat aircraft | 14 | 14 | 14 | 9 | 9 |
| • Transport aircraft | 7 | 7 | 7 | 8 | 8 |
| • Helicopters | 41 | 41 | 41 | 32 | 32 |
| **Air defense forces** | | | | | |
| • Light SAM launchers | 32 | 32 | 29 | 48 | 48 |
| **Navy** | | | | | |
| • Combat vessels | 3 | 3 | 5 | 7 | 7 |
| • Patrol craft | 50 | 50 | 48 | 44 | 36 |

*Note:* Beginning with data for 1997, we refer to quantities in active service. The numbers in parentheses refer to the total.

## Personnel

|  | Regular | Reserves | Total |
|---|---|---|---|
| Ground Forces | 8,500 |  | 8,500 |
| Air Force | 1,500 |  | 1,500 |
| Navy (including marine police) | 1,800 |  | 1,800 |
| **Total** | **11,800** |  | **11,800** |
| Paramilitary |  |  |  |
| • Armed police | 8,000 |  |  |

# Ground Forces

## Formations

|  | Independent brigade/group | Independent battalion | Battalions in brigade |
|---|---|---|---|
| Armored | 1 |  | 1 armd., 1 mech., 1 arty. |
| Mechanized |  | 4 |  |
| Royal Guard | 1 |  | 3 inf. batt. |
| Special forces |  | 1 |  |
| Artillery |  | 2 |  |
| Total | 2 | 7 |  |

## Tanks

| Model | Quantity | In service | Since | Notes |
|---|---|---|---|---|
| **MBTs** |  |  |  |  |
| **Medium and low quality** |  |  |  |  |
| • AMX-30 | 44 | 44 | 1978/1996 |  |
| Total | **44** | **44** |  |  |
| **On order** |  |  |  |  |
| • Challenger | 50 |  |  | Under negotiation |
| • Leclerc | 50 - 100 |  |  | Under negotiation |

## APCs/AFVs

| Model | Quantity | In service | Since | Notes |
|---|---|---|---|---|
| **APCs** |  |  |  |  |
| • VAB | 134 | 134 | 1978 | 4 mortar carriers, 24 mounted with HOT ATGM |

## APCs/AFVs *(continued)*

| Model | Quantity | In service | Since | Notes |
|---|---|---|---|---|
| • Fahd | 10 | 6 - 10 | | |
| • Saracen | 25 | 6 | 1970 | |
| Subtotal | 169 | 149 | | |
| **IFVs** | | | | |
| • V-150 Commando | 8 | 8 | 1986 | |
| • AMX-10P/VCI | 45 | 45 | 1978 | |
| • Piranha II | 4 | 4 | 1998 | Out of order of 40 LAVs |
| Subtotal | 57 | 57 | | |
| **Reconnaissance** | | | | |
| • VBL | 16 | 16 | 1994 | |
| • AMX 10RC | | | 1981 | Included with other models of AMX 10s |
| • Engesa EE-9 | 20 | 0 | 1978 | |
| • Saladin | 30 | 0 | 1970 | |
| • Ferret | 10 | 0 | 1968 | |
| Subtotal | 76 | 16 | | |
| **Total** | **302** | **222** | | |
| **On order** | | | | |
| • GKN Piranha | 40 | | | Being delivered |
| • VAB | | | | |
| • Fahd | | | | |

## Artillery

| Model | Quantity | In service | Since | Notes |
|---|---|---|---|---|
| **Self-propelled guns and howitzers** | | | | |
| • 155mm Mk F-3 (AMX) | 22 | 22 | 1984 | |
| **Towed guns and howitzers** | | | | |
| • 155mm G-5 | 12 | 12 | 1991 | |
| **Mortars, under 160mm** | | | | |
| • 120mm Brandt | 15 | 15 | | |
| • VPM 81mm SP | 4 | 4 | 1977 | Mounted on VAB APCs |
| Subtotal | 19 | 19 | | |
| **MRLs** | | | | |
| • 122mm BM-21 | | | | |
| • 127mm SS-30 or 180mm SS-40 Astros II | 3 | 3 | | |
| **Total** | **56** | **56** | | |

### Artillery *(continued)*

| Model | Quantity | In service | Since | Notes |
|---|---|---|---|---|
| **On order** | | | | |
| • 155mm Mk F-3 SP howitzers | | | | Undergoing upgrading (unconfirmed) |

### Anti-tank Weapons

| Model | Quantity | In service | Since | Notes |
|---|---|---|---|---|
| **Missiles** | | | | |
| • HOT | 48 | 48 | 1978 | 24 are mounted on VAB |
| • Milan | 60-100 | 60-100 | 1987 | |
| **Guns** | | | | |
| • 84mm Carl Gustav light recoilless rifle | | | 1978 | |

# Air Force

### Order of Battle

| Model | Quantity | In service | Notes |
|---|---|---|---|
| • Combat | 14 | 14 | |
| • Transport | 8 | 8 | |
| • Helicopters | 32 | 32 | |

### Combat Aircraft

| Model | Quantity | In service | Since | Notes |
|---|---|---|---|---|
| **Advanced multi-role** | | | | |
| • Mirage 2000 | 8 | 8 | 1997 | Delivery of 12 aircrafts commenced |
| **Multi-role** | | | | |
| • Mirage F-1E/B | 6 | 6 | 1984 | To be sold - 7 planes already sold to Spain |
| **Total** | **14** | **14** | | |
| **on order** | | | | |
| • Mirage-2000-5 | 12 | | | Being delivered |

## Transport Aircraft

| Model | Quantity | In service | Since | Notes |
|---|---|---|---|---|
| • Boeing 707 | 2 | 2 | 1977 | |
| • Airbus 340 | 1 | 1 | 1993 | |
| • Boeing 727 | 1 | 1 | 1979 | |
| • Britten-Norman BN-2 Islander | 1 | 1 | | |
| • Mystère-Falcon 900 | 3 | 3 | 1991 | |
| Total | 8 | 8 | | |

## Training and Liaison Aircraft

| Model | Quantity | In service | Since | Notes |
|---|---|---|---|---|
| With ground attack/ close air support capability | | | | |
| • Alpha jet | 6 | 6 | 1980 | |
| Total | 6 | 6 | | |
| On order | | | | |
| • Hawk 100 | 15-18 | | | |

## Helicopters

| Model | Quantity | In service | Since | Notes |
|---|---|---|---|---|
| Attack | | | | |
| • SA-342 Gazelle | 13 | 13 | 1983 | 2 employed as light helicopter with police |
| Medium transport | | | | |
| • AS-332 Super Puma/ AS 532 Cougar | 6 | 6 | 1987 | |
| • Westland Commando MK 2/MK 3 | 4 | 4 | 1982 | 4 out of 12 used for VIP transport |
| Subtotal | 10 | 10 | | |
| Naval combat | | | | |
| • Westland Commando MK 2/MK 3 | 8 | 8 | 1982 | |
| Total | 31 | 31 | | |
| On order | | | | |
| • Naval combat helicopter | | | | |

## Miscellaneous Aircraft

Target drones
• TTL BTT-3 Banshee:   Unconfirmed

## Advanced Armament

| | |
|---|---|
| Air-to-air missiles: | Mica (50), R-550 Magic II |
| Air-to-ground missiles: | AM-39 Exocet |

## Air Force Infrastructure

| | |
|---|---|
| Military airfields: | 2 |
| Doha; Al Ghariyeh | |

# Air Defense Forces

## Surface-to-Air Missiles

| Model | Launchers | Since | Notes |
|---|---|---|---|
| **Light missiles** | | | |
| • Rapier | 15 | 1984 | |
| • Roland 2 | 9 | | Number unconfirmed |
| • Mistral | 24 | | |
| Total | **48** | | |
| **Shoulder-launched missiles** | | | |
| • Blowpipe | 6 | 1986 | |
| • FIM-92A Stinger | 12 | | |
| Total | **18** | | |
| **On order** | | | |
| • Shorts Starburst | | | |

# Navy

## Combat Vessels

| Type | Original class name | Quantity | Length (m.)/ Displacement (t.) | Armament/ special equipment |
|---|---|---|---|---|
| **MFPBs** | | | | |
| • Barzan (new) | Vita Vosper Thornycroft | 4 | 56.3/376 | 8 x MM 40 Excocet SSMs<br>8 x Mistral SAMs<br>1 x 76mm gun<br>1x 30mm gun |

## Combat Vessels *(continued)*

| Type | Original class name | Quantity | Length (m.)/ Displacement (t.) | Armament/ special equipment |
|------|------|------|------|------|
| • Damsah class | Combattante III | 3 | 56/345 | 8 x MM 40 Exocet SSMs<br>1x 76mm gun<br>2x 40mm guns<br>4x 30mm guns |
| Total | | 7 | | |
| **Patrol craft** | | | | |
| • Barzan (old) class | Vosper Thornycroft | 4 | 33.5/120 | 4x 30mm guns |
| • Helmatic | | 3 | 16/20 | |
| • Damen | Polycat 1450 | 6 | 14.5/18 | 1x 20mm gun |
| • MV-45 | | 4 | 14.5/17 | 1x 20mm gun with police |
| • Fairey Marine Spear class | | 15 | 9.1/4.3 | |
| • P-1200 | | 4 | 11.9/4.3 | With police |
| Total | | 36 | | |
| **On order** | | | | |
| • Vosper Thornycroft PBs | | 2 | | |

## Coastal Defense

| Type | Batteries | Notes |
|------|------|------|
| • MM-40 Exocet | 3-4 | |

## Naval Infrastructure

**Naval bases:** Doha, Halul Island

# 15. SAUDI ARABIA

## General Data

**Official Name of the State:** The Kingdom of Saudi Arabia
**Head of State:** King Fahd ibn Abd al-Aziz al-Saud (also Prime Minister)
**First Deputy Prime Minister and Heir Apparent:** Crown Prince Abdallah ibn
Abd al-Aziz al-Saud (also Commander of the National Guard)
**Defense and Aviation Minister:** Prince Sultan ibn Abd al-Aziz al-Saud
(also Second Deputy Prime Minister)
**Chief of General Staff:** General Salih ibn Ali al-Muhaya
**Commander of the Ground Forces:** Lieutenant General Sultan ibn Ali
Al-Mutayri
**Commander of the Air Force:** Lieutenant General Abd al-Aziz ibn
Muhammad Hunaydi
**Commander of the Air Defense Forces:** Lieutenant General Majid ibn
Talhab al-Qutaibi
**Commander of the Navy:** Vice Admiral Talal ibn Salem al-Mufadhi

**Area:** 2,331,000 sq. km. (approximation; some borders undefined
or undemarcated)
**Population:** 19,480,000

## Demography

| | | |
|---|---|---|
| *Ethnic groups* | | |
| Arabs | 17,805,000 | 91.4% |
| Afro-Arabs | 974,000 | 5.0% |
| Others | 701,000 | 3.6% |
| *Religious groups* | | |
| Sunni Muslims | 17,941,000 | 92.1% |
| Shi'ite Muslims | 974,000 | 5.0% |
| Others (mainly Christians) | 565,000 | 2.9% |
| *Nationality subdivision:* | | |
| Saudis | 14,162,000 | 72.7% |
| Others | 5,318,000 | 27.3% |

## Economic Data

| | | 1993 | 1994 | 1995 | 1996 | 1997 |
|---|---|---|---|---|---|---|
| GDP current price, local currency | SR bn | 443.8 | 450.0 | 469.1 | 509.3 | 546.0 |
| GDP (US $) | $ bn | 118.50 | 120.16 | 125.26 | 135.99 | 145.79 |
| GDP per capita | $ | 6,829 | 6,765 | 6,863 | 7,218 | 7,484 |
| Real GDP growth | % | -0.6 | 0.5 | -0.8 | 2.3 | 2.5 |

## Economic Data *(continued)*

|  |  | 1993 | 1994 | 1995 | 1996 | 1997 |
|---|---|---|---|---|---|---|
| **Balance of payments** | | | | | | |
| • Exports fob | $ bn | 42.4 | 42.6 | 50.0 | 60.7 | 59.7 |
| • Imports fob | $ bn | 25.9 | 21.3 | 25.7 | 25.4 | 26.2 |
| • Account balance (including services and income) | $ bn | -17.3 | -10.5 | -5.3 | 0.7 | 0.3 |
| • External debt | $ bn | NA | NA | NA | NA | NA |
| **Government income and expenditure** | | | | | | |
| • Revenue, local currency | SR bn | 141 | 129 | 135 | 132 | 164 |
| • Expenditure, local currency | SR bn | 188 | 171 | 150 | 150 | 181 |
| • Defense expenditure | SR bn | 61.636 | 53.549 | 49.501 | 64.000 | 67.000 |
| • Defense expenditure/GDP | % | 13.88 | 11.89 | 10.55 | 12.56 | 12.27 |
| • Defense expenditure/CGE | % | 32.78 | 31.31 | 33.00 | 42.66 | 37.01 |
| • Population | m | 17.35 | 17.76 | 18.25 | 18.84 | 19.48 |
| • Official exchange rate | SR : 1 | 3.745 | 3.745 | 3.745 | 3.745 | 3.745 |

*Sources:* EIU quarterly report, EIU country profile, IMF statistical yearbook, SIPRI Yearbook

## Arms Procurement and Security Assistance Received

| Country | Type | Details |
|---|---|---|
| Belgium | • Arms transfers | Turrets for LAV IFVs |
| Britain | • Arms transfers | Combat aircraft (1998), trainer aircraft, helicopters, minesweepers, mortars, ARM missiles |
|  | • Military training | Foreign advisers/instructors/ serving personnel; trainees abroad |
| Canada | • Arms transfers | LAV APCs/IFVs (1998), naval simulators (1998) |
| Egypt | • Military training | Foreign advisers/instructors/service personnel (on individual basis, unconfirmed), trainees abroad (unconfirmed) |

## Arms Procurement and Security Assistance Received (continued)

| Country | Type | Details |
|---|---|---|
| France | • Arms transfers | Radars, SAMs, SP artillery, anti-ship AGMs, upgrading SAMs and missile frigates |
| | • Military training | Foreign advisers/instructors/ serving personnel; trainees abroad for Cougar helicopters |
| | • Maintenance aid | Naval vessels |
| Germany | • Arms transfers | Cougar helicopters (1998) |
| India | • Military training | Foreign advisers/instructors/ serving personnel |
| PRC | • Military training | Foreign advisers/instructors/ serving personnel for CSS-2 missiles |
| Sweden | • Arms transfers | Early warning system for GCC countries |
| Switzerland | • Arms transfers | Trainer aircraft co-produced with Britain |
| USA | • Arms transfers | AAMs, AGMs, combat aircraft, helicopters (1993), aircraft engines, SAMs, tanks, aircraft simulators, surveillance radars, integration of air defense system(1998), radio systems, surveillance radars |
| | • Military training | Foreign advisers/instructors/ serving personnel; trainees abroad |

## Arms Sales and Security Assistance Extended

| Country | Type | Details |
|---|---|---|
| Bosnia | • Arms transfers | Chinese-made small arms; 26 Russian Mi-8 helicopters; French-made Crotale/Shahine SAMs, Rapier SAMs, Stinger SAMs (1995) |
| | • Financial aid | Grant |
| GCC Peninsula Shield Force | • Facilities | 7,000-10,000 men at Hafr al-Batin; mostly Saudis, others from GCC forces, except Qatar |
| Lebanon | • Financial aid | $60 million grant in 1991 and additional grant in 1992 |
| Palestinian Authority | • Financial aid | In 1994 a commitment was made to donate $100 million to the Palestinian Authority in Gaza and Jericho |
| Syria | • Financial aid | Grants (with other GCC countries) |
| USA | • Facilities | HQ at Riyadh, AWACS a/c, U-2 a/c at Taif, approx. 48 F-16 and F-15 at Dhahran with C-130, F-111 EW a/c and KC-135 |

## Foreign Military Cooperation

| | Details |
|---|---|
| • Joint maneuvers | Britain, Egypt (1997), France, GCC countries, Pakistan, USA |

## Defense Production

| | M | P | A |
|---|---|---|---|
| **Ground forces equipment** | | | |
| • G-3 ARs | | √ | |
| • Small arms ammunition, electronic components | √ | | |
| • Al Fahd 8x8 APC | √ | | |
| • "Peninsula Shield" APCs | √ | | |
| **Aircraft and air ammunition** | | | |
| • Some accessories and components for foreign-made aircraft, flares and chaff | | √ | |
| **Electronics** | | | |
| • Radio transceivers, components of a/c radars, parts for EW equipment | | | √ |

*Note:* M - manufacture (indigenously developed)
P - production under license
A - assembly

## Weapons of Mass Destruction

**CW capabilities**

• Personal protective equipment; decontamination units; US-made CAM chemical detection systems; Fuchs (Fox) ABC detection vehicles

**Surface-to-surface missiles**

| Model | Launchers | Missiles | Since | Notes |
|---|---|---|---|---|
| • CSS-2 SSM (DF-3, East Wind, IRBM) | 8-12 | 30-50 | 1988 | No. of launchers unconfirmed |

# Armed Forces

**Major Changes:** The Saudi ground forces are assimilating their newly acquired M1A1 "Abrams" MBTs and their "Bradley" IFVs. The National Guard has deployed its LAV-25 IFVs. The Saudi Air Force received some 50 F-15S combat aircraft out of 75 ordered.

## Order of Battle

| Year | 1994 | 1995 | 1996 | 1997 | 1998 |
|---|---|---|---|---|---|
| **General data** | | | | | |
| • Personnel (regular) | 126,000 - 136,000 | 132,000 | 161,000 | 165,000 | 165,000 |
| • Number of brigades | 17 | 18 | 18 | 18 | 20 |
| • Number of battalions | 20 | 20 | 20 | 20 | 20 |
| **Ground forces** | | | | | |
| • Tanks | 700 | 900 | 1,015 | 865 (1,015) | 865 (1,015) |
| • APCs/AFVs | 3,400 | 4,040 | 4,050-4,100 | 5,220 | 5,287-5,337 (5,437) |
| • Artillery (incl. MRLs) | 770 | 770 | 770 | 404 (576) | 404 (776) |
| • SSM launchers | 8-12 | 8-12 | 8-12 | 8-12 | 8-12 |
| **Air force** | | | | | |
| • Combat aircraft | 270 | 250 | 249 | 321 | 346 |
| • Transport aircraft | 108 | 77 | 76 | 61 | 61 |
| • Helicopters | 171 | 180 | 180 | 175 | 160 |
| **Air defense forces** | | | | | |
| • Heavy SAM batteries | 23 | 23 | 23 | 22 | 22 |
| • Medium SAM batteries | 16 | 16 | 16 | 16 | 16 |
| **Navy** | | | | | |
| • Combat vessels | 26 | 27 | 27 | 24 | 24 |
| • Patrol craft | 82 | 82 | 102 | 92 | 80 |

*Note:* beginning with data for 1997, we refer to quantities in active service. The numbers in parentheses refer to the total.

## Personnel

| | Regular | Reserves | Total |
|---|---|---|---|
| Ground Forces | 70,000 | | 70,000 |
| Air Force | 20,000 | | 20,000 |
| Air Defense | 4,000 | | 4,000 |
| Navy (including a marine unit ) | 12,000 | | 12,000 |
| National Guard | 57,000 | 20,000 | 77,000 |
| Royal Guard | 2,000 | | 2,000 |
| **Total** | **165,000** | **20,000** | **185,000** |

## Personnel *(continued)*

|  | Regular | Reserves | Total |
|---|---|---|---|
| **Paramilitary** | | | |
| • Mujahidun | 30,000 | 30,000 | 30,000 |
| (affiliated with National Guard) | | | |
| • Coast Guard | 4,500 | | 4,500 |
| • Frontier Corps | 10,500 | | 10,500 |
| Total | **15,000** | | **45,000** |

*Note:* Coast Guard separated from Frontier Corps in 1992

# Ground Forces

## Formations (Ground Forces and National Guard)

|  | Independent brigade/group | Independent battalion |
|---|---|---|
| Armored (Ground Forces) | 4 | |
| Mechanized (5 Ground Forces, 3 National Guard) | 8 | |
| Infantry (Royal Guard) | 1 | |
| Infantry (National Guard) | 6 | 19 |
| Marines | 1 | |
| Airborne/Special forces (Ground Forces) | 1 | |
| Total | **20** | **20** |

*Note:* Saudi ground forces comprise of 9 brigades (5 mechanized, 3 armored, 1 airborne/infantry), plus one Royal Guard brigade; the National Guard has 8 brigades (3 mechanized, 5 infantry)

## Tanks

| Model | Quantity | In service | Since | Notes |
|---|---|---|---|---|
| **MBTs** | | | | |
| **High Quality** | | | | |
| • M-1 A2 | 315 | 315 | 1993 | |
| **Medium and low quality** | | | | |
| • AMX-30 | 300 | 150 | 1975 | 150 in store |
| • M-60 A3 | 400 | 400 | 1985 | |
| Subtotal | 700 | 550 | | |
| Total | **1,015** | **865** | | |

## APCs/AFVs

| Model | Quantity | In service | Since | Notes |
|---|---|---|---|---|
| **APCs** | | | | |
| • AMX-10/AMX-10P | 500 | 500 | 1975 | |
| • BMR-600 | 140 | 140 | 1985 | With marines |
| • Engesa EE-11 Urutu | some | some | | |
| • M-113 A1/A2 | 1,600 | 1,600 | 1976/1981 | |
| • M-3 (Panhard) | 150 | 150 | | |
| Subtotal | 2,390 | 2,390 | | |
| **IFVs** | | | | |
| • AML-60/90 | 350 | 200-250 | 1969 | |
| • Fox/Ferret | 200 | 200 | | Possibly phased out |
| • Piranha of various models | 1,117 | 1,117 | 1992 | Additional 73 120mm TDA rifled mortar carriers |
| • M-2/M-3 Bradley | 400 | 400 | | |
| • V-150 Commando | 980 | 980 | 1977 | Number unconfirmed |
| Subtotal | 3,047 | 2,897 - 2,947 | | |
| **Total** | **5,437** | **5,287 - 5,337** | | |
| **On order** | | | | |
| • Peninsula Shield | 50 | | | Initial order for 50 is to be followed by a second order for 150 |
| • Al Fahd AD-40-8-1 | | | | Size of order unknown (if any) |

## Artillery

| Model | Quantity | In service | Since | Notes |
|---|---|---|---|---|
| **Self-propelled guns and howitzers** | | | | |
| • 155mm M-109A2 SP | 280 | 110 | | |
| • 155mm GCT SP | 51 | 51 | 1980 | |
| Subtotal | 331 | 161 | | |
| **Towed guns and howitzers** | | | | |
| • 155mm FH-70 | 72 | 0 | | In storage |
| • 155mm M-198 | 90 | 60 | 1982 | |
| • 155mm M-114 | 50 | 50 | 1980 | |
| • 105mm M-102/M-101 | 100 | 0 | 1975 | In storage |
| Subtotal | 312 | 110 | | |

## Artillery *(continued)*

| Model | Quantity | In service | Since | Notes |
|---|---|---|---|---|
| **Mortars, under 160mm** | | | | |
| • 120mm TDA rifled mortar, SP | 73 | 73 | | On LAV-25s |
| • 107mm (4.2") M-30 mortar | | | 1981 | |
| **MRLs** | | | | |
| • 180mm SS-40 Astros II } | 60 | 60 | | |
| 127mm SS-30 Astros II } | | | | 10 batteries |
| Total | 776 | 404 | | |
| **Artillery/mortar-locating radars** | | | | |
| • AN/TPQ-37 | | | | |

### Logistic and Engineering Equipment

- M-123 Viper minefield crossing system, MK 3 (D) Flail, M-69 A1 bridging tanks, bridging equipment, AFV transporters (600), LAV recovery vehicles

### Anti-tank Weapons

| Model | Quantity | In service | Since | Notes |
|---|---|---|---|---|
| **Missiles** | | | | |
| • AMX-10P SP (carrying HOT) | | | 1982 | |
| • BGM-71C Improved TOW/BGM-71D TOW II | | | 1988 | |
| • M-47 Dragon | 1,000 | 1,000 | 1977 | |
| Total | **1,500** | **1,500** | | |
| **Guns** | | | | |
| • 106mm M-40 recoilless rifle | 50 | 50 | | |
| • 84mm Carl Gustav light recoilless rifle | 300 | 300 | | |

# Air Force

### Order of Battle

| Model | Quantity | In service | Notes |
|---|---|---|---|
| • Combat | 346 | 346 | |
| • Transport | 61 | 61 | |
| • Helicopters | 160 | 160 | |

## Combat Aircraft

| Model | Number | In service | Since | Notes |
|---|---|---|---|---|
| **Interceptors** | | | | |
| • F-15 C/D Eagle | 91 | 91 | 1982 | |
| • Tornado ADV (F Mk 3) | 24 | 24 | 1989 | |
| Subtotal | 115 | 115 | | |
| **Advanced multi-role** | | | | |
| • F-15S | 50 | 50 | 1995 | 50 estimated were supplied 75 aircraft were ordered |
| **Multi-role** | | | | |
| • Tornado IDS (GR Mk 1/GR-1A reconn. a/c) | 92 | 92 | 1986 | |
| • F-5E/F | approx. 64 | approx. 64 | 1973 | |
| • RF-5E | 10 | 10 | 1973 | |
| Subtotal | 166 | 166 | | |
| **Obsolete** | | | | |
| • F-5A/B | 15 | 15 | | Mostly employed as trainer a/c |
| Total | **346** | **346** | | |
| **On order** | | | | |
| • F-15S | 72 | | | Delivery 1998-99 (50 supplied) |
| • F-16 | | | | Under negotiation |

## Transport Aircraft

| Model | Quantity | In service | Since | Notes |
|---|---|---|---|---|
| • C-130E/H Hercules | 46 | 46 | 1970/1980 | |
| • CN-235 | 4 | 4 | 1987 | |
| • Gulfstream III | 1 | 1 | 1983 | |
| • Learjet 35 | 2 | 2 | 1981 | Employed in target-towing role |
| • Mystère-Falcon 20 | 2 | 2 | | |
| • VC-140 JetStar | 2 | 2 | 1969 | |
| • HS-125 | 4 | 4 | | |
| Total | **61** | **61** | | |

## Training and Liaison Aircraft

| Model | Quantity | In service | Since | Notes |
|---|---|---|---|---|
| With ground attack/close air support capability | | | | |
| • BAC-167 Strikemaster | 30 | 0 | 1968 | Possibly phased out |
| • Hawk Mk65 | 30 | 30 | 1987 | |
| Subtotal | 60 | 30 | | |
| Others | | | | |
| • BAe Jetstream 31 | 2 | 2 | 1987 | |
| • Cessna 172 G/H/L | 17 | 17 | 1967 | |
| • Pilatus PC-9 | 50 | 50 | 1987 | |
| Subtotal | 69 | 69 | | |
| Total | 129 | 99 | | |
| On order | | | | |
| • Hawk 100/200 | 20 | | | Under negotiation |

## Helicopters

| Model | Quantity | In service | Since | Notes |
|---|---|---|---|---|
| Attack (part of ground forces aviation) | | | | |
| • Bell 406CS | 15 | 15 | 1990 | Combat Scout |
| • AH-64A Apache | 12 | 12 | 1993 | |
| Subtotal | 27 | 27 | | |
| Naval combat | | | | |
| • AS-365 Dauphin 2/ AS-565MA | 27 | 27 | 1986 | Including small number medical evacuation role |
| • AS-332 Super Puma | 11 | 11 | 1992 | |
| Subtotal | 38 | 38 | | |
| Medium transport | | | | |
| • SH-3 (AS-61A) | 3 | 3 | 1978 | |
| • KV-107/KV-107 IIA | 17 | 17 | 1979 | |
| • AB-212/Bell-205 | 25 | 25 | 1977 | Number unconfirmed |
| • UH-60A Black Hawk/ Desert Hawk/Medevac | 20 | 20 | 1990 | |
| Subtotal | 65 | 65 | | |
| Light transport | | | | |
| • AB-206 JetRanger | 30 | 30 | 1967 | |
| Total | 160 | 160 | | |

## Helicopters *(continued)*

| Model | Quantity | In service | Since | Notes |
|-------|----------|-----------|-------|-------|
| **On order** | | | | |
| • British helicopters | 80-88 | | | Reportedly WS-70 (UH-60A) or EH-101, probably cancelled |
| • AH-64A | 12-24 | | | Under negotiation |
| • AS-532 Cougar | 12 | | | |

## Miscellaneous Aircraft

| Model | Quantity | In service | Since | Notes |
|-------|----------|-----------|-------|-------|
| **AEW/AWACS aircraft** | | | | |
| • E-3A AWACS | 5 | 5 | 1986 | |
| **Tankers** | | | | |
| • KC-130H | 7 | 7 | 1973 | |
| • KE-3/Boeing 707 | 8 | 8 | 1986 | |
| **Target drones** | | | | |
| • TTL BTT-3 Banshee | | | | |
| • MQM-74C Chukar II UAV | | | | |

## Advanced Armament

### Air-to-air-missiles
• AIM-7F Sparrow; AIM-7M; AIM-9J/P Sidewinder; AIM-9L/M Sidewinder; AIM-9P-4; AIM-9S, Red Top; Sky Flash

### Air-to-ground missiles
• AGM-65A Maverick (partly AGM-65D/G); ALARM anti-radiation missiles; AM-39 Exocet; AS-15TT anti-ship missile; Sea Eagle anti-ship missile

### Bombs
• Laser-guided bombs; CBU-86; CBU-87; BL-755 CBU; JP-233 anti-runway bombs; Paveway II laser-guided; GBU-10/12/15

## Air Force Infrastructure

### Aircraft shelters
For combat aircraft

**Military airfields:**   20-25

Abqaiq, al-Ahsa, al-Sulayyil, Dhahran, al-Hufuf, Jidda, Jubail, Khamis Mushayt, al-Kharj, Medina, Riyadh, Sharawra, Tabuk, Taif, Gizan, 5-10 additional airfields

# Air Defense Forces

## Surface-to-Air Missiles

| Model | Batteries | Launchers | Since | Notes |
|---|---|---|---|---|
| **Heavy missiles** | | | | |
| • MIM-104 Patriot | 5 | | 1991 | |
| • MIM-23B Improved HAWK | 17 | | 1982 | One used for training |
| Total | **22** | | | |
| **Medium missiles** | | | | |
| • Crotale | 16 | 93 | | Some are sheltered mounted for fixed sites |
| • Shahine I/II | | | 1981 | To be upgraded |
| Total | **16** | **93** | | |
| **Shoulder-launched missiles** | | | | |
| • FIM-92A/C Stinger | | 400 | 1984 | |
| • MIM-43A Redeye | | 500 | | |
| • Mistral | | 900 | | |
| Total | | **1,800** | | |
| **On order** | | | | |
| • FIM-92C Stinger SAMs | | 50 | | |
| • Crotale NG II batteries | | | | |
| • Mistral SAMs | | | | |

## Other Air Defense Systems

| Model | Quantity | In service | Since | Notes |
|---|---|---|---|---|
| **Air defense systems (missiles, radars and guns)** | | | | |
| • 35mm Skyguard AD system | 60 | 60 | | |
| **Short-range guns** | | | | |
| • 35mm Oerlikon-Buhrle 35x2 GDF | 150 | 150 | | |
| • 20mm M-163 Vulcan SP | 72 | 72 | | |
| • 30mm x 2 Wildcat SP | 52 | 52 | | |
| Total | **274** | **274** | | |
| **Radars** | | | | |
| • AN/FPS-117 (Seek Igloo) | 17 | 17 | | |
| • AN/TPS-43G | 28 | 28 | | |
| • AN/TPS-59 | | | | |
| • AN/TPS-63 | 35 | 35 | | |

## Other Air Defense Systems *(continued)*

| Model | Quantity | In service | Since | Notes |
|---|---|---|---|---|
| Command and control system | | | | |
| • C³I Peace Shield System | | | | Currently installed |
| Aerostat with airborne radars | | | | |
| • LASS | | | | Small number |

# Navy

### Combat Vessels

| Type | Original class name | Quantity | Length (m.)/ Displacement (t.) | Armament/ special equipment |
|---|---|---|---|---|
| **Missile frigates** | | | | |
| • Madina class | F-2000 | 4 | 115.0/2,000 | In process of upgrading 1xSA.365 helicopter 8xOtomat SSMs 1x8 Crotale Naval 1x100mm gun 4x40mm guns 4x533mm torpedo tubes |
| **Missile corvettes** | | | | |
| • Badr class | PCG-1 class (Tacoma boatbuilding) | 4 | 74.7/870 | 8xHarpoon SSMs 1x76mm gun 2x20mm AA guns 1x20mm Phalanx 6x324mm torpedo tubes |
| **MFPBs** | | | | |
| • Al Siddiq | PGG-1 class (Peterson Builders) | 9 | 58.1/425 | 4xHarpoon SSMs 1x76mm gun 2x20mm AA guns 1x20mm Phalanx gun |
| **Mine warfare vessels** | | | | |
| • Addriyah | MSC-322 class minesweeper | 4 | 46.6/320 | 1x20mm AA gun magnetic sweepers |

## Combat Vessels *(continued)*

| Type | Original class name | Quantity | Length (m.)/ Displacement (t.) | Armament/ special equipment |
|---|---|---|---|---|
| • Al Jawf | Sandown class | 3 | 52.7/450 | 2x30mm guns 2 PAP 104 Mk. 5 |
| Subtotal | | 7 | | |
| Total | | 24 | | |

### Patrol craft
(Mostly with coast guard)

| Type | Original class name | Quantity | Length (m.)/ Displacement (t.) | Armament/ special equipment |
|---|---|---|---|---|
| • Al-Jubatel | Abeking-Rasmussen | 2 | 26.2/96 | 1x20mm gun (with coast guard) |
| • Al Jouf | Blohm & Voss | 4 | 38.6/210 | 2x20mm guns (with coast guard) |
| • Halter type | | 17 | 23.8/56 | 2x25mm guns |
| • Sea guard | | 2 | 22.5/56 | 2xMM-15TT SSMs 2x20mm guns (with coast guard) |
| • Simonneau Type 51 | | 40 | 15.8/22 | 1x20mm gun |
| • Skorpion class | | 15 | 17.0/33 | light armament (with coast guard) |
| Total | | 80 | | |

**on order**

| Type | Original class name | Quantity | Length (m.)/ Displacement (t.) | Armament/ special equipment |
|---|---|---|---|---|
| • Lafayette class frigates | Type 3000 | 3 | 128/4,100 | Delivery in 1999 and 2002 1x AS 365 helicopter 8x MM40 SSM 8x Crotale Naval 1x 100mm gun 2x 20mm guns |
| • Sandown class mine sweepers | | 3 | | |

*Note:* Coast guard has some 650 small patrol craft.

## Landing Craft

| Type | Original class name | Quantity | Length (m.)/ Displacement (t.) | Armament/ special equipment |
|---|---|---|---|---|
| • LCM-6 class | | 4 | 17.1/62 | 34 tons or 80 troops |
| • Slingsby SAH 2200 hovercraft | | 3 | 10.6/- | 2.2 tons or 24 troops with coast guard |

## Landing Craft *(continued)*

| Type | Original class name | Quantity | Length (m.)/ Displacement (t.) | Armament/ special equipment |
|---|---|---|---|---|
| • US 1610 class LCU | | 4 | 41.1/375 | 170 tons or 120 troops |
| Total | | 11 | | |
| On order | | | | |
| • Slingsby SAH 2200 hovercraft | | 4 | | |

## Auxiliary Vessels

| Type | Original class name | Quantity | Length (m.)/ Displacement (t.) | Armament/ special equipment |
|---|---|---|---|---|
| • Tabouk training ship | | 1 | 60/585 | 1x 20mm gun |
| • Dammam | Jaguar class | 3 | 42.5/160 | Ex-gunboat now used for training |
| • Royal yacht, 1,450 dwt | | 1 | | |
| • Royal yacht, 670 ton | | 1 | | |
| • Royal yacht al-Yamama | | 1 | | |
| • Royal yacht, 112-ton | | 1 | | |
| • Royal yacht Pegasus | | 1 | | |
| • Durance class tanker | | 2 | 135.0/11,200 | 4x 40mm guns 2 helicopter pads |
| • Ocean tugs , 680 ton | | 3 | | |
| • Coastal tugs | | 13 | | |
| • Small tankers | | 3 | 28.7/233 | |
| • Training ship | | 1 | 21.4/75 | With coast guard |
| • Brooke marine firefighting craft | | 1 | 24.5/82 | Fire fighting with coast guard |

## Coastal Defense

| Type | Quantity | Notes |
|---|---|---|
| • Otomat coastal defense missile | 4 | |

## Naval Infrastructure

**Naval bases (Including coast guard):** 13
- al-Dammam, Aziziya (coast guard), al-Haql (coast guard), Jidda, Jizan, Jubayl, Makna (coast guard), al-Qatif, Ras al-Mishaab, Ras Tanura, al-Sharma, al-Wajh, Yanbu

### Ship maintenance and repair facilities:
- Repair of vessels, dependent on foreign experts; 22,000-ton and 62,000-ton floating docks at Dammam; 45,000-ton and 16,000-ton floating docks at Jidda

# 16. SUDAN

## General Data

**Official Name of the State:** The Republic of Sudan
**Head of State:** Lieutenant General Omar Hassan Ahmad al-Bashir
**Speaker of Parliament and Secretary General of the National Islamic Front:** Hassan Abdallah al-Tourabi (political and religious leader)
**Defense Minister:** Ibrahim Suleiman Hassan
**Chief of General Staff:** Lieutenant General Ahmed Hamed Siraj
**Commander of the Air Force:** Major General Ali Mahjoub Mardi
**Commander of the Navy:** Commodore Abbas al-Said Othman

**Area:** 2,504,530 sq. km. (dispute with Egypt over the "Halaib triangle" area; the government has no effective control over part of the south)
**Population:** 28,100,000

## Demography

*Ethnic groups (exact percentages not known)*
   Arabs
   Nilotics and others
*Religious groups*
   Sunni Muslims
   Animists
   Christians (Coptic, Greek Orthodox, Catholic, Protestant)

## Economic Data

|  |  | 1993 | 1994 | 1995 | 1996 | 1997 |
|---|---|---|---|---|---|---|
| GDP current price, local currency | S£ bn | 968 | 2,180 | 3,830 | 9,322 | 15,979 |
| GDP (US $) | $ bn | 6.07 | 7.52 | 6.59 | 7.45 | 10.69 |
| GDP per capita | $ | 216 | 259 | 246 | 272 | 380 |
| Real GDP growth | % | 4.3 | 4.5 | 4.4 | 4.5 | 4.0 |
| **Balance of payments** | | | | | | |
| • Exports fob | $ m | 306 | 524 | 556 | 620 | 594 |
| • Imports fob | $ m | 533 | 1,045 | 1,066 | 1,340 | 1,422 |
| • Account balance (including services and income) | $ m | -202 | -602 | -500 | -827 | -828 |
| • External debt | $ bn | 15.84 | 16.92 | 17.60 | 16.97 | 17.33 |

## Economic Data *(continued)*

| | | 1993 | 1994 | 1995 | 1996 | 1997 |
|---|---|---|---|---|---|---|
| **Government income and expenditure** | | | | | | |
| • Revenue, local currency | S£ bn | 131.9 | 285.2 | 365.4 | 629.5 | 1,073.9 |
| • Expenditure, local currency | S£ bn | 356.4 | 671.3 | 1,002.0 | 2,722.1 | 2,868.0 |
| • Defense expenditure | S£ bn | 29.50 | 49.90 | 80.60 | 208.20 | NA |
| • Defense expenditure/GDP | % | 3.04 | 2.28 | 2.10 | 2.23 | NA |
| • Defense expenditure/CGE | % | 8.27 | 7.43 | 8.04 | 7.64 | NA |
| • Population | m | 28.1 | 29.0 | 26.7 | 27.3 | 28.1 |
| • Official exchange rate (AV) | S£ : $1 | 159.31 | 289.61 | 580.87 | 1,250.79 | 1,494.00 |

*Sources:* EIU quarterly report, EIU country profile, IMF statistical yearbook, SIPRI Yearbook

## Arms Procurement and Security Assistance Received

| Country | Type | Details |
|---|---|---|
| Iran | • Arms transfers | Small arms, ammunition, EW equipment, vehicles, spare parts for Soviet and Chinese arms, tanks, aircraft, allegedly CW (1997) |
| | • Financial aid | Grant and loan (approx. $300 million) |
| | • Military training | Technicians and IRGC; trainees abroad |
| Kyrgyzstan | • Arms transfers | Combat helicopter (1997) |
| PRC | • Arms transfers | Combat aircraft (1996) |

## Arms Sales and Security Assistance Extended

| Country | Type | Details |
|---|---|---|
| Iran | • Facilities | Iranian IRGC, and facilities to Iranian ships at Port Sudan |
| Lebanon | • Facilities | Lebanese militia, camps with the popular defense forces |

## Weapons of Mass Destruction

### CW capabilities
• Personal protective equipment; unit decontamination equipment.
  Alleged CW from Iran unsubstantiated

# Armed Forces

**Major Changes:** No major change has been recorded in the Sudanese armed forces in 1998.

## Order of Battle

| Year | 1994 | 1995 | 1996 | 1997 | 1998 |
|---|---|---|---|---|---|
| **General data** | | | | | |
| • Personnel (regular) | 86,500 | 86,500 | 86,500 | 84,500 | 103,000 |
| • Divisions | 10 | 10 | 10 | 8 | 8 |
| • Number of brigades | + | + | + | 25 | 24 |
| **Ground forces** | | | | | |
| • Tanks | 450-500 | 450 | 450 | 290-340 | 290-340 (400) |
| • APCs/AFVs | 950 | 950 | 950 | 547 (686) | 547 (686) |
| • Artillery (including MRLs) | 360 | 360 | 360 | 753 (765) | 753 (765) |
| **Air Force** | | | | | |
| • Combat aircraft | 66 | 45 | 45 | 37 (53) | 34 (53) |
| • Transport aircraft | 24 | 25 | 25 | 26 | 26 |
| • Helicopters | 61 | 53 | 53 | 57 (67) | 63 (69) |
| **Air Defense Forces** | | | | | |
| • Heavy SAM batteries | 5 | 5 | 5 | 5 | 5 |
| **Navy** | | | | | |
| • Patrol craft | 10 | 10 | 23 | 22 | 22 |

*Note:* Beginning with data for 1997, we refer to quantities in active service. The numbers in parentheses refer to the total.

## Personnel

| | Regular | Reserves | Total |
|---|---|---|---|
| Ground Forces | 100,000 | | 100,000 |
| Air Force | 2,000 | | 2,000 |
| Navy | 1,000 | | 1,000 |
| **Total** | **103,000** | | **103,000** |
| **Paramilitary** | | | |
| • People's Defense Forces (loyal to Hassan Tourabi) | 15,000 | 85,000 | 100,000 |
| • Border Guard | 2,500 | | 2,500 |

*Note:* Sudan allegedly tried to mobilize up to 250,000 men in 1988, and up to 650,000 by year 2000 - the number seems unrealistic.

# Ground Forces

## Formations

|  | Divisions | Independent brigades/groups |
|---|---|---|
| Armored | 1 | |
| Mechanized/Infantry | 7 | 24 |
| Airborne | 1 | |
| Artillery | | 3 |
| Reconnaissance | | 1 |
| Engineering | 1 | |
| Total | 10 | 28 |

## Tanks

| Model | Quantity | In service | Since | Notes |
|---|---|---|---|---|
| **MBTs** | | | | |
| **High quality** | | | | |
| • M-60 A3 | 20 | 20 | 1981 | |
| **Medium and low quality** | | | | |
| • T-55/Type 59 } | 200-250 | 200-250 | | Number unconfirmed |
| • T-54 | + | + | | |
| • Type 62 | 70 | 70 | 1972 | |
| Subtotal | 270-320 | 270-320 | | |
| Total | 400 | 290-340 | | |

## APCs/AFVs

| Model | Quantity | In service | Since | Notes |
|---|---|---|---|---|
| **APCs** | | | | |
| • al-Walid | 150 | 100 | 1986 | |
| • AMX-VCI | small number | + | | |
| • M-113 | 80 | 36 | 1982 | |
| • BTR-152 | 80 | 80 | 1960 | |
| • BTR-50 | 20 | 20 | 1970 | |
| • Fahd | | | 1989 | Unconfirmed |
| • M-3 (Panhard) | | | 1983 | Unconfirmed |
| • OT-62 | 20 | 20 | | |
| • OT-64 | 55 | 55 | | |
| Subtotal | 405 | 311 | | |

## APCs/AFVs *(continued)*

| Model | Quantity | In service | Since | Notes |
|---|---|---|---|---|
| **IFVs** | | | | |
| • BMP-2 | 6 | 6 | | |
| • V-150 Commando | 100 | 55 | 1984 | |
| Subtotal | 106 | 61 | | |
| **Reconnaissance** | | | | |
| • AML-90 | 5 | 5 | | |
| • BRDM 1/2 | 60 | 60 | | |
| • Ferret | 60 | 60 | 1960 | |
| • Saladin | 50 | 50 | 1961 | |
| Subtotal | 175 | 175 | | |
| Total | **686** | **547** | | |

## Artillery

| Model | Quantity | In service | Since | Notes |
|---|---|---|---|---|
| **Self-propelled guns and howitzers** | | | | |
| • 155mm Mk F-3 (AMX) SP | 10 | 6 | 1984 | |
| **Towed guns and howitzers** | | | | |
| • 155mm M-114 | 20 | 12 | 1981 | |
| • 130mm Type 59 gun/M-46 | 75 | 75 | | |
| • 105mm M-101 | 20 | 20 | | |
| Subtotal | 115 | 107 | | |
| **Mortars, under 160mm** | | | | |
| • 120mm mortar | + | + | | |
| **MRLs** | | | | |
| • 122mm BM-21 | 90 | 90 | | |
| • 122mm Sakr | 50 | 50 | | |
| • 107mm Type 63 | 500 | 500 | | |
| Subtotal | 640 | 640 | | |
| Total | **765** | **753** | | |

## Anti-tank Weapons

| Model | Quantity | In service | Since | Notes |
|---|---|---|---|---|
| **Missiles** | | | | |
| • BGM-71C Improved TOW | + | + | | Not all serviceable |
| • Swingfire | + | 0 | | Not serviceable |
| • AT-3 (Sagger) | | | | |
| **Anti-tank guns** | | | | |
| • 100mm M-1955 field/AT gun | | | | |
| • 100mm M-1944 | 50 | 0 | | In storage |

### Anti-tank weapons *(continued)*

| Model | Quantity | In service | Since | Notes |
|---|---|---|---|---|
| • 85mm M-1945/ D-44 field/AT gun | 100 | 0 | | In storage |
| • 76mm M-1942 | + | 0 | | |
| On order | | | | |
| • 106mm M-40 recoilless | 100 | | | |

# Air Force

## Order of Battle

| Model | Quantity | In service | Notes |
|---|---|---|---|
| • Combat | 52-53 | 33-34 | low serviceability |
| • Transport | 26 | 26 | low serviceability |
| • Helicopters | 67 | 61-63 | low serviceability |

## Combat Aircraft

| Model | Quantity | In service | Since | Notes |
|---|---|---|---|---|
| Interceptors | | | | |
| • MiG-23 | 3-4 | 3-4 | 1987 | |
| Multi-role | | | | |
| • F-5E/F | 9 | 0 | 1984/1982 | |
| Obsolete | | | | |
| • A-5 (Fantan)/Q-5 | 10 | 10 | | |
| • F-6 Shenyang/J-6 | 11 | 11 | 1981 | |
| • MiG-21 (Fishbed)/F-7 | 19 | 9 | 1970 | |
| Subtotal | 40 | 30 | | |
| **Total** | **52-53** | **33-34** | | |

## Transport Aircraft

| Model | Quantity | In service | Since | Notes |
|---|---|---|---|---|
| • An-24 (Coke)/An-26 | 6 | 6 | | |
| • C-130H Hercules | 4 | 4 | 1978 | |
| • DHC-5D Buffalo | 3 | 3 | 1978 | |
| • Fokker F-27 | 1 | 1 | 1974 | |
| • Mystère-Falcon 50 | 1 | 1 | 1983 | |
| • Mystère-Falcon 20 | 1 | 1 | 1978 | |
| • C-212 | 4 | 4 | | |
| • EMB-110P | 6 | 6 | | |
| **Total** | **26** | **26** | | |

## Training and Liaison Aircraft

| Model | Quantity | In service | Since | Notes |
|---|---|---|---|---|
| With ground attack/close air support capability | | | | |
| • BAC-145 Jet Provost | 5 | 5 | 1969 | |
| • BAC-167 Strikemaster | 5 | 3 | 1984 | |
| Total | **10** | **8** | | |

## Helicopters

| Model | Quantity | In service | Since | Notes |
|---|---|---|---|---|
| **Attack** | | | | |
| • Mi-24 | 6 | 6 | | |
| **Medium transport** | | | | |
| • Mi-4 (Hound) | 3 | 3 | | Possibly phased out |
| • Mi-8 (Hip) | 14 | 6-8 | | |
| • SA-330 Puma/ IAR-330 Puma | 10 | 10 | 1985 | |
| • Bell 212/AB-212 | 5 | 5 | 1982 | |
| • AB-412 | 10 | 10 | | |
| Subtotal | 42 | 34-36 | | |
| **Light transport** | | | | |
| • MBB BO-105 | 18 | 18 | 1980 | Some serving with police |
| • Bell 206 | 3 | 3 | | |
| Subtotal | 21 | 21 | | |
| Total | **69** | **61-63** | | |

**On order**

• Helicopters from Russia

## Advanced Armament

**Air-to-air-missiles**

• AA-2 (Atoll)

## Air Force Infrastructure

**Military airfields:**  13

Atbara, al-Fasher, al-Geneina, Juba, Khartoum, Malakal, Merowe, al-Obeid, Port Sudan, Port Sudan (new), Wad Medani, Wadi Sayidina, Wau

# Air Defense Forces

## Surface-to-Air Missiles

| Model | Batteries | Launchers | Since | Notes |
|---|---|---|---|---|
| Heavy missiles | | | | ◢ |
| • SA-2 (Guideline) | 5 | | | |
| Shoulder-launched missiles | | | | |
| • SA-7 (Grail) | | 250 | | |
| • MIM-43A Redeye | | 25 | 1984 | |
| Total | | 275 | | |

## Other Air Defense Systems

| Model | Quantity | In service | Since | Notes |
|---|---|---|---|---|
| Short-range guns | | | | |
| • 57mm | + | + | | |
| • 40mm | 60 | 60 | | |
| • 37mm M-1939 | 110 | 110 | | |
| • 23mm ZU 23x2 | 50 | 50 | | |
| • 20mm M-3 VDA | 12 | 12 | | |
| • 20mm M-163 A-1 Vulcan SP | 8 | 8 | 1981 | |
| • 20mm M-167 Vulcan | 30 | 30 | | |
| Total | 270 | 270 | | |

# Navy

## Combat Vessels

| Type | Original class name | Quantity | Length (m.)/ Displacement (t.) | Armament/ special equipment |
|---|---|---|---|---|
| Patrol craft | | | | |
| • Abeking and Rasmussen | | 2 | 22.9/70 | 1 x 20mm gun YJ-1 SAM |
| • Ashoora I class | | 12 | 8.1/3 | |
| • Sewart class | | 4 | 12.9/92 | 1 x 7.62mm MG |
| • Kurmuk | Yugoslav type 15 | 4 | 16.9/19.5 | 1 x 20mm gun |
| Total | | 22 | | |

## Auxiliary Vessels

| Type | Original class name | Quantity | Length (m.)/ Displacement (t.) | Armament/ special equipment |
|---|---|---|---|---|
| • Yugoslav supply ships | | 7 | 47.3/410 | 1 x 20mm gun |

## Naval Infrastructure

**Naval bases:** 1
Port Sudan

# Non-governmental Military Organizations

## Personnel

| | Regular | Reserves | Total | Notes |
|---|---|---|---|---|
| • National Democratic Alliance (NDA) | | | | A coordinating organization of all active opposition organizations |
| • Sudan People's Liberation Army (SPLA) | 30,000 | 100,000 | 130,000 | The main non-governmental military organization active in south Sudan |
| • South Sudan Independence Movement (SSIM) | 10,000 | | 10,000 | Also known as SPLA United. In 1996 signed a truce with the government |
| • Sudan Alliance Forces | 1,000-2,000 | | 1,000-2,000 | Active in east Sudan |
| • Beja Congress Forces | 500 | | 500 | Active in east Sudan |
| • New Sudan Brigade | 2,000 | | 2˙000 | Recent activity unknown |

## Equipment

| Organiztion | Category | System | Notes |
|---|---|---|---|
| SPLA | Tanks | • T-54/55 | |
| | MRLs | • BM-21 | |
| | Artillery guns | • + | |
| | Mortars | • 120mm | |
| | | • 60mm | |
| | Air Defense | • SA-7 SAM | |
| | | • 14.5mm AA | |

# 17. SYRIA

## General Data

**Official Name of the State:** The Arab Republic of Syria
**Head of State:** President Hafez al-Assad
**Prime Minister:** Mahmoud al-Zuabi
**Minister of Defense:** Lieutenant General Mustafa al-Tlass
**Chief of General Staff:** General Ali Aslan
**Commander of the Air Force:** Major-General Muhammad al-Khouly
**Commander of the Navy:** Vice Admiral Wa'il Nasser

**Area:** 185,180 sq. km
**Population:** 15,100,000

### Demography

| | | |
|---|---|---|
| *Ethnic groups* | | |
| Arabs | 13,635,300 | 90.3% |
| Kurds, Armenians and Others | 1,464,700 | 9.7% |
| *Religious groups* | | |
| Sunni Muslims | 11,174,000 | 74.0% |
| Alawi, Druze, and Shi'ite Muslims | 2,416,000 | 16.0% |
| Christians (Greek Orthodox, Gregorian, Armenian, Catholics, Syrian Orthodox, Greek Catholics) | 1,510,000 | 10.0% |

### Economic Data

| | | 1993 | 1994 | 1995 | 1996 | 1997 |
|---|---|---|---|---|---|---|
| GDP current price, local currency | S£ bn | 413.8 | 502.4 | 551.7 | 672.6 | 688.8 |
| GDP (US $) | $ bn | 36.86 | 44.757 | 49.15 | 59.92 | 61.36 |
| GDP per capita | $ | 2,753 | 3,234 | 3,464 | 4,098 | 4,064 |
| Real GDP growth | % | 6.0 | 6.7 | 6.7 | 2.2 | 0.5 |
| **Balance of payments** | | | | | | |
| • Exports fob | $ bn | 3.203 | 3.329 | 3.858 | 4.178 | 4.057 |
| • Imports fob | $ bn | 3.476 | 4.604 | 4 | 4.516 | 3.603 |
| • Account balance (including services and income) | $ bn | -0.579 | -0.791 | 0.367 | 0.165 | 0.564 |
| • External debt | $ bn | 0.02 | 0.0206 | 0.0213 | 0.0214 | 0.0215 |

## Economic Data (continued)

|  |  | 1993 | 1994 | 1995 | 1996 | 1997 |
|---|---|---|---|---|---|---|
| Government income and expenditure |  |  |  |  |  |  |
| • Revenue, local currency | S£ bn | 123.018 | 144.162 | 125.7 | 156.913 | 180.5 |
| • Expenditure, local currency | S£ bn | 123.018 | 144.162 | 162 | 188.049 | 211.12 |
| • Defense expenditure | S£ bn | 29.95 | 37.27 | 40.5 | 41.74 | 43.86 |
| • Defense expenditure/GDP | % | 7.23 | 7.42 | 7.34 | 6.2 | 6.36 |
| • Defense expenditure/CGE | % | 24.34 | 25.85 | 25 | 22.2 | 20.77 |
| • Population | m | 13.39 | 13.84 | 14.19 | 14.62 | 15.1 |
| • Official exchange rate | S£ : $1 | 11.225 | 11.225 | 11.225 | 11.225 | 11.225 |

*Sources:* EIU quarterly report, EIU country profile, IMF statistical yearbook, SIPRI Yearbook

*Note:* Economic data is very unreliable. Unrealistic official exchange rate distorts data considerably.

## Arms Procurement and Security Assistance Received

| Country | Type | Details |
|---|---|---|
| Czech Republic | • Arms transfers | T-72 MBTs (1995) |
| India | • Arms transfers | Aircraft spare parts; CW chemical components (1996) |
| Iran | • Arms transfers | Assistance in MBTs upgrade (1997) |
|  | • Financial aid | Promised guarantees for debts to Russia (1997) |
| North Korea | • Arms transfers | Scud C SSMs (1996), including assistance in production. |
| Pakistan | • Arms transfers | Trainer aircraft (1994) |
| PRC | • Advisers |  |
| Russia | • Advisers | Approx. 50 |
|  | • Arms transfers | Kornet ATGMs (1998) |
|  | • Military training | 70 trainees in Russia (1998) |
| Saudi Arabia and other GCC countries | • Financial aid | $350 million promised in 1997 |
| Ukraine | • Arms transfers | Upgraded MBTs (1997) |

## Arms Sales and Security Assistance Extended

| Country | Type | Details |
|---------|------|---------|
| Kurds | • Facilities provided | Some facilities also in Syria |
| Lebanon | • Arms transfers | T-55 MBTs (1991) |
| | • Military training | Approx. 200 trainees annually, advisers |
| Palestinian "rejection front" organizations | • Facilities provided | Camps |
| | • Financial aid | Grant for Fatah-Intifada, al-Saiqa, PPSF, PLF and PFLP-GC |

## Foreign Military Cooperation

| | Details |
|---|---------|
| • Forces deployed abroad in | Lebanon--25,000 in Biqa', northern Lebanon (Tripoli area), and Beirut |

## Defense Production

| | M | P | A |
|---|---|---|---|
| **Army equipment** | | | |
| • Ammunition | √ | | |
| • Upgrading of tanks | | √ | |
| • Production and upgrading of SSMs (in cooperation with North Korea, plant under construction) | | √ | √ |
| **CW and BW:** | | | |
| • Production of chemical and biological agents, chemical warheads for SSMs | √ | | |

*Note:* M - manufacture (indigenously developed)
P - production under licence
A - assembly

## Weapons of Mass Destruction

### Nuclear capabilities
• Basic R&D; contract for purchase of a 27-KW research reactor from China; 3-MW research reactor on order from Argentina, deal suspended

### CW capabilities
• Personal protective equipment
• Soviet-type unit decontamination equipment
• Stockpiles of nerve gas, including Sarin, mustard gas,VX nerve gas
• Chemical warheads for SSMs
• Chemical armed aerial bombs

## Weapons of Mass Destruction *(continued)*

Biological warfare capabilities
• Biological weapons and toxins (unconfirmed)

Surface-to-Surface Missiles and Rockets

| Model | Launchers | Missiles | Since | Notes |
|---|---|---|---|---|
| • FROG-7 | 18 | | 1973 | |
| • SS-1 (Scud B) | 18 | 200 | 1974 | |
| • SS-1 (Scud C variant from North Korea) | 8 | 60 | 1992 | |
| • SS-21 (Scarab) | 18 | | 1983 | |
| Total | 62 | | | |

# Armed Forces

**Major Changes:** No major change has been recorded in the Syrian armed forces in 1998. The Syrian ground forces received some 1,000 AT-14 Kornet anti-tank missiles. This is the first arms deal with Russia in almost 10 years. There have been reports about a major arms deal with Russia, but none has materialized.

## Order of Battle

| Year | 1994 | 1995 | 1996 | 1997 | 1998 |
|---|---|---|---|---|---|
| **General data** | | | | | |
| • Personnel (regular) | 390,000 | 390,000 | 390,000 | 380,000 | 380,000 |
| • Divisions | 12 | 12 | 12 | 12 | 12 |
| • Total number of brigades | 59 | 59 | 59 | 68 | 68 |
| **Ground forces** | | | | | |
| • Tanks | 4,800 | 4,800 | 4,800 | 3,700 (4,800) | 3,700 (4,800) |
| • APCs/AFVs | 4,980 | 4,980 | 4,980 | 4,080 | 4,080 |
| • Artillery (Incl. MRLs) | 2,500 | 2,500 | 2,500 | 2,575 (2,975) | 2,575 (2,975) |
| • SSM launchers | 62 | 62 | 62 | 62 | 62 |
| **Air force** | | | | | |
| • Combat aircraft | 515 | 515 | 515 | 520 | 520 |
| • Transport aircraft | 23 | 23 | 23 | 23 (25) | 23 (25) |
| • Helicopters | 285 | 285 | 285 | 295 | 295 |
| **Air defense forces** | | | | | |
| • Heavy SAM batteries | 108 | 108 | 108 | 108 | 108 |
| • Medium SAM batteries | 70 | 70 | 70 | 65 | 65 |
| • Light SAM launchers | + | + | + | 55 | 55 |

## Order of Battle *(continued)*

| Year | 1994 | 1995 | 1996 | 1997 | 1998 |
|---|---|---|---|---|---|
| **Navy** | | | | | |
| • Combat vessels | 32 | 32 | 32 | 25 (30) | 24 (27) |
| • Patrol craft | 16 | 16 | 16 | 8 | 8 |
| • Submarines | 3 | 3 | 3 | 0 (3) | 0 (3) |

*Note:* Beginning with data for 1997, we refer to quantities in active service. The numbers in parentheses refer to the total.

## Personnel

| | Regular | Reserves | Total |
|---|---|---|---|
| Ground Forces | 306,000 | 100,000 | 406,000 |
| Air Force | 30,000 | 10,000 | 40,000 |
| Air Defense | 40,000 | 20,000 | 60,000 |
| Navy | 4,000 | 2,500 | 6,500 |
| **Total** | **380,000** | **132,500** | **512,500** |
| **Paramilitary** | | | |
| • Gendarmerie | 8,000 | | 8,000 |
| • Workers' Militia | | 400,000 | 400,000 |

*Note:* Syria can mobilize 750,000 reserves, not organized in units.

# Ground Forces

## Formations

| | Corps | Divisions | Independent brigades/groups | Brigades in division |
|---|---|---|---|---|
| All arms | 3 | | | |
| Armored | | 7 | 1 | 3 armd., 1 mech., 1 arty. each |
| Mechanized | | 3 | 1 | 2 mech., 2 armd. 1 arty. each |
| Republican Guard | | 1 | | 3 armd., 1 mech., 1 arty. each |
| Infantry/Special forces | | 1 | 3 | |
| Airborne/Special forces | | | 8 - 10 | |

## Formations *(continued)*

|  | Corps | Divisions | Independent brigades/groups | Brigades in division |
|---|---|---|---|---|
| Artillery |  |  | 2 |  |
| SSM forces |  |  | 3 |  |
| Anti-tank/Infantry |  |  | 2 |  |
| Total | 3 | 12 | 20 - 22 |  |

Note: one armored division is a reserve unit.

## Tanks

| Model | Quantity | In service | Since | Notes |
|---|---|---|---|---|
| **MBTs** |  |  |  |  |
| **High Quality** |  |  |  |  |
| • T-72/T-72M | 1,600 | 1,600 | 1979/1993 |  |
| **Medium and low quality** |  |  |  |  |
| • T-62 | 1,000 | 1,000 | 1974 |  |
| • T-55/T-54 | 2,200-2,300 | 1,100 | 1957 | Some upgraded |
| Subtotal | 3,200-3,300 | 2,100 |  |  |
| **Total** | **4,800** | **3,700** |  |  |

*Note:* 1,200 older models in storage.

## APCs/AFVs

| Model | Quantity | In service | Since | Notes |
|---|---|---|---|---|
| **APCs** |  |  |  |  |
| • BTR-152 | 560 | 560 | 1967 |  |
| • BTR-40/50/60 | 1,000 | 1,000 | 1956 |  |
| Subtotal | 1,560 | 1,560 |  |  |
| **IFVs** |  |  |  |  |
| • BMP-1 | 2,450 | 2,450 | 1977 |  |
| • BMP-2 | approx. 70 | approx. 70 | 1988 |  |
| Subtotal | 2,520 | 2,520 |  |  |
| **Reconnaissance** |  |  |  |  |
| • BRDM-2 |  |  |  | 900 under Antitank weapons |
| Total | 4,080 | 4,080 |  |  |

## Artillery

| Model | Quantity | In service | Since | Notes |
|---|---|---|---|---|
| **Self-propelled guns and howitzers** | | | | |
| • 152mm 2S3 | 50 | 50 | 1984 | |
| • 122mm 2S1 | 400 | 400 | 1982 | |
| • 122mm D30 | 55 | 55 | 1986 | Syrian |
| Subtotal | 505 | 505 | | |
| **Towed guns and howitzers** | | | | |
| • 180mm S-23 | 10 | 10 | | |
| • 152mm M-1943 | 50 | 50 | | |
| • 152mm D-20 | 20 | 20 | | |
| • 130mm M-46 | 800 | 800 | 1970 | |
| • 122mm D-30 | 500 | 500 | | |
| • 122mm D-74 | 400 | 0 | | In storage |
| • 122mm M-1938 | 150 | 150 | | |
| Subtotal | 1,930 | 1,530 | | |
| **Mortars, over 160mm** | | | | |
| • 240mm | 10 | 10 | | |
| • 160mm | 80 | 80 | | |
| Subtotal | 90 | 90 | | |
| **Mortars, under 160mm** | | | | |
| • 120mm | | | | |
| **MRLs** | | | | |
| • 122mm BM-21 | 250 | 250 | 1979 | |
| • 107mm Type 63 | 200 | 200 | | |
| Subtotal | 450 | 450 | | |
| **Total** | **2,975** | **2,575** | | |

## Logistic and Engineering Equipment

MTU-67 bridging tanks/MT-55 bridging tanks (approx. 90), tank-towed bridges, mine-clearing rollers, AFV transporters (800)

## Anti-tank Weapons

| Model | Quantity | In service | Since | Notes |
|---|---|---|---|---|
| **Missiles** | | | | |
| • AT-14 (Kornet) | 1,000 | 1,000 | 1998 | Being deliverd |
| • AT-4 (Spigot) | 150 | 150 | 1980 | |
| • AT-5 (Spandrel) | 40 | 40 | | |
| • AT-3 (Sagger) SP | 3,000 | 3,000 | 1974 | Mounted on BRDM-2 and BMP-1 |
| • Milan | 200 | 200 | 1980 | |
| **Total** | **4,390** | **4,390** | | |

# Air Force

## Order of Battle

| Model | Quantity | In service | Notes |
|---|---|---|---|
| • Combat | 520 | 520 | |
| • Transport | 25 | 23 | |
| • Helicopters | 295 | 295 | |

## Combat Aircraft

| Model | Quantity | In service | Since | Notes |
|---|---|---|---|---|
| Interceptors | | | | |
| • MiG-25 (Foxbat) | 35 | 35 | 1980 | |
| • MiG-29 (Fulcrum) | 20 | 20 | 1987 | |
| • MiG-23 ML/MF | 100 | 100 | 1974 | |
| Subtotal | 155 | 155 | | |
| Ground attack | | | | |
| • Su-24 (Fencer) | 20 | 20 | 1988 | |
| • MiG-23 U/BN (Flogger) | 35 | 35 | 1978 | |
| • Su-20/22 (Fitter C/D) | 100 | 100 | 1978 | |
| Subtotal | 155 | 155 | | |
| Obsolete | | | | |
| • MiG-21 MF/ BIS/U (Fishbed) | 200-210 | 200-210 | | Possibly some upgraded |
| Total | 520 | 520 | | |

On order

Su-24 (Fencer), MiG-29 (Fulcrum), Su-27

## Transport Aircraft

| Model | Quantity | In service | Since | Notes |
|---|---|---|---|---|
| • An-24/26 (Coke/Curl) | 6 | 6 | | |
| • IL-76 (Candid) | 4 | 4 | 1983 | |
| • Tu - 134 | 2 | 2 | | |
| • Mystère-Falcon 20/900 | 5 | 3 | | |
| • Piper Navajo | 2 | 2 | | |
| • Yak-40 (Codling) | 6 | 6 | | |
| Total | 25 | 23 | | |

## Training and Liaison Aircraft

| Model | Quantity | In service | Since | Notes |
|---|---|---|---|---|
| With ground attack/close air support capability | | | | |
| • L-39 Albatross | 90 | 90 | 1980 | |
| Others | | | | |
| • MBB 223 Flamingo | 40 | 40 | | |
| • Mushshak | 6 | 6 | 1994 | |
| Subtotal | 46 | 46 | | |
| Total | **136** | **136** | | |

## Helicopters

| Model | Quantity | In service | Since | Notes |
|---|---|---|---|---|
| Attack | | | | |
| • Mi-25 (Hind) | 55 | 55 | 1980 | |
| • SA-342 Gazelle | 45 | 45 | 1976 | |
| Subtotal | 100 | 100 | | |
| Medium transport | | | | |
| • Mi-8/Mi-17 (Hip H) | 160 | 160 | | |
| • Mi-2 | 10 | 10 | | Limited serviceability |
| Subtotal | 170 | 170 | | |
| Naval combat | | | | |
| • Ka-28 (Helix) | 5 | 5 | 1990 | |
| • Mi-14 (Haze) | 20 | 20 | | |
| Subtotal | 25 | 25 | | |
| Total | **295** | **295** | | |

## Miscellaneous Aircraft

| Model | Quantity | In service | Since | Notes |
|---|---|---|---|---|
| Reconnaissance aircraft | | | | |
| Mig 25 R | 7 | 7 | | |
| UAVs and mini-UAVs | | | | |
| • Shmel/Malachit | | 0 | | |

## Advanced Armament

**Air-to-air missiles**
AA-2 (Atoll), AA-6 (Acrid), AA-7 (Apex), AA-8 (Aphid), AA-10 (Alamo),
AA-11 (Archer)

**Air-to-ground missiles**
AS-7 (Kerry), AS-9 (Kyle), AS-10 (Karen), AS-11 (Kegler), AS-12, AS-14 (Kedge),
AT-2 (Swatter), HOT

## Air Force Infrastructure

**Aircraft shelters**
In all airfields, for combat aircraft
**military airfields:**              21
Abu Duhur, Afis North, Aleppo, Damascus (international), Damascus (Meze),
   Dir ez-Zor, Dumayr, Hama, Jarah, Khalkhala, Latakia, Marj-royal (Bley),
   Nassiriyah, Tudmur, al-Qusayr, Rasm al-Aboud, Sayqal, Shayarat, al-Suweida,
   T-4, Tabaka

# Air Defense Forces

## Surface-to-air Missiles

| Model | Batteries | Launchers | Since | Notes |
|-------|-----------|-----------|-------|-------|
| **Heavy missiles** | | | | |
| • SA-2 (Guideline) and SA-3 (Goa) | 100 | 600 | 1971 | |
| • SA-5 (Gammon) | 8 | 24 | 1983 | |
| **Total** | **108** | **624** | | |
| **Medium missiles** | | | | |
| • SA-8 (Gecko) | 14 | 56 | 1982 | |
| • SA-6 (Gainful) | 50 | 200 | 1973 | |
| **Total** | **64** | **256** | | |
| **Light missiles** | | | | |
| • SA-9 (Gaskin) | | 20 | 1978 | |
| • SA-13 (Gopher) | | 35 | | |
| **Total** | | **55** | | |
| **Shoulder-launched missiles** | | | | |
| • SA-7 (Grail) | | | 1973 | |
| • SA-14 (Gremlin) | | | | |
| • SA-16 | | | | |
| **On order** | | | | |
| SA-10 (Grumble) | | | | |

## Other Air Defense Systems

| Model | Quantity | In service | Since | Notes |
|-------|----------|------------|-------|-------|
| **Short-range guns** | | | | |
| • 57mm S-60 | 700 | approx 400 | | Partly phased out |
| • 37mm M-1939 | 300 | | | In storage |
| • 23mm ZSU 23x4 SP | 400 | 400 | | |
| • 23mm ZU 23x2 | 600 | approx. 300 | | |
| **Total** | **2,000** | **approx. 1,100** | | |

## Other Air Defense Systems *(continued)*

| Model | Quantity | In service | Since | Notes |
|-------|----------|-----------|-------|-------|
| Radars | | | | |

Long Track, P-14 (Tall King), P-15 (Flat Face), P-12 (Spoon Rest), P-30, P-35, P-80, PRV-13, PRV-16.

# Navy

## Combat Vessels

| Type | Original class name | Quantity | Length (m.)/ Displacement (t.) | Armament/ special equipment |
|------|---------------------|----------|-------------------------------|----------------------------|
| **Submarines** | | | | |
| • R class (Romeo) | Type 633 | 0 | 76.6/1,830 | 8 x 533mm torpedoes 28 mines 3 Unserviceable |
| **MFPBs** | | | | |
| • Komar | | 0 | 27/85 | 2 x SS-N-2A Styx SSM 2 x 25mm guns 3 Unserviceable |
| • Ossa I | | 6 | 38.6/210 | 4 x SS-N-2A Styx SSM 4 x 30mm guns |
| • Ossa II | | 10 | 38.6/245 | 4 x SS-N-2C Styx SSM 4 x 30mm guns |
| Subtotal | | 16 | | Some possibly phased out |
| **ASW vessels** | | | | |
| • Petya II submarine chaser frigate | | 2 | 81.8/950 | 5-16 x 400mm torpedoes 4 x RBU 2500 ASW mortars 22 mines 4 x 76mm guns |
| **Mine warfare vessels** | | | | |
| • Sonya class | Type 1265 | 1 | 48/450 | 2 x 30mm guns 2 x 25mm guns |
| • Yevgenia class | | 5 | 24.6/77 | 2 x 25mm guns 2 x 14.5mm MGs |
| Subtotal | | 6 | | |
| **Total** | | **24** | | |

## Combat Vessels *(continued)*

| Type | Original class name | Quantity | Length (m.)/ Displacement (t.) | Armament/ special equipment |
|---|---|---|---|---|
| **Patrol craft** | | | | |
| • Zhuk class | Type 1400M | 8 | 24/39 | 4 x 14.5mm MGs |
| Total | | 8 | | |

## Landing Craft

| Type | Original class name | Quantity | Length (m.)/ Displacement (t.) | Armament/ special equipment |
|---|---|---|---|---|
| • Polnochny B-class LCT | Type 771 | 3 | 75/760 | 180 troops or 350 tons 2 x 140mm MRLs 4 x 30mm guns |
| Total | | 3 | | |

## Auxiliary Vessels

| Type | Original class name | Quantity | Length (m.)/ Displacement (t.) | Armament/ special equipment |
|---|---|---|---|---|
| • Training ship (al-Assad) | | 1 | 105/3,500 | |
| • Natya | Type 226 | 1 | 61/804 | 2 x SA-N-5 Grail SAMs 4 x 30mm guns formerly a minesweeper, now converted to oceanographic research |
| • T-43 class | | 1 | 60/580 | 16 mines 4 x 37mm guns 4 x 14.5mm MGs |
| • Sekstan class | | 1 | 40.8/400 | 115 tons |
| • Poluchat torpedo recovery vessel | | 1 | 29.6/100 | 2 x 14.5mm MGs |
| • Rotork Sea Truck | | 6 | 14.5/12 | |
| Total | | 11 | | |

## Advanced Armament

**Surface-to-surface missiles**
SS-N-2 Styx/SS-N-2C

## Coastal Defense

| Type | Launchers | Missiles | Since | Notes |
|------|-----------|----------|-------|-------|
| **Missiles** | | | | |
| • SSC-1B Sepal | 12 | | | |
| • SSC-3 | 12 | | 1966 | Armed with SS-N-2C missiles |
| **Guns** | | | | |
| • 130mm | 36 | | | |

## Naval Infrastructure

Naval bases:     3
Latakia, Minat al-Baida, Tartus

**Ship maintenance and repair facilities:**
repairs at Latakia

# 18. TUNISIA

## General Data

**Official Name of the State:** The Republic of Tunisia
**Head of State:** President General Zayn al-Abedine Bin Ali
(also Defense Minister)
**Prime Minister:** Hamid al-Karaoui
**Minister of National Defense:** Habib Ben Yahia
**Secretary of State for Security:** Mohamed Ali Ghenzoui
**Minister, Chief of General Staff:** Mohamed Jegham
**Commander of the Ground Forces:** Lieutenant General Muhammad
Hadi Bin Hassin
**Commander of the Air Force:** Major General Rida Hamuda Atar
**Commander of the Navy:** Commodore al-Shadli Sharif

**Area:** 164,206 sq. km.
**Population:** 9,200,000

## Demography

| Ethnic groups | | |
|---|---|---|
| Arabs/Berbers | 9,016,000 | 98.0% |
| Europeans | 92,000 | 1.0% |
| Others | 92,000 | 1.0% |
| Religious groups | | |
| Sunni Muslims | 9,016,000 | 98.0% |
| Christians | 92,000 | 1.0% |
| Others | 92,000 | 1.0% |

## Economic Data

| | | 1993 | 1994 | 1995 | 1996 | 1997 |
|---|---|---|---|---|---|---|
| GDP current price, local currency | TD bn | 14.66 | 15.81 | 17.03 | 19.07 | 21.02 |
| GDP (US $) | $ bn | 14.55 | 15.70 | 18.03 | 19.49 | 19 |
| GDP per capita | $ | 1,691 | 1,784 | 2,004 | 2,141 | 2,066 |
| Real GDP growth | % | 2.1 | 3.2 | 2.3 | 7.0 | 5.4 |
| **Balance of payments** | | | | | | |
| • Exports fob | $ bn | 3.746 | 4.643 | 5.470 | 5.519 | 5.559 |
| • Imports fob | $ bn | 5.810 | 6.210 | 7.459 | 7.280 | 7.514 |

## Economic Data *(continued)*

|  |  | 1993 | 1994 | 1995 | 1996 | 1997 |
|---|---|---|---|---|---|---|
| • Account balance (including services and income) | $ bn | -1.323 | -0.564 | -0.755 | -0.512 | -0.639 |
| • External debt | $ bn | 8.7 | 9.3 | 9.8 | 9.9 | 9.6 |
| **Government income and expenditure** | | | | | | |
| • Revenue, local currency | TD bn | 3.86 | 4.17 | 4.26 | 4.5 | 4.87 |
| • Expenditure, local currency | TD bn | 4.3 | 4.58 | 4.97 | 5.37 | 5.8 |
| • Defense expenditure | TD bn | 0.346 | 0.364 | 0.326 | 0.343 | 0.369 |
| • Defense expenditure/GDP | % | 2.36 | 2.3 | 1.9 | 1.8 | 1.75 |
| • Defense expenditure/CGE | % | 8.04 | 7.94 | 6.55 | 6.38 | 6.36 |
| • Population | m | 8.6 | 8.8 | 9 | 9.1 | 9.2 |
| • Official exchange rate | TD : $1 | 1.004 | 1.012 | 0.946 | 0.973 | 1.106 |

*Sources:* EIU quarterly report, EIU country profile, IMF statistical yearbook, SIPRI Yearbook

## Arms Procurement and Security Assistance Received

| Country | Type | Details |
|---|---|---|
| Czech Republic | • Arms transfers | Trainer and transport aircraft (1996) |
| Germany | • Arms transfers | Naval vessels (1993) |
| USA | • Financial aid | $27 million grant (1993) and a higher grant in 1994 |

## Foreign Military Cooperation

| | Details |
|---|---|
| • Joint maneuvers with | France, USA, Spain (unconfirmed) |

## Defense Production

| | M | P | A |
|---|---|---|---|
| **Naval Craft** | | | |
| • 20 meter patrol craft, with assistance from South Korea | | √ | |

*Note:*  M - manufacture (indigenously developed)
P - production under license
A - assembly

# Armed Forces

**Major Changes:** No major change has been recorded in the Tunisian armed forces in 1998.

## Order of Battle

| Year | 1994 | 1995 | 1996 | 1997 | 1998 |
|---|---|---|---|---|---|
| **General data** | | | | | |
| • Personnel | 35,500 | 35,500 | 35,500 | 35,500 | 35,500 |
| • Total number of brigades | 8 | 8 | 8 | 5 | 5 |
| **Ground forces** | | | | | |
| • Tanks | 192 | 200 | 200 | 139 (144) | 139 (144) |
| • APCs/AFVs | 316 | 316 | 316 | 281 | 281 |
| • Artillery | 91 | 91 | 91 | 205 (215) | 205 (215) |
| **Air force** | | | | | |
| • Combat aircraft | 14 | 13 | 13 | 12 | 12 |
| • Transport aircraft | 6 | 11 | 11 | 10 (11) | 10 (11) |
| • Helicopters | 42 | 35 | 35 | 40 | 40 |
| **Air defense forces** | | | | | |
| • Light SAM launchers | + | + | + | 73 | 73 |
| **Navy** | | | | | |
| • Combat vessels | 16 | 19 | 19 | 11 | 11 |
| • Patrol craft | 17 | 17 | 17 | 36 | 36 |

*Note:* Beginning with data for 1997, we refer to quantities in active service. The numbers in parentheses refer to the total.

## Personnel

| | Regular | Total |
|---|---|---|
| Ground Forces | 27,000 | 27,000 |
| Air Force | 4,000 | 4,000 |
| Navy | 4,500 | 4,500 |
| **Total** | **35,500** | **35,500** |
| **Paramilitary** | | |
| • Gendarmerie | 2,000 | 2,000 |
| • National guard | 7,000 | 7,000 |

# Ground Forces

## Formations

|  | Independent brigades/groups | Regiments in brigade |
| --- | --- | --- |
| Mechanized/Infantry | 3 | 1 armd., 2 mech., 1 arty. each |
| Commando/Paratroops | 1 | |
| Sahara brigade | 1 | |
| Total | 5 | |

## Tanks

| Model | Quantity | In service | Since | Notes |
| --- | --- | --- | --- | --- |
| MBTs | | | | |
| Medium and low quality | | | | |
| • M-60 A1/A3 | 89 | 84 | 1984 | |
| Light tanks | | | | |
| • SK-105 (Kurassier) | 55 | 55 | 1983 | |
| Total | 144 | 139 | | |

## APCs/AFVs

| Model | Quantity | In service | Since | Notes |
| --- | --- | --- | --- | --- |
| APCs | | | | |
| • M-113 A1/A2/ M-125/M-577 | 85 | 85 | 1980 | 35 M-901 ITV in anti-tank weapons |
| • Fiat Type 6614 | 110 | 110 | 1980 | |
| Subtotal | 195 | 195 | | |
| IFVs | | | | |
| • Engesa EE-11 | | | 1982 | Included with Engesa EE-9 |
| Reconnaissance | | | | |
| • Engesa EE-9 | 36 | 36 | 1982 | |
| • Saladin | 20 | 20 | 1962 | |
| • AML-60/AML-90 | 30 | 30 | 1969 | |
| Subtotal | 86 | 86 | | |
| Total | 281 | 281 | | |

## Artillery

| Model | Quantity | In service | Since | Notes |
|---|---|---|---|---|
| **Self-propelled guns and howitzers** | | | | |
| • 105mm M-108 | 10 | 0 | 1950 | Possibly phased out |
| **Towed guns and howitzers** | | | | |
| • 155mm M-198 | 48 | 48 | 1987 | |
| • 155mm M-114 | 18 | 18 | 1970 | |
| • 105mm M-101 | 45 | 45 | 1980 | |
| Subtotal | 111 | 111 | | |
| **Mortars, under 160mm** | | | | |
| • 120mm Brandt | 18 | 18 | 1987 | |
| • 107mm | 40 | 40 | 1980 | |
| • 107mm SP | 36 | 36 | 1987 | |
| Subtotal | 94 | 94 | | |
| Total | **215** | **205** | | |

On order
• 155mm M-109

## Logistic and Engineering Equipment

On order
US-made AFV transporters

## Anti-tank Weapons

| Model | Quantity | In service | Since | Notes |
|---|---|---|---|---|
| **Missiles** | | | | |
| • BGM-71A TOW | 100 | 100 | 1982 | |
| • M-901 ITV SP | 35 | 35 | 1987 | TOW under armor |
| • Milan | 500 | 500 | 1982 | |
| Total | **635** | **635** | | |
| **Guns** | | | | |
| • 106mm M-40A1 | | 70 | | Recoilless rifle |

# Air Force

## Order of Battle

| Model | Quantity | In service | |
|---|---|---|---|
| • Combat | 12 | 12 | |
| • Transport | 11 | 10 | |
| • Helicopters | 40 | 40 | |

## Combat Aircraft

| Model | Quantity | In service | Since | Notes |
|---|---|---|---|---|
| **Multi-role** | | | | |
| • F-5E/F-5F | 12 | 12 | 1984 | |
| Total | **12** | **12** | | |

## Transport Aircraft

| Model | Quantity | In service | Since | Notes |
|---|---|---|---|---|
| • C-130H Hercules | 8 | 7 | 1985 | |
| • L-410 | 3 | 3 | 1994 | |
| Total | **11** | **10** | | |

## Training and Liaison Aircraft

| Model | Quantity | In service | Since | Notes |
|---|---|---|---|---|
| **With ground attack/close air support capability** | | | | |
| • Aermacchi MB-326 B/KT/LT | 10 | 10 | 1974 | |
| • L-59 | 12 | 12 | 1995 | |
| Subtotal | 22 | 22 | | |
| **Others** | | | | |
| • SIAI-Marchetti SF-260WT/C | 18 | 18 | 1974 | |
| • S 208A/M | 2 | 2 | 1979 | |
| • Piper Cub | 10 | 10 | | |
| Subtotal | 30 | 30 | | |
| Total | **52** | **52** | | |

## Helicopters

| Model | Quantity | In service | Since | Notes |
|---|---|---|---|---|
| **Attack** | | | | |
| • SA-342 Gazelle | 5 | 5 | | |
| **Medium Transport** | | | | |
| • AB-205/Bell-205/UH-1H | 19 | 19 | 1978 | |
| • AS 365 Dauphin II | 1 | 1 | 1986 | |
| Subtotal | 20 | 20 | | |
| **Light Transport** | | | | |
| • Alouette II/III | 9 | 9 | 1964 | |
| • AS-350 Ecureuil | 6 | 6 | 1982 | |
| Subtotal | 15 | 15 | | |
| Total | **40** | **40** | | |

## Advanced Armament

**Air-to-air missiles**
AIM-9J Sidewinder

## Air Force Infrastructure

**Military airfields:**        5
Bizerta (Sidi Ahmad), Gabes, Gafsa, Sfax, one additional

# Air Defense Forces

## Surface-to-Air Missiles

| Model | Launchers | Since | Notes |
|---|---|---|---|
| Light missiles | | | |
| • MIM-72A Chaparral | 25 | 1977 | |
| • RBS-70 | 48 | 1982 | |
| Total | 73 | | |
| Shoulder-launched missiles | | | |
| • SA-7 (Grail) | + | | |

## Other Air Defense Systems

| Model | Quantity | In service | Since | Notes |
|---|---|---|---|---|
| Short-range guns | | | | |
| • 40mm | 12 | 12 | 1964 | |
| • 37mm M-1939 | 15 | 15 | 1980 | |
| • 20mm M-55 | 100 | 100 | | |
| Total | 127 | 127 | | |
| Radars | | | | |
| • TRS-2100 Tiger S | | | | |

# Navy

## Combat Vessels

| Type | Original class name | Quantity | Length (m.)/ Displacement (t.) | Armament/ special equipment |
|---|---|---|---|---|
| **MFPBs** | | | | |
| • Combattante III | | 3 | 56/345 | 8 x MM40 Exocet SSMs<br>1 x 76mm guns<br>2 x 40mm guns<br>4 x 30mm guns |
| • Bizerte class | P-48 | 3 | 48/250 | 8 x SS - 12M SAMs<br>4 x 37mm guns |
| Subtotal | | 6 | | |
| **Gunboats/MTBs** | | | | |
| • Shanghai II class | | 2 | 38.8/113 | 4 x 37mm guns<br>4 x 25mm guns |
| • Modified Shanghai II class | | 3 | 41/170 | 4 x 14.5mm MGs |
| Subtotal | | 5 | | |
| Total | | 11 | | |
| **Patrol craft** | | | | |
| • Kondor I class | | 4 | 51.9/377 | 2 x 25mm guns<br>formerly a minesweeper, now with coast guard |
| • Coastal patrol craft | Ch. Navals de l'Esterel | 4 | 31.5/60 | 2 x 20mm guns |
| • Tazarka class | Vosper Thornycroft | 2 | 31.4/125 | with coast guard<br>2 x 20mm guns<br>2 x 14.5mm MGs |
| • Coastal patrol craft | Ch. Navals de l'Esterel | 6 | 25/38 | 1 x 20mm gun |
| • Bremse class | | 5 | 22.6/42 | 2 x 14.5mm MGs<br>with coast guard |
| • Coastal patrol craft | Socomena | 11 | 20.5/32 | 1 x 12.7mm MG<br>with coast guard |
| • Gabes class | | 4 | 12.9/18 | 2 x 12.7mm MGs<br>with coast guard |
| Total | | 36 | | |

## Auxiliary Vessels

| Type | Original class name | Quantity | Length (m.)/ Displacement (t.) | Armament/ special equipment |
|---|---|---|---|---|
| • Robert Conrad class | | 1 | 63.7/1,370 | Survey ship |
| • Guesette class | | 1 | 11/8.5 | Survey ship |
| Total | | 2 | | |
| on Order | | | | |
| • T-AGS-33 | | 1 | | |

## Naval Infrastructure

Naval bases:          5

Bizerta, Kelibia, Sfax, Sousse, Tunis

**Ship maintenance and repair facilities:**

4 dry-docks and 1 slipway in Bizerta, 2 pontoons and 1 floating dock at Sfax.
Capability for maintainance and repair of existing vessels

# 19. TURKEY

## General Data

**Official Name of the State:** Republic of Turkey
**Head of State:** President Suleyman Demirel
**Prime Minister:** Bulent Ecevit
**Minister of Defense:** Sabahattin Cakmakoglu
**Head of Turkish Chiefs of Staff:** General Huseyin Kivrikoglu
**Commander of Ground Forces:** General Atilla Ates
**Commander of the Air Force:** General Ilhan Kilic
**Commander of the Navy:** Admiral Salim Dervisoglu

**Area:** 780,580 sq. km.
**Population:** 62,600,000

## Demography

| | | |
|---|---|---|
| *Ethnic groups* | | |
| Turkish | 50,080,000 | 80% |
| Kurdish | 12,520,000 | 20% |
| *Religious groups* | | |
| Sunni Muslims | 49,955,000 | 79.8% |
| Alevis (Shi'ite Muslims) | 12,520,000 | 20.0% |
| Other (Christians and Jews) | 125,000 | 0.2% |

## Economic Data

| | | 1993 | 1994 | 1995 | 1996 | 1997 |
|---|---|---|---|---|---|---|
| GDP current price, local currency | TL tr | 1,997.4 | 4,026 | 7,926 | 14,320 | 29,158 |
| GDP (US $) | $ bn | 181,830 | 103,961 | 132,875 | 132,869 | 141,816 |
| GDP per capita | $ | 3,051 | 1,715 | 2,157 | 2,119 | 2,223 |
| Real GDP growth | % | 8.1 | -5.0 | 6.7 | 7.3 | 7.6 |
| **Balance of payments** | | | | | | |
| • Exports fob | $ bn | 15.61 | 18.39 | 21.98 | 32.45 | 32.67 |
| • Imports fob | $ bn | 29.7 | 22.61 | 35.19 | 43.03 | 48.03 |
| • Account balance (including services and income) | $ bn | -6.44 | 2.63 | -2.34 | -2.44 | -2.88 |
| • External debt | $ bn | 68.8 | 66.3 | 73.8 | 79.8 | 89.2 |
| **Government income and expenditure** | | | | | | |
| • Revenue, local currency | TL bn | 351,392 | 745,116 | 1,404,023 | 2,702,034 | 5,854,331 |

## Economic Data *(continued)*

|  |  | 1993 | 1994 | 1995 | 1996 | 1997 |
|---|---|---|---|---|---|---|
| • Expenditure, local currency | TL bn | 485,249 | 897,296 | 1,720,646 | 3,940,102 | 8,032,178 |
| • Defense expenditure | TL bn | 77,717 | 156,724 | 302,864 | 611,521 | 1,101,665 |
| • Defense expenditure/GDP | % | 3.89 | 3.89 | 3.82 | 4.27 | 3.78 |
| • Defense expenditure/CGE | % | 16.02 | 17.47 | 17.6 | 15.52 | 13.71 |
| • Population | m | 59.6 | 60.6 | 61.6 | 62.7 | 63.8 |
| • Official exchange rate | TL : $1 | 10,985 | 38,726 | 59,650 | 107,775 | 205,605 |

*Sources:* EIU quarterly report, EIU country profile, IMF statistical yearbook, SIPRI Yearbook

## Arms Procurement and Security Assistance Received

| Country | Type | Details |
|---|---|---|
| Britain | • Arms transfers | APCs (1995), Rapier SAMs (1999) |
| France | • Arms transfers | Helicopters (1997), Circe minesweepers (1998) |
|  | • Cooperation in arms production | Eryx ATGMs (1998 - suspended) |
| Germany | • Arms transfers | Meko frigates (1996), Preveze submarine (1996), aircraft (1993), APCs (1993), tanks (1993), SP artillery (1994), SAMs (1994) |
|  | • Maintenance of equipment | Transport aircraft |
| Israel | • Arms transfers | Upgrade of F-4s and F-5s (1997), Popeye guided missiles (1998), Radars (1998) |
|  | • Facilities provided | Training facilities for Turkish aircraft (1998) |
| Italy | • Arms transfers | AB-412 Helicopters (1998), APCs (1995) |
| Jordan | • Facilities provided | Training facilities for Turkish aircraft (1998) |
| Kuwait and Saudi Arabia | • Financial aid | $500 million annually from special Gulf War fund (1998) |
| Netherlands | • Arms transfers | aircraft (1996) |
| Romania | • Arms transfers | Bombs (1998) |
| Russia | • Arms transfers | Mi-17 helicopters (1996), APCs (1992) |
| Spain | • Arms transfers | CN-235 aircraft (1997) |

## Arms Procurement and Security Assistance Received *(continued)*

| Country | Type | Details |
|---------|------|---------|
| USA | • Arms transfers | Knox frigates (1997), F-4 aircraft (1994), ATACM SSMs (1997), Seahawk helicopters (1997), MLRS (1992), APCs (1997), Harpoon missiles (1998) |
|  | • Financial aid | $ 122 million US foreign aid to be terminated in 1999. |

## Arms Sales and Security Assistance Extended

| Country | Type | Details |
|---------|------|---------|
| Albania | • Financial aid | $7 million for harbor reconstruction (1998) |
|  | • Military training | Advisers |
| Algeria | • Arms transfers | Armored Land Rovers (1996) |
| Bosnia | • Arms transfers | Artillery (1995) |
|  | • Financial aid | $10 million (1997) |
|  | • Military training | Trainees in Turkey |
| China | • Cooperation in arms production/ assembly/R&D |  |
| Croatia | • Arms transfers | CN-235 aircraft (1998) |
| Egypt | • Arms transfers | F-16s (1996) |
| Georgia | • Arms transfers | Gunboats (1998) |
|  | • Military training |  |
| Israel | • Facilities provided | Training facilities for IAF (1997) |
|  | • Cooperation in arms production/ assembly/R&D | Joint development of ATBM project (1998) |
|  | • Arms transfers | Armored Land Rovers (1998) |
| Jordan | • Arms transfers | CN-235 aircraft (on lease - 1998) |
|  | • Facilities provided | Training facilities for Jordanian aircraft (1998) |
|  | • Military training | Flight simulation (1998) |
| KDP (Kurds) | • Arms transfers | Tanks, small arms (1997) |
|  | • Financial aid |  |
| Macedonia | • Arms transfers | F-5 Aircraft (1998) |
| NATO | • Facilities provided | HQ Landsoutheast, HQ 6 ATAF |
| Pakistan | • Arms transfers | Armored Land Rovers (1996) |
| Poland | • Military training |  |
| UAE | • Arms transfers | FMC- Nurol AAPCs (1998) |

## Foreign Military Cooperation

| | Details |
|---|---|
| • Forces deployed abroad in | Albania; Cyprus (30,000 troops); northern Iraq (1,000 troops); Adriatic Sea (Sharp Guard operation); Bosnia (UNPROFOR); Georgia (UNIMiG); Iraq/Kuwait (UNIKOM); Italy (Deny Flight operation) |
| • Joint maneuvers with | Albania (naval), Israel, Jordan, Georgia (naval), Pakistan, Poland, NATO states, USA |

## Defense Production

| | M | P | A |
|---|---|---|---|
| **Army equipment** | | | |
| • Land Rover APCs, FMC-Nurol AAPCs and AIFVs | √ | | |
| • Trucks and wheeled tactical vehicles | √ | | |
| • ERYX ATGMs | | √ | |
| • Chines WS-1 SSMs | √ | | |
| • 107mm and 122mm MRLs | √ | | |
| • 35mm Oerlikon anti-aircraft guns | | √ | |
| • 25mm cannons | | | √ |
| • Upgrade of 105mm and 155mm SP guns | √ | | |
| • Small arms | √ | | |
| • Explosives | √ | | |
| • M48 tank guns | √ | | |
| **Aircraft and air ammunition** | | | |
| • F-16s | | √ | |
| • UH-1H helicopters, under negotiations | | | √ |
| • Cougar helicopters | | | √ |
| • SF-260D basic trainers | | √ | |
| • CN-235 light transport aircraft | | √ | |
| • UAVs | √ | | |
| • Modification of S-2E maritime patrol aircraft | | | |
| • Stinger SAMs and SP Stinger systems | √ | √ | |
| • Jet engines | | √ | |
| • Popeye air-launched rockets | | √ | |
| • Rapier missiles | | √ | √ |
| **Naval crafts** | | | |
| • Atilay class submarines | | | √ |
| • Berk class missile frigates | | | √ |
| • Yildiz class and Dogan class MFPBs | | | √ |
| • Yonca PBs | | √ | |
| • Osman Gazi landing craft | | | √ |

## Defense Production *(continued)*

| | M | P | A |
|---|---|---|---|
| **Electronics** | | | |
| • Land-based and naval EW sets | √ | | |
| • Navigation systems | √ | | |
| • Ground surveillance radars | √ | | |
| • Tactical communication systems | √ | | |
| • Artillery fire-control systems | √ | | |
| • HF/SSB radios | | √ | |
| • ALQ-178 EW systems for F-4s and F-16s | | √ | |
| • TRS-22 air search radars | | √ | |
| • C³I systems | | √ | |
| **Optronics** | | | |
| • Optical targeting devices | √ | | |
| • Night-vision equipment | √ | | |
| • Laser range-finders | √ | | |

Note: M - manufacture (indigenously developed)
P - production under license
A - assembly

## Weapons of Mass Destruction

### Nuclear capabilities
• Turkey intends to order a 1,000MW power reactor. As a member of NATO, nuclear weapons were deployed in Turkey in the past, and might be deployed again.

### CW capabilities
• No details available

### Biological warfare capabilities
• No details available

### Surface to Surface Missiles and Rockets

| Model | Launchers | Missiles | Since | Notes |
|---|---|---|---|---|
| • ATACMS | 36 | | 1997 | Out of 72 being delivered |
| **On order** | | | | |
| • ATACMS | 72 | | | Being delivered |

# Armed Forces

**Major Changes:** The Turkish armed forces have launched a major rearmament project for all military branches. Nevertheless, this procurement program has had no major effect yet on the Turkish Order of Battle in 1998, except for the navy. The navy has received its 3rd Preveze class submarine, and ordered 4 additional. It also received its 3rd Oliver Hazard Perry frigates from the US.

## Order of Battle

| Year | 1994 | 1995 | 1996 | 1997 | 1998 |
|---|---|---|---|---|---|
| **General data** | | | | | |
| • Personnel (regulars) | 503,800 | 507,800 | 515,800 | 639,000 | 633,000 |
| • Divisions | 2 - 3 | 2 - 3 | 2 - 3 | 5 | 5 |
| • Total number of brigades | 64 | 60 | 63 | 67 | 67 |
| **Ground forces** | | | | | |
| • Tanks | 4,330 | 4,300 | 4,280 | 4,115 | 4,115 |
| | | | | (4,190) | (4,190) |
| • APCs/AFVs | 3,360 | 4,711 | 4,046 | 4,743 | 4,520 |
| • Artillery (incl. MRLs) | 4,275 | 4,341 | 4,128 | 4,113 | 4,312 |
| | | | | (4,412) | (4,611) |
| **Air force** | | | | | |
| • Combat aircraft | 555 | 374 | 434 | 461 | 461 |
| • Transport aircraft | 88 | 70 | 62 | 87 | 87 |
| • Helicopters | 323 | 305 | 304 | 381 | 381 |
| **Air defense forces** | | | | | |
| • Heavy SAM batteries | 40 | 30 | 30 | 24 | 24 |
| • Light SAM launchers | 24 | 24 | 24 | 86 | 86 |
| **Navy** | | | | | |
| • Combat vessels | 60 | 61 | 63 | 75 | 51 |
| • Patrol craft | 27 | 27 | 32 | 96 | 88 |
| • Submarines | 15 | 16 | 16 | 17 | 16 |

*Note:* Beginning with data for 1997, we refer to quantities in active service. The numbers in parentheses refer to the total.

## Personnel

| | Regular | Reserves | Total |
|---|---|---|---|
| Ground Forces | 525,000 | 259,000 | 784,000 |
| Air Force | 57,000 | 74,000 | 131,000 |
| Navy | 51,000 | 65,000 | 116,000 |
| **Total** | **633,000** | **398,000** | **1,031,000** |

## Personnel *(continued)*

|  | Regular | Reserves | Total |
|---|---|---|---|
| **Paramilitary** |  |  |  |
| • Coast Guard | 2,200 |  |  |
| • Gendarmerie/ National Guard | 180,000 | 50,000 |  |

# Ground Forces

## Formations

|  | Corps | Divisions | Independent brigades/ groups | Independent battalions | Battalions in brigade |
|---|---|---|---|---|---|
| All arms | 4 armies 9 corps |  |  |  |  |
| Armored |  |  | 15 |  | 2 armd., 2 mech., 1 arty. each |
| Mechanized |  | 2 | 18 |  | 1 armd., 2 mech., 1 arty. each |
| Infantry |  | 3 | 9 |  | 4 inf., 1 arty. each |
| Commando |  |  | 4 |  | 3 inf., 1 arty. each |
| Presidential guard |  |  | 1 (reg.) |  |  |
| Border Defense |  |  | 5 (reg.) | 26 |  |
| Coastal Defense (reserve) |  |  | 4 |  |  |
| Marines |  |  | 1 |  | 3 inf., 1 arty. each |
| **Total** |  | 5 | 57 | 26 |  |

## Tanks

| Model | Quantity | In service | Since | Notes |
|---|---|---|---|---|
| **MBTs** |  |  |  |  |
| **Medium and low quality** |  |  |  |  |
| • Leopard A1/A3 | 307 | 307 |  |  |
| • M-60 A1/A3 | 932 | 932 |  |  |
| • M-48T | 2,876 | 2,876 |  | Possibly some in storage |
| • M-47 | 75 | 0 |  | In storage |
| **Total** | **4,190** | **4,115** |  |  |

## APCs/AFVs

| Model | Quantity | In service | Since | Notes |
|---|---|---|---|---|
| **APCs** | | | | |
| • FMC- Nurol AAPC | 730 | 730 | 1997 | Additional 170 mortar carriers and 48 ATV |
| • M-113 A1/A2 | 2,815 | 2,815 | | |
| • BTR - 80 | 240 | 240 | | |
| • BTR - 60 | 340 | 340 | | |
| • S - 55 | 40 | 40 | | |
| Subtotal | 4,165 | 4,165 | | |
| **IFVs** | | | | |
| • Condor | 25 | 25 | | |
| • UR - 416 | 35 | 35 | | |
| • FMC- Nurol AIFV | 280 | 280 | 1997 | |
| Subtotal | 340 | 340 | | |
| **Reconnaissance** | | | | |
| • Scorpion (Akrep) | some | some | 1994 | |
| **Total** | **4,520** | **4,520** | | |

## Artillery

| Model | Quantity | In service | Since | Notes |
|---|---|---|---|---|
| **Self-propelled guns and howitzers** | | | | |
| • 203mm M-110 | 219 | 219 | | |
| • 203mm M-55 | 9 | 9 | | |
| • 175mm M-107 | 36 | 36 | | |
| • 155mm M-44T | 222 | 222 | | |
| • 105mm M-52T | 365 | 365 | | |
| • 105mm M-108 | 26 | 26 | | |
| Subtotal | 877 | 877 | | |
| **Towed guns and howitzers** | | | | |
| • 203mm M-115 | 162 | 162 | 1983 | |
| • 155mm M-114 | 517 | 517 | | |
| • 155mm M-59 | 171 | 0 | | |
| • 150mm Skoda | 128 | 0 | 1975 | |
| • 105mm | | | | |
| • M-101/M-102 | 640 | 640 | | |
| Subtotal | 1,618 | 1,319 | | |
| **Mortars, under 160mm** | | | | |
| • 120mm | 578 | 578 | | |
| • 107mm M-30 | 1,265 | 1,265 | | |

## Artillery *(continued)*

| Model | Quantity | In service | Since | Notes |
|---|---|---|---|---|
| • 107mm M-106 SP | some | some | | |
| • FMC- Nurol AMV | 170 | 170 | 1997 | |
| Subtotal | 2,020 | 2,020 | | |
| **MRLs** | | | | |
| • 227mm MLRS | 12 | 12 | | |
| • 107mm | 48 | 48 | 1975 | |
| Subtotal | 96 | 96 | | |
| Total | **4,611** | **4,312** | | |

### Artillery/mortar-locating radars

• AN/TPQ- 37
• AN/TPQ- 36
• Ranging radars

## Logistic and Engineering Equipment

Mine laying and clearing, bar mine-clearing system, crossing equipment

## Anti-tank Weapons

| Model | Quantity | In service | Since | Notes |
|---|---|---|---|---|
| **Missiles** | | | | |
| • Cobra | 186 | 186 | 1977 | |
| • Milan | 392 | 392 | 1984 | |
| • TOW SP | 365 | 365 | | 48 of which are on FMC-Nurol ATV |
| Total | **943** | **943** | | |
| **Guns** | | | | |
| • 106mm M-40A1 | 2,330 | 2,330 | | |
| • 75mm | 620 | 620 | | |
| • 57mm M-18 | 925 | 925 | | |
| Total | **3,875** | **3,875** | | |

# Air Force

## Order of Battle

| Model | Quantity | In service | Notes |
|---|---|---|---|
| • Combat | 416 | 416 | |
| • Transport | 93 | 93 | |
| • Helicopters | 381 | 381 | |

## Combat Aircraft

| Model | Quantity | In service | Since | Notes |
|---|---|---|---|---|
| Advanced multi-role | | | | |
| • F-16C/D | 174 | 174 | 1987 | |
| Multi-role | | | | |
| • F-4E | 136 | 136 | 1973 | |
| Obsolete | | | | |
| • F-5A/B | 106 | 106 | 1965 | |
| Total | 416 | 416 | | |
| On Order | | | | |
| • F-15E | | | | Under negotiations |
| • F-16 C/D | 232 | | | Total order |
| • F-5 | 48 | | | To be upgraded |
| • F-4E | 54 | | | To be upgraded, all others for storage |

## Transport Aircraft

| Model | Quantity | In service | Since | Notes |
|---|---|---|---|---|
| • C-160D | 19 | 19 | 1971 | |
| • KC-135R | 9 | 9 | 1995 | Tanker |
| • C-130 | 13 | 13 | 1964 | |
| • Citation (VIP) | 2 | 2 | 1985 | |
| • CN-235 | 50 | 50 | 1991 | |
| Total | 93 | 93 | | |
| On order | | | | |
| • CN-235 | 12 | | | Being delivered, 9 for maritime patrol |

## Training and Liaison Aircraft

| Model | Quantity | In service | Since | Notes |
|---|---|---|---|---|
| With ground attack/close air support capability | | | | |
| • T-33 | 34 | 34 | 1982 | |
| • T-38 (F-5) | 70 | 70 | 1965 | |
| • Cessna 318 (T-37) | 60 | 60 | 1960 | |
| Subtotal | 164 | 164 | | |
| Others | | | | |
| • SF-260D | 40 | 40 | 1990 | |
| • Cessna 172 (T-41) | 51 | 51 | 1972 | 28 in army aviation |
| Subtotal | 91 | 91 | | |
| Total | 255 | 255 | | |

## Helicopters

| Model | Quantity | In service | Since | Notes |
|-------|----------|------------|-------|-------|
| **Attack** | | | | |
| • AH-1W/P | 37 | 37 | 1990 | With army aviation |
| **Medium transport** | | | | |
| • AB-212 | 15 | 15 | 1985 | 13 in the navy, in ASW roll and 3 in army aviation |
| • AS-532 Cougar | 17 | 17 | 1995 | With army aviation |
| • Mi - 17 | 19 | 19 | 1995 | With gendermeire |
| • UH-60 Black Hawk | 39 | 39 | 1992 | 35 with gendarmeire |
| • UH-1H/AB-204/AB-205 | 190 | 190 | 1966 | 160 in army aviation and 3 in navy |
| Subtotal | 282 | 282 | | |
| **Light transport** | | | | |
| • AB 206 | 20 | 20 | 1968 | 3 with coast guard |
| • H-300C | 28 | 28 | 1982 | With army aviation |
| • OH-58B | 3 | 3 | 1994 | With army aviation |
| Subtotal | 51 | 51 | | |
| **Total** | **371** | **371** | | |
| **On order** | | | | |
| • AB-412 | 5 | | | |
| • S - 70B | 8 | | | With navy |
| • Cougar AS- 532 | 30 | | | |

## Miscellaneous Aircraft

| Model | Quantity | In service | Since | Notes |
|-------|----------|------------|-------|-------|
| **Reconnaissance aircraft** | | | | |
| • RF-4E | 39 | 39 | 1977 | |
| ELINT | | | | |
| • CN 235 | | | 1991 | 2 listed under transport aircraft |
| **UAVs and mini-UAVs** | | | | |
| • CL-89 | | | | |
| • Gnat 750 | 6 | 6 | | |
| **Maritime surveillance aircraft** | | | | |
| • Maule MX 7 | 1 | 1 | 1993 | With coast guard |
| • S-2A/E Tracker | 9 | 0 | | Reportedly grounded |

379

## Miscellaneous Aircraft

| Model | Quantity | In service | Since | Notes |
|-------|----------|-----------|-------|-------|
| **On order** | | | | |
| • CN-235 | 9 | | | Maritime surveillance, listed under transport |

## Advanced Armament

**Air-to-air missiles**
AIM-120 AMRAAM, AIM-9S Sidewinder, AIM-7E Sparrow
**Air-to-ground missiles**
AGM-88 HARM, AGM-65 A/G Maverick, AGM-142 Popeye (100)
**Avionics**
LANTIRN          24
**On order**
LANTIRN (approx. 10)

## Air Force Infrastructure

**Military airfields:**          23
Adnan-menderes, Afyon, Akhisar, Akinci, Ankara-güvercinlik, Balikesit, Bandirma, Dalaman, Diyarbakir, Elazig, Erhac, Erkilet, Erzincan, Eskisehir, Istanbul-Sarigazi, Izmir-Kaklic, Kayseri, Konya, Malatya, Merzifon, Murted, Yalova, Yesilkoy

# Air Defense Forces

## Surface-to-Air Missiles

| Model | Batteries | Launchers | Since | Notes |
|-------|-----------|-----------|-------|-------|
| **Heavy missiles** | | | | |
| • Nike Hercules | 24 | 72 | | 8 squadrons, 24 batteries |
| **Light missiles** | | | | |
| • Rapier | | 86 | | |
| **Shoulder-launched missiles** | | | | |
| • Stinger | | 108 | | |
| • Red-eye | | 790 | | |
| **Total** | | **898** | | |
| **On order** | | | | |
| • Rapier B1X | | 78 | | Upgrading of the original Rapier launchers - due to end by May 1999. |

## Other Air Defense Systems

| Model | Quantity | In service | Since | Notes |
|---|---|---|---|---|
| **Short-range guns** | | | | |
| • 40mm L60/70 | 800 | 800 | 1980 | |
| • 40mm T1 | 40 | 40 | | |
| • M-42 A1 | 260 | 260 | | |
| • 35mm GDF-003 | 120 | 120 | 1984 | |
| • 20mm GAI-DO1 | 440 | 440 | 1975 | |
| Total | **1,660** | **1,660** | | |
| **Radars** | | | | |
| • AN/TPS-59 | | | | |

# Navy

## Combat Vessels

| Type | Original class name | Quantity | Length (m.)/ Displacement (t.) | Armament/ special equipment |
|---|---|---|---|---|
| **Submarines** | | | | |
| • Atilay | Type 1200 | 6 | 61.2/1,185 | 8 x 533mm torpedoes |
| • Çannakale class | Guppy III | 1 | 99.5/2,450 | 10 x 533mm torpedoes<br>40 mines |
| • Burakreist class | Guppy II A | 4 | 93.2/2,440 | 10 x 533mm torpedoes<br>40 mines |
| • Hizzirreis | Tang | 2 | 87.4/2,700 | 8 x 533mm torpedoes<br>mines |
| • Preveze | Type 1400 | 3 | 62/1,586 | 2 x Sub Harpoon SSMs<br>8 x 533mm torpedoes<br>mines |
| Total | | **16** | | |
| **Destroyers** | | | | |
| • Alcitepe | Carpenter class | 2 | 119/2,425 | ASROC Mk112 8<br>torpedo launcher<br>6 x 324mm torpedoes<br>2 x 127mm guns<br>2 x 76mm guns<br>2 x 35mm guns |

## Combat Vessels

| Type | Original class name | Quantity | Length (m.)/ Displacement (t.) | Armament/ special equipment |
|------|------|------|------|------|
| • Yücetepe | Gearing class | 2 | 119/2,425 | Helicopter pad<br>1 x Harpoon SSM<br>ASROC Mk112<br>8 torpedo launchers<br>6 x 324mm torpedoes<br>4 x 127mm guns<br>2 x 35mm guns |
| Subtotal | | 4 | | |
| **Frigates** | | | | |
| • Barbaros | Modified MEKO | 2 | 116.7/3,350 | AB 212 ASW helicopter<br>8 x Harpoon SSMs<br>1 x Seasparrow 8 SAMs<br>6 x 324mm torpedoes<br>1 x 127mm gun<br>3 x Oerlicon 25mm AD guns |
| • Berk | | 2 | 95/1,450 | Helicopter pad<br>2 x Hedgehog Mk11 24 ASW rocket launchers<br>6 x 324mm torpedoes<br>4 x 76mm guns |
| • Oliver Perry class | | 3 | 135.6/3,638 | 2 x AB 212 helicopters<br>4 x Harpoon SSMs<br>36 x Standard SAMs<br>6 x 324mm torpedoes<br>1 x 76mm gun<br>1 x 20mm Phalanx AD gun |
| • Muavenet | Knox class | 8 | 134/3,011 | AB 212 ASW helicopter<br>8 x Harpoon SSMs<br>ASROC Mk112 8 torpedo launcher<br>4 x 324mm torpedoes<br>1 x 20mm Vulcan Phalanx AD gun<br>1 x 127mm gun |

## Combat Vessels *(continued)*

| Type | Original class name | Quantity | Length (m.)/ Displacement (t.) | Armament/ special equipment |
|------|---------------------|----------|-------------------------------|------------------------------|
| • Yavuz | MEKO 200 | 4 | 115.5/2,414 | AB 212 ASW helicopter 8 x Harpoon SSMs 6 x 324mm torpedoes 1 x Seasparrow 8 SAMs 1 x 127mm gun 3 x Oerlicon 25mm AD gun |
| Subtotal | | 19 | | |
| **MFPBs** | | | | |
| • Doğan class | Lürssen | 8 | 58.1/436 | 8 x Harpoon SSMs 1 x 76mm gun 2 x 35mm guns |
| • Kilic class | Lürssen | 1 | | 8 x Harpoon SSMs 1 x 76mm gun 1 x 40mm guns |
| • Yildiz class | | 2 | 57.8/433 | 8 x Harpoon SSMs 1 x 76mm gun 2 x 35mm guns |
| • Kartal | Jaguar class | 8 | 42.5/160 | 2-4 Penguin SSMs 2 x 533mm torpedoes 2 x 40mm guns 4 mines |
| Subtotal | | 19 | | |
| **Mine warfare vessels** | | | | |
| • Nurset | | 1 | 77/1,880 | 4 x 76mm guns 400 mines |
| • Mehmecik class | YMP class | 1 | 39.6/540 | |
| • Karamürsel | Vegasack class | 6 | 47.3/362 | Active mine detectors 2 x 20mm guns |
| • Circe minehunters | | 1 | 50.9/495 | 1 x 20mm gun robot seeker/destroyer |
| Subtotal | | 9 | | |
| **Total** | | **51** | | |

## Combat Vessels *(continued)*

| Type | Original class name | Quantity | Length (m.)/ Displacement (t.) | Armament/ special equipment |
|------|------|------|------|------|
| **Patrol craft** (mostly with coast guard) | | | | |
| • Girne class | | 1 | 58.1/341 | 2 x Mousetrap Mk 20 4 ASW rocket launchers 2 x 40mm guns 2 x 20mm guns |
| • Bora class | Ashville | 1 | 50.1/225 | 1 x 76mm gun 1 x 40mm gun 4 x 12.7mm MGs |
| • Hisar class | PC - 1638 | 6 | 53/325 | 1 x Hedgehog Mk 15 24 ASW rocket launchers 1 x 40mm gun 4 x 20mm guns |
| • Trabzon class | | 4 | 50/370 | 1 x 40mm gun 2 x 12.7mm MGs |
| • Turk class | | 12 | 40.2/170 | 1 x Mousetrap Mk 20 4 ASW rocket launcher 1-2 x 40mm guns 1 x 20mm gun 2 x 12.7mm MGs |
| • PGM -71 class | | 4 | 30.8/130 | 2 x Mousetrap Mk 22 8 ASW rocket launchers 1 x 40mm gun 4 x 20mm guns |
| • Coast guard type | | 4 | 25.3/63 | 2 x Mousetrap Mk 20 8 ASW rocket launchers 2 x 20mm guns |
| • Large patrol craft | | 12 | 40.7/187 | 1 x 40mm gun 2 x 12.7mm MGs |
| • Sar 33 Type | | 10 | 34.6/180 | 1 x 40mm gun 2 x 12.7mm MGs |
| • Sar 35 Type | | 4 | 36.6/210 | 1 x 40mm gun 2 x 12.7mm MGs |

## Combat Vessels *(continued)*

| Type | Original class name | Quantity | Length (m.)/ Displacement (t.) | Armament/ special equipment |
|---|---|---|---|---|
| • KW 15 class | | 8 | 28.9/70 | 1 x 40mm gun<br>2 x 20mm guns |
| • Coastal patrol craft | KW 15 Class | 1 | 26.7/56 | 2 x 20mm guns |
| • Coastal patrol craft | US Mk 5 | 6 | 16.8/25 | 1 x 12.7mm MG |
| • Coastal patrol craft | | 12 | 14.6/29 | 1 x 25mm or<br>1 x 12.7mm MG |
| • Inshore patrol craft | | 1 | 11.6/10 | 1 x 12.7mm MG |
| • Harbor patrol craft | | 2 | 17/15 | |
| Total | | 88 | | |
| **On Order** | | | | |
| • Yonca PBs | | 10 | | |
| • Prevese class submarines | | 5 | | Being delivered |
| • Circe class minesweepers | | 5 | | Being supplied |
| • Oliver Hazard Perry frigates | | 3 | | From US drow down |
| • Meko class frigates | | 2 | | To be supplied 1999 |
| • Yildiz (Kilic) class | | 2 | | To be supplied 1999 |

## Landing Craft

| Type | Original class name | Quantity | Length (m.)/ Displacement (t.) | Armament/ special equipment |
|---|---|---|---|---|
| • Osman Gazi | | 1 | 105/3,773 | 900 troops,<br>15 tanks<br>4 LCVPs<br>3 x 40mm guns<br>2 x 35mm guns |
| • Sarucabey | | 2 | 92/2,600 | 600 troops,<br>11 tanks<br>2 LCVPs<br>2 x 40mm guns<br>4 x 20mm guns |

## Landing Craft *(continued)*

| Type | Original class name | Quantity | Length (m.)/ Displacement (t.) | Armament/ special equipment |
|---|---|---|---|---|
| • Çakabey | | 1 | 77.3/1,600 | 400 troops, 9 tanks<br>2 LCVPs<br>4 x 40mm guns<br>4 x 20mm guns |
| • Ertugan | Terrebonne Parish class | 2 | 117.1/5,800 | 395 troops 2,200 tons<br>4 LCVPs<br>6 x 76mm guns |
| • LCM - 8 | | 22 | 22/113 | 160 troops or 60 tons<br>2 x 12.7mm MGs |
| • LCT | | 28 | 59.6/600 | 100 troops, 5 tanks<br>2 x 20mm guns<br>2 x 12.7mm MGs |
| • Edic Type | | 7 | 57/580 | 100 troops, 5 tanks<br>2 x 20mm guns<br>2 x 12.7mm MGs |
| • Bayraktar | LST | 2 | 100/1,653 | 6 x 40mm guns |
| • LCU | | 2 | 44.3/405 | 2 x 20mm guns |
| Total | | 71 | | |

## Auxiliary Vessels

| Type | Original class name | Quantity | Length (m.)/ Displacement (t.) | Armament/ special equipment |
|---|---|---|---|---|
| • Tankers | | 6 | 1,440-19,000 | 2 x 20mm guns |
| • Water tankers | | 15 | 300-1,200 ton | |
| • Salvage/Rescue | | 3 | 1,200-1,600 ton | 2-4 20mm, 76mm or 40mm guns |
| • Survey | | 3 | 680 ton | 2 x 20mm guns |
| • Intelligence vessel | | 1 | 1,497 ton | |
| • Training ships | | 2 | 2,370 ton | 2 x 100mm guns<br>4 x 40mm guns |
| • Transport | | 34 | Various sizes | |
| • Tugs | | 10 | 750, 1,235 ton | |
| • Repair | | 12 | | 400 - 16,000 ton Lift |
| • Boom defense | | 3 | 560 - 780 ton | 3-4 20mm, 76mm or 40mm guns |

## Naval Infrastructure

| | |
|---|---|
| Naval bases: | 16 |

Aksaz, Aksaz Bay, Ankara (HQ), Çanakkala, Erdek, Eregli, Foça, Gölcük, Iskanderun, Istanbul, Izmir, Karamürsel (training), Marmaris, Mersin, Samsun, Trabzon

| | |
|---|---|
| Ship maintenance and repair facilities: | 2 |

Gölcük, Taskiçak

| | |
|---|---|
| Naval aviation bases: | 4 |

Antalia, Cigli, Topel, Trabzon

# Non-governmental Paramilitary Forces

## Personnel

| | Active |
|---|---|
| • PKK | 8,000 |

## Equipment

| Organization | System | Model | Number | Notes |
|---|---|---|---|---|
| PKK | Air defense | • SA - 7 (Garil) | | |

# 20. UNITED ARAB EMIRATES (UAE)

## General Data

**Official Name of the State:** United Arab Emirates*
**Head of State:** President Shaykh Zayid ibn Sultan al-Nuhayan, Emir of
  Abu Dhabi (also Supreme Commander of the Armed Forces)
**Prime Minister:** Shaykh Maktum ibn Rashid al-Maktum, Emir of Dubai
  (also Vice President)
**Minister of Defense:** Shaykh Muhammad ibn Rashid al-Maktum
**Chief of General Staff:** HRH Lieutenant General Muhammad ibn
  Zayid al-Nuhayan
**Commander of the Air Force and Air Defense Forces:** Brigadier General
  Atik Gum'a al-Hamli
**Commander of the Navy:** Captain Muhammad al-Muhairi


**Area:** Approximately 82,900 sq. km. (borders with Oman, Saudi Arabia and
  Qatar partly undemarcated and/or disputed)
**Population:** 2,620,000 (estimate)

---

* The UAE consists of seven principalities: Abu Dhabi, Dubai, Ras al-Khaima,
  Sharja, Umm al-Qaiwain, Fujaira, and Ajman.

## Demography

| | | |
|---|---|---|
| *Ethnic groups* | | |
| Arabs | 1,310,000 | 50.0% |
| Southeast Asians | 1,147,500 | 43.8% |
| Others (Europeans, Persians) | 162,500 | 6.2% |
| *Religious groups* | | |
| Sunni Muslims | 1,637,500 | 62.5% |
| Shi'ite Muslims | 393,000 | 15.0% |
| Others | 589,500 | 22.5% |
| *National groups* | | |
| UAE nationals | 498,000 | 19.0% |
| Alien Arabs | 602,500 | 23.0% |
| Southeast Asians | | |
| (Indians, Pakistanis, Thais, Filipinos) | 1,310,000 | 50.0% |
| Others (Europeans, Iranians) | 209,500 | 8.0% |

## Economic Data

| | | 1993 | 1994 | 1995 | 1996 | 1997 |
|---|---|---|---|---|---|---|
| GDP current price, local currency | Dh bn | 130.5 | 134.6 | 147 | 163.8 | 165.8 |
| GDP (US $) | $ bn | 35.54 | 36.66 | 40.04 | 44.61 | 45.16 |
| GDP per capita | $ | 17,086 | 16,439 | 16,823 | 18,282 | 17,236 |
| Real GDP growth | % | 0.4 | -1.7 | 1.0 | 0.8 | 0.3 |
| **Balance of payments** | | | | | | |
| • Merchandise exports fob | $ bn | 26.67 | 27.38 | 29.34 | 33.60 | 32.98 |
| • Merchandise Imports cif | $ bn | 19.52 | 21.02 | 20.98 | 22.64 | 29.95 |
| • Account balance (including services and income) | $ bn | 4.06 | 4.70 | 7.39 | 9.84 | 2 |
| • External debt | $ bn | 9.85 | 12.22 | 9.50 | 10.88 | 10.89 |
| **Government income and expenditure** | | | | | | |
| • Revenue, local currency | Dh bn | 15.90 | 16.85 | 16.92 | 20.58 | 18.87 |
| • Expenditure, local currency | Dh bn | 17.63 | 17.82 | 17.94 | 17.02 | 18.78 |
| • Defense expenditure | Dh bn | 7.7 | 7.3 | 7.1 | 7.4 | NA |
| • Defense expenditure/GDP | % | 5.90 | 5.42 | 4.82 | 4.51 | NA |
| • Defense expenditure/CGE | % | 43.67 | 40.96 | 39.57 | 43.47 | NA |
| • Population | m | 2.08 | 2.23 | 2.38 | 2.44 | 2.62 |
| • Official exchange rate | Dh : $1 | 3.671 | 3.671 | 3.671 | 3.671 | 3.671 |

*Sources:* EIU quarterly report, EIU country profile, IMF statistical yearbook, SIPRI Yearbook

## Arms Procurement and Security Assistance Received

| Country | Type | Details |
|---|---|---|
| Britain | • Arms transfers | AFV transporters, PGMs, long range A/G missiles (1998), sonar |
| France | • Arms transfers | Combat aircraft (Mirage 2000-9), helicopters, AGMs, Leclerc tanks (1998), maritime patrol a/c (with Indonesia), radio sets, thermal imaging night vision systems, Shoulder-launched SAMs, ARVs, torpedo, C$^3$I systems |

## Arms Procurement and Security Assistance Received *(continued)*

| Country | Type | Details |
|---------|------|---------|
| Germany | • Arms transfers | Trainer a/c (1997 ) |
| | • Military training | Trainees abroad |
| Indonesia | • Maintenance of equipment | Transport a/c (1993), maritime patrol a/c (with France) |
| Italy | • Arms transfers | Helicopters |
| Netherlands | • Arms transfers | Frigates , artillery surveillance radar, CIWS, SP howitzers (1998) |
| | • Military training | Trainees abroad (1998) |
| Norway | • Arms transfers | Navy simulator |
| Romania | • Arms transfers | Romanian-built French-model helicopters |
| Russia | • Arms transfers | BMP-3 IFVs (1997), Smerch long-range MRLs (1998), ATGMs |
| South Africa | • Arms transfers | Artillery (1995) |
| Sweden | • Arms transfers | Early warning system |
| Switzerland | • Arms transfers | Trainer aircraft |
| USA | • Military training | Foreign advisors/instructors/serving personnel (some civilians); trainees abroad |
| | • Arms transfers | F-16 Block 60 a/c, AMRAAM, Aircraft training simulator, transport aircraft, SAMs, light reconnaissance vehicles, radio systems, AH-64A helicopters (1994), AGM missiles, two missile frigates; early warning system, LANTIRN on order; reconnaissance satellite, under negotiation |

## Arms Sales and Security Assistance Extended

| Country | Type | Details |
|---------|------|---------|
| Bosnia | • Arms transfers | AMX-30 MBTs |
| Britain | • Facilities | Logistical facilities |
| Netherlands | • Arms transfers | Artillery (1997) |
| USA | • Facilities | Storage facilities for naval equipment at Jebel Ali and Fujaira, and pre-positioning of equipment for an armored brigade under negotiation |

## Foreign Military Cooperation

| | Details |
|---|---------|
| • Forces deployed abroad | In Saudi Arabia (part of GCC Peninsula Shield Force) |
| • Joint maneuvers | France, GCC countries, USA, India(1996) |
| • Security agreement | France, Germany |

## Defense Production

| | M | P | A |
|---|---|---|---|
| **Naval equipment** | | | |
| • Construction of patrol boats at Ajman (with British cooperation) | | √ | |

Note:  M= manufacture (indigenously developed)
P= production under license
A= assembly

## Weapons of Mass Destruction

**CW capabilities**
• Personal protective equipment; unit decontamination equipment

# Armed Forces

**Major Changes:** The ground forces of the United Arab Emirates are in the process of deploying the new Leclerc MBT (436 have been ordered), its BMP-3 IFVs and its M-109A3 SP howitzers. Another major deal is for a command, control and communication system which was ordered from France. The Air Force placed an order for some new Mirage 2000-9, and is planning to upgrade its existing Mirage 2000 aircraft to the 2000-9 standard. The Air Force is still negotiating its largest deal, for 80 F-16 Block 60 combat aircraft. The Navy is assimilating its two Abu Dhabi class (Kortenaer) frigates, and ordered one more Oliver Hazard Perry class frigate from the USA

## Order of Battle

| Year | 1994 | 1995 | 1996 | 1997 | 1998 |
|---|---|---|---|---|---|
| **General data** | | | | | |
| • Personnel (regular) | 48,000 | 46,500 | 46,500 | 46,500 | 46,500 |
| • Number of brigades | 6 | 6 | 6 | 9 | 8 |
| **Ground forces** | | | | | |
| • Tanks | 216 | 212 | 216 | 366 (416 - 466) | 330 (416 - 466) |
| • APCs/AFVs | 893 | 1,100 | 1,100 | 955 (1,115) | 955 (1,115) |
| • Artillery (including MRLs) | 270 | 264 | 264 | 411 (434) | 411 (434) |

## Order of Battle (continued)

| Year | 1994 | 1995 | 1996 | 1997 | 1998 |
|---|---|---|---|---|---|
| **Air Force** | | | | | |
| • Combat aircraft | 76 | 65 | 66 | 54 (66) | 54 (66) |
| • Transport aircraft | 40 | 36 | 36 | 31 (34) | 31 (34) |
| • Helicopters | 69 | 85 | 85 | 93 (95) | 93 (95) |
| **Air Defense Forces** | | | | | |
| • Heavy SAM batteries | 7 | 5-7 | 5-7 | 5-7 | 5-7 |
| • Medium SAM batteries | 3 | 3 | 3 | + | + |
| • Light SAM launchers | + | + | + | 113 | 113 |
| **Navy** | | | | | |
| • Combat vessels | 28 | 10 | 10 | 12 | 12 |
| • Patrol craft | 12 | 50 | 121 | 119 | 105 |

*Note:* Beginning with data for 1997, we refer to quantities in active service. The numbers in parentheses refer to the total.

## Personnel

| | Regular | Total |
|---|---|---|
| Ground forces | 40,000 | 40,000 |
| Air Force | 4,500 | 4,500 |
| Navy | 2,000 | 2,000 |
| **Total** | **46,500** | **46,500** |
| **Paramilitary** | | |
| • Coast Guard | | + |
| • Frontier Corps | | + |

# Ground Forces

## Formations

| | Independent brigade/group |
|---|---|
| Armored | 3 |
| Mechanized | 4 |
| | (including two brigades under Dubai National Command) |
| Royal Guard | 1 |
| Artillery | 1 |
| **Total** | **9** |

## Tanks

| Model | Quantity | In service | Since | Notes |
|---|---|---|---|---|
| **MBTs** | | | | |
| **High quality** | | | | |
| • Leclerc | 200-250 | 150 | 1995 | estimated number supplied out of a total order of 388 |
| **Medium and low quality** | | | | |
| • AMX-30 | 100 | 64 | 1981 | |
| • OF-40 Lion Mk 2 | 36 | 36 | 1982 | |
| Subtotal | 136 | 100 | | |
| **Light tanks** | | | | |
| • Scorpion | 80 | 80 | 1975 | |
| **Total** | **416-466** | **330** | | |
| **On order** | | | | |
| • Leclerc tanks | 436 (total order) | | | 388 MBTs, 46 recovery vehicles and 2 training vehicles |

## APCs/AFVs

| Model | Quantity | In service | Since | Notes |
|---|---|---|---|---|
| **APCs** | | | | |
| • AMX-VCI | 10 | 10 | 1978 | |
| • Engesa EE-11 Urutu | + | 30 | 1985 | |
| • Saracen | 30 | 0 | | In storage |
| • VAB | 20 | 20 | 1980 | |
| • VCR | + | + | | |
| • M-3 (Panhard) | 300 | 300 | 1977 | |
| • Fahd | 100 | 100 | | |
| • AT-105 Saxon | 20 | 20 | | Possibly with police |
| subtotal | approx. 510 | approx. 480 | | |
| **IFVs** | | | | |
| • AMX-10P | 20 | 20 | 1980 | |
| • BMP-3 | 250 | 250 | 1980 | |
| Subtotal | 270 | 270 | | |
| **Reconnaissance** | | | | |
| • AML-60/AML-90 | 105 | 105 | 1980 | |
| • Engessa EE-9 Cascavel | + | 100 | | |
| • Ferret | 60 | 0 | | In storage |

## APCs/AFVs *(continued)*

| Model | Quantity | In service | Since | Notes |
|---|---|---|---|---|
| • Saladin | 70 | 0 | | In storage |
| • VBC-90 | + | + | | |
| Subtotal | 335 | 205 | | |
| **Total** | **1,115** | **955** | | |
| On order | | | | |
| • M-2/M-3 Bradley | 200 | | | |
| • BMP-3 | 120 | | | Status uncertain |
| • AAPC | 136 | | | From Turkey, delivery 1999 |

## Artillery

| Model | Quantity | In service | Since | Notes |
|---|---|---|---|---|
| **Self-propelled guns and howitzers** | | | | |
| • 155mm Mk F3 (AMX-13) | 20 | 20 | 1976 | |
| • 155mm G-6 | 78 | 78 | | |
| • 155mm M-109A3 | 85 | 85 | 1995 | Deliveries in progress |
| Subtotal | 183 | 183 | | |
| **Towed guns and howitzers** | | | | |
| • 155mm M-198 | + | 12 | | |
| • 130mm Type 59 | + | 30 | | |
| • 105mm L-118 light gun | 81 | 81 | | |
| • 105mm M-102 | 50 | 50 | | |
| • 105mm M-56 Pack | 18 | 18 | | |
| Subtotal | 191+ | 191 | | |
| **Mortars, under 160mm** | | | | |
| • 120mm | 12 | 12 | | |
| **MRLs** | | | | |
| • 122mm Firos-25/30 | 48 | 25 | | |
| **Total** | **434+** | **411** | | |
| On order | | | | |
| • 227mm MLRS | | | | |

## Logistic and Engineering Equipment

• Matenin automatic mine layers, Mk 3 (D) Flail

### Anti-tank Weapons

| Model | Quantity | In service | Since | Notes |
|---|---|---|---|---|
| **Missiles** | | | | |
| • BGM-71B Improved TOW | 24 | 24 | 1983 | |
| • HOT | 50 | 50 | | launchers |
| • Milan | 230 | 230 | | |
| Total | approx. 300 | approx. 300 | | **launchers** |
| **Guns** | | | | |
| • 120mm BAT L-4 recoilless rifle | | | | |
| • 84mm Carl Gustav M-2 light recoilless rifle | 250 | 250 | | |

# Air Force

### Order of Battle

| Model | Quantity | In service | Notes |
|---|---|---|---|
| • Combat | 66 | 54 | |
| • Transport | 34 | 31 | |
| • Helicopters | 95 | 93 | |

### Combat Aircraft

| Model | Quantity | In service | Since | Notes |
|---|---|---|---|---|
| **Advanced multi-role** | | | | |
| • Mirage 2000 | 36 | 36 | 1989 | 8 are reconnaissance |
| **Obsolete** | | | | |
| • Mirage V--AD/RAD/DAD | 18 | 18 | 1974 | |
| • Mirage III | 12 | 0 | | |
| Subtotal | 30 | 18 | | |
| Total | **66** | **54** | | |
| **on order** | | | | |
| • Mirage 2000-9 | 30 | | | 14 new and 13 ex-French AF. The existing aircraft are to be upgaded to the same standard |
| • F-16 Block 60 | 80 | | | |

396

## Transport Aircraft

| Model | Quantity | In service | Since | Notes |
|---|---|---|---|---|
| • BAe 125 | 1 | 1 | | |
| • Boeing 747 | 3 | 3 | 1985 | |
| • Boeing 737 | 1 | 1 | 1976 | |
| • Boeing 707 | 2 | 2 | 1976 | |
| • Britten-Norman BN-2 Islander | 1 | 1 | 1983 | |
| • C-130H Hercules/L-100-30 | 6 | 6 | 1975/1981 | |
| • CASA C-212 | 4 | 4 | 1982 | Employed in EW role |
| • CN-235 | 7 | 7 | 1993 | Some in maritime patrol role |
| • DHC-4 Caribou | 3 | 0 | | Possibly not serviceable |
| • G-222 | 1 | 1 | | Number unconfirmed |
| • IL-76 | 4 | 4 | 1994 | On lease |
| • Mystère-Falcon 20 | 1 | 1 | | |
| Total | 34 | 31 | | |

**On order**
- C-130
- CN-235

## Training and Liaison Aircraft

| Model | Quantity | In service | Since | Notes |
|---|---|---|---|---|
| **With ground attack/close air support capability** | | | | |
| • Aermacchi MB-326 KD/LD | 8 | 8 | 1974 | |
| • Aermacchi MB-339 | 5 | 5 | 1984 | |
| • Hawk Mk 102 | 26 | 26 | 1993 | |
| • Hawk Mk 61/63 | 22 | 22 | 1983/1984 | |
| Subtotal | 61 | 61 | | |
| **Others** | | | | |
| • Cessna 182 Skylane | 1 | 1 | | |
| • Pilatus PC-7 | 23 | 23 | 1982 | |
| • G-115T (Grob) | 12 | 12 | 1997 | |
| • SIAI-Marchetti SF-260 WD | 5 | 5 | 1983 | |
| Subtotal | 41 | 41 | | |
| Total | 102 | 102 | | |

**On order**
- G-115Ton (Grob) — Option for additional 12

## Helicopters

| Model | Quantity | In service | Since | Notes |
|---|---|---|---|---|
| **Attack** | | | | |
| • AH-64A Apache | 20 | 20 | 1993 | |
| • SA-342K Gazelle | 12 | 10 | 1980 | |
| • Alouette III | 7 | 7 | | |
| Subtotal | 39 | 37 | | |
| **Medium transport** | | | | |
| • AB-205/Bell 205 | 8 | 8 | 1969 | |
| • AB-212 | 3 | 3 | 1977 | |
| • AB-214 | 4 | 4 | 1981 | |
| • AB-412 | 5 | 5 | 1994 | Possibly with police |
| • SA-330 Puma/ possibly IAR-330 | 11 | 11 | 1972 | |
| Subtotal | 31 | 31 | | |
| **Light transport** | | | | |
| • A-109 | 3 | 3 | 1995 | Possibly with police |
| • AB-206 JetRanger/ Bell 206L | 10 | 10 | 1984 | |
| • BO-105 | 5 | 5 | 1992 | Employed in liaison role, number unconfirmed |
| Subtotal | 18 | 18 | | |
| **Naval combat** | | | | |
| • AS-332/532 Super Puma/Cougar | 7 | 7 | 1982 | |
| **Total** | **95** | **93** | | |
| **On order** | | | | |
| • AH-64A | 10 | | | Total order 30 |
| • AS-565 Panther | 7 | | | Naval combat |

## Miscellaneous Aircraft

| Model | Quantity | In service | Since | Notes |
|---|---|---|---|---|
| **EW aircraft** | | | | |
| • C-130 EW | | | | Listed under transport |
| **Target drones** | | | | |
| • TTL BTT-3 Banshee | | | | |
| **UAVs and mini-UAVs** | | | | |
| • Beech MQM-107A UAV | 20 | 20 | | |

## Advanced Armament

**Air-to-air-missiles**
- AIM-9L Sidewinder, R-550 Magic

**Air-to-ground missiles**
- AS-11, AS-12, AS-30L, AM-39 Exocet, al-Hakim (PGM-1/PGM-2)

**Bombs**
- BAP-100 anti-runway

**On order**
- AS-15TT air-to-surface (anti-ship) missiles; AM-39, AIM-120, Black Shahin, Harpoon, ASRAAM, Pave Way

## Air Force Infrastructure

**Aircraft shelters**
- For combat aircraft at Abu Dhabi and Jabil (Jebel) Ali AF bases

**Military airfields:** 7
- Abu Dhabi (international), al-Dhafra (Sharja), Bateen (Abu Dhabi), Dubai (international), Fujaira, Sharja, Mindhat

# Air Defense Forces

### Surface-to-Air Missiles

| Model | Batteries | Launchers | Since | Notes |
|---|---|---|---|---|
| **Heavy missiles** | | | | |
| • MIM-23B improved HAWK | 5-7 | 30-40 | 1989 | |
| **Medium missiles** | | | | |
| • Crotale | + | 9 | 1978 | |
| • Rapier | + | 12 | 1976 | |
| Total | + | 21 | | |
| **Light missiles** | | | | |
| • RBS-70 | | 13 | 1980 | |
| • Mistral | | 100 | 1993 | |
| • Javelin | | + | | |
| • Tigercat | | + | | Probably phased out |
| Total | | 113 | | |
| **Shoulder-launched missiles** | | | | |
| • Blowpipe | | 20+ | | Probably phased out |

399

### Surface-to-Air Missiles *(continued)*

| Model | Batteries | Launchers | Since | Notes |
|---|---|---|---|---|
| • FIM-92A Stinger | | + | | |
| • SA-7 (Grail) | | + | | |
| • SA-14 (Gremlin) | | + | | |
| • SA-16 (Gimlet) | | 10 | | |
| Total | | 30+ | | |
| **On order** | | | | |
| • MIM-104 Patriot | | | | Under negotiation |
| • SA-10 | | | | |
| • SA-12 (S-300V) | | | | Under negotiation |

### Other Air Defense Systems

| Model | Quantity | In service | Since | Notes |
|---|---|---|---|---|
| **Air defense systems (missiles, radars, and guns)** | | | | |
| • Skyguard AA system | 7 | 7 | | |
| **Short-range guns** | | | | |
| • 30mm x2 M-3 SP | | | | |
| • 20mm x2 GCF-BM2 SP | | | | |
| **Radars** | | | | |
| • AN/TPS-70 | 3 | 3 | | |
| • Watchman | | | | |

**On order**

Westinghouse air defense command, control and communication system; LASS; Crotale-NG SAMs (under negotiation); Mistral SAMs; Oerlikon ADATS (under negotiation); Starburst (under negotiation)

# Navy

### Combat Vessels

| Type | Original class name | Quantity | Length (m.)/ Displacement (t.) | Armament/ special equipment |
|---|---|---|---|---|
| **Missile frigates** | | | | |
| • Abu Dhabi | Kortenaer class | 2 | 130.5/3,050 | 2 x helicopters<br>8 x Harpoon SSM<br>4 x 324mm torpedoes<br>8 x Sea Sparrow SAM<br>1 x 76mm gun |

## Combat Vessels *(continued)*

| Type | Original class name | Quantity | Length (m.)/ Displacement (t.) | Armament/ special equipment |
|---|---|---|---|---|
| **Missile corvettes** | | | | |
| • Muray-Jib | Lürssen 62 | 2 | 63/630 | 1 x Alouette helicopter<br>8 x Exocet MM40 SSMs<br>8 x Crotale<br>Navale SAM<br>1 x 76mm gun<br>1 x 30mm Goal-keeper |
| **MFPBs** | | | | |
| • Ban-Yas | Lürssen TNC-45 | 6 | 44.9/260 | 4 x Exocet MM40 SSMs<br>1 x 76mm gun |
| • Mubarraz class | Lürssen | 2 | 44.9/260 | 4 x Exocet MM40 SSMs<br>1 x 6 Mistral SAM<br>1 x 76mm gun |
| Subtotal | | 8 | | |
| Total | | 12 | | |
| **Patrol craft** | | | | |
| (Some with coast guard) | | | | |
| • Ardhana | Vosper Thornycroft type | 6 | 33.5/110 | 2 x 30mm guns<br>1 x 20mm gun |
| • Camcraft | | 5 | 23.4/70 | 2 x 20mm guns<br>with coast guard |
| • Camcraft | | 16 | 19.8/50 | 1 x 20mm gun<br>with coast guard |
| • Watercraft | | 8 | 13.7/25 | |
| • Boghammar | | 3 | 13m | With police |
| • Baglietto GC-23 | | 6 | 24/50.7 | 1 x 20mm gun<br>with coast guard |
| • Baglietto | | 3 | 18.1/22 | With coast guard |
| • Arctic | | 8 | 8.5/4 | |
| • Harbor patrol craft | | 40 | 6.6-10m | With coast guard |
| • Dhafeer + Spear | | 10 | 9-12m | With police |
| Total | | 105 | | |
| **On order** | | | | |
| • Oliver Hazard Perry missile frigates | | 2 | | From US drawdown |

## Landing Craft

| Type | Original class name | Quantity | Length (m.)/ Displacement (t.) | Armament/ special equipment |
|------|------|------|------|------|
| • al-Feyi | Siong Huat LSL | 3 | 50/650 | |
| • LCM | | 1 | 40/100 | |
| • LCT | | 2 | | |
| • Serana class | | 2 | 26.3/105 | 45 ton or 100 troops |
| Total | | 8 | | |

## Auxiliary Vessels

| Type | Original class name | Quantity | Length (m.)/ Displacement (t.) | Armament/ special equipment |
|------|------|------|------|------|
| • Diving tender | | 1 | 31.4/100 | |
| • Coastal tug | | 1 | 35.0/795 | |
| • Diving tender (coast guard) | | 2 | | |
| **On order** | | | | |
| • Crestitalia 30-meter diver support vessels | | 2 | | |

## Coastal Defense

| Type | Quantity | Notes |
|------|------|------|
| • MM-40 Exocet | | Unconfirmed |

## Naval Infrastructure

| Naval bases: | 11 | Including coast guard |

• Ajman, Dalma (Abu Dhabi), Fujaira, Mina Jabil (Jebel) Ali (Dubai), Mina Khalid (Sharja), Mina Khor Fakkan (Sharja), Mina Rashid (Dubai), Mina Saqr (Ras al-Khaima), Mina Sultan (Sharja), Taweela, Mina Zayd (Abu Dhabi)

### Ship maintenance and repair facilities

• Dubai wharf for maintenance and repair of merchant and naval vessels, two dry-docks available, a new ship repair facility from the USA on order

# 21. YEMEN

## General Data

**Official Name of the State:** Republic of Yemen
**Head of State:** President Lieutenant General Ali Abdallah Salih
**Prime Minister:** Abd al-Karim al Iryani
**Minister of Defense:** Major General Muhammad Dayfallah
**Chief of General Staff:** Major General Abdallah Ali Aliwah
**Commander of the Air Force:** Colonel Muhammad Salih al-Ahmar
**Commander of the Navy:** Captain Ali Qasim Talib

**Area:** 527,970 sq. km. (borders with Saudi Arabia partly undemarcated and/or disputed)
**Population:** 16,500,000

## Demograpy

| Ethnic groups | | |
|---|---|---|
| Arabs | 15,130,000 | 91.7% |
| Afro-Arabs | 1,039,000 | 6.3% |
| Others | 330,000 | 2.0% |
| Religious groups | | |
| Sunni Muslims | 10,230,000 | 62.0% |
| Shi'ite Zaydi Muslims | 5,940,000 | 36.0% |
| Shi'ite Ismaili Muslims | 82,000 | 0.5% |
| Others | 247,000 | 1.5% |

## Economic Data

|  |  | 1993 | 1994 | 1995 | 1996 | 1997 |
|---|---|---|---|---|---|---|
| GDP current price, local currency | YR bn | 220.9 | 268.8 | 447.8 | 654.2 | 740.6 |
| GDP (US $) | $ bn | 4.542 | 3.328 | 3.679 | 5.103 | 5.727 |
| GDP per capita | $ | 369 | 223 | 238 | 320 | 347 |
| Real GDP growth | % | 2.8 | -0.8 | 9.1 | 5.1 | 5.7 |
| **Balance of payments** | | | | | | |
| • Exports fob | $ bn | 1.17 | 1.82 | 1.94 | 2.26 | 2.26 |
| • Imports fob | $ bn | 3.21 | 2.17 | 1.95 | 2.66 | 2.75 |
| • Account balance (including services and income) | $ bn | -1.248 | 0.366 | 0.183 | 0.106 | 0.159 |
| • External debt | $ bn | 5.923 | 6.121 | 6.212 | 6.356 | 4.223 |

## Economic Data (continued)

|  |  | 1993 | 1994 | 1995 | 1996 | 1997 |
|---|---|---|---|---|---|---|
| **Government income and expenditure** | | | | | | |
| • Revenue, local currency | YR bn | 42.9 | 88 | 155.9 | NA | NA |
| • Expenditure, local currency | YR bn | 87.1 | 124.1 | 181.4 | NA | NA |
| • Defense expenditure | YR bn | 19.752 | 30.273 | 3.897 | NA | NA |
| • Defense expenditure/GDP | % | 11.63 | 11.26 | 0.87 | NA | NA |
| • Defense expenditure/CGE | % | 22.67 | 24.39 | 2.14 | NA | NA |
| • Population | m | 12.3 | 14.9 | 15.4 | 15.9 | 16.5 |
| • Official exchange rate | YR : $1 | 48.63 | 80.75 | 121.69 | 128.18 | 129.30 |

*Sources:* EIU quarterly report, EIU country profile, IMF statistical yearbook, SIPRI Yearbook

## Arms Procurement and Security Assistance Received

| Country | Type | Details |
|---|---|---|
| Bulgaria | • Arms transfers | T-62 tanks, small arms |
| France | • Military training | Trainees abroad |
| Moldova | • Arms transfers | MiG-29, of Russian origin (1995), MRLs |
| USA | • Arms transfers | Spare parts for American made systems (1996) |

## Arms Sales and Security Assistance Extended

| Country | Type | Details |
|---|---|---|
| Iraq | • Facilities | Refuge to a few Iraqi aircraft (unconfirmed) |

## Weapons of Mass Destruction

**Surface-to-surface missiles and Rockets**

| Model | Launchers | Missiles | Since | Notes |
|---|---|---|---|---|
| • FROG-7 | 12 | | | |
| • SS-1 (Scud B) | 6 | | | |
| • SS-21 (Scarab) | 4 | | 1988 | |
| **Total** | **22** | | | |

*Note:* Serviceability of missiles and launchers unknown.

# Armed Forces

All figures are rough estimates, due to 1994 civil war.

**Major Changes:** No major change has been recorded in the Yemeni armed forces in 1998.

## Order of Battle

| Year | 1994 | 1995 | 1996 | 1997 | 1998 |
|---|---|---|---|---|---|
| **General data** | | | | | |
| • Personnel (regular) | 62,500-66,500 | 62,500-66,500 | 62,500-66,500 | 60,000-64,000 | 60,000-64,000 |
| • Number of brigades | 41 | 30 | 30 | 33 | 33 |
| **Ground forces** | | | | | |
| • Tanks | 1,300 | 1,000 | 1,040 | 575 (1,040) | 575 (1,040) |
| • APCs/AFVs | 950 | 870 | 1,320 | 480 (1,165) | 480 (1,171) |
| • Artillery (including MRLs) | 1,130 | 1,020 | 1,020 | 659 (1,019) | 659 (993) |
| • SSM launchers | 22 | 22 | 22 | 22 | 22 |
| **Air Force** | | | | | |
| • Combat aircraft | 170 | 166 | 166 | 55 (147) | 46 (147) |
| • Transport aircraft | 23 | 23 | 23 | 18 (23) | 18 (23) |
| • Helicopters | 77 | 67 | 67 | 27 (67) | 27 (67) |
| **Air defense forces** | | | | | |
| • Heavy SAM batteries | 25 | 25 | 25 | 25 | 25 |
| • Medium SAM batteries | + | + | + | + | + |
| • Light SAM launchers | + | + | + | 120 | 120 |
| **Navy** | | | | | |
| • Combat vessels | 19 | 12 | 13 | 11 | 11 |
| • Patrol craft | 12 | 11 | 7 | 7 | 3 |

*Note:* Beginning with data for 1997, we refer to quantities in active service. The numbers in parentheses refer to the total.

### Personnel

| | Regular | Reserves (only partly trained) | Total |
|---|---|---|---|
| Ground Forces | 55,000-59,000 | 200,000 | 255,000-259,000 |
| Air Force | 3,000 | | 3,000 |
| Navy | 2,000 | | 2,000 |
| Total | 60,000-64,000 | 200,000 | 260,000-264,000 |

### Paramilitary

| | Regular | Reserves (only partly trained) | Total |
|---|---|---|---|
| Central security force (for internal purposes) | 50,000 | | 50,000 |

The military forces are a combination of personnel of former YAR and PDRY; no information regarding reorganization is available.

# Ground Forces

### Formations

| | Independent brigade/group | Independent battalion |
|---|---|---|
| Armored | 7 | |
| Mechanized | 5 | |
| Infantry (mostly skeleton or undermanned units) | 18 | |
| Artillery | 4 | |
| SSM | 1 | |
| Air Defense | | 2 |
| Commando/ Paratroops | 1 | |
| Special forces | 1 | |
| Central Guards | 1 | |
| Total | 38 | 2 |

## Tanks

| Model | Quantity | In service | Since | Notes |
|---|---|---|---|---|
| **Medium and low quality** | | | | |
| • T-62 | 200 | 75 | 1979 | |
| • M-60 A1 | 140 | 50 | 1979 | |
| • T-54/55 | 700 | 450 | 1971 | |
| Total | **1,040** | **575** | | |

## APCs/AFVs

| Model | Quantity | In service | Since | Notes |
|---|---|---|---|---|
| **APCs** | | | | |
| • al-Walid | | | | |
| • BTR-152 | | | | |
| • BTR-40/50/60 } | 650 | 180 | | |
| • M-113 A1 | 76 | 70 | 1979 | including several derivatives |
| Subtotal | 726 | 250 | | |
| **IFVs** | | | | |
| • BMP-1/BMP-2 | 150 | 100 | | |
| **Reconnaissance** | | | | |
| • AML-90/AML-60 | 125 | 80 | 1975 | |
| • BRDM-2 | 100 | 50 | | |
| • Ferret | 10 | + | | Possibly phased out |
| • Saladin | 60 | + | | Possibly phased out |
| Subtotal | 295 | 130 | | |
| Total | **1,171** | **480** | | |

## Artillery

| Model | Quantity | In service | Since | Notes |
|---|---|---|---|---|
| **Self-propelled guns and howitzers** | | | | |
| • 122mm M-1974 | + | + | | |
| • 100mm SU-100 | 30 | 0 | | Obsolete |
| Subtotal | 30 | 0 | | |
| **Towed guns and howitzers** | | | | |
| • 155mm M-114 | 12 | 12 | 1980 | |
| • 152mm D-20 | 10 | + | | |
| • 130mm M-46 | 75 | 60 | | |
| • 122mm D-30 | 150 | 130 | | |
| • 122mm M-1938 | 100 | 40 | | |
| • 122mm M-1931/7 | 30 | 30 | | |
| • 105mm M-101 | 30 | 25 | | |
| Subtotal | 407 | 297 | | |

## Artillery *(continued)*

| Model | Quantity | In service | Since | Notes |
|---|---|---|---|---|
| **Mortars, over 160mm** | | | | |
| • 160mm | 100 | 100 | | |
| **Mortars, under 160mm** | | | | |
| • 120mm | 100 | 100 | | |
| • 107mm | 12 | 12 | | |
| Subtotal | 112 | 112 | | |
| **MRLs** | | | | |
| • 240mm BM-24 | 35 | + | | Unconfirmed |
| • 140mm BM-14 | 14 | + | | |
| • 132mm BM-13 | 15 | + | | |
| • 122mm BM-21 | 280 | 150 | | |
| Subtotal | 344 | 150 | | |
| Total | 993 | 659 | | |

### Anti-tank Weapons

| Model | Quantity | In service | Since | Notes |
|---|---|---|---|---|
| **Missiles** | | | | |
| • AT-3 (Sagger) | + | + | | |
| • BGM-71A Improved TOW | 12 | + | 1979 | |
| • M-47 Dragon | 24 | + | 1982 | |
| **Guns** | | | | |
| • 107mm B-11 recoilless rifle | + | + | | |
| • 100mm M-1955 field/ AT gun | 20 | + | | |
| • 85mm M-1945/ D-44 field/AT gun | 100 | 90 | | |
| • 82mm recoilless rifle | + | + | | |
| • 76mm M-1942 divisional gun | 100 | 70 | | |
| • 75mm recoilless rifle | + | + | | |
| • 57mm gun | | | | |

# Air Force

### Order of Battle

| Model | Quantity | In service | Notes |
|---|---|---|---|
| • Combat | 147 | 46 | Some in storage |
| • Transport | 23 | 18 | |
| • Helicopters | 67 | 27 | |

## Combat Aircraft

| Model | Quantity | In service | Since | Notes |
|---|---|---|---|---|
| **Interceptors** | | | | |
| • MiG-29 (Fulcrum) | 4-5 | + | 1994 | |
| • MiG-23/27 (Flogger B/D) | 15 | 0 | 1980 | |
| Subtotal | 20 | + | | |
| **Multi-role** | | | | |
| • F-5E/B | 10 | 10 | 1980 | |
| **Ground attack** | | | | |
| • Su-20/22 (Fitter C) | 35 | 15 | 1980 | |
| **Obsolete** | | | | |
| • MiG-21 (Fishbed) | 82 | 21 | 1979 | Some in storage |
| • MiG-17 (Fresco)/ | | | | In training role, |
| MiG-15 (Faggot/Midget) | | | | some not |
| | | | | serviceable |
| Subtotal | 82 | 21 | | |
| Total | **147** | **46** | | |
| **On order** | | | | |
| • Su-20/22 | 12 | | | |
| • MiG-29 | 30 | | | Possibly some |
| | | | | delivered |

## Transport Aircraft

| Model | Quantity | In service | Since | Notes |
|---|---|---|---|---|
| • An-24/An-26 (Coke/Curl) | 15 | 10 | 1984/1985 | |
| • C-130H Hercules | 2 | 2 | 1979 | |
| • IL-14 (Crate) | 4 | 4 | | |
| • Short Skyvan Srs. 3 | 2 | 2 | | |
| Total | **23** | **18** | | |

## Training and Liaison Aircraft

| Model | Quantity | In service | Since | Notes |
|---|---|---|---|---|
| • YAK-11 | 15 | 0 | | |

## Helicopters

| Model | Quantity | In service | Since | Notes |
|---|---|---|---|---|
| **Attack** | | | | |
| • Mi-24 (Hind) | 12 | 6 | 1980 | |
| **Medium transport** | | | | |
| • AB-212 | 5 | 3 | 1980 | |
| • AB-204 | 2 | 2 | | |

### Helicopters *(continued)*

| Model | Quantity | In service | Since | Notes |
|---|---|---|---|---|
| • AB-205 | 2 | 2 | | |
| • Mi-8/Mi-17 (Hip) | 40 | 10 | | |
| Subtotal | 49 | 17 | | |
| **Light transport** | | | | |
| • AB-206 JetRanger | 6 | 4 | | |
| Total | 67 | 27 | | |

### Advanced Armament

**Air-to-air-missiles**
• AA-2 (Atoll)
**Air-to-ground missiles**
• AT-2 (Swatter)

### Air Force Infrastructure

**Military airfields (approx. 18)**
• Aden (Khormaksar), al-Anad, Ataq, Bayhan, al-Qasab, Ghor Ubyad, al-Hudaydah, Ir-Fadhl, Kamaran Island, Lawdar, al-Mukalla, Nugaissa, al Riyan (Rayane), San'a, Socotra, approx. three others

# Air Defense Forces

### Surface-to-Air Missiles

| Model | Batteries | Launchers | Since | Notes |
|---|---|---|---|---|
| **Heavy missiles** | | | | |
| • SA-2 (Guideline) | | | | |
| • SA-3 | | | | |
| Total | 25 | | | |
| **Medium missiles** | | | | |
| • SA-6 | + | | | |
| **Light missiles** | | | | |
| • SA-9 (Gaskin) | | 120 | | |
| **Shoulder-launched missiles** | | | | |
| • SA-7 (Grail) | | 100-200 | | |

## Other Air Defense Systems

| Model | Quantity | In service | Since | Notes |
|---|---|---|---|---|
| **Short-range guns** | | | | |
| • 57mm ZSU 57x2 SP | + | + | | |
| • 57mm S-60 | 150 | 100 | | |
| • 37mm M-1939 | 150 | 150 | | |
| • 23mm ZSU 23x4 SP (Shilka) | 10 | + | | |
| • 23mm ZU 23x2 | 30 | 30 | | |
| • 20mm M-163 Vulcan SP | 20 | 20 | | |
| • 20mm M-167 Vulcan | 52 | 20 | | |
| **Total** | **412** | **320** | | |

# Navy

## Combat vessels

| Type | Original class name | Quantity | Length (m.)/ Displacement (t.) | Armament/ special equipment |
|---|---|---|---|---|
| **Missile corvettes** | | | | |
| • Tarantul | Type 1241 | 2 | 56.1/385 | 4 x Styx SS-N-2C SSMs<br>4 x SA-N-5 Grail SAMs<br>1 x 76mm gun<br>2 x 30mm guns |
| **MFPBs** | | | | |
| • Huang-Feng | | 3 | 33.6/171 | 4 x YJ-1 (C-801) SSMs<br>4 x 25mm guns |
| **Mine warfare vessels** | | | | |
| • Yevgenia class | Type 1258 | 5 | 24.6/177 | 2 x 25mm guns |
| • Natya class | Type 266ME | 1 | 61/804 | Acoustic & magnetic sweeps<br>4 x 30mm guns<br>4 x 25mm guns<br>2 x RBU 1200 A/S mortars<br>10 mines |
| Subtotal | | 6 | | |
| **Total** | | **11** | | |

## Combat vessels *(continued)*

| Type | Original class name | Quantity | Length (m.)/ Displacement (t.) | Armament/ special equipment |
|------|------|------|------|------|
| **Patrol craft** | | | | |
| • Broadsword class (customs) | | 1 | 32/90.5 | 2 x 25mm guns 2 x 14.5mm MGs 2 x 12.7mm MGs |
| • Zhuk class | Type 1400M | 2 | 24/39 | 4 x 14.5mm MGs |
| Total | | 3 | | |
| **On order** | | | | |
| • CMN-15-60 patrol craft | | 6 | | |

## Landing Craft

| Type | Original class name | Quantity | Length (m.)/ Displacement (t.) | Armament/ special equipment |
|------|------|------|------|------|
| • Ondatra LCU | Type 1176 | 2 | 24/145 | 1 tank |
| • Ropucha LST | Type 775 | 1 | 112.5/4,080 | 4 x SA-N-5 SAMs 4 x 57mm guns 2 x 122mm MRLs 92 mines 10 tanks & 190 troops |
| Total | | 3 | | |

## Auxiliary Vessels

| Type | Original class name | Quantity | Length (m.)/ Displacement (t.) | Armament/ special equipment |
|------|------|------|------|------|
| • Toplivo class | | 2 | 53.7/1,029 | 500 tonnes |

## Coastal Defense

| Type | Launchers | Notes |
|------|------|------|
| • Land based SS-N-2 Styx | 8 | |

## Naval Infrastructure

Naval bases:          6
• Aden, al-Hudaydah; anchorage at Kamaran Island (unconfirmed); al-Mukalla, Perim Island, Socotra

## Ship maintenance and repair facilities
• National Dockyards, Aden 4,500-ton floating dock and 1,500-ton slipway

# Part III

# Charts and Tables

## The Middle East Military Balance at a glance

| | General data | | | Ground Forces | | | |
| | Personnel | | | Tanks (Total) | Fighting Vehicles (Total) | Artillery Pieces | Ballistic Missile Launchers |
| | Regular | Reserves | Total | | | | |
|---|---|---|---|---|---|---|---|
| **Eastern Mediterranean** | | | | | | | |
| Egypt | 455,000 | 244,000 | 699,000 | 2,785 | 3,160 | 3,510 | 36 |
| Jordan | 94,200 | 60,000 | 154,200 | 872 | 1,475 | 788 | |
| Lebanon | 51,400 | | 51,400 | 280 | 730 | 323 | |
| Palestinian Authority | 34,000 | | 34,000 | 0 | 45 | | |
| Syria | 380,000 | 132,500 | 512,500 | 3,700 | 4,980 | 2,575 | 62 |
| Turkey | 633,000 | 398,000 | 1,031,000 | 4,115 | 4,505 | 4,312 | 36 |
| Israel | 186,500 | 445,000 | 631,500 | 3,895 | 8,040 | 1,348 | 12 |
| Subtotal | **1,834,100** | **1,279,500** | **3,113,600** | **15,647** | **22,935** | **12,856** | **146** |
| **The Gulf** | | | | | | | |
| Bahrain | 7,400 | | 7,400 | 187 | 277 | 48 | |
| Iraq | 432,500 | 650,000 | 1,082,500 | 2,000 | 2,000 | 1,950 | 34 |
| Iran | 518,000 | 350,000 | 868,000 | 1,520 | 1,235 | 2,640 | 39 |
| Kuwait | 19,500 | 24,000 | 43,500 | 318 | 436 | 75 | |
| Oman | 34,000 | | 34,000 | 131 | 135 | 148 | |
| Qatar | 11,800 | | 11,800 | 55 | 222 | 56 | |
| Saudi Arabia | 165,000 | 20,000 | 185,000 | 865 | 5,337 | 404 | 12 |
| UAE | 46,500 | | 46,500 | 330 | 955 | 411 | |
| Subtotal | **1,234,700** | **1,044,000** | **2,278,700** | **5,406** | **10,597** | **5,732** | **85** |
| **North Africa and Others** | | | | | | | |
| Algeria | 127,000 | 150,000 | 227,000 | 860 | 1,930 | 900 | |
| Libya | 76,000 | | 76,000 | 746 | 2,770 | 2,220 | 128 |
| Morocco | 145,500 | 150,000 | 295,500 | 454 | 1,074 | 967 | |
| Sudan | 103,000 | | 103,000 | 340 | 547 | 753 | |
| Tunisia | 35,500 | | 35,500 | 154 | 281 | 205 | |
| Yemen | 64,000 | 200,000 | 264,000 | 575 | 480 | 659 | 22 |
| Total Forces | **3,619,800** | **2,823,500** | **6,393,300** | **24,182** | **40,614** | **24,292** | **381** |

## The Middle East Military Balance at a glance *(continued)*

| | Air Force | | | Air Defense | | Navy | | |
|---|---|---|---|---|---|---|---|---|
| | Combat Aircraft (Total) | Transport Aircraft | Helicopters (Total) | Surface to Air Missiles | | Sub-marines | Combat Vessels | Patrol craft |
| | | | | Heavy Batteries | Medium Batteries | | | |
| **Eastern Mediterranean** | | | | | | | | |
| Egypt | 498 | 38 | 224 | 105 | 44 | 6 | 66 | 83 |
| Jordan | 101 | 12 | 68 | 14 | | | | 13 |
| Lebanon | 0 | | 16 | | | | | 39 |
| Palestinian Authority | 0 | 2 | 2 | | | | | 13 |
| Syria | 365 | 23 | 295 | 108 | 64 | | 24 | 8 |
| Turkey | 416 | 87 | 370 | 24 | | 16 | 51 | 88 |
| Israel | 624 | 77 | 289 | 22 | | 4 | 21 | 35 |
| Subtotal | 2,004 | 239 | 1,264 | 273 | 108 | 26 | 162 | 279 |
| **The Gulf** | | | | | | | | |
| Bahrain | 24 | 2 | 41 | 1 | 2 | | 11 | 19 |
| Iraq | 180 | 10 | 366 | 60 | | | 2 | |
| Iran | 145 | 91 | 293 | 35 | | 6 | 31 | 139 |
| Kuwait | 40 | 5 | 27 | 6 | | | 6 | 21 |
| Oman | 31 | 38 | 37 | | | | 9 | 23 |
| Qatar | 14 | 8 | 31 | | | | 7 | 36 |
| Saudi Arabia | 346 | 61 | 160 | 22 | 16 | | 24 | 80 |
| UAE | 54 | 31 | 93 | 7 | | | 12 | 105 |
| Subtotal | 834 | 246 | 1,048 | 131 | 18 | 6 | 102 | 423 |
| **North Africa and Others** | | | | | | | | |
| Algeria | 145 | 39 | 114 | 11 | 18 | 2 | 29 | 21 |
| Libya | 166 | 85 | 127 | 31 | 6 | | 34 | 2 |
| Morocco | 70 | 43 | 130 | | | | 13 | 48 |
| Sudan | 34 | 26 | 63 | 5 | | | | 22 |
| Tunisia | 12 | 10 | 40 | | | | 11 | 36 |
| Yemen | 46 | 18 | 27 | 25 | | | 11 | 3 |
| Total Forces | 3,311 | 706 | 2,813 | 476 | 150 | 34 | 362 | 834 |

# The Syria-Israel Military Balance

### Personnel

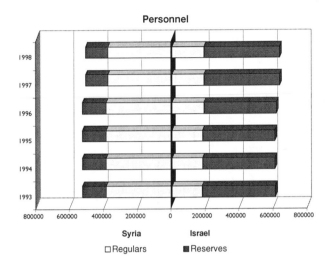

### Armor

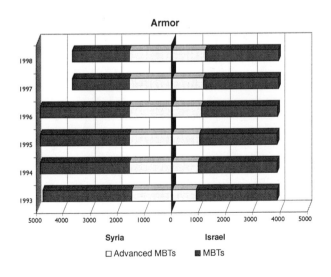

# The Syria-Israel Military Balance *(continued)*

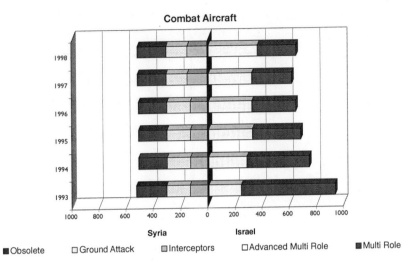

## Combat Aircraft

Syria — Israel

■ Obsolete   □ Ground Attack   ▨ Interceptors   □ Advanced Multi Role   ■ Multi Role

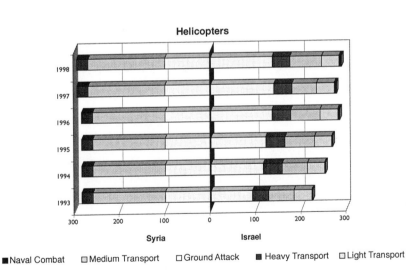

## Helicopters

Syria — Israel

■ Naval Combat   □ Medium Transport   □ Ground Attack   ■ Heavy Transport   □ Light Transport

417

# The Syria-Israel Military Balance *(continued)*

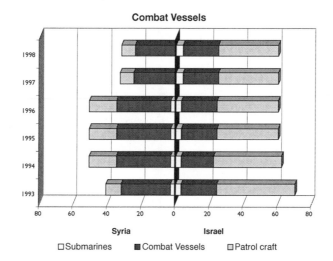

Combat Vessels

Syria · Israel

☐ Submarines ■ Combat Vessels ☐ Patrol craft

# The Iran-Iraq Military Balance

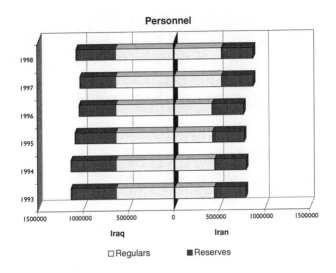

**Personnel**

Iraq — Iran

☐ Regulars     ■ Reserves

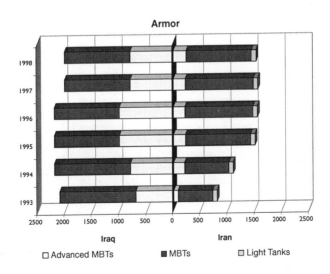

**Armor**

Iraq — Iran

☐ Advanced MBTs     ■ MBTs     ☐ Light Tanks

# The Iran-Iraq Military Balance *(continued)*

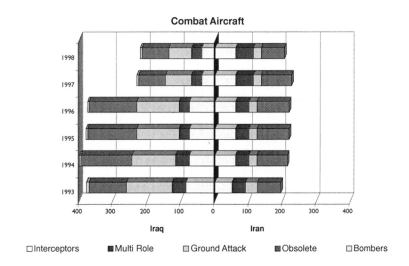

**Combat Aircraft**

□ Interceptors  ■ Multi Role  □ Ground Attack  ■ Obsolete  □ Bombers

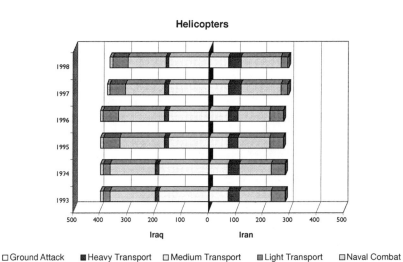

**Helicopters**

□ Ground Attack  ■ Heavy Transport  □ Medium Transport  ■ Light Transport  □ Naval Combat

420

# The Iran-Iraq Military Balance *(continued)*

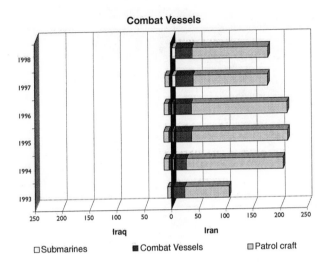

**Combat Vessels**

Iraq     Iran

□ Submarines     ■ Combat Vessels     ▨ Patrol craft

# Military Power in the Arab-Israeli Subregion

## Personnel

Regulars in Thousands

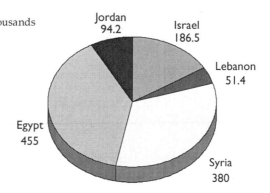

Jordan
94.2

Israel
186.5

Lebanon
51.4

Egypt
455

Syria
380

## Tanks

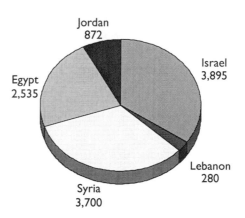

Jordan
872

Israel
3,895

Egypt
2,535

Lebanon
280

Syria
3,700

## Armored Fighting Vehicles

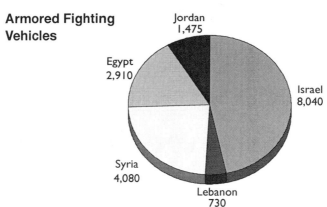

Jordan
1,475

Egypt
2,910

Israel
8,040

Syria
4,080

Lebanon
730

# Military Power in the Arab-Israeli Subregion *(continued)*

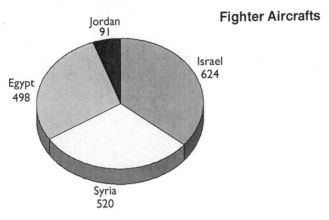

**Fighter Aircrafts**

Jordan
91

Israel
624

Egypt
498

Syria
520

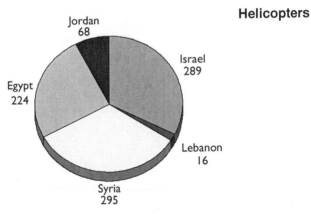

**Helicopters**

Jordan
68

Israel
289

Egypt
224

Lebanon
16

Syria
295

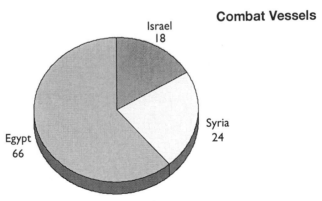

**Combat Vessels**

Israel
18

Syria
24

Egypt
66

# Military Power in the Gulf

## Personnel
Thousands

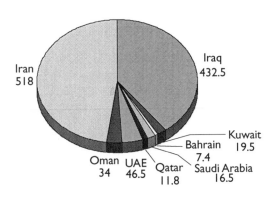

## Tanks

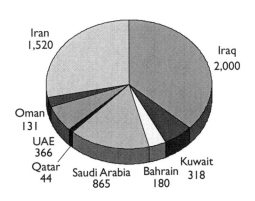

## Armored Fighting Vehicles

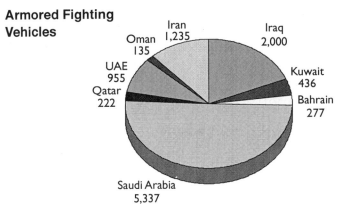

## Military Power in the Gulf *(continued)*

### Fighter Aircrafts

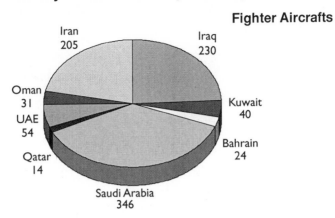

Iran
205

Iraq
230

Oman
31

UAE
54

Kuwait
40

Qatar
14

Bahrain
24

Saudi Arabia
346

### Helicopters

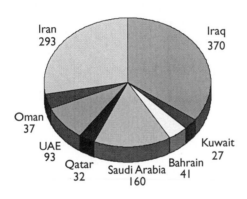

Iran
293

Iraq
370

Oman
37

UAE
93

Qatar
32

Saudi Arabia
160

Bahrain
41

Kuwait
27

### Combat Vessels

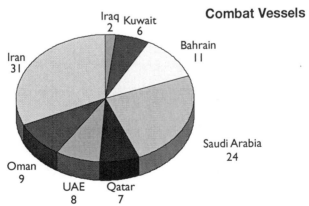

Iraq
2

Kuwait
6

Bahrain
11

Iran
31

Saudi Arabia
24

Oman
9

UAE
8

Qatar
7

## Part IV

# GLOSSARY OF
# WEAPONS SYSTEMS

# LAND FORCES EQUIPMENT

## Armor

### Tanks

| Type | Crew | Combat weight/ Power-to-weight ratio (hp/t) | Gun | Ammunition | Max. ope. range (km) | Country of origin | Notes |
|---|---|---|---|---|---|---|---|
| **Main battle tanks – high quality** | | | | | | | |
| Challenger 2 | 4 | 62.5/19.2 | 120mm L30 | Up to 50 Shells | 450 road, 250 cross country | Britain | |
| Khalid | 4 | 58/20.68 | 120mm | 64 shells | | Jordan | Jordanian improved version of Chieftain Mk 5 |
| Leclerc | 3 | 54.5/27.52 | 120mm | 40 shells | 550 | France | |
| Leopard A1/A3 | 4 | 42.4/20.75 | 105mm L7A3 | 60 shells | 600 road, 450 cross country | Germany | |
| M-1A1 | 4 | 57.15/26.24 | 105mm | 40 shells | 465 | USA | |
| M-1A2 | 4 | 54.54/27 | 120mm | 55 shells | 500 | USA | |
| M-84 A | 3 | 42/23.8 | 125mm | 42 shells | | Yugoslavia | Improved version of T-72 |
| Merkava Mk.1 | 4 | 60/15 | 105mm | 62 shells | 400 | Israel | |
| Merkava Mk.2 | 4 | 61/15 | 105mm | 62 shells | 400 | Israel | |
| Merkava Mk. 3 | 4 | 61/19.67 | 120mm | 50 shells | 500 | Israel | The Egyptian version is fitted with a 120mm gun |

## Tanks (continued)

| Type | Crew | Combat weight/ Power-to-weight ratio (hp/t) | Gun | Ammunition | Max. ope. range (km) | Country of origin | Notes |
|---|---|---|---|---|---|---|---|
| T-72 | 3 | 44.5/18.9 | 125mm 2A46 | 45 shells (including 6 ATGW) | 480 | Russia | |
| Zulfikar | | 40/25 | 125mm | | | Iran | |
| **Medium and low quality tanks** | | | | | | | |
| AMX-30 | 4 | 37/20 | 105mm | 47 shells | 450 | France | |
| Centurion (upgraded) | 4 | 51.8/12.54 | 105mm | 64 shells | 190 | Britain | |
| Chieftain Mk. 5 | 4 | 55/13.63 | 120mm L11A5 | 64 shells | 400-500 road, 200-300 cross country | Britain | |
| Chieftain Mk.3 | 4 | 54.1/13.49 | 120mm | 53 shells | 400-500 road, 200-300 cross country | Britain | |
| M-47 | 5 | 46.17/17.54 | 90mm | 71 shells | 130 | USA | |
| M-47M | 4 | 46.8/16.1 | 90mm | 79 shells | 600 | USA | |
| M-48A1 | 4 | 47.173/17.17 | 90mm M41 | 60 shells | 113 (without external fuel tanks) | USA | |
| M-48A5 | 4 | 48.98/15.89 | 105mm M68 | 54 shells | 500 | USA | |

## Tanks (continued)

| Type | Crew | Combat weight/ Power-to- weight ratio (hp/t) | Gun | Ammunition | Max. ope. range (km) | Country of origin | Notes |
|---|---|---|---|---|---|---|---|
| M-60 A1 | 4 | 52.61/14.24 | 105mm M68 | 63 shells | 500 | USA | |
| M-60 A3 | 4 | 52.61/14.24 | 105mm M68 | 63 shells | 480 | USA | |
| OF-40 Mk.2 | 4 | 45.5/18.24 | 105mm | 57 shells | 600 | Italy | Omani version of |
| Qayd al-Ard | 4 | 55/13.63 | 120mm | 64 shells | | Britain | Chieftain Mk 5 |
| Shot Kal | 4 | 51.8/12.54 | 105mm | 72 shells | | | Israeli improved version of Centurion |
| T-54 | 4 | 36/14.44 | 100mm D-10 | 35 shells | 510 | Russia | |
| T-55 | 4 | 36.5/16.3 | 100mm D-10T2S | 43 shells | 460 | Russia | |
| T-55 (Safir-74) | | | 105mm? | | | Iraq | Iraqi upgrade |
| T-55/Type-69 | 3 | | 125mm? | | | Iraq | Iraqi upgrade |
| T-62 | 4 | 40/14.5 | 115mm 2A20 | 40 shells | 450 road 320 cross country | Russia | |
| Tariq | 4 | 51.8/12.8 | 105mm | 64 shells | 190 | | Jordanian Improved Version of Centurion |
| Type 59 | 4 | 36/14.44 | 100mm | 34 shells | 420–440 | PRC | (Chinese T-54) |
| Type 69 | 4 | 36.5/15.9 | 100mm | 34 shells | | PRC | |
| Vickers Mk. 1 | 4 | 38.6/16.8 | 105mm L7 | 44 shells | 480 | Britain | |

## Tanks (continued)

| Type | Crew | Combat weight/Power-to-weight ratio (hp/t) | Gun | Ammunition | Max. ope. range (km) | Country of origin | Notes |
|---|---|---|---|---|---|---|---|
| **Light tanks** | | | | | | | |
| AMX-13 | 3 | 15/16.6 | 90mm | 32 shells | 350-400 | France | There are versions with 75mm and 105mm guns |
| PT-76 | 3 | 14.6/16.4 | 76.2mm | 40 shells | 400 | Russia | |
| Scorpion | 3 | 8/23.5 | 76mm | 40 shells | 644 road | Britain | |
| SK-105 | 3 | 17.7/18.1 | 105mm 105G1 | 41 shells | 500 | Austria | |

## Armored Personnel Carriers

| Type | Crew | Combat weight/Power-to-weight ratio (hp/ton) | Configuration | Country of origin | Notes |
|---|---|---|---|---|---|
| AAPC | 13 | 12.94/23.16 | Tracked | Turkey | |
| Achzarit | 3+7 | | Tracked | Israel | Based on T-55 MBT hull |
| AT-105 | 2+8 | 11.66/14.06 | 4x4 | Britain | |
| BMR-600 | 2+10 | 14/22 | 6x6 | Spain | |
| BTR-152 | 2+17 | 9/12.29 | 6x6 | Russia | |
| BTR-40 | 2+8 | 5.3/15 | 4x4 | Russia | |
| BTR-50 | 2+20 | 14.2/16.9 | Tracked | Russia | |
| BTR-60PA | 2+16 | 10/18.03 | 8x8 | Russia | |
| BTR-80 | 3+7 | 13.6/19.11 | 8x8 | Russia | |

## Armored Personnel Carriers *(continued)*

| Type | Crew | Configuration | Combat weight/ Power-to-weight ratio (hp/ton) | Country of origin | Notes |
|---|---|---|---|---|---|
| Engesa EE-11 | 13 | 6x6 | 14/18.6 | Brazil | |
| al-Fahd | 2+10 | 4x4 | 10.9/15.4 | Egypt | |
| al-Fahd 240 | 2+10 | 4x4 | 10.9/22 | Egypt | |
| al-Fahd | 2+12 | 8x8 | | Saudi Arabia | also known as AD-40-8-1 |
| FIAT OtoBreda 6614 | 1+10 | 4x4 | 8.5/18.82 | Italy | |
| FUG-70/ PSZH-IV | 3+6 | Wheeled | 7.6/13.15 | Hungary | |
| GKN- Defence Piranha | 15 | 8x8 | 12.3/24.4 | Britain | |
| M-113A1 | 2+11 | Tracked | 11.07/19.27 | USA | |
| M-113A2 | 2+11 | Tracked | 11.25/18.51 | USA | |
| M-125A1 | 6 | Tracked | 11.26/19.09 | USA | |
| M-2 halftrack | 10 | Halftrack | 8.89/14.39 | USA | |
| M-3 halftrack | 13 | Halftrack | 8.89/14.39 | USA | |
| M-3 Panhard | 2+10 | 4x4 | 6.1/14.75 | France | |
| M-60P | 3+10 | Tracked | 11/12.73 | Slovenia | |
| MT-LB | 2+11 | Tracked | 11.9/20.16 | Russia | |
| Nagmachon | 8 | Tracked | | Israel | based on MBT hull |
| Nagmashot | 8 | Tracked | | Israel | based on Centurion MBT hull |
| Nakpadon | | Tracked | | Israel | |

433

## Armored Personnel Carriers (continued)

| Type | Crew | Configuration | Combat weight/ Power-to-weight ratio (hp/ton) | Country of origin | Notes |
|---|---|---|---|---|---|
| OT-62B | 2+18 | Tracked | 15/20 | Czech Republic/ Poland | Czech/Polish BTR-50 |
| OT-64C(1) SKOT-2A | 2+10 | 8x8 | 14.5/12.41 | Czech Republic/ Poland | |
| Peninsula Shield | 9 | 6x6 | 16/22.8 | Saudi Arabia | See also Armored Rec. Vehicles |
| RBY | 2+6 | 4x4 | 4/30 | Israel | |
| S-55 | 2+6 | 4x4 | 3.6/31.2 | Britain | |
| Saracen FV603 (C) | 2+10 | 6x6 | 10.17/15.73 | Britain | |
| UR-416 | 2+8 | 4x4 | 7.6/16.5 | Germany | |
| VAB-VTT | 2+10 | 4x4 | 13/16.92 | France | |
| VAB-VTT | 2+10 | 6x6 | 14.2/16.54 | France | |
| VCR | 3+9 | 6x6 | 7.9/18.35 | France | |
| al-Walid | 2+10 | 4x4 | | Egypt | |
| YW-531 | 2+13 | Tracked | 12.6/25.39 | PRC | |

## Infantry Fighting Vehicles

| Type | Crew | Configuration | Combat weight/ Power-to-weight ratio (hp/ton) | Armament | Country of origin/Notes |
|------|------|---------------|-----------------------------------------------|----------|-------------------------|
| AIFV | 13 | Tracked | 13.68/21.92 | 25mm gun | Turkey |
| AMX-10P | 3+8 | Tracked | 14.5/17.93 | 20mm gun | France |
| AMX-VCI | 3+10 | Tracked | 15/16.67 | 20mm gun | France |
| BMD-1 | 3+4 | Tracked | 7.5/32 | 73mm 2A28 gun; launcher rail for AT-3 'Sagger' ATGW | Russia |
| BMP-1 | 3+8 | Tracked | 13.5/22.22 | 73mm 2A28 gun; launcher rail for AT-3 'Sagger' ATGW | Russia |
| BMP-2 | 3+7 | Tracked | 14.3/20.30 | 30mm 2A42 gun 1 launcher for AT-5 'Spandrel' or AT-4 'Spigot' ATGW | Russia |
| BMP-3 | 3+7 | Tracked | 18.7/26.73 | 100mm 2A70 gun; 30mm 2A72 gun; AT-10 'Stabber' ATGW | Russia |
| Boragh | 2+13 | Tracked | 12.8/22 | 73mm gun ATGW | Iranian WZ-503 (BMP-1) |
| Condor | 2+12 | 4x4 | 12.4/13.54 | 20mm gun 7.62 MG | Germany |
| Desert Warrior | 3+7 | Tracked | 25.7/21.4 | 25mm gun 2-tube TOW ATGW launchers | Britain |
| Engesa EE-11 | 3+5 | 6x6 | 14/18.6 | 90mm gun | Brazil |
| al-Fahd 240/240-30 | 2+10 3+10 | 4x4 | 12.5/19.2 | 30mm 2A42 gun; AT-5 'Spandrel' ATGW | Egypt |
| LAV-25 | 3+6 | 8x8 | 12.79/21.49 | 25mm gun | Canada |
| M-2 Bradley IFV | 3+6 | Tracked | 22.94/20.38 | 25mm gun 2- tube TOW launcher | USA |

435

## Infantry Fighting Vehicles (continued)

| Type | Crew | Configuration | Combat weight/ Power-to-weight ratio (hp/ton) | Armament | Country of origin/Notes |
|------|------|---------------|-----------------------------------------------|----------|--------------------------|
| M-3 Bradley CFV | 3+2 | Tracked | 22.44/20.51 | 25mm gun | USA |
| Pandur | 2+8 | 6x6 | 13/25.3 | 30mm gun | Austria |
| Ratel 20 | 11 | 6x6 | 18.5/15.24 | 20mm gun | South Africa |
| Ratel 90 | 10 | 6x6 | 19/14.84 | 90mm gun | South Africa |
| V-150 | 3+2 | 4x4 | 9.88/20.42 | 20mm gun | USA |
| V-150 S | 3+2 | 4x4 | 10.88/22.96 | 20mm gun | USA |
| V-300 | 3+9 | 6x6 | 14.96/18.94 | 90mm gun or 76mm gun or 25mm gun or 20mm gun | USA |
| VAB-VCI | 2+10 | 4x4 | 13/16.92 | 20mm gun | France |
| VAB-VCI | 2+10 | 6x6 | 14.2/15.49 | 20mm gun | France |
| YPR-765 | 3+7 | Tracked | 13.68/19.29 | 25mm gun | Netherlands |

## Armored Reconnaissance Vehicles

| Type | Crew | Configuration | Combat weight/ Power-to-weight ratio (hp/ton) | Armament | Country of origin/Notes |
|------|------|---------------|-----------------------------------------------|----------|--------------------------|
| Akrep (Scorpion) | 4 | 4x4 | 3.6/37 | | Turkey |
| AML-60 | 3 | 4x4 | 5.5/16.36 | 60mm mortar | France |
| AML-90 | 3 | 4x4 | 5.5/16.36 | 90mm gun | France |
| AMX-10RC | 4 | 6x6 | 15.88/16.45 | 105mm gun | France |

## Armored Reconnaissance Vehicles (continued)

| Type | Crew | Configuration | Combat weight/Power-to-weight ratio (hp/ton) | Armament | Country of origin/Notes |
|---|---|---|---|---|---|
| BRDM-1 | 5 | 4x4 | 5.6/16.08 | | Russia |
| BRDM-2 | 4 | 4x4 | 7/20 | 14.5mm KPVT MG or 23mm gun AT-3 (Sagger) ATGW | Russia |
| EBR-75 | 4 | 8x8 | 13.5/14.81 | 75mm gun | France |
| Engesa EE-9 | 3 | 6x6 | 13.4/15.82 | 90mm gun | Brazil |
| al-Fahd | 3 | 8x8 | | Various turrets can be fitted, up to a three-man model with a 105mm gun | Saudi Arabia also known as AD-40-8-2 |
| Ferret | 2 | 4x4 | 4.4/29.35 | 2xVigilance ATGW launchers | Britain |
| Ferret Mk 1/2 | 3 | 4x4 | 4.37/29.51 | | Britain |
| FIAT OtoBreda 6616 | 3 | 4x4 | 8/20.2 | 20mm gun | Italy |
| Fox | 3 | 4x4 | 6.12/30.04 | | Britain |
| M-3 (Panhard) | | 4x4 | 6.1/14.75 | HOT ATGW | France (see Armored personnel carriers) |
| M-901 ITV | 4 | Tracked | 11.8/18 | TOW ATGW | USA |
| Peninsula Shield | 3 | 6x6 | 18.5/22.8 | 90mm Mk.7 gun | Saudi Arabia (see Armored personnel carriers) |
| Saladin | 3 | 6x6 | 11.6/14.66 | | Britain |
| VBC-90 | 3 | 6x6 | 13.5/16 | 90mm gun | France |
| VCR/TH | 3 | 6x6 | 7.9/18.33 | HOT ATGW | France |

# Artillery

## Guns, Howitzers and Mortars

| Caliber | Designation | Type | Range (km) | Country of origin | Notes |
|---|---|---|---|---|---|
| 240mm | M-240 | Towed mortar | 9.7km | Russia | |
| 210mm | al-Faw | SP gun | 57 (base bleed and RAP ammunition) | Iraq | with assistance of companies from Belgium and Britain |
| 203mm/8″ | M-110 A1 | SP howitzer | 16.8 | USA | |
| 203mm/8″ | M-115 | Towed howitzer | 16.8 | USA | |
| 180mm | S-23 | Towed gun | 32 | Russia | |
| 175mm | M-107 | SP gun | 32.7 | USA | |
| 160mm | M-43/53 | Towed mortar | 5.1 | Russia | |
| 160mm | M-66 | SP mortar | 9.3 | Israel | |
| 155mm | FH-70 | Towed howitzer | 24 | FRG | |
| 155mm | G-5 | Towed gun/howitzer | 30 | South Africa | |
| 155mm | G-6 | SP howitzer | 30.8 (39 with base bleed ammunition) | South Africa | |
| 155mm | GCT | SP howitzer | 23.5 | France | |
| 155mm | GHN-45 | Towed howitzer/gun | 17.8 | Austria | |
| 155mm | L-33 (Sherman/ Soltam) | SP howitzer | 21 | Israel | gun-Israel; chassis-obsolete US-made tanks |
| 155mm | M-109 A1/A2/A6 | SP howitzer | 21 | USA | |

## Guns, Howitzers and Mortars (continued)

| Caliber | Designation | Type | Range (km) | Country of origin | Notes |
|---|---|---|---|---|---|
| 155mm | M-109 Doher | SP howitzer | | USA/Israel | upgrading of M-109 |
| 155mm | M-114 A2 | Towed howitzer | 14.6 | USA | |
| 155mm | M-1950 | Towed howitzer | 17.5 | France | |
| 155mm | M-198 A1 | Towed howitzer | 18.1 | USA | |
| 155mm | M-41 | Towed gun | 30 | Iraq/Austria | a combination of the 130mm gun chassis and Austrian 155mm barrels |
| 155mm | M-44 | SP howitzer | 14.6 | USA | |
| 155mm | M-50 (Sherman) | SP howitzer | 17.5 | Israel | gun - France; chassis - USA, improved in Israel |
| 155mm | M-59 (Long Tom) | Towed gun | 22 | USA | |
| 155mm | M-71 | Towed gun/howitzer | 24 | Israel | |
| 155mm | Majnoon | SP howitzer | 30.2 | Iraq | with assistance from a company in Belgium |
| 155mm | Mk F-3 (AMX) | SP howitzer | 18 | France | |
| 155mm | Palmaria | SP howitzer | 24 | Italy | |
| 152mm | D-20 | Towed howitzer/gun | 18 | Russia | |
| 152mm | M-1943 (D-1) | Towed howitzer | 12.4 | Russia | |
| 152mm | M-1946 2A36 | Towed howitzer | 27 | Russia | |
| 152mm | M-1973 | SP howitzer | 18 | Russia | |
| 130mm | M-46 | Towed gun | 27.1 | Russia | |

**Guns, Howitzers and Mortars (continued)**

| Caliber | Designation | Type | Range (km) | Country of origin | Notes |
|---|---|---|---|---|---|
| 130mm | Type 59 | Towed gun | 27.4 | PRC | copy of Soviet 130mm M-46 |
| 122mm | AR-122 | SP howitzer | 15.4 | Russia (gun)/ Egypt | conversion to SP with US aid |
| 122mm | D-30 | Towed howitzer | 16 | Russia | |
| 122mm | D-74 | Towed gun | 24 | Russia | |
| 122mm | ISU | SP gun | 16 | Russia | |
| 122mm | M-1938 | Towed howitzer | 11.8 | Russia | |
| 122mm | M-1974 | SP howitzer | 15.3 | Russia | |
| 122mm | Saddam | Towed howitzer | 16 | Iraq/Russia | Russian 122mm D-30, produced in Iraq, with assistance from Yugoslavia |
| 120mm | | SP mortar | 11.5 | Iraq | Mounted on Russian-made MT-LB carrier |
| 120mm | Brandt | SP mortar | | France (mortar)/ Canada (vehicle) | On LAV chassis |
| 120mm | Brandt M-50/M-60 | Towed mortar | 6.6 | France | |
| 120mm | M-43 | Towed mortar | 5.7 | Russia | |

## Guns, Howitzers and Mortars (continued)

| Caliber | Designation | Type | Range (km) | Country of origin | Notes |
|---|---|---|---|---|---|
| 120mm | M-65 | Towed mortar | 6.3 | Israel | Available as SP, mounted on US made M-2 halftrack |
| 120mm | TDA | SP rifled mortar; | 13 | France | Mounted on Mowag Piranha 8x8 APC |
| 107mm (4.2″) | M-30 | SP/towed mortar | 5.6 | USA | SP on M-106 A2 carrier, a derivative of M-113 APC |
| 105mm | L-118 | Towed light gun | 17.2 | Britain | |
| 105mm | M-101 A1 | Towed howitzer | 11.3 | USA | |
| 105mm | M-102 A1 | Towed howitzer | 11.5 | USA | |
| 105mm | M-108 | SP howitzer | 11.5 | USA | |
| 105mm | M-52 | SP howitzer | 11.3 | USA | |
| 105mm | M-56 | Towed Pack howitzer | 10.6 | Italy | |
| 105mm | Mk 61 | SP howitzer | 15 | France | |
| 100mm | M-1955 | Towed field/AT gun | 21 | Russia | |
| 100mm | SU-100 | SP gun | | Russia | |
| 87mm (25lb.) | | Towed howitzer | 12.2 | Britain | |
| 85mm | M-1945/D-44 | Towed field/AT gun | 15.8 | Russia | |
| 76mm | M-1942 (ZIS-3) | Towed divisional gun | 13.3 | Russia | |

## Surface-to-Surface Missiles

| Designation | Range (km) | Propulsion/CEP | Payload (kg) | Country of origin | Notes |
|---|---|---|---|---|---|
| al-Hussein | 590-640 | Single stage liquid/3-4 km | 300 | Iraq | Extended range Scuds |
| CSS-2 (East Wind) | 2,700 | Single stage liquid/3-4 km | 2,045 | PRC | |
| M-7 (CSS-8) | 150 | Single stage liquid | 190 | PRC | This is derived from HQ-2 SAM for export |
| GHAURI-I | 1,300-1,500 | Single stage liquid | 750 | Pakistan | Possibly based on the No Dong |
| GHAURI-II | 2,000-2,300 | 2 stage liquid | 1,000 | Pakistan | |
| Jericho I | 450 | 2 stage solid | 500 | Israel | According to foreign publications |
| Jericho II | 800 | 2 stage solid | 500 | Israel | According to foreign publications |
| Jericho II B | N/A | | | Israel | According to foreign publications |
| Kachlilit | N/A | | N/A | Israel | Anti-radar missile |
| Keres | 40 | Solid | N/A | Israel | Anti-radar missile. A derivative of US RGM-66D |
| M-9 | 600 | Single stage solid/600m | 500 | PRC | |
| M-11 | 280 | Single stage solid/600m | 500 | PRC | |
| MGM-52C Lance | 75 | Single stage liquid/150m | 225 | USA | |
| MGM-140 ATACMS | 135 | Single stage solid/225m | 450 | USA | |
| Nodong | 1,000 | | 1,000 | North Korea | |
| Saqr 80 | 80 | Single stage solid/3-4 km | 200 | Egypt | Uses a FROG - 7 launcher |
| Shahab-3 | 1,300 | | 1,000 | Iran | Possibly based on Nodong |
| Shahab-4 | 2,000 | 2 stage liquid (?) | | Iran | |
| SS-1 (Scud B, R-17 or 9K72) | 280 | Single stage liquid/1 km | 800-1,000 | Russia | |

## Surface-to-Surface Missiles

| Designation | Range (km) | Propulsion/CEP | Payload (kg) | Country of origin | Notes |
|---|---|---|---|---|---|
| Scud C | 550 | Single stage, liquid/2-3 km | 500-700 | North Korea | Upgrading of Russian SS-1 Scud B |
| SS-21 (Scarab, OTR-21 or Tochka) | 70 | Single stage solid/150m | 120 | Russia | Tochka U has a range of 120km |
| Shaheen | 750 | Single stage solid | 1,000? | Pakistan (China?) | Possibly based on Chinese M-9 |
| Soumoud | 150(?) | Single stage, liquid | N/A | Iraq | Formally developed within the restrictions of the UNSC resolutions, but probably exceeds the limitations considerably |
| Taepo Dong 1 | 1,700-2,200 | 2 stage liquid | 700-1,000 | North Korea | |
| Taepo Dong 2 | 4,000-6,000 | 2 stage liquid | 700-1,000 | North Korea | |
| Tamuz 1 | 2,000 | 2 stage liquid | | Iraq | Not operational |

## Surface to Surface Rockets and Multiple Rocket Launchers

| Caliber | Designation | Number of rails/tubes | Range (Km) | Country of origin | Notes |
|---|---|---|---|---|---|
| 540mm | FROG-7 (Luna-M or 9K52) | 1 | 70 | Russia | |
| 540mm | Laith 90 | 1 | 90 | Iraq | Extended range version of the Russian FROG-7 |
| 400mm | Ababil-100 | 4 | 100 | Iraq | Improved version of Yugoslavia's 262mm LRSV M-87 |
| 355mm | Nazeat | N/A | 90 | Iran | |
| 333mm | Shahin 2 | N/A | 20 | Iran | |
| 300mm | Sajeel 60 | 4 | 60 | Iraq | Copy of Brazilian 300mm SS-60 |

## Surface to Surface Rockets and Multiple Rocket Launchers *(continued)*

| Caliber | Designation | Number of rails/tubes | Range (Km) | Country of origin | Notes |
|---|---|---|---|---|---|
| 300mm | SS-60 | 4 | 60 | Brazil | |
| 300mm | BM-9A52-2 Smerch | 12 | 70 | Russia | |
| 290mm | MAR 290 | 4 | 25 | Israel | |
| 262mm | Ababil-50 | 12 | 50 | Iraq | Copy or production under license of Yugoslavia's 262mm LRSV M-87 |
| 240mm | BM-24 | 12 | 10.2 | Russia | |
| 240mm | Fajr 3 | N/A | N/A | Iran | |
| 230mm | Oghab | 3 | 80 (unconfirmed) | Iran | Improved version of PRC's Type 83 273mm rocket |
| 227mm | MLRS | 12 | 30 | USA | |
| 180mm | Sajeel 40 | 16 | 35 | Iraq | Copy of Brazilian 180mm SS-40 |
| 180mm | SS-40 Astros II | 16 | 35 | Brazil | |
| 140mm | BM-14-16 | 16 | 9.8 | Russia | |
| 140mm | RPU-14 | 16 | 9.8 | Russia | |
| 140mm | Teruel | 40 | 18.2 | Spain | |
| 132mm | BM-13-16 | 16 | 9 | Russia | |
| 130mm | M-51 (RM-130) | 32 | 8.2 | Romania/Russia | |
| 130mm | M-51 | 32 | 8.2 | Czech Republic | |
| 130mm | Type 63 | 19 | 10.4 | PRC | |
| 128mm | M-63 | 32 | 8.5 | Yugoslavia | |
| 127mm | Sajeel 30 | 32 | 30 | Iraq | Copy of Brazilian 127mm SS-30 |
| 127mm | SS-30 Astros II | 32 | 30 | Brazil | |
| 122mm | BM-11 | 30 | | North Korea | A variant of Soviet BM-21 |

## Surface to Surface Rockets and Multiple Rocket Launchers *(continued)*

| Caliber | Designation | Number of rails/tubes | Range (Km) | Country of origin | Notes |
|---|---|---|---|---|---|
| 122mm | BM-21 | 40 | 20.8 | Russia | |
| 122mm | Firos-25 | 40 | 25 | Italy | |
| 122mm | RM-70 | 40 | 20.4 | Czech Republic | Similar to Soviet BM-21 |
| 122mm | Saqr 10 and Saqr 18 | | 18 | Egypt | |
| 122mm | Saqr 30 | | 22.5 | Egypt | |
| 122mm | Saqr 36 | | 20.4 | Egypt | |
| 107mm | | 12 | 8 | Iraq | Copy of 107mm from PRC or RM-11 from North Korea |
| 107mm | RM-11 | | 8.1 | North Korea | |
| 107mm | Type 63 | 12 | 8.5 | PRC | |

## Artillery and Ground Surveillance Radars

| Designation | Detection range (km) | Frequency | Country of origin |
|---|---|---|---|
| AN/PPS-15A | | | USA |
| AN/TPQ-37 | 50 | | USA |
| Blindfire | | | Britain |
| Cymbeline | 30 | I band | Britain |
| EL/M-2310 | | | Israel |
| Rasit | 40 | I/J band | France |

445

**Artillery Ammunition Carriers**

| Designation | Configuration | Country of origin | Notes |
|---|---|---|---|
| M - 992 | Tracked | USA | |
| MT-LB | Tracked | Russia | also serves as prime mover for towed artillery and APC |

# Anti-Tank Equipment

**Anti-Tank Guns**

| Caliber | Designation and type | Country of origin | Notes |
|---|---|---|---|
| 120mm | BAT L-4 recoilless rifle | Britain | |
| 107mm | B-11 recoilless rifle | Russia | |
| 106mm | M-40 A1C / A2 recoilless rifle | USA/Israel | |
| 100mm | M-1955 gun field / AT gun | Russia | see Guns and Howitzers |
| 90mm | light gun, low recoil | Belgium | used on AFVs |
| 85mm | M-1945/D-44 field / AT gun | Russia | see Guns and Howitzers |
| 84mm | Carl Gustav light recoilless rifle | Sweden | |
| 82mm | B-10 recoilless rifle | Russia | |
| 76mm | M-1942 (ZIS-3) field / AT gun | Russia | see Guns and Howitzers |
| 75mm | M-20 recoilless rifle | USA | |
| 57mm | AT gun | Czech Republic | |

## Anti-Tank Guided Missiles

| Designation | Range (m.) | Guidance | Country of origin | Notes |
|---|---|---|---|---|
| AT-1 (Snapper) | 2,300 | Wire | Russia | |
| AT-2 (Swatter) | 2,500 | Radio | Russia | |
| AT-3 (Sagger) | 3,000 | Wire | Russia | |
| AT-4 (Spigot) | 2,500 | Wire | Russia | |
| AT-5 (Spandrel) | 3,600 | Wire | Russia | |
| AT-6 (Spiral) | 5,000 | Radio | Russia | |
| AT-14 (Kornet) | 5,500 | Laser | Russia | |
| Dandy (NT-D) | 6,000 | IIR + optical wire | Israel | Tandem warhead |
| Dragon I/II | 1,000 | Wire | USA | |
| Dragon II+/III (Superdragon) | 2,000 | Wire | USA | |
| Eryx | 600 | Wire | France/Canada | |
| Gil (NT-G) | 2,500 | IIR + optical wire | Israel | Tandem warhead |
| Hellfire | 8,000 | Laser | USA | |
| HOT | 4,000 | Wire | France/Germany | |
| Mapats | 5,000 | Laser | Israel | |
| MILAN | 2,000 | Wire | France/Germany | |
| Nimrod | 26,000 | Laser | Israel | Land-based variant of Nimrod AGM |
| SS-11 | 3,000 | Wire | France | |
| SS-12 | 5,000 | Wire | France | can be employed as ATGM or as antiship missile launched from ground, helicopter, or ship |

447

## Anti-Tank Guided Missiles (continued)

| Designation | Range (m.) | Guidance | Country of origin | Notes |
|---|---|---|---|---|
| Spike (NT-S) | 4,000 | IIR fire and forget | Israel | |
| Swingfire | 4,000 | | Britain/Egypt | |
| T-1/T-16 | | | Russia | ATGM system/tank destroyer (unconfirmed) |
| TOW (BGM 71A/C/D) | 3,750 | Wire | USA | |
| BGM-71E TOW IIA | 3,750 | Wire | USA | Tandem warhead |
| BGM-71F TOW IIB | 3,750 | Wire | USA | Tandem warhead programmed for top attack |
| Trigat | 2,000 | Laser | France | |

# Engineering and Logistics

## Engineering Equipment

| Designation | Country of Origin | Notes |
|---|---|---|
| Bar mine-lying system | Britain | |
| EWK pontoon bridge (Faltschwimmbrucke) | Germany | |
| Gilois motorized bridge | France | Bridge and ferry system |
| GSP | Russia | Heavy amphibious self propelled ferry |
| M-60 AVLB | USA | Bridging tank |
| M-69 A1 | USA | Bridging tank |
| M-123 Viper | USA | Minefield - crossing system |
| Matenin SA | France | Automatic mine layers |

## Engineering Equipment (continued)

| Designation | Country of Origin | Notes |
|---|---|---|
| Mk 3(D) flail | France | Antimine vehicle |
| MT-55 | Russia | Bridging tank |
| MTU-55 | Russia | Bridging tank |
| MTU-67 | Russia | Bridging tank |
| PMP pontoon bridge | Russia | Heavy folding pontoon bridge |
| Pomins II | Israel | Portable (infantry) mine neutralization system |
| PRP motorized bridge | Russia | |
| Puma | Israel | A combat vehicle carrying a squad of combat engineers and some equipment (an improvement of existing foreign tank chassis) |
| TAB, tactical assault bridge | Israel | |
| TLB, trailer-launched bridge | Israel | |
| TPP, pontoon bridge | Russia | Can be used as a pontoon bridge or a raft |
| TWMP, tread-width mine ploughs | Israel | |
| UDK-1, bridge | Britain | |

## Recovery Vehicles

| Designation | Type | Combat weight (ton) | Lifting/towing capaility | Country of origin | Notes |
|---|---|---|---|---|---|
| M-88 A1 | Armored recovery vhicle | 50.8 | Up to 22.7 tones when using a stabilizing blade. Two winches: max. capacity of 40.8 ton at 6 m/min | USA | Based on the M48 main battle tank |
| M-578 | Light armored recovery vehicle | 24.3 | Crane maximum lift capability – 6.7 ton. Two winches with max. capacity of 27 ton on a bare drum | USA | Hull is similar to that of the 175mm M107 and 203mm M110 SPGs |
| T-55 | Armored recovery vehicle | 34 | Lifting capability of between 10 to 20 ton (depending on model) | Russia | Additional models were developed by the Czech Republic, Poland and Germany |
| T-62 | Armored recovery vehicle | 38 | | Russia | |

# AIR DEFENSE EQUIPMENT

## Anti-Aircraft Guns

| Caliber | Designation | SP, tracked or wheeled (when relevant) | Country of origin | Notes |
|---------|-------------|----------------------------------------|-------------------|-------|
| 57mm | ZSU 57x2 | SP, tracked | Russia | |
| 57mm | S-60 | | Russia | |
| 40mm | M-42 (twin 40mm) | SP, tracked | USA | |
| 40mm | Bofors L-70 | | Sweden | |
| 40mm | Bofors L-60 | | Sweden | |
| 37mm | M-1939 | | Russia | |
| 35mm | Contraves Skyguard | | | See Air Defense Systems |
| 35mm | Gepard | SP | Germany | |
| 35mm | Oerlikon-Buhrle 35x2 GDF-002 | | Switzerland | May be part of 35mm Skyguard system |
| 30mm | AMX DCA 30 (twin 30mm) | SP, tracked | France | |
| 30mm | Artemis (twin 30mm) | | Greece | Based on 30mm Mauser AAG, Germany |
| 30mm | 30x2 M-53/59 | SP, wheeled | Czech Republic | |
| 30mm | Oerlikon | | Switzerland | |
| 30mm | 30x2 Wildcat | SP, wheeled | Germany | |
| 30mm | 30x2 M-3 | SP | France | |
| 23mm | ZSU 23x4 (Gun Dish) | SP, tracked | Russia | Russian designation: Shilka |
| 23mm | ZU 23x2 | | Russia | |
| 20mm | 20x2 VDAA | SP (on VAB APC) | France | |

## Anti Aircraft Guns *(continued)*

| Caliber | Designation | SP, tracked or wheeled (when relevant) | Country of origin | Notes |
|---|---|---|---|---|
| 20mm | TCM-20x2 | SP | Israel | Israeli mounting of French gun on US-made M-3 halftrack |
| 20mm | Oerlikon GAI | | Switzerland | |
| 20mm | M-163 A1 Vulcan | SP | USA | |
| 20mm | M-167 Vulcan | | USA | |
| 20mm | 20x2 | SP | France | Mounted on Panhard VCR 6x6 |
| 20mm | 20x3 M-55 A4 | | Slovenia | |
| 20mm | VDAA | SP | France | Mounted on VAB 6x6 |

## Air Defense Systems

| Caliber | Designation | Missiles | Country of origin | Notes |
|---|---|---|---|---|
| 20mm | Mahbet | Stinger | Israel | Based on M-163 Vulcan |
| 35mm | Skyguard (Contraves Skyguard) 2x35 | Aspide or RIM-7M Sparrow | Italy | Gun - Switzerland, SAM - Italy, or USA; chassis and radar - Italy or Austria; Egyptian designation Amoun |
| 23mm | Sinai 23 | 4x SA-7 | Egypt | Gun + SAM - Russia or Egypt; chassis - USA |

## Air defense missiles

| Model | Range (Km) | Guidance | Configuration | Country of origin |
|-------|-----------|----------|---------------|-------------------|
| **Heavy Missiles** | | | | |
| HAWK | 35 | Semi-active Radar | Towed | USA |
| Improved HAWK (MIM-23B) | 40 | Semi-active Radar | Towed | USA |
| HQ-2J | 34 | Command | Towed | China |
| Nike Hercules | 155 | Command | Towed | USA |
| Patriot (MIM-104) | 160 | Command, Semi-active Radar | Trucked | USA |
| SA-10 (S-300P/300V) | 70/150 | Command, Active radar | Trucked | Russia |
| SA-2 | 35 | Command | Towed | Russia |
| SA-3 | 22 | Command | Towed | Russia |
| SA-5 | 250 | Command, Active radar | Static | Russia |
| **Medium Missiles** | | | | |
| ADAMS | 12 | Command | SP | Israel |
| Crotale | 9 | Command | SP | France |
| Crotale NG | 11 | Command, IR, Optical | SP | France |
| SA-11 | 28 | Semi-active radar | SP | Russia |
| SA-6 (Kub) | 24 | Semi-active radar | Trucked | Russia |
| Shahine I/II | 8-11 | Command, IR, Optical | SP | France |
| **Light Missiles** | | | | |
| ADATS | 8 | Laser | SP | Switzerland |
| Avenger | 4.5 | IR | SP | USA |
| Chaparral (MIM-72A) | 8 | Active IR | SP | USA |
| Mistral | 6 | Optical, IR | Portable | France |
| Rapier | 7 | Command, Optical command | Towed | Britain |

## Air defense missiles

| Model | Range (Km) | Guidance | Configuration | Country of origin |
|---|---|---|---|---|
| RBS - 70 | 6 | Laser | Portable | Sweden |
| Roland I/II | 6.3 | Command | SP | France |
| SA-8 (Osa romb) | 9.9 | Command | SP | Russia |
| SA-9 | 8 | Optical, IR | SP | Russia |
| SA-13 (Strella 10) | 5 | Optical, IR | SP | Russia |
| Tigercat | 5.5 | Optical command | Towed | Britain |
| **Man-portable Missiles** | | | | |
| Ain al-Saqr | 4.4 | Optical, IR | Portable | Egypt |
| Blowpipe | 3.5 | Optical command | Portable | Britain |
| HN-5 | 4 | Optical, IR | Portable | China |
| Javelin | 5 | Optical command | Portable | Britain |
| Redeye (MIM-43A) | 5.5 | Optical, IR | Portable | USA |
| SA-7 (Strella) | 3.5 | Optical, IR | Portable | Russia |
| SA-14 (Strella 3) | 6 | Optical, IR | Portable | Russia |
| SA-16 (Igla) | 5 | Optical, IR | Portable | Russia |
| Starburst | 4 | Laser | Portable | Britain |
| Stinger (FIM - 92A) | 4.5 | Optical, IR | Portable | USA |

# AIR FORCE EQUIPMENT

## Aircraft

### Fighter aircraft

| Model | Radius of action (Km) | Radar | Air-to-air missiles | Air-to-ground missiles | Navigation and fire-control instrumentation | Country of origin |
|---|---|---|---|---|---|---|
| **Interceptors** | | | | | | |
| F-14 | | AVG-12 (315 km) | Sparrow; Phoenix | | Infra-red seeker | USA |
| F-15C/D | | APG-63 Look-down/shoot-down capability | Sidewinder Sparrow AMRAAM | | ATLIS II Laser illumination pod | USA |
| MIG-25 | 1,130 | 'Fox Fire' limited look-down/ shoot-down | AA-6 AA-7 (R-23) AA-8 (R-60) | | ECCM pods | Russia |
| Tornado ADV Mk 3 | 740 | Foxhunter multi-mode, ground mapping | Skyflash Sidewinder | | Internal ECM/ ECCM TI FL radar | Britain, Germany |
| MIG-23 MF/ML | 1,150 (AA) 700 (AG) | 'High Lark' Look-down (85km) | AA-7 (R-23) AA-8 (R-60) | | Infra-red seeker | Russia |
| MIG-29 | | RLS RP-29 'Slot Back' look-down/shoot-down | AA-8 (R-60) AA-10 (R-27) AA-11 (R-73) | | Infra-red seeker | Russia |

## Fighter aircraft (continued)

| Model | Radius of action (Km) | Radar | Air-to-air missiles | Air-to-ground missiles | Navigation and fire-control instrumentation | Country of origin |
|---|---|---|---|---|---|---|
| Advanced multi-role | | | | | | |
| F-15E | 1,270 | APG-70 Look-down/shoot-down capability | Sidewinder Sparrow AMRAAM | Maverick (TV/IIR); Paveway GBU - 10/12/15 laser/TV guided | FLIR Lantirn targeting pod | USA |
| F-16 A/B | 925 | APG-66 Look-down/shoot-down capability | Sidewinder AMRAAM | Maverick (TV/IIR); HARM/Shrike | FLIR ALQ- 119/131 ECM; Pave Penny laser pod | USA |
| F-16 C/D | 925 | APG-68V air-to-air/air-to-ground | Sidewinder AMRAAM Sparrow Python 4 | Maverick (TV/IIR); Paveway GBU - 10/12/15 laser/TV guided; HARM/Shrike; Harpoon; Popeye II | FLIR ALQ- 131/187 ECM; Pave Penny laser pod; Lantirn; Orpheus (recce.); Atils laser pod | USA |
| F-18 C/D | 537 (hi-lo-hi) | APG-65 air-to-air/air-to-ground | Sidewinder AMRAAM Sparrow | Maverick (TV/IIR); Paveway GBU - 10/12 laser guided; HARM/Shrike; Harpoon | AAS -38 FLIR; ALQ- 126/165 ECM; ASQ-173 laser pod | USA |

**Fighter aircraft** *(continued)*

| Model | Radius of action (Km) | Radar | Air-to-air missiles | Air-to-ground missiles | Navigation and fire-control instrumentation | Country of origin |
|---|---|---|---|---|---|---|
| Phantom 2000 (IAI) | 1,145 (hi-lo-hi) | APG - 76 | Python 3 Sidewinder | Griffin laser guided; Popeye | Integrated navigation system; WDNS weapon and navigation computer; internal ECM | Israel |
| Mirage 2000 | 1,200 (hi-lo-hi) 925 (lo-lo-lo) | RDM/RDY multi-mode | R 530/550 Magic Mica | ARMAT Exocet; AS-30L; laser guided bombs | Atlis laser pod; SLAR reconnaissance pods; ECM pods Astac ELINT pod | France |
| **Multi-role** | | | | | | |
| Mirage F1 | 425 (hi-lo-hi) | Cyrano IV Doppler navigation radar | R 530/550 Magic Sidewinder | ARMAT Exocet AS-30L laser guided bombs | Navigation/bombing computer; Atlis laser pod; SLAR reconnaissance pods; ECM pods | France |
| Tornado IDS Mk 1 | 1,390 (hi-lo-lo-hi) | TI FL radar Decca doppler terrain following radar | Sidewinder | AS- 30L; Maverick TV/IIR/ laser guided; GBU- 10/12/15 laser/TV guided; Sea Eagle munitions dispenser | Digital attack/ navigation system; Ferranti laser pod; internal ECM | Britain, Germany |

**Fighter aircraft (*continued*)**

| Model | Radius of action (Km) | Radar | Air-to-air missiles | Air-to-ground missiles | Navigation and fire-control instrumentation | Country of origin |
|---|---|---|---|---|---|---|
| Jaguar | 1,400 (hi-lo-hi) 917 (lo-lo-lo) | Agave | R 550 Magic; Sidewinder | AS 37 anti-radar | HUDWAC weapons computer; reconnaissance pod TV night sensors | Britain |
| F-4E | | APQ-72 | Sparrow III; Sidewinder | Bullpup (radio guidance); Maverick (TV/IIR) Standard/Shrike; Paveway GBU -10/12 laser guided | ASQ-19 navigation package; AJB-3 bombing system; laser pod | USA |
| F-5 E/F | 222 (lo-lo-lo) 890 (hi-lo-hi) | APQ-159 (37km) | Sidewinder | Paveway GBU - 10/12 laser guided; | Laser pod | USA |
| Hawk 200 | 945 (hi-lo-hi) | APG-66H multi-mode | Sky Flash; Sidewinder | Sea Eagle; Maverick | HUDWAC weapons computer; FLIR Reconnaissance pod | Britain |
| **Obsolete** | | | | | | |
| F-5 A/B | 350 | | Sidewinder; | | | USA |
| Mirage III-E | 1,200 | Cyrano II | R 530 Magic | AS-30 IR/command | Nav/bombing computer; | France |
| Mirage V | 1,300 (hi-lo-hi) 650 (lo-lo-lo) | Agave | R 530/550 Magic; Sidewinder | AS-30 IR/command | Laser rangefinder; refuelling pod | France |

## Fighter aircraft (continued)

| Model | Radius of action (Km) | Radar | Air-to-air missiles | Air-to-ground missiles | Navigation and fire-control instrumentation | Country of origin |
|---|---|---|---|---|---|---|
| MIG-21 MF/BIS | 740 (hi-lo-hi) | 'Jay Bird' (20km) | AA-2 C/D (K-13) | | | Russia |
| F-6 | 685 | Izumrud | PL-2 PL-5 | | | China |
| F-7 | 600 (hi-lo-hi) | Ranging radar | PL-2 PL-5 PL-7 | | HUDWAC weapons computer | China |
| | 370 (lo-lo-lo) | | R 550 Magic | | | |
| **Ground attack** | | | | | | |
| OV-10 | 367 | Doppler navigation radar | Sidewinder | Paveway GBU- 10/ 12 laser guided | TV/laser designation pod | USA |
| Su-20/22 | 2,300 (hi-hi-hi) | SRD-5M ranging radar; | AA-8 (R-60) | AS-7; AS-9; AS-10 | Laser pod; reconnaissance pod; ECM pod | Russia |
| | 1,400 (lo-lo-lo) | ASP-5ND fire control system | | | | |
| Su-24 | 322 (lo-lo-lo) | PNS-24M terrain-following/ | AA-8 (R-60) | AS-10; AS-11; AS-12; AS-14 | Kaira-24 laser/ TV guidance system; laser pod; internal ECM | Russia |
| | 950 (lo-lo-hi) | navigation system | | | | |
| | 1,050 (hi-lo-hi) | | | | | |
| Su-25 | 400 (lo-lo-lo) | Kinzhal ground radar; | AA-8 (R-60) | AS-10; AS-11; AS-14 KAB-500 laser guided bombs | Voskhod nav./attack system; internal TV/laser guiding system; Internal ECM IIR pod | Russia |
| | 630 (hi-hi-hi) | doppler navigation system | | | | |
| MIG-23BN | 700 | Doppler navigation radar | AA-8 (R-60) | AS-7 | Laser rangefinder | Russia |

## Fighter aircraft (continued)

| Model | Radius of action (Km) | Radar | Air-to-air missiles | Air-to-ground missiles | Navigation and fire-control instrumentation | Country of origin |
|---|---|---|---|---|---|---|
| **Bombers** | | | | | | |
| Tu-16 | 3,150 | | | AS-5 AS-6 | | Russia |
| Tu-22 | 2,200 (hi-hi-hi) 1,500 (lo-lo-lo) | 'Down Beat' navigation radar | | AS-4 | | Russia |

## Helicopter

| Model | Number of passengers | External payload (kg) | Max range (km) | Armament | Avionics | Country of origin |
|---|---|---|---|---|---|---|
| **Light Transport** | | | | | | |
| 300C | 1+2 | 408 | 370 | | | USA |
| 500D | 6 | | 482 531 | | | USA |
| 530F | 6 | 907 | 371 429 | | FLIR | USA |
| AS-350 Ecureuil | 6 | 907 | 720 | Machine guns 20mm guns; rockets | | France |
| Bell 206B | .3-4 | | 645 | | | USA |
| Bell 406 (OH-58B) Kiowa | 2+2 | | 556 | | Doppler navigation system; night vision | USA |

## Helicpoter *(continued)*

| Model | Number of passengers | External payload (kg) | Max range (km) | Armament | Avionics | Country of origin |
|---|---|---|---|---|---|---|
| BK- 117 | 7 | | 500 | | Laser-1 doppler navigation system | Japan |
| Mi-2 | 8 | 800 | 440 | | | Russia |
| SA- 315 Lama | 1+4 | 1,135 | 515 | | | France |
| SA- 318C Alouette II | 1+4 | 600 | 300 | | | France |
| SA- 316 Alouette III | 6 | 750 | 290 | | | France |
| UH-12 | 1+2 | 454 | 346 | | | USA |
| **Medium Transport** | | | | | | |
| AS- 330 Puma | 16 | 3,200 | 572 | Machine guns; 20mm gun rockets | Doppler navigation radar Decca navigation system; rolling map | France |
| AS-61/SH-3D | 31 | 3,630 | 582 | | Doppler navigation system | USA |
| AS- 332 Super Puma/ AS-532 Cougar | 21-25 | 4,500 | 870 | Machine guns; 20mm gun rockets | Doppler navigation radar Decca navigation system; rolling map | France |
| AS- 365 Dauphin II | 10 | 1,600 | 250 | | Digital navigation system | France |
| Bell 204 | 7-8 | 1,360 | 615 | Machine-guns; rocket launchers; torpedoes | Sonar | USA |

**Helicopter (continued)**

| Model | Number of passengers | External payload (kg) | Max range (km) | Armament | Avionics | Country of origin |
|---|---|---|---|---|---|---|
| UH-1H (Bell 205, 212) | 11-14 | 1,760 | 511 | Machine-guns; rocket launchers | | USA |
| Bell 214 | 18 | | 678 | | | Italy |
| Bell 412 | 14 | 1,814 | 656 / 804 | | Doppler navigation radar | Italy |
| KV-107 | 26 | | 175 | | Doppler navigation radar | Japan |
| Mi-8/17 | 24 | 3,000 | 500 | Machine guns; rockets; bombs | Doppler navigation radar | Russia |
| S-70/UH-60A | 11 | 3,630 | 600 | Machine guns | Doppler navigation radar night vision; | USA |
| SA-321 Super Frelon | 27 | 4,500 | 630 | | ALQ-144 ECM Doppler radar; | France |
| Westland Commando | 28 | 2,720 | 445 | | internal navigation system Doppler navigation radar | Britain |
| **Heavy Transport** | | | | | | |
| CH-47D Chinook | 44 | 12,700 | 185 | | Doppler navigation radar | USA |
| CH-53D | 64 | 14,515 | 413 | | | USA |
| Mi-6 | 70 | 8,000 | 620 | Machine guns; rockets | | Russia |
| **Ground Attack** | | | | | | |
| 500MD | | | 389 (S/L) 428 (5,000 ft) | TOW missiles Stinger missiles | TV/FLIR targeting system | USA |
| A-109A Mk II | 7 | 907 | 550 | Machine guns; rocket launchers; TOW missiles | Doppler navigation radar TV targeting system | Italy |

**Helicopter** *(continued)*

| Model | Number of passengers | External payload (kg) | Max range (km) | Armament | Avionics | Country of origin |
|---|---|---|---|---|---|---|
| AH-1 G/J/P | | | 574 | Minigun; TOW missiles | Optical targeting system | USA |
| AH-1W | | | 635 | 20mm Gun TOW missiles; Hellfire missiles | Optical targeting system laser designator | USA |
| AH-64A | | 771 | 482 | 30mm Gun; Hellfire missiles; rockets; Stinger missiles | Doppler navigation system ALQ-136/144 ECM; TV/FLIR targeting system laser designator | USA |
| BO-105 | 1+4 | | 575 (S/L) 657 (5,000 ft) | HOT missiles TOW missiles | Doppler navigation system; optical targeting system | Germany |
| Mi-24 | 8 | | 450 | AT-2 missiles; Machine guns; rockets; bombs | Doppler navigation system; optical targeting system Internal ECM | Russia |
| OH-58D Kiowa warrior (bell 406) | | | 556 | Machine guns; TOW missiles; Stinger missiles | Doppler navigation system TV/IIR targeting system Laser designator; night vision | USA |
| SA-316 Alouette III | 6 | 750 | 290 | Machine guns; 20mm gun; AS-11/12 missiles; | Optical targeting system | France |
| SA-342 Gazelle | 1+4 | 700 | 670 | AS-12 missiles Hot; missiles Rockets; machine guns | Optical targeting system laser designator (342 L) | France |

**Helicpoter (continued)**

| Model | Number of passengers | External payload (kg) | Max range (km) | Armament | Avionics | Country of origin |
|---|---|---|---|---|---|---|
| **Naval Combat** | | | | | | |
| AS- 332 Super Puma / AS-532 Cougar | | 4,500 | 870 | Exocet missiles; AS- 15TT missiles; Torpedoes | Doppler navigation radar; Decca navigation system; RDR 1400/1500 search radar or Varan ASW radar; sonar; magnetic sweep sonobuoys | France |
| AS- 365 Dauphin II | 10 | 1,600 | 250 | AS- 15TT; Torpedoes | Agrion 15 plan position radar or Omera ORB 32 search radar; Croyzet magnetic sweep; HS 12 sonar; digital navigation system | France |
| AS-61/SH-3D | 31 | 3,630 | 582 | Torpedoes; depth charges | Doppler ASW navigation system; APS-707 radar; AQS- 13/18 sonar | USA |
| Bell 204 | | 1,360 | 615 | Torpedoes | Sonar | USA |
| Bell 212 | | 1,760 | 511 | Torpedoes | Doppler ASW navigation system; AQS-13 B/F sonar | USA |
| Bell 412 | | 1,814 | 656 (S/L); 804 (5,000 ft) | 25mm gun; Sea Skua anti-ship | Doppler radar TV/FLIR targeting system ALQ-144 ECM | Italy |

**Helicpoter (continued)**

| Model | Number of passengers | External payload (kg) | Max range (km) | Armament | Avionics | Country of origin |
|---|---|---|---|---|---|---|
| Kamov 28 | | | 200 | Torpedoes; depth charges | Doppler navigation radar; magnetic sweep; OKA-2 sonar; sonobuoys | Russia |
| Mi-14 PL | | | 1,135 | Torpedoes; depth charges | Doppler navigation radar; 12M radar; magnetic sweep; OKA-2 sonar; sonobuoys | Russia |
| SA-321 Super Ferlon | | 4,500 | 630 | Torpedoes | Doppler radar OR Sylphe ASW radar; internal navigation system sonar | France |
| SH-2G | 4 | 1,814 | 885 | Torpedoes | LN-66HP radar; magnetic and acoustic sweeps; 15 sonobuoys; FLIR | USA |
| Westland Sea King Mk 47 | | | 1,230 | Torpedoes; depth charges | AD 580 doppler navigation system; AW 391 radar; AQS-13B/plessey sonar; sonobuoys | Britain |

## Training Aircraft

| Model | Range (Km) | External weight (Kg) | Armament | Avionics | Country of origin |
|---|---|---|---|---|---|
| **With Close support capability** | | | | | |
| Alpha Jet | 555 | 2,500 | 30mm gun; rockets; bombs; Magic AA missiles | Weapon aiming computer; camera reconnaissance pod | France, Germany |
| BAC 167 | 900 | 1,360 | Machine guns; bombs; rockets | | Britain |
| C- 101 | 964 | 2,250 | 30mm gun; rockets; bombs | Internal navigation system; optical sight laser designator; reconnaissance pod; ECM pod | Spain |
| Cessna 318/T-37B | 1,400 | | Machine gun; rockets; bombs | Internal navigation system; computing gun-sight; gun camera; reconnaissance pod | USA |
| CM 170 Fuga Magister | 910 | 500 | Machine guns; rockets | Gyro gun-sight | France |
| G2-A Galeb | | 700 | Machine guns; bombs; rockets | Fixed gunsight | Yugoslavia |

**Training Aircraft (continued)**

| Model | Range (Km) | External weight (Kg) | Armament | Avionics | Country of origin |
|---|---|---|---|---|---|
| Hawk Mk 60 | 998 | 3,084 | 30mm gun; rockets; bombs; Magic/Sidewinder AA missiles; Maverick AS missiles; Sea Eagle anti-ship missiles | Internal navigation system gunsight/camera; camera reconnaissance pod | Britain |
| Hawk Mk 100 | 998 | 3,084 | 30mm gun; rockets; bombs Magic/Sidewinder AA missiles; Maverick AS missiles; Sea Eagle anti-ship missiles | Internal navigation system; gunsight/camera; HUDWAC weapon system; FLIR; camera reconnaissance pod; ECM pod | Britain |
| L-29 Delfin | 397 | | Machine guns; rockets; bombs | Gyro gun-sight or gun camera | Czech Republic |
| L-39 Albatros | | 1,100 | 23mm gun; rockets; bombs; IR missiles | Camera reconnaissance pod; gyro gun-sight | Czech Republic |
| L-59 | 1,210 | 1,700 | 23mm gun; bombs; rockets | HUD mission computer | Czech Republic |

467

**Training Aircraft (continued)**

| Model | Range (Km) | External weight (Kg) | Armament | Avionics | Country of origin |
|---|---|---|---|---|---|
| MB 326 | 648 | 1,814 | Machine guns; rockets; bombs; AS-12 anti-tank missiles | Internal navigation system fixed/gyro gunsight; gunsight camera; camera reconnaissance pod | Italy |
| MB 339 | 593 | 1,815 | 30mm guns; bombs; rockets; Magic/Sidewinder | Internal navigation system; fixed/gyro gunsight; camera reconnaissance. Pod; ECM pod | Italy |
| T-33 | | | AA missiles Machine gun | | USA |
| **Others** | | | | | |
| AS- 202 Bravo | 965 | | | | Switzerland |
| Bae SA-3-120 Bulldog | 1,000 | | | | Britain |
| Bonanza F 33C | 1,326 | | | | USA |
| CAP 10 | 1,000 | | | | France |
| Cessna 150 | 909 | | | | USA |
| Cessna 172/T-41 | 963 | | | Internal navigation system | USA |
| Cessna 180/185 | 1,100 | | | Internal navigation system | USA |
| Cessna 182 | 1,380 | | | Internal navigation system | USA |
| Cessna U-206 | 1,045 | | Minigun; bombs | | USA |
| EMB- 312 | 1,844 | 625 | Machine gun; rockets; bombs | Fixed gun-sight | Brazil |

## Training Aircraft *(continued)*

| Model | Range (Km) | External weight (Kg) | Armament | Avionics | Country of origin |
|---|---|---|---|---|---|
| G-115T Acro | 1,310 | | | | Germany |
| MBB 223 Flamingo | 500 | | | | Germany, Spain |
| Mushshak | | 300 | Machine guns; rockets | | Pakistan |
| PC-7/9 | 1,200 | | | Computer navigation system (PC-9) | Switzerland |
| PC-6 | 1,050 | | | | Switzerland |
| SF 260 Warrior | 556 | 300 | Machine guns; bombs; rockets | Camera reconnaissance pod | USA |
| Sierra 200 | 1,270 | | | | USA |
| T-34C | 555 | 544 | Machine guns; rockets; bombs; AGM- 22A missiles | | USA |
| T-38 Talon (F-5) | | | | Internal navigation system | USA |
| TB 20/21/200 | 1,170 | | | | France |
| Zlin 142 | 525 | | | | Czech Republic |

**Transport Aircraft**

| Model | Passengers | Range (Km) | Payload (Kg) | Country of origin |
|---|---|---|---|---|
| Airbus A340 | 295 | 12,416 | 47,127 | France |
| An-12 | 90 | Max. load: 3,600 Max. fuel: 5,700 | 20,000 | Russia |
| An-24 | 44-50 | Max. load: 550 Max. fuel: 2,400 | 5,500 | Russia |
| An-26 | 40 | Max. load: 1,100 Max. fuel: 2,550 | 5,500 | Russia |
| Arava | 20 | Max. load: 486 Max. fuel: 1,400 | 2,350 | Israel |
| BAe 125/HS 125 | 8/12 | 3,120 | 857 | Britain |
| BN-2B Islander | 10 | Max. load: 672 Max. fuel: 2,027 | 1,200 | Britain |
| Boeing 707 | 181 | 4,235 | 24,950 | USA |
| Boeing 727 | 145 | 4,390 | 18,144 | USA |
| Boeing 737 | 130 | 4,180 | 17,223 | USA |
| Boeing 747-200 | 452 | 10,562 | | USA |
| Boeing 747-200F | | 8,060 | 109,315 | USA |
| C-130H | 92 | Max. load: 3,790 Max. fuel: 7,876 | 19,356 | USA |
| C-140 Jetstar | 10 | Max. load: 3,410 Max. fuel: 3,595 | 1,327 | USA |
| C-160 | 93 | Max. load: 1,853 Max. fuel: 5,095 | 16,000 | Germany |
| CASA C-212 | 16 | Max. load: 720 Max. fuel: 1,920 | 2,000 | Spain |
| Citation III | 11 | 4,815 | | USA |
| CN-235 | 48 | 4,350 | 6,000 | Spain |
| Commander 690 | 8 | 2,116 | | Britain |
| DC-3 Dakota | 38 | 1,853 | 2,500 | USA |
| DC-8 | 189 | 11,410 | 30,240 | USA |
| DC-9 | 105 | 3,100 | 12,743 | USA |
| DC-10 | 380 | 7,400 | 43,300 | USA |
| DHC-4 | 32 | Max. load: 390 Max. fuel: 2,100 | 3,965 | Canada |
| DHC-5 | 41 | Max. load: 815 Max. fuel: 3,490 | 6,280 | Canada |

**Transport Aircraft *(continued)***

| Model | Passengers | Range (Km) | Payload (Kg) | Country of origin |
|---|---|---|---|---|
| Dornier Do 228 | 15/20 | 1,740 | 2,200 | Germany |
| Dove | 11 | 620 | 670 | Canada |
| EMB 110P | 18 | 2,000 | 1,681 | Brazil |
| Falcon 10 | 7 | 3,370 | 603 | France |
| Falcon 20 | 8/14 | 3,540 | 1,380 | France |
| Falcon 50 | 8 | 6,480 | 1,570 | France |
| Falcon 900 | 8 | 7,229 | 2,185 | France |
| Fokker F-27 | 44 | 2,213 | 6,438 | Netherlands |
| G222L | 53 | Max. load: 1,890 Max. fuel: 5,100 | 9,000 | Italia |
| Gulfstream II/III | 19 | 7,590 | 907 | USA |
| Gulfstream V | 19 | 12,038 | 2,948 | USA |
| IL-14 | 18 | 2,600 | 5,300 | Russia |
| IL-76 | 120 | 6,700 | 48,000 | Russia |
| IL-78 Tanker | | 2,500 | 60,000 Fuel | Russia |
| KC-130 Tanker | | 1,850 | 23,587 Fuel | USA |
| KC-135 Tanker | | 4,630 | 92,210 Fuel | USA |
| King Air B100/B200/200T | 8/14 | 2,456 | | USA |
| L-100-30 | 128 | Max. load: 2,585 Max. fuel: 10,000 | 23,679 | USA |
| L-1011-500 | 246 | Max. load: 9,900 Max. fuel: 11,286 | 42,000 | USA |
| L-410 UVP | 15 | Max. load: 390 Max. fuel: 1,140 | 1,310 | Czech Republic |
| Learjet 25 | 8 | 2,650 | | USA |
| Piper Navajo | 6 | 1,800 | | USA |
| Skyvan Srs 3M | 22 | Max. load: 386 Max. fuel: 1,075 | 2,358 | Britain |
| Tu-124 | 44 | Max. load: 1,220 Max. fuel: 3,500 | 6,000 | Russia |
| Tu-134 | 80 | Max. load: 2,400 Min. load: 3,500 | 8,165 | Russia |
| Yak-40 | 27 | Max. load: 1,000 Max. fuel: 1,480 | 2,300 | Russia |

# Advanced Armament

## Air-to-Air Missiles

| Type | Guidance | Range (Km) | Counter measures | Country of origin |
|---|---|---|---|---|
| AA-2C/D | Semi-active radar/IR | 8/3 | | Russia |
| AA-6 | Semi-active radar/IR | 30 | | Russia |
| AA-7 | Semi-active radar/IR | 25/15 | IRCM | Russia |
| AA-8 | IR | 3-5 | | Russia |
| AA-10 | Semi-active radar/IR | 50/40 | IRCM | Russia |
| AA-11 | IR | 30 | Improved IRCM | Russia |
| AMRAAM | Active radar | 50 | | USA |
| Mica | Active radar/Imaging IR | 50 | Enhanced IRCM | France |
| Phoenix | Active radar | 150 | ECCM | USA |
| PL-2 | IR | 3 | | PRC |
| PL-5 | IR | 3 | | PRC |
| PL-7 | IR | 3 | | PRC |
| Python 3 | IR | 5 | IRCM | Israel |
| Python 4 | IR | 8 | IRCM | Israel |
| R530 | Semi-active radar/IR | 15/3 | | France |
| Super 530F/D | Semi-active radar | 30/40 | Improved ECCM | France |
| R 550 Magic II | IR | 5 | Improved IRCM | France |
| Shafrir 2 | IR | 3 | | Israel |
| Sidewinder | IR | 8 | Improved IRCM | USA |
| Sky Flash | Semi-active radar | 40 | Improved ECCM | Britain |
| Sparrow | Semi-active radar | 45 | Improved ECCM | USA |

## Air-to-Surface Missiles

| Type | Purpose | Guidance | Range (Km) | Country of origin |
|---|---|---|---|---|
| ALARM | Anti radiation | Passive radar homing | 45 | Britain |
| ARMAT | Anti radiation | Passive radar homing | 90 | France |
| AS 4 | Anti radiation | Passive radar homing | 400 | Russia |
| AS 9 | Anti radiation | Passive radar homing | 90 | Russia |
| AS 11 | Anti radiation | Passive radar homing | 50 | Russia |
| AS 12 | Anti radiation | Passive radar homing | 35 | Russia |
| HARM | Anti radiation | Passive radar homing | 25 | USA |
| Shrike | Anti radiation | Passive radar homing | 12 | USA |
| Standard | Anti radiation | Passive radar homing | 55 | USA |
| AM 39 Exocet | Anti ship | Active radar | 50 | France |
| AS 15TT | Anti ship | Radar command | 15 | France |
| AS 5 | Anti ship | Active radar | 180 | Russia |
| C-801 | Anti ship | Active radar | 40 | China |
| Gabriel | Anti ship | Active radar | 35 | Israel |
| Harpoon | Anti ship | Active radar | 120 | USA |
| Penguin | Anti ship | IR | 30 | Norway |
| Sea Eagle | Anti ship | Active radar | 110 | Britain |
| Sea Skua | Anti ship | Semi-active radar | 18 | Britain |
| AS 11 | Anti tank | Manual wire-guided | 3 | France |
| AS 12 | Anti tank | Manual wire-guided | 5 | France |
| AT 2 | Anti tank | Radio command | 4 | Russia |
| AT 6 | Anti tank | Radio command | 5 | Russia |
| Hellfire | Anti tank | Laser/IIR | 8 | USA |
| HOT | Anti tank | Auto. Wire-guided | 4 | France |

## Air-to-Surface missiles *(continued)*

| Type | Purpose | Guidance | Range (Km) | Country of origin |
|------|---------|----------|-----------|-------------------|
| TOW | Anti tank | Auto. Wire-guided | 4 | USA |
| Trigat 3LR | Anti tank | IIR | 4.5 | France |
| AS 6 | Ground attack | Internal/passive radar | 400 | Russia |
| AS 7 | Ground attack | Radio command | 5 | Russia |
| AS 10 | Ground attack | Laser | 10 | Russia |
| AS 14 | Ground attack | Laser/TV | 12 | Russia |
| AS 30 | Ground attack | Radio command/Laser | 10 | France |
| Bullpop | Ground attack | Radio command | 10 | USA |
| Griffin | Ground attack | Laser guided bombs | 10 | Israel |
| Maverick | Ground attack | TV/IIR/Laser | 8/25/20 | USA |
| Opher | Ground attack | IR guided bombs | | Israel |
| Paveway | Ground attack | Laser guided bombs | 7 | USA |
| PGM 1/2/3 | Ground attack | Laser/IR | 20 | Britain |
| Popeye | Ground attack | TV/IIR | 80 | Israel |
| Pyramid | Ground attack | TV guided bombs | | Israel |
| Skipper | Ground attack | Laser guided bombs | 7 | USA |

# ABBREVIATIONS

| | |
|---|---|
| AA | anti-aircraft |
| AAG | anti-aircraft gun |
| AAM | air-to-air missile |
| AEW | airborne early warning |
| AFB | air force base |
| AFV | armored fighting vehicle |
| AGM | air-to-ground missile |
| AP | anti-personnel |
| APC | armored personnel carrier |
| AR | assault rifle |
| ARV | armored reconnaissance vehicle ; armored recovery vehicle |
| Arty. | artillery |
| ARV | armored reconnaissance vehicle |
| ASW | anti-submarine warfare |
| AT | anti-tank |
| ATGM | anti-tank guided missile |
| ATRL | anti-tank rocket launcher |
| AWACS | airborne warning and control system |
| batt. | battalion/battery |
| bn. | billion |
| CAS | close air support |
| CBU | cluster bomb unit |
| CEW | counter-electronic warfare |
| CLGP | cannon-launched guided projectile |
| CW | chemical warfare |
| div. | division |
| dwt | deadweight tons |
| ECM | electronic countermeasures |
| ECCM | electronic counter-countermeasures |
| ESM | electronic surveillance measures |
| EW | electronic warfare |
| FAE | fuel air explosive |
| FLIR | forward-looking infrared |
| FOB | free on board |
| ft. | feet |
| GBU | glide bomb unit |
| GCC | Gulf cooperation council |
| GDP | gross domestic product |
| GHQ | general headquarters |
| GPMG | general purpose machine gun |
| GRT | gross registered tons |

## ABBREVIATIONS *(continued)*

| | |
|---|---|
| h. | hours |
| HMG | heavy machine gun |
| HQ | headquarters |
| HUD | head up display (in combat a/c) |
| IAF | Israel Air Force |
| IAI | Israel Aircraft Industries |
| IDF | Israel Defense Forces |
| IFV | Infantry fighting vehicle |
| IIR | imaging infrared |
| kg. | kilograms |
| km. | kilometers |
| laser | light amplification by stimulated emission of radiation |
| LCM | landing craft, mechanized |
| LCT | landing craft, tank |
| LCU | landing craft, utility |
| LMG | light machine gun |
| LSM | landing ship, mechanized |
| LST | landing ship, tank |
| LT | light tank |
| m. | meter ; millions |
| MBT | main battle tank |
| MFPB | missile fast patrol boat |
| MG | machine gun |
| mil. | millions |
| MLRS | multiple-launch rocket system |
| mm | millimeter |
| MMG | medium machine gun |
| MRL | multiple-rocket launcher |
| MTB | motor torpedo boat |
| Naval SSM | sea-to-sea missile |
| NCO | non-commissioned officer |
| PGM | precision-guided munition |
| PKK | Kurdish workers party |
| PLA | Palestine liberation army |
| PLO | Palestine liberation organization |
| port. | portable |
| PRC | People's republic of china |
| reg. | regular; regiment |
| res. | reserve |
| R&D | research and development |
| RPV | remotely piloted vehicle; see also UAV |

## ABBREVIATIONS *(continued)*

| | |
|---|---|
| SAR | semi-automatic rifle |
| SAM | surface-to-air missile |
| SDV | swimmer delivery vehicle |
| SLAR | sideways-looking airborne radar |
| SMG | submachine gun |
| SP | self-propelled |
| sq. | square |
| SSB | single side band (radio transceiver) |
| SSM | surface-to-surface missile |
| Sys. | system |
| STOL | short take-off/landing |
| TALD | tactical air-launched decoy |
| TEL | transporter-erector-launcher (for SSMs or SAMs) |
| TOE | table of organization and equipment |
| TOW | tube-launched, optically wire-guided (anti-tank) missile |
| UAV | unmanned aerial vehicle; RPV is remotely piloted, UAV is either remotely piloted or a drone. |
| unconf. | unconfirmed |

# Notes on Contributors

**Shlomo Brom**

Brig. Gen. (res.) Shlomo Brom joined the Jaffee Center as a Senior Research Associate in late 1998. From 1970 to 1987, he held several posts in the Israeli Air Force. From 1988 to 1990, he served as Defense Attaché at the Israeli Embassy in the Republic of South Africa. In 1990-1998 he served as Deputy Chief and then Chief of the IDF's Strategic Planning Division.

**Yiftah Shapir**

Yiftah Shapir joined the Jaffee Center in 1993 as an associate of the Center's Project on Security and Arms Control in the Middle East where he followed proliferation of weapons of mass destruction (WMD) in the Middle East. Since 1996, he is responsible for the quantitative part of *The Middle East Military Balance*. Before joining the Center, Shapir served as an officer in the Israeli Air Force. He holds a B.Sc. degree in Physics and Chemistry from the Hebrew University of Jerusalem, and an MBA from the Recanati School of Business Administration at Tel Aviv University.

**Shmuel Even**

Col. (res.) Shmuel Even received his BA and MA in economics at Ben-Gurion University of the Negev, and earned a B.Sc. in industry and management from the Technion Israel Institute of Technology in Haifa. Even served in the IDF's Military Intelligence Branch. Since 1995, Even is associated with the Jaffee Center, specializing in oil and the economy of the Middle East.

## Shmuel Gordon

Col. (res.) Dr. Shmuel Gordon served in the Israeli Air Force as a fighter pilot, squadron commander, and commander of the IAF's C$^3$I Center (1964-1997). From 1988 to 1992, he was a senior analyst in military doctrine and advanced systems at the RAND Corporation. Dr. Gordon is currently a defense consultant to various Israeli government agencies.

## Yoram Schweitzer

Yoram Schweitzer is a Research Associate at the International Policy Institute for Countering Terrorism (Herzlia, Israel). During 1982-1987, he was a research assistant at the Jaffee Center's Project on Terrorism. From 1987-1998, he held several postings in the IDF's Military Intelligence Branch.

## Eli Oren

Navy Capt. (res.) Eli Oren retired in 1998 from the IDF after more than 25 years of service in Israeli Naval Intelligence and the IDF's Strategic Planning Division. Since his retirement, he serves as coordinator for NATO and European Security Organizations under the Deputy Director General for External Relations and Arms Control of Israel's Ministry of Defense.

## Moshe Matri

Col. (res.) Moshe Matri retired from the IDF in 1992 after a long career in the Military Intelligence Branch and the Strategic Planning Division. He serves as an advisor for strategic planning to the City of Haifa municipality and to other local and government agencies.

## The Robert and Renée Belfer Center
## for Science and International Affairs

Graham T. Allison, Director
John F. Kennedy School of Government
Harvard University
79 JFK Street, Cambridge MA 02138
(617) 495-1400

The Belfer Center for Science and International Affairs (BCSIA) is the hub of research, teaching, and training in international security affairs, environmental and resource issues, and science and technology policy at Harvard's John F. Kennedy School of Government. The Center's mission is to provide leadership in advancing policy-relevant knowledge about the most important challenges of international security and other critical issues where science, technology, and international affairs intersect.

BCSIA's leadership begins with the recognition of science and technology as driving forces transforming international affairs. The Center integrates insights of social scientists, natural scientists, technologists, and practitioners with experience in government, diplomacy, the military, and business to address these challenges. The Center pursues its mission in four complementary research programs:

• The International Security Program (ISP) addresses the most pressing threats to U.S. national interests and international security.

• The Environment and Natural Resources Program (ENRP) is the locus of Harvard's interdisciplinary research on resource and environmental problems and policy responses.

• The Science, Technology, and Public Policy (STPP) program analyzes ways in which science and technology policy influence international security, resources, environment, and development, and such cross-cutting issues as technological innovation and information infrastructure.

• The Strengthening Democratic Institutions (SDI) project catalyzes support for three great transformations in Russia, Ukraine, and the other republics of the former Soviet Union—to sustainable democracies, free market economies, and cooperative international relations.

The heart of the Center is its resident research community of more than one hundred scholars: Harvard faculty, analysts, practitioners, and each year a new, interdisciplinary group of research fellows. BCSIA sponsors frequent seminars, workshops, and conferences, many open to the public; maintains a substantial specialized library; and publishes a monograph series and discussion papers. The Center's International Security Program, directed by Steven E. Miller, publishes the BCSIA Studies in International Security and sponsors and edits the quarterly journal *International Security*.

The Center is supported by an endowment established with funds from Robert and Renée Belfer, the Ford Foundation, and Harvard University, by foundation grants, by individual gifts, and by occasional government contracts.